EMPTY WORDS

Empty Words

Buddhist Philosophy and Cross-Cultural Interpretation

Jay L. Garfield

UNIVERSITY PRESS

2002

OXFORD
UNIVERSITY PRESS

Oxford   New York
Athens   Auckland   Bangkok   Bogotá   Buenos Aires   Cape Town
Chennai   Dar es Salaam   Delhi   Florence   Hong Kong   Istanbul   Karachi
Kolkata   Kuala Lumpur   Madrid   Melbourne   Mexico City   Mumbai   Nairobi
Paris   São Paulo   Shanghai   Singapore   Taipei   Tokyo   Toronto   Warsaw

and associated companies in
Berlin   Ibadan

Copyright © 2002 by Oxford University Press, Inc.

Published by Oxford University Press, Inc.
198 Madison Avenue, New York, New York 10016

Oxford is a registered trademark of Oxford University Press

Library of Congress Cataloging-in-Publication Data
Garfield, Jay L., 1955–
Empty words : Buddhist philosophy and
cross-cultural interpretation / Jay L. Garfield.
p. cm.
Includes bibliographical references and index.
ISBN 0-19-514551-8; 0-19-514672-7 (pbk.)
1. Mādhyamika (Buddhism)   2. Yogācāra (Buddhism)
3. Philosophy, Buddhist.   I. Title.
BQ7457 . G37 2000
181'.043—dc21   00-068162

1 3 5 7 9 8 6 4 2

Printed in the United States of America
on acid-free paper

For the ven Geshe Ngawang Samten,

colleague, teacher, friend,
and co-conspirator in cross-cultural philosophy,
without whom none of these thoughts could have
been thought, with gratitude and in friendship

Preface

I OFFER HERE FOURTEEN ESSAYS on topics in Buddhist philosophy, many of which have appeared before, but in scattered places, and two of which are published here for the first time. This work represents my thinking about these matters over the past decade. I hope that presenting these essays together will make more explicit the connections I see between Madhyamaka and Yogācāra; between Buddhist metaphysics and Buddhist ethics; between the practice of philosophy and the practices of reading and interpretation; and between all of this and the ethics and politics of scholarship. These connections have always been in the forefront of my thinking as I have worked on these cross-cultural philosophical themes. But because so many of these pieces have appeared in places disconnected from the others, the connections may not have been apparent to my readers. I hope, therefore, that these essays will be read and considered in concert.

Much of this book can also be read (or used in courses) in conjunction with *Fundamental Wisdom of the Middle Way: Nāgārjuna's* Mūlamadhyamakakārikā (Garfield 1995). Some of these chapters (1 and 2) were early versions of material that now appears in that volume. Others (chaps. 3–5) represent further thoughts and developments of ideas I present in that book regarding Nāgārjuna's philosophy, and have been at least partly inspired by criticisms and questions from students and colleagues about my presentation of Nāgārjuna's text. Still others (chaps. 6 and 9) situate Nāgārjuna's text in the context of debates between Madhyamaka and Cittamātra.

Since the publication of *Fundamental Wisdom of the Middle Way*, I have turned much of my attention to Cittamātra philosophy, especially the work of Vasubandhu and Sthiramati. The essays here can be understood as contributing to two broad debates about that school: First, in the debate regarding whether Cittamātra really is idealistic, I argue that Vasubandhu and Sthiramati, at least, are idealists in the classical sense of that term, and that their views can be usefully juxtaposed (though not identified) with those of Western idealists such as Berkeley, Kant, and Schopenhauer. (chaps. 6, 7, 8, and 9) In the second debate—on the so-called "continuity thesis" regarding Madhyamaka and Yogācāra—I defend the view that these are indeed very different philosophical systems and that the debate between them is a real one (chaps. 4 and 9). In fact, as I hope these essays demonstrate, I find Vasubandhu and Sthiramati to provide us with one of the deepest and most systematic explorations of the implications of idealism in any philosophical tradition. Inasmuch as Madhyamaka and Yogācāra are in the Indian and subsequent Tibetan literature so inextricably intertwined in exposition, in debate, and in the development of Buddhist epistemology, it is crucial, to understand either, to understand both.

I prefer to think of my enterprise in these pages as an exploration of cross-cultural philosophy rather than as an exercise in "comparative philosophy." That is, my goal is not so much to juxtapose texts from distinct traditions to notice similarities and differences as it is to do philosophy, with lots of texts, lots of perspectives, and lots of hermeneutical traditions—to make the resources of diverse traditions and their scholars available to one another and to create new dialogues. Several of these essays (chaps. 8, 11, 13) focus explicitly on these methodological concerns. Others, I hope, demonstrate the technique in practice. I would draw attention especially to chapters 2, 5, and 10 in this regard.

Ethical concerns are central to Buddhist philosophy, and it would be difficult, misleading, and even perverse to study Buddhist metaphysics and epistemology without attending to the ethical side of the tradition. This concern in part motivates my attention in this volume to moral theory. But philosophy itself as a practice raises moral and political problems, chief among them questions regarding the appropriate approach to the intellectual and cultural traditions less powerful and accorded less respect in the West than our own. I explore these questions in chapters 13 and 14. But more broadly, cross-cultural philosophy ought to have something to say about moral and political questions concerning global justice and peace, particularly since both the Western and the Buddhist philosophical traditions locate morality close to the core of their concerns. Chapters 10, 11, and 12 explicitly bring together Western and Buddhist thinking about human rights, democracy, Satyagraha, and compassion. They represent an attempt to engage Buddhist and Western philosophical dialogue with concrete political questions.

I have made a few editorial changes in some of these essays, replacing a few old translations by other scholars cited in the previouly published versions with my own newer translations, clarifying a few obscure points, and correcting errors of various sorts. Though there are no major changes, the versions of the essays printed here supersede those already in print. Unless otherwise noted all translations are my own, and unless otherwise noted these come from the Paljor Press edition of the sDe dge edition of the Tibetan Canon.

Acknowledgments

I AM GRATEFUL to many for support and assistance as I undertook this work. Many are thanked in acknowledgemnt notes in the individual essays themselves. But the following colleagues and students deserve special note: In Tasmania I benefited enormously from regular discussion with Anna Alomes, Khristos Nizamis, and the Ven. Sonam Thakchöe and the Ven. Gareth Sparham, as well as from the sage advice and administrative assistance of Jennifer Dunbabin. John Powers, Graham Priest, Guy Newland, Meredith Michaels, Janet Gyatso, Mark Siderits, Susan Levin, Jamie Hubbbard, Purushottama Bilimoria, and Roy Perrett have been valued philosophical colleagues on the Western side of the enterprise. I owe huge intellectual debts to each. My Tibetan colleagues the Ven. Geshe Ngawang Samten, the Most Ven. Prof. Samdhong Rinpoche, the Ven. Lobsang Norbu Shastri, the Ven. Geshe Yeshes Thab khas, the late Ven. Geshe Lobsang Gyatso, and the almost-Tibetan Ven. Sherab Gyatso have been enormously generous with their time and have contributed a great deal not only to my understanding of Buddhist philosophical material but also to my understanding of the nature of cross-cultural philosophy. Their commitment to that enterprise and enthusiastic participation has been a source of great intellectual inspiration. I thank my research assistants over this period, Yeshi Tashi Shastri, Jamyang Norbu Gurung, Sara Streett, and Tricia Perry, as well as Donna Gunn, the late Ruth Hammen, Leni Bowen, Sandra Kellett, Jennifer Dunbabin, Eliza Goddard, and Elizabeth Cowan.

I gratefully acknowledge the support of the Australian Research Council through a three-year Large Grant, which supported much of the research on Cittamātra; the Indo-American Fellowship, which supported me for one year in India; and the University of Tasmania, Hampshire College, and Smith College, each of which has generously supported the academic exchange with the Tibetan exile academic community that undergirds much of this work. I note particularly Malcolm Waters, Gregory Prince, and John Connolly, each of whom has extended himself personally to make these exchanges successful. Finally I thank my colleagues at the Central Institute of Higher Tibetan Studies, at the Institute of Buddhist Dialectics, in the School of Cognitive Science and Cultural Studies at Hampshire College, in the School of Philosophy at the University of Tasmania, and in the Department of Philosophy at Smith College for providing congenial philosophical homes, and my family, especially my wife, Blaine Garson, for providing my real home.

Chapter 1, "Epochē and Śūnyatā: Scepticism East and West," originally appeared in *Philosophy East and West,* vol. 40, no 3, 1990. It is reprinted with permission of the editors.

Chapter 2, "Dependent Arising and the Emptiness of Emptiness: Why Did Nāgārjuna start with Causation?" First appeared in *Philosophy East and West,* vol. 44, no. 2, 1994. It is reprinted with permission of the editors.

Chapter 3, "Emptiness and Positionlessness: Do the Mādhyamika Relinquish All Views?" originally appeared *in Journal of Indian Philosophy and Religion,* vol. 1, 1996. It is reprinted with permission of the editors.

Chapter 4, "Nāgārjuna's Theory of Causality: Implications Sacred and Profane," is forthcoming in *Philosophy East and West,* 2001. It is printed with permission of the editors.

Chapter 5, "Nāgārjuna and the Limits of Thought" (with Graham Priest), is forthcoming in *Philosophy East and West,* vol. 53, no. 1, 2003.

Chapter 6, "Three Natures and Three Naturelessnesses: Comments on Cittamātra Conceptual Categories," originally appeared in *The Journal of Indian Philosophy and Religion,* vol. 2, 1997. It is reprinted with permission of the editors.

Chapter 7, "Trisvabhāvanirdeśa: A Translation and Commentary," originally appeared in *Asian Philosophy,* vol. 7, no. 2, 1997. It is reprinted with permission of the editors.

Chapter 8, "Western Idealism through Indian Eyes: Reading Berkeley, Kant and Schopenhauer through Vasubandhu," originally appeared in *Sophia,* vol. 37, no. 1, 1998. It is reprinted with permission of the editors.

Chapter 10, "Human Rights and Compassion: Toward a Unified Moral Framework," originally appeared in *Journal of Buddhist Ethics,* Online Conference on Buddhism and Human Rights, 1995, *http://jbe.la.psu.edu/1995conf/garfield.txt,* and in *Buddhism and Human Rights,* edited by Damien V. Keown, Charles S. Prebish, and Wayne R Husted. Richmond, Surrey: Curzon Press, 1998. It is reprinted with permission of the publisher.

Chapter 11, "Buddhism and Democracy," appeared in *Paidea: Proceedings of the XX'th World Congress of Philosophy*, 2000. It is printed with permission of the publisher.

Chapter 12, "The 'Satya' in Satyagraha: Samdhong Rinnpoche's Theory of Non-violence," appeared in *In Search of Truth: Essays in Honour of Samdhong Rinpoche*, edited by S. Gyatso et al., Central Institute of Higher Tibetan Studies Press, 1999. It is reprinted with permission of the publisher.

Chapter 13, "Temporality and Alterity: Dimensions of Hermeneutic Distance," originally appeared in *Polylog*, June 2000. It is reprinted with permission of the editors.

Contents

PART I

Madhyamaka

Epochē and Śūnyatā

Skepticism East and West

The whole modern conception of the world is founded on the
illusion that the so-called laws of nature are the explanations of
natural phenomena.

Thus people today stop at the laws of nature, treating them as
something inviolable, just as God and Fate were treated in past
ages.

And in fact both are right and both wrong: though the view
of the ancients is clearer in so far as they have a clear and acknowledged terminus, while the modern system tries to make it
look as if *everything* were explained.

> *Wittgenstein,* Tractatus Logico-Philosophicus, *6.371,*
> *6.372, trans. B. F. McGuiness*

Sextus empiricus regarded skepticism not as a nihilistic attack
on our cognitive life, but rather—as he emphasizes in a variety of medical
metaphors—as a form of philosophical therapy, to cure us of the cognitive
and emotional ills born of extreme metaphysical, moral, or epistemological positions.

> The Sceptic's end, where matters of opinion are concerned, is mental tran-
> quility; in the realm of things unavoidable, moderation of feeling is the
> end. . . . Upon his suspension of judgment there followed, by chance, men-
> tal tranquility in matters of opinion. For the person who entertains the
> opinion that anything is by nature good or bad is continually disturbed.
> When he lacks those things that seem to him to be good, he believes he
> is being pursued, as if by the Furies, by those things which are by nature
> bad, and pursues what he believes to be the good things. . . . On the other
> side there is the man who leaves undetermined the question of what things
> are good and bad by nature. He does not exert himself to avoid anything
> or to seek after anything, and hence he is in a tranquil state. (Hallie 1985,
> p. 41)

> The Sceptic wishes, from considerations of humanity, to do all he can with the arguments at his disposal to cure the self-conceit and rashness of the dogmatists. And so just as healers of bodily ailments keep remedies of various potency, and administer the powerful ones to those whose ailments are violent and the lighter ones to those with light complaints, in the same manner the Sceptic too propounds arguments ... capable of forcibly removing the condition of dogmatist self-conceit. (ibid., p. 128)

(Wittgenstein also adopts the medical metaphor, "The philosopher's treatment of a question is like the treatment of an illness" [*Philosophical Investigations* 255]). As far as Sextus was concerned, Skepticism is a *moderate* position, as compared with the available alternatives. Moreover, Sextus argued, the serene equanimity that is the goal of skeptical practice is to be attained by the achievement of the "suspension of belief" upon which one's cognitive and practical life comes to be governed by "the guidance of nature, the compulsion of the feelings, the tradition of laws and customs, and the instruction of the arts" (ibid., p. 40). Again, it is important to note that whatever Sextus has in mind by the "suspension of disbelief" or the "refusal to assert," he *does not mean* that we are to become cognitively inert, inactive, or disengaged, epistemically or otherwise. For such an attitude is encouraged by neither art, custom, perception, nor appetite. Moreover, such a life or attitude towards knowledge would be *extreme*, and, again, skepticism is a *moderate* position. And finally, by any standards, this rejection of epistemic and moral life would reveal, in a straightforward sense, a sickness for which skepticism is intended as a cure.

I emphasize these points because many modern writers—following Kant and earlier usage introduced by Berkeley, a usage muddied (though in constructive ways) by Hume—urge that a central task of philosophy is to "answer the skeptic": to show, presumably, that what the skeptic denies to be possible is in fact not only possible, but actual. To adopt a later medical metaphor, this endeavor strikes me as a form of philosophical *resistance* in the psychoanalytic sense, a consequence of the very disease of which the skeptic intends to cure philosophers. It is more appropriate, I will argue, not to resist skeptical arguments, but to attend carefully to them. In particular, I will argue that resistance to skepticism rests on a confusion of skepticism with one of its extreme targets—typically what those Buddhist skeptics known as "mādhyamikas" called "nihilism." Such a confusion mistakes the point of skeptical arguments, the conclusions of the critical portions of the skeptical enterprise, and, most important, the skeptical solutions, as Hume and more recently Kripke (1982, pp. 66–68) have described them, that skepticism offers to the puzzles it generates.

Much of the confusion I hope to clear up is understandable given the expositions of skepticism with which many of us are most familiar. I have in mind those of Sextus, Hume, and Wittgenstein, along with appropriate ancillary figures.

For a variety of historical, rhetorical, and other reasons, these expositions have not placed at center stage either the opposition of extremes against which skeptical critical attacks are addressed, or the ways in which the skeptical solutions to the problems ostensibly solved by these extreme positions constitute what can simultaneously be seen as a *via media* between, and a complete rejection of, those extreme positions. But skeptical philosophy is a cross-cultural phenomenon. A rich skeptical tradition is present in Madhyamaka Buddhist philosophy; the *Prāsaṅgika-Madhyamaka* tradition particularly is startlingly akin to the Western skeptical tradition, in terms of its aims, methodology, and philosophical problematic. Nāgārjuna and Candrakīrti, like Sextus, emphasize the therapeutic nature of philosophy:

39   Since ultimately action is empty,
       If it is understood it is seen to be that way.
       Since action does not exist,
       That which arises from action does not exist either.

73   When one understands that this arises from that,
       All of the false views are thereby refuted.
       Hatred, anger and delusion are eliminated,
       And undefiled, one achieves nirvāna.
              (Nāgārjuna *Śūnyatāsaptati*)

They, too, are concerned to develop skeptical problems and skeptical solutions thereto regarding personal identity and the existence of the external world, the self, morality, and meaning. The arguments are immediately accessible and familiar to Western philosophers.

But these Buddhist skeptics, because of their cultural and philosophical contexts are a bit more explicit about certain features of the skeptical method than their European counterparts. In particular, the theory of the relation of skeptical positions to dogmatic positions is more carefully worked out; the nature of the suspension of belief or "positionlessness" is more explicitly characterized; and the relation between skeptical methodlogy and the role of convention in the life of the skeptic is more apparent in these accounts. There are numerous other interesting points of similarity and difference between the traditions, but I want to trade on these three expository advantages, using the Prāsaṅgika-Madhyamaka formulation of skepticism to motivate and to illuminate certain obscurities in the skepticism of Europe. This is an essay with a complex agenda. I hope to demonstrate the possibility and desirability of European and Buddhist skeptical arguments together, as a vehicle for their mutual illumination. Finally, I hope to defend the skeptical enterprise as a much-needed corrective to some contemporary philosophical confusions. This is too large a task to accomplish in a single essay, and this discussion must accordingly be regarded as a programmatic beginning.

After undertaking a cross-cultural expository defense of skepticism as a moderate solution to the problems posed by metaphysical extremism, I will undertake a bit of therapy. For much of contemporary philosophy, I would argue, is seriously and dogmatically ill. One physician on one house call can cure only one patient. I will endeavor to cure a prominently diseased dogmatist, Jerry Fodor, of one of the more epidemic dogmatic ills—that of causal realism—by a judicious application of the skeptical physic. My hope is that this cure will serve as a model, and that its ease will inspire much self-treatment.

THE STRUCTURE OF SKEPTICISM

The Prāsaṅgika-Madhyamaka Buddhists[1] refer to their opponents as "extremists" connoting just about what Sextus has in mind when he refers to his opponents as "dogmatists." They identify, for each philosophical problem subject to skeptical treatment, a reificationist and a nihilistic extreme. This taxonomy is important. For while it will be clear that, for example, both Sextus and Wittgenstein have both extreme views in mind, the failure in the European formulation of skeptical arguments to be explicit on this distinction leads to the easy and dangerous conflation of skepticism with nihilism, and the attendant disparagement and rejection of skepticism. Reificationism, in this philosophical taxonomy, asserts the ultimate reality of something whose reality (or reality in that sense) the skeptic denies (for example, of material substance, of a persistent self, of an independent realm of mathematical or moral truth, of a "third world" of meanings, or of primitive semantic facts), while nihilism is the philosophical denial of the existence of that which—at least in some sense—clearly exists, or more accurately of the warrant of what are in fact clearly warranted claims. A nihilist hence might deny that any of our statements about external objects, about ourselves or our moral responsibility, or about the meanings of words are true or warranted, or that one can make sense of any of the practices associated with such beliefs.

Nihilism is a forensic device for skepticism. In the language of Hume, aptly appropriated by Kripke, the nihilistic challenges to our beliefs and practices pose "skeptical problems." The task of the skeptic is to provide "skeptical solutions"—to respond to the nihilistic attack on the reality or warrant of a class of entities, beliefs, or practices in a way that at the same time does not capitulate to the metaphysical excesses of reificationism.

> A *skeptical* solution of a philosophical problem begins . . . by conceding that the skeptic's negative assertions are unanswerable. Nevertheless our ordinary practice or belief is justified because—contrary appearances notwithstanding—it need not require the justification the sceptic has shown

to be untenable. And much of the value of the sceptical argument consists precisely in the fact that he has shown that an ordinary practice, if it is to be defended at all, cannot be defended in a certain way. (Kripke 1982, pp. 66–67)

As Kripke points out in the context of his exposition of Wittgenstein's skeptical response to semantic nihilism,[2] this form of skeptical response typically consists in *granting* the principal arguments of the nihilist against the possibility of the *kind* of knowledge, certainly justification, or entity the nihilist repudiates. It also points out that in fact the practices the nihilist seeks to undermine are not grounded on things of *that* kind but are rather founded in conventions that remain untouched by nihilistic arguments and in no way presuppose the reification of the entities whose existence is at issue between nihilist and reificationist extremes. In this sense skepticism constitutes a "middle way" or a moderate position.

A few quick examples whose details are familiar may clarify this critical distinction between skepticism and nihilism and the relation between them. Consider skepticism about the existence of the external world. The reificationist argues that since we apprehend qualities, there must be some material substance in which they inhere—that there is a substantial, independent external world, whose furniture consists in material substance and its attributes. The nihilist, on the other hand (perhaps Berkeley or a Yogācāra fellow-traveler[3]), argues that we can make no sense of the concept of such material substance or substratum, or that if we can, we can never have knowledge of it. So, she or he argues, there is no external world, or at least we have no knowledge of any such world.[4]

The skeptic concedes to the nihilist that we have no idea of material substance as a permanent substratum for attributes, or that if we had a concept of such a thing, we could never have knowledge of its existence. Think of Hume ("that unintelligible chimera of a substance" [1922, p. 222]) or Nāgārjuna ("[47] Form is not apprehended as inherently existing").[5] Candrakīrti puts it this way (*Prasannapadā* 42a): "One might think: Even though a cause of material form is unintelligible it could be that inasmuch as form exists as effect, since that exists, it will have to exist as cause as well. If form existed as effect, that would be so. But, it doesn't exist." But the skeptic denies that our ordinary discourse about and use of material objects in any way implicates the concept of a substance with attributes. Instead, the skeptic argues, our conventions and practices regarding the use of, talk about, and justification of knowledge claims regarding external objects get their point just from their role in our individual and collective lives. It is these practices that give sense to talk about objects, and not the existence of substance.

Or consider skepticism with regard to the existence of the self. The reificationist (for example, Descartes or the typical Hindu philosopher) argues that experience presupposes a persistent self as its subject. The nihilist (Hume in setting up the problem, or Sextus) argues that in view of the incoherence of such a notion, or its unknowability, there can be no such self, or at least no self-knowledge. The skeptical reconstruction proceeds by noting that the self is, as Hume puts it, a "forensic" or, as Tsong khapa puts it, a "conventional" concept. The identification and discussion of selves presupposes not a substance to which we have privileged access, but conventions regarding the applications of names, attribution of responsibility, and so forth.

Think of skepticism with regard to meaning. The reificationist (Frege, Old Testament Wittgenstein) argues that there are particular semantic facts that constitute or determine the meanings of words and that we grasp when we know word meaning. The semantic nihilist (Bhartṛhari on some readings or Wittgenstein's imaginary interlocutor in the New Testament) argues that there can be no such facts, or that we could never know them, and hence that there is nothing that constitutes the meaning or correct use of terms. The skeptical solution developed by Wittgenstein and Tsong khapa concedes the lack of any such special semantic facts but requires us to note that word meaning and the assertability of correctness regarding word use rest not upon such facts but upon a network of social conventions regarding word use.

Consider next the example with which I will be most centrally concerned later. The reificationist with regard to causation argues that the regularities we observe in nature are to be explained by a fundamental causal power that causes have to bring about their effects—a necessary connection. The nihilist argues that because we can have no clear idea of such a causal power or natural necessity, causal explanation is impossible. The skeptical solution to the problem thus posed regarding the possibility of scientific explanation—as Hume, Wittgenstein, Nāgārjuna, and Candrakīrti argue—is, rather than to understand regularity as vouchsafed by causation, to understand causal explanation as grounded in regularities.[6]

All of these examples, to be sure, are presented in telegraphic form. But I hope they illustrate the constructive response skepticism provides to the challenges posed by nihilistic critiques of reificationist positions. There is an important additional characteristic of the relationship between skepticism and the dogmatic extremes against which it is counterposed that warrants emphasis. And it is only by appreciating this feature of skepticism that we can understand the sense in which the skeptic can be claiming to "suspend belief" or be "positionless." To suspend belief in the sense Sextus[7] has in mind is not to shrug one's shoulders in indecision regarding competing claims. To understand suspension this way is to see skepticism as a wholly negative position. I want to emphasize the essentially *constructive* character of skeptical argument, however, which requires a subtler understanding of suspension. To suspend judgment in this sense is to refuse to assent to a position, while refusing to assert its negation, since either would commit one to a false or misleading metaphysical presupposition. To suspend judgment is hence to refuse to enter into a misguided discourse. For the skeptic, European or Buddhist, both members of any dogmatic pair, despite their apparent antagonism, share some common metaphysical thesis as a presupposition of their respective positions. And it is in the rejection of this position—and in the consequent suspension of judgment regarding the opposing dogmatic positions— that skepticism consists.[8] The dogmatic thesis in the case of the existence of the external world is that the existence of physical objects and the truth of claims about them presuppose the existence of material substance. With respect to the existence of the self, the thesis is that personal identity and self-knowledge are possible *iff* there is a persistent soul; with respect to meaning, it is that conditions for the correct use of words presuppose the existence and grasp of semantic facts. Finally, the causal reificationist and nihilist agree that causal explanation is possible only if the regularities it exploits are grounded in independent causal links. In each case, the reificationist and the nihilist differ only on the issue whether the metaphysical presupposition in question is satisfied. The skeptic rejects the presupposition of the dispute.

The skeptical move in each case consists in rejecting exactly the thesis that the apparently diametrically opposed dogmatic positions share. That is what makes skepticism so radical, so deep, and so apparently nihilistic when viewed uncritically. For in each case, the thesis rejected is an unquestioned fundamental presupposition of much mainstream philosophical thought—"the decisive move in the conjuring trick." In each case, however, the skeptic determines to argue that these shared fundamental metaphysical assumptions regarding the necessary ontological conditions of knowledge must be rejected in order to understand and explain epistemic practice.

When Sextus urges us to suspend belief, he is referring to the metaphysical beliefs that lead to dogmatic opposition; we should, in addition, absent ourselves from the debates concerning them. When he says "not more," he urges that the external world is not more than what we observe, that personal identity is not more than an aggregation of experiences and capacities, that meaning is not more than convention, that causation is not more than regularity. Custom and the particular practices of the arts and sciences, he urges, yield all the knowledge, certainty, and justification we need to navigate the world, identify ourselves and others, speak intelligibly, and explain natural phenomena.

> Now, we cannot be entirely inactive when it comes to the observances of everyday life. Therefore, while living undogmatically, we pay due regard to appearances. This observance of the requirements of everyday life seems to be fourfold, with the following particular heads: the guidance of nature, the compulsion of the feelings, the tradition of laws and customs, and the instruction of the arts. It is by the guidance of nature that we are capable of sensation and thought. It is by the compulsion of the feelings that hun-

ger leads us to food and thirst leads us to drink. It is by virtue of the tradition of laws and customs that in everyday life we accept piety as good and impiety as evil. And it is by virtue of the instruction of the arts that we are not inactive in those arts which we employ. All these statements, however, we make without prejudice. (Hallie 1985, p. 40)

This thought is echoed by Wittgenstein's observation that when we hit explanatory bedrock, we find not certain propositions, but practices:

204. Giving grounds, however, justifying the evidence, comes to an end;— but the end is not certain propositions' striking us immediately as true, *i.e.* it is not a kind of *seeing* on our part; it is our *acting* which lies at the bottom of the language game.

344. My *life* consists in my being content to accept many things. (*On Certainty*)

When the Mahāyānists argue that phenomena are all empty, the same insight is being expressed: material objects are devoid of substance in the metaphysician's sense; persons are empty of immaterial souls that persist through change; words are empty of special semantic facts that determine their meanings; and regularity in nature is empty of special causal powers that provide its underpinnings.

The constructive side to the skeptical enterprise has a characteristic strategy, involving two moves. In the first place, it involves what I like to call the "skeptical inversion" of the order of explanation: the nihilist challenges us to explain the apparently problematic by reference to what, according to the reificationist, should be the unproblematic, and argues that we cannot. The skeptic grants the force of this argument but demonstrates that in fact the *explanans*—or at least the forms of discourse involving vocabulary pertaining thereto—is what is problematic and obscure. Moreover, the skeptic argues, the very reality—such as it is—of that *explanans* is in fact grounded in what was originally problematized by the skeptical challenge.

This is a highly abstract characterization. A few familiar examples should clarify the point. Hume accepts that we can never explain the regularity of nature by appeal to a causal link and inverts the order of explanation by arguing that our talk about causation is to be explained by our familiarity with regularities. Nāgārjuna makes the same move. Wittgenstein and Tsong khapa grant that the ability of a community of language users to use words in roughly the same way cannot be explained by the private grasping by each member of the community of the meanings of words, and they invert the order of explanation, arguing that the possibility of an individual using a word meaningfully is to be explained by reference to the regularity of practices in the community. Sextus, Hume, and Nāgārjuna argue that our conventions regarding the identification of person are not to be understood as grounded in the reference of each person's "I" to a particular enduring mental substance; rather, the talk of myself as an individual (and of others as individuals) is explained by reference to our conventions of personal individuation, conventions that are, as Hume notes, "forensic."

This second characteristic of the skeptical inversion, which should now be obvious from this brief survey of examples, is that an appeal to social conventions is central to the skeptical reconstruction of our heretofore metaphysically or epistemologically confused discourse. In the private-language case this is obvious. It should also be clear in the case of personal identity and in that of the skeptical reconstruction of morality. Though Hume and Sextus are less explicit on this point, Nāgārjuna, Candrakīrti, and Tsong khapa emphasize—and Hume and Sextus would undoubtedly agree—social convention is also hard at work in skeptical reconstructions of discourse about the existence of physical objects and causation. For the boundaries of physical objects are not given by nature, nor are the classes of events that count as "the same type" that underlie the generalizations that vouchsafe the attributions of explanatory significance involving words like *because*. The canonizations of sortals and of object-boundaries drawn in space, time, and composition require social and linguistic conventions. Tsong khapa puts the point this way:

> With respect to earth and solidity, etc as definition and definiendum—if one presents them as definiendum and definition whose meaning is determined through engagement with a basis of conventional engagement *found through previous analysis*, this will prove incoherent; instead, they can only be presented through their mutual interrelationship. (1998, 200)

> Prāsaṅgikas use the above-mentioned analysis into whether or not things have any independent defining characteristics only to determine whether or not they exist ultimately. As it is presented in the previous scriptural quotations, existents are merely names and symbols and conventions, as has been explained many times. "Being name only" means, as I have previously explained, that if the conventional meaning is investigated, nothing is found; *not* that name exists but the object does not, *nor* that without a name no object exists. So, not *everything* posited nominally by a conventionally designative mind as conventionally existent is accepted; but nor is anything *not* posited through the power of a conventionally designative mind as conventionally existent accepted as empirically real. (1998, 201)

When the skeptic follows the custom of his or her country and participates in its linguistic conventions in asserting the existence of material objects, he or she does so in the recognition that these linguistic, explanatory, and allied conventions justify such talk, rather than a belief in the givenness of objects as independent entities or in the givenness of sortals as naturally determined. And in particular, the conception of objects as substances and their properties as essential or accidental attributes inherent in them is rejected by the skeptic as it is by the nihilist. But the skeptic rejects this conception with the realization—not shared by the reificationist who is the nihilist's target—that none of our ordinary epistemic or social practices regarding material objects presupposes such a view anyway.

All of this allows us to characterize more explicitly the paradoxical skeptical recommendations of equipoise (Sextus: "to come first of all to a suspension of judgement and then to mental tranquility" [Hallie 1985, p. 33]. Or " 'All things are false,' for example, asserts its own falsity together with that of all other things ... (p. 36), or positionlessness (Nāgārjuna: "If I had any proposition at all, thereby I would have that fault. Since I don't have a proposition, I don't have any fault at all." [*Vigrahavyāvartanī* 29]).

These recommendations are often regarded as paradoxical, because they at least appear themselves to be assertions of the kind that the skeptic rejects, or to constitute positions of the kind the Mahāyānist refuses to adopt. But closer inspection should indicate that they are not so, and Sextus's metaphor of the laxative that purges itself together with the ill it aims at curing can be as useful here.[9] The ills that skepticism aims to cure are philosophical ills—specifically metaphysical and epistemological ones characterized by the obsessive search for epistemologically or ontologically primitive foundations of knowledge, meaning, explanation, or morality that undergird our collective epistemic, linguistic, scientific, and moral practices. The *positions* the skeptic is concerned to undermine are specifically philosophical.[10] They are positions regarding the necessary or sufficient underpinnings of what the skeptic wants to reveal as practices that need no grounding in independent facts. The skeptic does not reject these practices. On the contrary, Sextus recommends exactly that we follow nature, feeling, custom, and the instruction of the arts, and Nāgārjuna explains that

71   The statement, "This arises depending on that"
       Is not contradicted from the mundane perspective.
       But since dependent phenomena lack essence,
       How could they truly exist? That is how it must be.
                              (Śūnyatāsaptatikārikā)

That is, to understand the conventional *as conventional*, and as empty of any reality or foundation beyond convention, is the goal of philosophical inquiry. Consider this remark of Tsong khapa:

> Moreover, the meaning [of the *Saṃdhinirmocana-sūtra*] is explained in order to eliminate grasping and reification that would prevent one from developing an understanding of the ultimate, such as the repudiation of conventional reality; the reification of the non-conventional existence of permanent phenomena, etc, and of form and so forth existing in the way they appear. This is accomplished by rejecting the literal readings of such

statements as those asserting non-production and by teaching non-arising and non-cessation, etc, from the ultimate point of view. It is hence necessary to accept arising, ceasing, etc conventionally and thus repudiation is avoided. (1998; 171)

The pill is skeptical inquiry. But when the poison is purged, the inquiry is no longer necessary. The inquiry does not involve adopting one or the other of the disputing dogmatic positions but rather making peace by rejecting both—and not in favor of a third dogmatism, but rather of not seeking the chimerical foundations that spark the dispute in the first place.

It is in this sense that all skeptical philosophers from Sextus and the historical Buddha to Wittgenstein and contemporary Mahāyānists have regarded skeptical philosophy as a form of therapy: the goal is not simply the search for truth for its own sake, or the critical appraisal of arguments, or intellectual entertainment. The goal is rather to cure the philosopher of the confusion attendant upon the fundamental misconceptions underlying dogmatism—that any reasonable practice must be grounded in some set of certain propositions, which in turn must be grounded in some convention-independent, ontologically determinate reality given to us and underlying our conventions. Such misconceptions engender endless sophistical dialectic and block clear thinking about language, explanation, morality, and ontology. The skeptic endeavors to replace such dogmatic impediments to understanding not with an alternative theory about the chimerical substratum of our practices but rather with a contentment with those practices on their own terms, and with their conventional status. Wittgenstein makes the same point in these remarks from *On Certainty*.

> 7. That is to say the *questions* that we raise and our *doubts* depend on the fact that some propositions are exempt from doubt, are as it were like hinges on which those turn.
> 8. That is to say, it belongs to the logic of our scientific investigations that certain things are *in deed* not doubted.
> 9. But it isn't that the situation is like this: We just *can't* investigate everything, and for that reason we are forced to rest content with assumption. If I want the door to turn, the hinges must stay put. (*On Certainty*)

A DOGMATIC ILLNESS DIAGNOSED

All of this would be beside the point if philosophical dogmatisms were merely diseases of a remote past, or if they were merely benign philosophical playthings. But dogmatisms in many forms are alive and well, and are, in fact, wreaking philosophical havoc. In order to recommend the skeptical purgative, I will consider one contemporary case of the reificationist infection and attempt to effect a skeptical cure. The variety of the disease I have in mind is causal reificationism, a disease one might have thought to have been stamped out by the Humean vaccine. But it is still with us, giving rise to much needless confusion in the philosophical foundations of cognitive science, among other places. I will articulate its consequences in Fodor's hands and demonstrate that a careful skeptical analysis frees cognitive science from artificial dogmatic methodological bonds.

Fodor, in *Psychosemantics* (Fodor 1987), attempts to demonstrate that *all* scientific taxonomy is individualistic—that science never does, and must never, identify phenomena for theoretical purposes *qua* relational, because all such taxonomy depends upon the causal powers of the phenomena to be classified, and because causal powers are always local. This claim is important and controversial, for as many (Garfield 1988, Milikan 1987, Burge 1979, Baker 1988, and others) have argued, psychology often at least apparently *does* individuate phenomena in its domain relationally. In particular, phenomena such as the propositional attitudes are arguably relational and are arguably essential to much psychological explanation.

This is also metaphysically rich stuff—the stuff of dogmatic reificationism with respect to causation. I will argue that while scientific—including psychological—taxonomy must cleave nature at causally relevant joints, there is good empirical reason to believe that the resulting cuts are often relational, and no good metaphysical reason to believe that they cannot be. Moreover, and most importantly for disarming this new realism about causation, nothing in causal individuation requires one to discover any *causal powers* that things *have*. Explanation does not require such an occult metaphysics. And once we appreciate the force of this conclusion, psychological, intentional causal relations between naturalistically[11] characterized relata have as much claim to reality as any microphysical causal relations linking individualistically characterized phenomena.

I will begin by rehearsing Fodor's argument in some detail, explaining just how and where its bizarre metaphysical commitments enter. Once the argument is clearly in view, I will argue directly for its unsoundness and present an alternative, more moderate skeptical account of the nature of causation, and of the nature of causal taxonomy in cognitive science inspired by Nāgārjuna, Sextus, and Hume. After considering and dismissing some possible Fodorian replies, I will conclude with some general morals of this discussion for practice in cognitive science. Fodor's initial argument proceeds as follows:

1. We want science to give causal explanations to such things . . . as can be causally explained. (1987, p. 34)
2. Giving such explanations essentially involves projecting and confirming causal generalizations. And causal generalizations subsume the things they apply to in virtue of the causal properties of the things they apply to. (ibid., p. 34)

3. *And ... [consider]* the property of being a mental state of a person who lives in a world where there is XYZ rather than H_2O in the puddles [as opposed to being that of a person who lives in an H_2O world]. These sorts of differences in the relational properties of psychological (/brain/ particle) states are irrelevant to their causal powers, hence irrelevant to scientific taxonomy.

   ... [I]f you're interested in causal explanation, it would be mad to distinguish between Oscar's brain states, and Oscar 2's; their brain states have identical causal powers. That's why we individuate brain states individualistically. And if you're interested in causal explanation, it would be mad to distinguish between Oscar's *mental* states and Oscar 2's; their mental states have identical causal powers. (ibid., p. 34)

4. So, [relational] taxonomy won't do for the purposes of psychology. Q.E.D. ... It's true that when I say "water" I get water and when my Twin says "water" he gets XYZ. But that's irrelevant to the question about identity of causal powers, *because these utterances (/thoughts) are being imagined to occur in different contexts.* ... What *is* relevant to the question of identity of causal powers is the following pair of counterfactuals: (a) If his utterance (/thought) had occurred in my context, it *would have had* the effects that his utterance (/thought) did have; and if my utterance (/thought) had occurred in my context, it *would have had* the effects that my utterance (/thought) did have. For our utterances (/thoughts) to have the same causal powers, both of these counterfactuals have to be true. But both of those counterfactuals *are* true. ... (1987, pp. 34–35)

Fodor then brings this all together:

> So, then, to bring this all together: you can affect the relational properties of things in all sorts of ways—including by stipulation, But for one thing to affect the causal powers of another, there must be a mediating law of mechanism. It's a mystery what this could be in the Twin (Oscar) cases; not surprisingly, since it's surely plausible that the only mechanisms that *can* mediate environmental effects on the causal powers of mental states are neurological. The way to avoid making this mystery is to count the mental states—and, *mutatis mutandis,* the behaviors—of Twins (Oscars) as having the same causal powers, hence as taxonomically identical. (ibid., p. 41)

So here is Fodor's position: we individuate phenomena by referring to their causal powers. Causation is local in the case of psychological phenomena, so psychological taxonomy must be individualistic. Individualistic psychological taxonomy identifies psychological phenomena with neurological phenomena. So, in order for psychological explanations to be causal, and hence scientific, psychological phenomena must be individualistic in character. And this is true just because for Fodor causal explanations must carve nature at her joints by characterizing *explanans* and *explananda* under sortals that capture phenomena that in fact have genuine *causal powers*—the ability to bring about effects of the right kind or to be brought about by causes of the right kind—powers that inhere in precisely those phenomena.

THE SKEPTICAL MEDICINE

1   Neither from itself, nor from another
       Nor from both,
       Nor without a cause
       Does anything, whatever, anywhere arise.

(That is, there are no *sui generis* phenomena, nor any power by means of which one event or state can *bring about* another. Nor can any such power be found in any combination of phenomena or in any non-natural arena.)

2   There are four conditions: efficient condition,
       Percept-object condition, immediate condition,
       Dominant condition, just so.
       There is no fifth condition.

(Natural phenomena have no essences independent of their place in the network of explanatory relationships and regularities in which they occur, and there is no privileged ontological scheme. But there are multiple dimensions of interdependence and each is relevant to explanation. These constitute interdependence.)

3   The essence of entities
       Is not present in the conditions, etc.
       If there is no essence,
       There can be no otherness-essence.

(The explanatorily useful relations phenomena bear to one another—natural regularities—are not, when conceived clearly, due to any independently present *power*. Ontology depends upon explanatory interests.)

10   Power to act does not have conditions.
       There is no power to act without conditions.
       There are no conditions without power to act.
       Nor do any have the power to act.

(The conditions are explanatorily useful, and we can indeed explain events by reference to the events that preceded them, that are simultaneous with them, into which they decompose, or by reference to our purposes. But none of these explanations involves the addition of any occult causal power mediating between conditions and that which they condition.)

11   These give rise to those,
      So these are called conditions.
      As long as those do not come from these,
      Why are these not non-conditions?

(None of this is to say that no natural regularities are usefully exploited in scientific explanation. Some are, but this is all that there is to interdependence and explanatory utility.)[12]

In these famous (though obscure and diversely interpreted) opening verses of the *Mūlamadhyamakakārikā*, Nāgārjuna defends a middle way between nihilism and strong realism with respect to causation. Against the nihilist he urges that there are natural regularities and that they can be and are exploited in explanation. Against the realist—who (with Fodor) is committed to a reification of such regularities in a cement-of-the-universe model of causation—he argues that natural regularities themselves lie at the base of explanation. The use of these regularities in explanations, Nāgārjuna argues, neither demands nor profits by the interposition of a force. For then cause and effect would each need to be individually connected to that force by. . . . [13]

This moderate skepticism about causation—which finds echo in Sextus and Hume and in the remarks of Wittgenstein quoted at the beginning of this chapter—provides the key to understanding the fundamental errors in Fodor's excessive causal realism. To begin with, consider the odd pair of conclusions concerning the predicates that exemplify *is a belief that p* and the predicate *is a planet: is a planet* counts, for Fodor, as a useful astronomical predicate despite its relational character because being a planet affects planets' causal powers, namely the power to bump or not into various things. It is puzzling that possession of these causal powers is presumed to be constant across counterfactual contexts in which the nonrelational properties of the planet are held constant— that is what makes this predicate, in Fodor's mind, individualistic despite being at the same time relational. *Believes that there is water on Mars*, however, unless it can be identified with a local property of its bearer's brain—unless it is non-relational—fails to be individualistic and hence fails to count as a scientifically useful predicate. For, as Twin-Earth examples show, when relationally individuated, its causal powers are not constant across counterfactual contexts.

But this putative distinction cannot be maintained. The causal powers of Uranus are not constant across counterfactual contexts. Consider the world where it orbits a sun with a different mass or is a different distance from Neptune. There, of course, its trajectory differs, and so, then, does that of what it might or might not bump into. There is no principled respect in which this variability in powers differs from that of inscriptions, or if Burge, Baker, and I are right, of individualistically described psychological states. They, too, have different causal powers in different counterfactual circumstances. The only difference is that in these cases, it is not the variation of mass of nearby astronomical bodies that issues in covariation in trajectory, but rather the variation in social conventions and behaviorally relevant environment that issues in covariation in semantic character, in the conditions under which they would be uttered, and in their probable consequences—hence in the psychological or linguistic type of significant tokens. And to suggest that the descriptive vocabulary appropriate to describing these properties and the variations therein is ruled out a priori is groundlessly to beg the question at issue. Why not rule out trajectory talk? Just as the latter is essential to practice in astrophysics, the former is essential to practice in cognitive science.

Fodor might object at this point that in each of these pairs of cases something is constant—the physical counterfactual dispositions of the planets on the one hand and of the twins on the other. And the fact that these physical dispositions remain constant across counterfactual contexts privileges the physical vocabulary for scientific purposes. But there are at least two things wrong with this reply. First, as I noted above, it begs the question against the claim that intentional predicates are as appropriate to psychology as nonintentional ones are to astronomy, and that the intentional properties of the twins differ. Second, it betrays an unmotivated natural essentialism. For asserting in this context that what makes a rock the object that it is for any and all scientific purposes are just its individualistic properties is to plump for a particular set of predicates as constituting a necessary description of it, regardless of one's descriptive or explanatory purposes. And how would one defend such metaphysical extravagance? (A bit later on I will consider some slightly more sophisticated forms of this Fodorian objection.)

The source of the error has yet to be identified and examined. And here is where Nāgārjuna's insight can be applied. Nāgārjuna pointed out, as Hume would some sixteen centuries later, that while regularities are to be found in nature, and while explanation must exploit regularities, appeal to some occult causal nexus joining *explanans* to *explanandum*, or predecessor event to successor event is both otiose and ultimately incoherent. But it is this misguided, unreflective image of such a "cement of the universe" that holds the natural order together, and at that in very thin mortar joints, that underlies causal reificationism. There are, of course, as Nāgārjuna insists, *conditions*—explanatorily necessary and sufficient conditions of *explananda* (and moreover lots of types of them as everybody (except for Hempel and a few others) from Aristotle to Pylyshyn has emphasized). We explain—correctly—the ignition of the match by its striking in the presence of oxygen, my dialing 911 by my desire to get help, and the clicking on of the thermostat by reference to its regulatory function. And explanation presupposes both regularity and the possibility of describing *explanans* and *explanandum* in the vocabulary in which these regularities are properly expressed. But that is all that is presupposed. No set of individual facts about the individual match, its striking, and its ignition at a particular time constitutes the fact that the striking caused the ignition. Rather, the regularity of such successions makes it appropriate to say that *this* striking *so described* caused *this* ignition *so described.*

The addition of *causation* or a causal *power* in the "cause" or of *effectual potential* in the "effect" is unwarranted, unnecessary, and explanatorily impotent: It is unwarranted because there can be no evidence for such a mysterious, occult causal link. There is plenty of evidence for the occurrences of the phenomena putatively so linked, and in the right cases there may be plenty of inductive or theoretical evidence for the regularity of their association. But no such evidence can be even relevant to some mysterious necessity—some unknown force or glue—beyond what can be observed or measured. Moreover, explanation proceeds quite smoothly, as does prediction, in the absence of any such causal glue.[14] And this is the central point: our natural laws, functional generalizations, structural explanations, and narratives provide coherence and intelligibility without interpolating causal glue or ascribing any modal powers to the phenomena they subsume. And even if we did add cement, the regressive problem would remain: what empowers causes to generate causal power, and what enables causal power to bring about effects?[15]

Once we replace Fodor's loose, metaphysically luxurious talk about causal powers with more commonsense and methodologically sound—that is to say, skeptical—talk about explanatorily useful regularities, the central methodological project underwritten by this metaphysical currency collapses. For it was the claim that causal powers inhere in an individual object by virtue of its particular natural type (leaving aside the incoherence of Fodor's account of what constitutes an appropriate natural type) that grounded the claim that scientific individuation must be individualistic. And if I am right, the obscure and unacknowledged image of causation as a kind of immaterial superglue that can bond only adjacent surfaces of natural kinds is what lies behind the (undefended—presumably obvious) assertion that causal powers are possessed only by individualistically characterized individuals.

But such grand causal realism is incoherent. Regularity is as real as connection can become, and subsumability under explanatorily useful regularities is as real as a natural kind gets. But here is the point: there is nothing about regular association in any of its forms that demands spatiotemporal locality of the regularly associated phenomena. And there is nothing, at least nothing obvious, that blocks their relational individuation. In a particular domain the truth or falsity of individualism or naturalism would hence appear to be an empirical matter. And given the irreducibility that Fodor acknowledges in general between the vocabularies of the "special sciences," there is no reason to feel queasy about an individualistic ontology in a science of the interior, say, of a person whose behavior in situ is best explained in terms of regularities captured by a vocabulary that individuates that person's states relationally.

This is, of course, but a case study, and its implications must be treated with appropriate caution. But this much, I think, emerges: reification in regard to causation is not philosophically benign. It issues in a commitment a priori to an ontologically radical and methodologically restrictive vision of the nature of mind and of cognitive science. This vision and its attendant strictures on the conduct of science and the construction of theories are seen to be gratuitous when subjected to the constructive critical analysis suggested by skepticism with respect to causation. Such an analysis does not undermine the possibility of psychology or our faith in its explanations. Rather, it facilitates a more naturalistically conceived theoretical posture in that discipline—one that corresponds more closely to actual practice.

Relapse Avoided

I can imagine discomfort with this skeptical view. The hyperrealist metaphysics of causation I have been attacking is indeed well entrenched. So I will consider several plausible replies.

The reply that Fodor implicitly endorses might be called "the argument from the unity of science" or perhaps "the argument from physics." The wording is something like this: The laws of the special sciences are not properly laws at all— they are rough generalizations that demand copious, ineliminable, ceteris paribus clauses. What underlies their verisimilitude is the truth of closed, exceptionless, *really* true laws—the laws of the millennial physics. But these laws employ an individualistic taxonomy. So, insofar as a special science generalization is true, it too must employ an individualistic taxonomy. Chemistry, physiology, and neuroscience promise reduction and hence their own volumes in the *Encyclopedia of Unified Science* (Fodor 20XX?) just because their individuation schemes promise, when suitably refined, to coincide with that of physics. But if psychology recognizes naturalistically individuated phenomena, and seeks generalizations that will subsume them, it does so at the cost of a gerrymander of the natural world that will forever condemn it to theoretical excommunication.

This argument has a certain nostalgic power, but, I fear, there is not much else in its favor. To note two salient difficulties: there is no reason to believe that explanatory utility and reducibility to physics go hand in hand. Good economics is possible even despite variations in media of exchange, and good linguistics does not suppose that larynxes, ink, chalk, and other media of expression share any essential physical properties. (A more sober and careful argument for this point is to be found in Garfield 1988.) More significant, though, and closer to the heart of my difficulty with Fodor's position is this: the laws of physics—even the laws of the best physics—are fraught with ceteris paribus clauses. They do not (as Cartwright [1978] has so eloquently argued) describe any actual physical phenomena. Nor are scientific laws meant to. Laws of nature are true only of ideal types, and idealization is an ineliminable aspect of scientific explanation—the ground of the possibility of the universality to which they aspire. This is no less true of physical laws than it is of psychological laws. So if the point of striving for an individualistic ontology is unity with physics, and if the point of that is the attainment of exceptionless truth when instantiated by actual empirical phenomena, the point is chimerical. And the source, I suspect, of this faith in the perfectibility of physical science is intuition that it is onto *causal powers*.[16]

A closely related reply concerns *forces*. After all, one might argue, physics does recognize causal powers. In fact, it recognizes at present approximately four of them, or maybe three if the electroweak unification is successful. And if further unification occurs—the ultimate unification—we will have an account of the genuine causal power, the actual cement of the universe. This would be all well and good if physics characterized forces as powers that physical phenomena *have*, or as things that have *powers* over physical phenomena. But that is just not what they are. Forces represent dynamic relations between physical parameters. Period. They do not inhere in physical phenomena, nor do they exist independently of them and act on them. Physicists seem to have read their Hume, or their Nāgārjuna.[17]

A final argument can be anticipated, and this one really betrays the metaphysics that Nāgārjuna, Hume, and Wittgenstein are all concerned to debunk: regularities are cheap. Not all of them are explanatory. Take the regular coincidence of the noon whistle and the noon train, for example. In order for a regularity to be explanatory, what must underlie it is a *real causal link—the causal power of the cause to bring about the effect*. So if there are explanatory regularities, and not mere cosmic coincidences, there must be causal powers. But here is where we must recall the powerful argument from the *Tractatus* with which I opened this chapter. The addition of a causal cement between cause and effect can add nothing explanatory to an explanation. For one would still need (as noted in the Third Man argument offered earlier) an explanation of how the cause brought about the cement, and of how the cement brought about the effect. And as any good mason will tell you, adding an additional loose joint will do nothing to improve the bond. As Hume emphasized, regularities vouchsafe individual attributions of causation, and networks of regularities vouchsafe particular regularities. Counterfactuals are supported by confidence and success, and not by occult metaphysics. And as the skeptic—Buddhist or European—will be quick to emphasize, this amounts to the adoption of positionlessness as a guiding principle in the interpretation of scientific theories. I neither assert the existence of occult causal powers, nor do we deny the explanatory utility of our theories by virtue of their absence.[18]

Someone might well object at this point that any claim of skeptical cure is at least premature. For, it might be argued, the skeptic has not demonstrated that his or her account of causal discourse as grounded in regularity is devoid of metaphysical commitment. For one thing, the account so far is sketchy, and it might well turn out to involve non-obvious metaphysical commitments as it is elaborated. And does the skeptic of owe us some account of why the practice of exploiting regularities in nature for the purposes of explanation is itself justified? There is a point to this objection, and the skeptical response illuminates the structure of the enterprise. It may indeed be that the skeptic unwittingly dog-matizes. But if she or he does, that fact will emerge and be treatable by subsequent skeptical therapy. Skeptical analysis may well be interminable analysis. But that does not undermine its utility. (On the other hand, of course, it might well be—as it appears in this case—that the skeptic does not dogmatize, in which case the therapy is short-term.) And practices, including the broadest explanatory ones, are subject to criticism and often can be justified or shown to be unjustified. But the justification of a practice does not necessarily consist in producing a set of true or indubitable sentences about the worlds upon whose truth or certainty the practice rests. The justification of practices can often be simply pragmatic. The work, or that's the way we do things—if one wants to engage in *this enterprise*, one does it this way. Scientific explanation and the identification of causes may be like that. So it in no way follows from the inability of the skeptic to produce decisive arguments for the truth of competing theories concerning causation, the nature of the physical world, or of the self, that the enterprise is bankrupt. The activity of producing such theories is just what the skeptic wants us to abandon. And if the skeptic is guilty of dogmatizing, that only shows that more analysis is required.

IMMUNIZATION

I conclude by drawing attention to the several skeptical morals of these discus-sions for metaphysics and method in science. None of these conclusions is new, but since all are called into question by what I think is a very popular dogmatic causal hyperrealism, it is worth repeating them in one place.

First, while it is certainly true that scientific taxonomy—including that of both physics and psychology—individuates phenomena in response to the demands of explanation, this does not in any way entail individualism. For, when stripped of incoherent and otiose metaphysical baggage, all that the phrase "causal powers" could ever indicate is *explanatorily useful relations*. And there is no good reason, once this rich metaphysics of causation is abandoned, to believe that such relations always comprise individualistically characterized relata. Moreover, the claim that the relational categories of physical science are somehow more individualistic than those of the special sciences, for example, cognitive science, is false. Naturalism is hence not simply a hallmark of special science, let alone *immature* cognitive science.

Second, reducibility to a more fundamental, or physical, science—in particular reduction by demonstrating a token-identity relation between phenomena recognized by the respective taxonomies of reduced and reducing science—is no prerequisite for respectability in the cognitive sciences, or, for that matter, any science. The ground for that belief is another belief in the special insight of physics into occult causal powers. But this belief is groundless, or at best is grounded on a mistaken mythology of the peculiar perfection of physical laws and a failure to recognize the central and universal role of idealization and ceteris paribus instantiation of ideal types in scientific explanation.

Third, a unitary, broadly physicalist ontology is compatible with ontological pluralism at the level of the taxonomy of nature and does not entail the unity of science, or even the unity of *good* science. One does not need to be some kind of Cartesian substance-pluralist to endorse the disunity of science.

Finally, and most important, the philosophy of science can do without any rich metaphysics of causation or causal powers. The superstition that, for an ontology to grip nature by the throat to carve her at the joints, it must first discover *real* relations between phenomena underwritten by *causal powers* as opposed to "mere" regularities is just that—a superstition. Explanatory regularities and the taxonomies they induce are certainly real enough, as real as anything can be.

Moreover, I should emphasize that I have presented but a single case history. If the general thrust of the initial portion of my discussion is correct, there is an epidemic to be addressed, and many of us are victims. This is but one example of the cure that can be wrought by skeptical analysis. The cure may be difficult, and it may leave many of us dissatisfied with what we now take to be the goals and nature of philosophy, and with many of our own positions and arguments. Fortunately, however, skeptical medicine has one salient side effect: it is good philosophical fun. I hope that this provides encouragement for the view that the appropriate response to the skeptic is not to search for a reply, but to take one's medicine and wake up to regularity.

Dependent Arising and the Emptiness of Emptiness

Why Did Nāgārjuna Start with Causation?

N̄ĀGĀRJUNA, WHO LIVED IN SOUTH INDIA in approximately the first century C.E., is undoubtedly the most important, influential, and widely studied Mahāyāna Buddhist philosopher. He is the founder of the Madhyamaka, or Middle Path, schools of Mahāyāna Buddhism. His considerable corpus includes texts addressed to lay audiences, letters of advice to kings, and the set of penetrating metaphysical and epistemological treatises that represent the foundation of the highly skeptical and dialectical analytic philosophical school known as Madhyamaka. Most important of these is his largest and best known text *Mūlamadhyamakakārikā*, in English *Fundamental Verses on the Middle Way*. This text in turn inspires a huge commentarial literature in Sanskrit, Tibetan, Chinese, Korean, and Japanese. Divergences on interpretation of *Mūlamadhyamakakārikā* often determine the splits between major philosophical schools. So, for instance, the distinction between two of the three major Mahāyāna philosophical schools, *Svātantrika-Madhyamaka* and *Prāsaṅgika-Madhyamaka* reflect, inter alia, distinct readings of this text, itself taken as fundamental by scholars within each of these schools.

The treatise itself is composed in very terse, often cryptic verses, with much of the explicit argument suppressed, generating significant interpretive challenges. But the uniformity of the philosophical methodology and the clarity of the central philosophical vision expressed in the text together provide a considerable fulcrum for exegesis. The central topic of the text is *emptiness*—the Buddhist technical term for the lack of independent existence, inherent existence, or essence in things. Nāgārjuna relentlessly analyzes phenomena or processes that appear to exist independently and argues that they cannot so exist, and yet, though lacking the inherent existence imputed to them either by naive common sense or sophisticated realistic philosophical theory, these phenomena are not nonexistent; they are, he argues, conventionally real.

This dual thesis of the conventional reality of phenomena together with their lack of inherent existence depends upon the complex doctrine of the Two Truths or Two Realities—a conventional or nominal truth and an ultimate truth—and upon a subtle and surprising doctrine regarding their relation. It is, in fact, this sophisticated development of the doctrine of the Two Truths as a vehicle for understanding Buddhist metaphysics and epistemology that is Nāgārjuna's greatest philosophical contribution. If the analysis in terms of emptiness is the substantial heart of *Mūlamadhyamakakārikā*, the method of reductio ad absurdum is the methodological core. Nāgārjuna, like Western skeptics, systematically eschews the defense of positive metaphysical doctrines regarding the nature of things, demonstrating rather that any such positive thesis is incoherent, and that in the end our conventions and our conceptual framework can never be justified by demonstrating their correspondence to an independent reality. Rather, he suggests, what counts as real depends precisely upon our conventions.[1]

For Nāgārjuna and his followers this point is connected deeply and directly with the emptiness of phenomena. That is, for instance, when a mādhyamika philosopher says of a table that it is empty, that assertion by itself is incomplete. It invites the question, "Empty of what?" And the answer is, "Empty of inherent existence, or (a more literal translation of the Sanskrit *svabhāva* or the Tibetan *rang bzhin*) self-nature, or, in more Western terms, *essence*." Now, to say that the table is empty is hence simply to say that it *lacks essence*, and importantly *not* to say that it is completely nonexistent. To say that it lacks essence, the mādhyamika philosopher will explain, is to say, as the Tibetans like to put it, that it does not exist "from its own side": that its existence *as the object that it is—as a table—* depends not on *it*, nor on any purely nonrelational characteristics, but depends upon *us* as well. That is, if our culture had not evolved this manner of furniture, what appears to us to be an obviously unitary object might instead be correctly described as five objects: four quite useful sticks absurdly surmounted by a pointless slab of stick-wood waiting to be carved. It is also to say that the table depends for its existence on its parts, on its causes, on its material, and so forth. Apart from these, there is no table. The table, we might say, is a purely arbitrary slice of space-time chosen by us as the referent of a single name, and not an entity demanding, on its own, recognition and a philosophical analysis to reveal its essence. That independent character is precisely what it lacks on this view.

And this analysis in terms of emptiness—an analysis refusing to characterize the nature of any thing, precisely because it denies that we can make sense of the idea of a thing's nature—proceeding by the relentless refutation of any attempt to provide such a positive analysis, is applied by Nāgārjuna to all phenomena, including, most radically, emptiness itself. For if Nāgārjuna merely argued that all phenomena are empty, one might justly indict him for in fact merely replacing one analysis of things with another; that is, with arguing that emptiness is in fact the essence of all things. But Nāgārjuna, as we shall see, argues that emptiness itself is empty. It is not a self-existent void standing behind the veil of illusion represented by conventional reality, but merely an aspect of conventional reality. And this, as we shall see, is what provides the key to understanding the deep unity between the Two Truths.

While Nāgārjuna is a powerfully original thinker, he is clearly and self-consciously operating squarely within the framework of Buddhist philosophy. As such, Nāgārjuna accepts, and takes it as incumbent upon him, to provide an account of the Four Noble Truths. Moreover, he takes it as a fundamental philosophical task to provide an understanding of what Buddhist philosophy refers to as *pratītya-samutpāda*—dependent co-origination. This term denotes the nexus between phenomena by virtue of which events depend on other events, composites depend upon their parts, and so on. Just how this dependency is spelled out, and just what its status is, is a matter of considerable debate within Buddhist philosophy, just as the nature of causation and explanation is a matter of great dispute within Western philosophy. Nāgārjuna is very much concerned to stake out a radical and revealing position in this debate. I will argue that this position provides the key to understanding his entire text.

Mūlamadhyamakakārikā is divided into twenty-seven chapters.[2] The first chapter addresses dependent origination. While many Western commentators assert that this chapter opens the text simply because it addresses a "fundamental doctrine of Buddhism" (Kalupahana 1986), I will argue that Nāgārjuna begins with causation for deeper, more systematic reasons. In chapters 2 through 23, Nāgārjuna addresses a wide range of phenomena, including external perceptibles, psychological processes, relations, putative substances, and attributes, arguing that all are empty. In the final four chapters, Nāgārjuna replies to objections and generalizes the particular analyses into a broad theory concerning the nature of emptiness itself and the relation between the Two Truths, emptiness and dependent arising itself. It is generally, and in my view correctly, acknowledged that chapter 24, the examination of the Four Noble Truths, is the central chapter of the text and the climax of the argument. One verse of this chapter, verse 18, has received so much attention that interpretations of it alone represent the foundations of major Buddhist schools in East Asia:

18   Whatever is dependently co-arisen,
       That is explained to be emptiness.
       That, being a dependent designation,
       Is itself the middle way.

Here Nāgārjuna asserts the fundamental identity of (1) emptiness, or the ultimate truth; (2) the dependently originated—that is, all phenomena; and (3) verbal convention. Moreover, he asserts that understanding this relation is itself the middle-way philosophical view he articulates in *Mūlamadhyamakakārikā*. This verse and the discussion in the chapters that follow provide the fulcrum for Candrakīrti's more explicit characterization of the emptiness of emptiness as an interpretation of Nāgārjuna's philosophical system—the interpretation that is definitive of the Prāsaṅgika-Madhyamaka school. In what follows I will provide an interpretation of this central verse and its context that harmonizes with Candrakīrti's and argue that in fact this doctrine is already to be found in the opening chapter of the text—the examination of conditions. Reading the text in this way, I will argue, locates the doctrine of the emptiness of emptiness not only as a dramatic philosophical conclusion to be drawn at the end of twenty-four chapters of argument, but as the perspective implicit in the argument from the very beginning, and only rendered explicit in chapter 24. Reading the text in this way, I will suggest, also shows us exactly how 24: 18 is to be understood, and just why a proper understanding of causality is so central to Buddhist philosophy.

I will begin by offering a philosophical reading of chapter I. I will argue that Nāgārjuna distinguishes two possible views of dependent origination or the causal process—one according to which causes bring about their effects by virtue of causal powers and one according to which causal relations simply amount to explanatorily useful regularities—and defends the latter. This, I will argue, when suitably fleshed out, amounts to Nāgārjuna's doctrine of the emptiness of causation. I will then turn immediately to chapter 24, focusing on the link between emptiness, dependent origination, and convention, and developing the theory of the emptiness of emptiness. With this in hand, we will return to chapter 1, showing how this doctrine is anticipated in the initial discussion of causation. Then I will show quickly how this way of reading the texts changes the way we would read subsequent chapters, and I will make a few general remarks about the moral of this textual exercise for an understanding of the centrality of causation to metaphysics and for an understanding of the remarkably pragmatic outlook of Madhyamaka philosophy.

Chapter I—Examination of Conditions

Central to this first chapter is the distinction between causes and conditions (Skt: *hetu* and *pratyaya*, Tib: *rgyu* and *rkyen*). This distinction, variously drawn and controversial,[3] is arguably differently understood in Sanskrit and Tibetan. The way I will understand it here, I argue, makes good coherent sense not only of this chapter, but of *Mūlamadhyamakakārikā* as a whole. Briefly, we will understand this distinction as follows: when Nāgārjuna uses the word *cause (hetu, rgyu)*, he has in mind an event or state that has in it a *power (kriyā, bya ba)* to bring about its effect, and has that power as part of its essence or nature (*svabhāva, rang bzhin*). When he uses the term *condition*, on the other hand (*pratyaya, rkyen*), he has in mind an event, state, or process that can be appealed to in explaining another event, state or process, without any metaphysical commitment to any occult connection between *explanandum* and *explanans*. In chapter I, Nāgārjuna, we shall see, argues against the existence of causes and for the existence of a variety of kinds of conditions.[4]

The argument against causation is tightly intertwined with the positive account of dependent arising and of the nature of the relation between conditions and the conditioned. Nāgārjuna begins by stating the conclusion (1: 1):

1   Neither from itself nor from another,
      Nor from both,
      Nor without a cause,
      Does anything whatever, anywhere arise.

2   There are four conditions: efficient condition;
      Percept-object condition; immediate condition;
      Dominant condition, just so.
      There is no fifth condition.

Entities are neither self-caused nor brought about through the power of other entities. That is, there is no causation, when causation is thought of as involving causal activity.[5] Nonetheless, he notes (1: 2) there are conditions, in fact four distinct kinds, that can be appealed to in the explanation and prediction of phenomena. An example might be useful to illustrate the difference between the four kinds of condition, and the picture Nāgārjuna will paint of explanation: suppose that you ask, "Why are the lights on?" I might reply as follows: (1) Because I flicked the switch. I have appealed to an efficient condition; or (2) Because the wires are in good working order, the bulbs haven't burned out, and the electricity is flowing. These are supporting conditions; or (3) The light is the emission of photons each of which is emitted in response to the bombardment of an atom by an electron, and so on. I have appealed to a chain of immediate conditions; or (4) So that we can see. This is the dominant condition. Any of these would be a perfectly good answer to the "Why?" question. But note that none of them makes reference to any causal powers or necessitation.

The next three verses are crucial.

3   The essence of entities
      Is not present in the conditions, etc.
      If there is no essence,
      There can be no otherness-essence.

4   Power to act does not have conditions.
      There is no power to act without conditions.
      There are no conditions without power to act.
      Nor do any have the power to act.

5   These give rise to those,
      So these are called conditions.
      As long as those do not come from these,
      Why are these not non-conditions?

Nāgārjuna first notes (1: 3) that in examining a phenomenon and its relations to its conditions, we do not find that phenomenon somehow contained potentially in those conditions. Now, on the reading of this chapter, I will suggest, we can see conditions simply as useful *explanans*. Using this language, we can see Nāgārjuna as urging that even distinguishing clearly between *explanans* and *explanandum* as distinct entities, with the former containing potentially what the latter has actually, is problematic. What we are typically confronted with in nature is a vast network of interdependent and continuous processes, and carving out particular phenomena for explanation or for use in explanations depends more on our explanatory interests and language than on joints nature presents to us. Through addressing the question of the potential existence of an event in its conditions, Nāgārjuna hints at this concealed relation between praxis and reality.

Next, Nāgārjuna notes (1: 4) that in exploiting an event or entity as a condition in explanation we do not thereby ascribe it any causal power. Our desire for light does not exert some occult force on the lights. Nor is there anything to be found in the flicking of the switch other than the plastic, metal, movement, and connections visible to the naked eye. Occult causal powers are singularly absent. On the other hand, Nāgārjuna points out in the same breath that this does not mean that conditions are explanatorily impotent. In a perfectly ordinary sense—not that the metaphysicians of causation have in mind, our desire is active in the production of light, but not in the sense that it contains light potentially, or some special causal power that connects our minds to the bulbs.[6]

What is it, then, about some sets of event pairs, but not others, that makes them dependently related, if not some causal link present in some cases but not in others? Nāgārjuna replies (1: 5) that it is the regularities that count. Flickings give rise to illuminations. So they are conditions of them. If they did not, they would not be. Period. Explanation relies on regularities. Regularities are explained by reference to further regularities. Adding active forces or potentials contributes nothing of explanatory utility to the picture.[7]

In reading the next few verses, we must be hermeneutically cautious, paying careful attention to Nāgārjuna's use of the term *existent* (*satah, yod pa*) and its negative contrastive "nonexistent" (*asatah, med pa*). For Nāgārjuna is worried here about the false opposition between inherent existence and complete nonexistence, as opposed to conventional existence or nonexistence. Though this will become clearer as we go along, keep in mind for the present that for a thing to exist inherently is for it to exist in virtue of possessing an essence; for it to exist independently of other entities, and independently of convention. For a thing to be completely nonexistent is for it to not exist in any sense at all—not even conventionally or dependently.

With this in mind, we can see how Nāgārjuna defends dependent arising while rejecting causation.

6   For neither an existent nor a nonexistent thing
        Is a condition appropriate.
        If a thing is nonexistent, how could it have a condition?
        If a thing is already existent, what would a condition do?

7   When neither existents nor
        Nonexistents nor existent nonexistents are established,
        How could one propose a "productive cause?"
        If there were one, it would be pointless.

8   An existent entity (a mental episode)
        Has no object.
        Since a mental episode is without an object,
        How could there be any percept-condition?

9   Since things are not arisen,
        Cessation is not acceptable.
        Therefore, an immediate condition is not reasonable.
        If something is ceased, how could it be a condition?

He notes (1: 6) that if entities are conceived as inherently existent, they exist independently and hence need no conditions for their production. Indeed, they could not be produced if they exist in this way. On the other hand, if things exist in no way whatsoever, it follows trivially that they have no conditions. This verse and the following three (1: 6–10) make this point with regard to each of the four kinds of conditions.

What is important about this strand of the argument? Nāgārjuna is drawing attention to the connection between a causal power view of causation and an essentialist view of phenomena on the one hand, and between a condition view of dependent arising and a conventional view of phenomena on the other. Here is the point: if one views phenomena as having and as emerging from casual powers, one views them as having essences and as being connected to the essences of other phenomena. This, Nāgārjuna suggests, is ultimately incoherent, since it forces one at the same time to assert the *inherent existence* of these things, in virtue of their essential identity, and to assert their *dependence* and *productive* character, in virtue of their causal history and power. But such dependence and relational character, he suggests, are incompatible with their inherent existence. If, on the other hand, one regards things as dependent merely on conditions, one regards them as merely conventionally existent. And to regard something as merely conventionally existent is to regard it as without essence and without power. And this is to regard it as existing dependently. This provides a coherent mundane understanding of phenomena as an alternative to the metaphysics of reification Nāgārjuna criticizes.

Verse 10 is central in this discussion.

10   If things did not exist
        Without essence,
        The phrase, "When this exists so this will be,"
        Would not be acceptable.

Nāgārjuna is replying here to the causal realist's inference from the reality of causal powers to their embodiment in real entities whose essences include those powers. He turns the tables on the realist, arguing that precisely because there is no such reality to things—and hence no entities to serve as the bearers of the causal powers the realist wants to posit—the Buddhist formula expressing the truth of dependent arising[8] can be asserted. It could *not* be asserted if in fact there were real entities. For if they were real in the sense important for the realist, they would be independent. So if the formula were interpreted in this context as pointing to any causal power, it would be false. It can only be interpreted, it would follow, as a formula expressing the regularity of nature.

In the next three verses (1: 11–13), Nāgārjuna anticipates and answers the causal realist's reply:

11   In the several or united conditions
        The effect cannot be found.
        How could something not in the conditions
        Come from the conditions?

12   However, if a nonexistent effect
        Arises from these conditions,
        Why does it not arise
        From non-conditions?

13   If the effect's essence is in the conditions,
        But the conditions don't have their own essence,
        How could an effect whose essence is in the conditions
        Come from something that is essenceless?

First, the realist argues that the conclusion Nāgārjuna draws from the unreality of causal power—the nonexistence of things (where *existence* is read "inherent existence")—entails the falsity of the claim that things dependently arise (1: 11). For if there are no things, surely nothing arises. This charge has a double edge: if the argument is successful, it not only shows that Nāgārjuna's own position is vacuous, but also that it contradicts one of the most fundamental tenets of Buddhist philosophy, that all phenomena are dependently arisen. Moreover, the opponent charges (1: 11), on Nāgārjuna's view, that the *explanandum* is not to be found potentially in the *explanans*; there is no explanation of how the former is to be understood as depending upon the latter. As Nāgārjuna will emphasize in 1: 14, however, the very structure of this charge contains the seeds of its reply.

The very emptiness of the effect, an effect presupposed by the opponent to be non-empty, in fact follows from the emptiness of the conditions and of the relationship between conditions and effect. Nāgārjuna can hence reply to the opponents' attempted refutation by embracing the conclusion of his *reductio* together with the premises it supposedly refutes.

How, the opponent asks, are we to distinguish coincidental sequence from causal consequence? And why (1: 12) do things not simply arise randomly from events that are non-conditions, since no special connection is posited to link consequents to their proper causal antecedents? Finally, the opponent asks (1: 13), since the phenomena we observe clearly have natures, how could it be, as Nāgārjuna argues, that they proceed by means of a process with no essence, from conditions with no essence? Whence do the natures of actual existents arise? Nāgārjuna again replies to this last charge by pointing out that since on his view the effects indeed have no essence, the opponent's presupposition is ill-founded. This move also indicates a reply to the problem posed in (1: 12): That problem is grounded in the mistaken view that a phenomenon's lack of inherent existence entails that it, being nonexistent, could come into existence from nowhere. But "from nowhere," for the opponent, means from something lacking inherent existence. And indeed, for Nāgārjuna, this is exactly the case: effects lacking inherent existence depend precisely upon conditions that themselves lack inherent existence.

Nāgārjuna's summary of the import of this set of replies (I: 14) is terse and cryptic.

14   Therefore, neither with conditions as their essence,
        Nor with non-conditions as their essence are there any effects.
        If there are no such effects,
        How could conditions or non-conditions be evident?

But unpacking it with the aid of what has gone before provides an important key to understanding the doctrine of the emptiness of causation that is the burden of this chapter. First, Nāgārjuna points out, the opponent begs the question in asserting the genuine existence of the effects in question. They, like their conditions, and like the process of dependent origination itself, are nonexistent from the ultimate point of view. Hence the third charge fails. As a consequence, in the sense in which the opponent supposes that these effects proceed from their conditions—namely that their essence is contained potentially in their causes, which themselves exist inherently—these effects need not be so produced. And so, finally, the effect-containing conditions that the opponent charges Nāgārjuna with being unable to explain are themselves unnecessary. In short, while the reificationist critic charges the Madhyamika with failing to come up with a causal link sufficiently robust to link ultimately real phenomena, for the Madhyamika philosopher the core reason for the absence of such a causal link is the very absence of such phenomena in the first place.

We are now in a position to characterize explicitly the emptiness of causation, and the way this doctrine is identical with the that of dependent origination from conditions adumbrated in this chapter. It is best to offer this characterization using the via media formulation most consonant with Nāgārjuna's philosophical school. We will locate the doctrine as a midpoint between two extreme philosophical views. That midpoint is achieved by taking conventions as the foundation of ontology, hence rejecting the very enterprise of a philosophical search for the ontological foundations of convention (chapter 1 of this volume). To say that causation is non-empty or inherently existent is to succumb to the temptation to ground our explanatory practice and discourse in genuine causal powers linking causes to effects. That is the reificationist extreme that Nāgārjuna clearly rejects. To respond to the arguments against the inherent existence of causation by suggesting that there is then no possibility of appealing to conditions to explain phenomena—that there is no dependent origination at all—is the extreme of nihilism, also clearly rejected by Nāgārjuna. To assert the emptiness of causation is to accept the utility of our causal discourse and explanatory practice, but to resist the temptation to see these as grounded in reference to causal powers or as demanding such grounding. Dependent origination simply is the explicability and coherence of the universe. Its emptiness is the fact that there is no more to it than that.

Now this is certainly philosophically interesting stuff in its own right. But as I suggested at the outset, there is more to it than just an analysis of causation and dependent arising. For, as we shall see, for Nāgārjuna among the most important means of demonstrating the emptiness of phenomena is to argue that they are dependently arisen. And so the claim that dependent arising itself is empty will turn out to be the claim that the emptiness of phenomena is itself empty—the central and deepest claim of Madhyamaka ontology.

CHAPTER 24—EXAMINATION OF THE FOUR NOBLE TRUTHS

While chapter 24 ostensibly concerns the Four Buddhist Truths and the way they are to be understood from the vantagepoint of emptiness, it is really about the nature of emptiness itself, and about the relation between emptiness and conventional reality. As such, it is the philosophical heart of *Mūlamadhyamakakārikā*. The first six verses of the chapter (24: 1–6) reply to Nāgārjuna's doctrine of emptiness by an opponent charging the doctrine with nihilism. The next eight verses (24: 7–14) are primarily rhetorical, castigating the opponent for his misunderstanding of Madhyamaka. The important philosophical work begins with 24:15.

From this point Nāgārjuna offers a theory of the relationship between emptiness, dependent origination, and convention and argues not only that these three can be understood as correlative, but that if conventional things (or emptiness itself) were *non-empty*, the very nihilism with which the reificationist opponent charges Madhyamaka would ensue. This tactic of arguing not only against each extreme but also that the contradictory extremes are in fact mutually entailing is a dialectical trademark of Nāgārjuna's philosophical method. Because of the length of this chapter, I will not provide a verse-by-verse reading here, but only a general gloss of the argument, with special attention to critical verses (see Garfield 1995 for a detailed discussion of this chapter).

1   If all of this is empty,
Neither arising nor ceasing,
Then for you, it follows that
The Four Noble Truths do not exist.

2   If the Four Noble Truths do not exist,
Then knowledge, abandonment,
Meditation, and manifestation
Will be completely impossible.

3   If these things do not exist,
The four fruits will not arise.
Without the four fruits, there will be no attainers of the fruits.
Nor will there be the faithful.

4   If so, the spiritual community will not exist.
Nor will the eight kinds of person.
If the Four Noble Truths do not exist,
There will be no true Dharma.

5   If there is no doctrine and spiritual community,
How can there be a Buddha?
If emptiness is conceived in this way,
The three jewels are contradicted.

6   Hence you assert that there are no real fruits.
And no Dharma. The Dharma itself
And the conventional truth
Will be contradicted.

The opponent opens the chapter by claiming that if the entire phenomenal world were empty nothing would in fact exist, a conclusion absurd on its face and, more important, contradictory to fundamental Buddhist tenets such as the Four Noble Truths (24: 1–6) as well as to conventional wisdom. The implicit dilemma with which Nāgārjuna confronts himself is elegant (24: 6). For as we have seen, the distinction between the Two Truths, or two vantagepoints—the ultimate and the conventional—is fundamental to his own method. So when the opponent charges that the assertion of the nonexistence of such things as the Four Noble Truths, and of the arising, abiding, and ceasing of entities is contradictory both to conventional wisdom and to the ultimate truth (that is, on one straightforward interpretation, that all phenomena are impermanent, that is, merely arising, abiding momentarily, and ceasing), Nāgārjuna is forced to defend himself on both fronts and to comment on the connection between these standpoints.

Nāgārjuna launches the reply by charging the opponent with foisting the opponent's own understanding of emptiness to Nāgārjuna. Though this is not made as explicit in the text as one might like, the understanding Nāgārjuna has in mind, in the terms of Madhyamaka, reifies emptiness itself. 24: 16 provides a clue.

16   If the existence of all things
     Is perceived in terms of their essence,
     Then this perception of all things
     Will be without the perception of causes and conditions.

The opponent thinks that to exist actually is to exist as a discrete entity with an essence. It would follow that for the opponent the reality of emptiness would entail that emptiness itself is an entity, and at that an inherently existing entity. To see emptiness in this way is to see it as radically different from conventional, phenomenal reality. It is to see the conventional as illusory and emptiness as the reality standing behind it. To adopt this view of emptiness is indeed to deny the reality of the entire phenomenal, conventional world. It is also to ascribe a special, nonconventional, nondependent hyper-reality to emptiness itself. Ordinary things would be viewed as nonexistent; emptiness as substantially existent. (It is important and central to the Madhyamaka dialectic to see that these go together—that nihilism about one kind of entity is typically paired with reification of another.) This view is not uncommon in Buddhist philosophy, and Nāgārjuna is clearly aware that it might be suggested by his own position. So Nāgārjuna's reply must begin by distancing himself from this reified view of emptiness itself and hence from the dualism it entails. Only then can he show that to reify emptiness in this way would indeed entail the difficulties his imaginary opponent adumbrates, difficulties not attaching to Nāgārjuna's own view. This brings us to the central verses of this chapter:

18   Whatever is dependently co-arisen,
     That is explained to be emptiness.
     That, being a dependent designation,
     Is itself the middle way.

19   Something that is not dependently arisen,
          Such a thing does not exist.
          Therefore a non-empty thing,
          Does not exist.

These verses demand careful scrutiny. In 24: 18 Nāgārjuna establishes a critical
three-way relation between emptiness, dependent origination, and verbal convention and asserts that this relation itself is the Middle Way toward which his entire
philosophical system is aimed. As we shall see, this is the basis for understanding
the emptiness of emptiness itself. First, Nāgārjuna asserts that the dependently
arisen is emptiness. Emptiness and the phenomenal world are not two distinct
things, but rather two characterizations of the same thing. To say of something
that it is dependently co-arisen is to say that it is empty. To say of something
that it is empty is another way of saying that it arises dependently.

Moreover, whatever is dependently co-arisen is verbally established. That is,
the identity of any dependently arisen thing depends upon verbal conventions.
To say of a thing that it is dependently arisen is to say that its identity as a single
entity is nothing more than its being the referent of a word. The thing itself,
apart from conventions of individuation, is nothing but an arbitrary slice of an
indefinite spatiotemporal and causal manifold. To say of a thing that its identity
is a merely verbal fact about it is to say that it is empty. To view emptiness in
this way is to see it neither as an entity nor as unreal—but instead to see it as
conventionally real. Moreover, *emptiness* itself is asserted to be a dependent designation (*prajñaptir-upādāya, brten nas gdags pa*). Its referent, emptiness itself, is
thereby asserted to be merely dependent and nominal—conventionally existent
but ultimately empty. This is hence a middle path with regard to emptiness. To
view the dependently originated world in this way is to see it neither as non-
empty nor as completely nonexistent. It is, viewed in this way, conventionally
existent, but empty. We hence have a middle path with regard to dependent
origination. To view convention in this way is to view it neither as ontologically
insignificant—it determines the character of the phenomenal world—nor as ontologically efficacious: it is empty. Hence we also have a middle way with regard
to convention. And finally, given the nice ambiguity in the reference of *that* (*de
ni*), not only are *dependent arising* and *emptiness* asserted to be dependent designations, and hence merely nominal, but the very relation between them is asserted to be so dependent, and hence to be empty.[9]

These morals are driven home in 24: 19, where Nāgārjuna emphasizes that
everything—and this must include emptiness—is dependently arisen. So everything, including emptiness, lacks inherent existence. So nothing lacks the three
co-extensive properties of emptiness, dependent-origination, and conventional
identity.

With this in hand, Nāgārjuna can reply to the critic: he first points out (24: 20–35; see Garfield 1995 for details) that by virtue of the identity of dependent origination and emptiness on the one hand and of ontological independence and intrinsic reality on the other, such phenomena as arising, ceasing, suffering, change, enlightenment, and so on—the very phenomena the opponent charges Nāgārjuna with denying—are possible only if they are empty. The tables are thus turned: it appeared that Nāgārjuna, in arguing for the emptiness of these phenomena, was arguing that in reality they do not exist, precisely because, for the reifier of emptiness, existence and emptiness are opposites. But in fact, because of the identity of emptiness and conventional existence, it is the reifier who, by virtue of denying the emptiness of these phenomena, denies their existence. And it is hence the reifier of emptiness who is impaled on both horns of the dilemma she or he presented to Nāgārjuna: contradicting the ultimate truth, she or he denies that these phenomena are empty; contradicting the conventional, she or he is forced to deny that they even exist! And so Nāgārjuna can conclude:

36   He who rejects the emptiness
      Of dependent origination,
      He rejects all
      Worldly conventions.

To assert the non-emptiness of phenomena and of their interrelations, Nāgārjuna suggests, when emptiness is properly understood, is not only philosophically deeply confused, but contradictory to common sense. We can make sense of this argument in the following way: common sense neither posits nor requires intrinsic reality in phenomena or a real causal nexus. Common sense holds the world to be a network of dependently arisen phenomena. So common sense holds the world to be empty. Again, the standpoint of emptiness is not at odds with the conventional standpoint, only with a particular philosophical understanding of it—that which takes the conventional to be more than merely conventional. What is curious—and, from the Buddhist standpoint, sad—about the human condition, on this view, is the naturalness and seductiveness of that philosophical perspective.[10]

The Emptiness of Emptiness

Let us consider now what it is to say that emptiness itself is empty. The claim, even in the context of Buddhist philosophy, does have a somewhat paradoxical air. (This paradox is explored in detail in chapter 5 of this volume.) For emptiness is, in Mahāyāna philosophical thought, the ultimate nature of all phenomena. And the distinction between the merely conventional nature of things and their ultimate nature would seem to mark the distinction between the apparent and the real. While it is plausible to say that what is merely apparent is empty of reality, it seems nihilistic to say that what is ultimately real is empty of reality, and as we have seen the Madhyamaka are quite consciously anti-nihilistic. But again, when we say that a phenomenon is empty, we say, inter alia, that it is impermanent, that it depends upon conditions, and that its identity depends upon convention. Do we really want to say of each phenomenon that its emptiness—the fact that it is empty—is itself impermanent; itself dependent on something else; itself dependent upon conventions? It might at least appear that even if all other properties of conventional entities were so, their emptiness would be an eternal, independent, essential fact.

It may be useful to approach the emptiness of emptiness by first asking what it would be to treat emptiness as non-empty. When we say that a phenomenon is empty, we mean that when we try to specify its essence, we come up with nothing. When we look for the substance that underlies the properties, or the bearer of the parts, we find none. When we ask what it is that gives a thing its identity, we stumble not upon ontological facts but upon conventions. For a thing to be non-empty would be for it to have an essence discoverable upon analysis; for it to be a substance independent of its attributes, or a bearer of parts; for its identity to be self-determined by its essence. A non-empty entity can be fully characterized nonrelationally.

For emptiness to be non-empty would be for it to be a substantial entity; an independent existent; a nonconventional phenomenon. On such a view, arguably held by certain Buddhist philosophical schools, emptiness is entirely distinct from any conventional phenomenon. It is, on such a view, the object of correct perception, while conventional phenomena are the objects of delusive perception. While conventional phenomena depend upon conventions, conditions, or the ignorance of obstructed minds, emptiness, on such a view, is apparent precisely when one sees through those conventions, dispels that ignorance, and overcomes those obstructions. It has no parts or conditions, and no properties. Though such a position might appear metaphysically extravagant, it is hardly unmotivated. For one thing, it seems that emptiness does have an identifiable essence—namely the lack of inherent existence. So if to be empty is to be empty of essence, emptiness fails on that count to be empty. Moreover, since all phenomena, on the Madhyamaka view, are empty, emptiness would appear to be eternal and independent of any particular conventions, and hence not dependently arisen. The Two Truths, on such an ontological vision, are indeed radically distinct from one another.

But this position is, from Nāgārjuna's perspective, untenable. The best way to see that follows: suppose that we take a conventional entity, such as a table. We analyze it to demonstrate its emptiness, finding that there is no table apart from its parts, that it cannot be distinguished in a principled way from its antecedent and subsequent histories, and so forth. So we conclude that it is empty. But now let us analyze that emptiness—the emptiness of the table, to see what we find.

What do we find? Nothing at all but the table's lack of inherent existence. The emptiness depends upon the table. No conventional table—no emptiness of the table. To see the table as empty, for Nāgārjuna, is not to somehow see "beyond" the illusion of the table to some other, more real entity. It is to see the table as conventional, as dependent. But the table that we so see when we see its emptiness is the very same table, seen not as the substantial thing we instinctively posit, but rather as it is. Emptiness is hence not different from conventional reality—it is the fact that conventional reality is conventional. Hence it must be dependently arisen, since it depends upon the existence of empty phenomena. Hence emptiness itself is empty. This is perhaps the deepest, most radical step in the Madhyamaka dialectic, but it is also, as we shall see, the step that saves the dialectic from falling into metaphysical extravagance and brings it back to sober pragmatic scepticism.

Now, this doctrine of the emptiness of emptiness emerges directly from 24: 18.

18   Whatever is dependently co-arisen,
        That is explained to be emptiness.
        That, being a dependent designation,
        Is itself the middle way.

For the emptiness of emptiness, as we have just seen, simply amounts to the identification of emptiness with the property of being dependently arisen, and with the property of having an identity just in virtue of conventional, verbal designation. It is the fact that emptiness is no more than this that makes it empty, just as it is the fact that conventional phenomena in general are no more than conventional, and no more than their parts and status in the causal nexus that makes them empty.[11]

So the doctrine of the emptiness of emptiness can be seen as inextricably linked to Nāgārjuna's distinctive account of the relation between the Two Truths. For Nāgārjuna, as is also evident in this crucial verse, it is a mistake to distinguish conventional from ultimate reality—the dependently arisen from emptiness—at an ontological level. Emptiness just is the emptiness of conventional phenomena. To perceive conventional phenomena as empty is just to see them as conventional, and as dependently arisen. The difference—such as it is—between the conventional and the ultimate is a difference in the way phenomena are conceived/perceived. The point must be formulated with some delicacy, and cannot be formulated without a hint of the paradoxical: conventional phenomena are typically represented as inherently existent. We typically perceive and conceive of external phenomena, ourselves, causal powers, moral truths, and so on as independently existing, intrinsically identifiable, and substantial. But though this is, in one sense, the conventional character of conventional phenomena—the manner in which they are ordinarily experienced—to see them this way is precisely not to see them *as conventional*. To see that they are merely conventional, in the sense adumbrated above and defended by Nāgārjuna and his followers, is thereby to see them as empty, and this is their ultimate mode of existence. These are the Two Truths about phenomena: on the one hand they are conventionally existent and the things we ordinarily say about them are in fact true, to the extent that we get it right on the terms of the everyday. Snow is indeed white, and there are indeed tables and chairs in this room. On the other hand, they are ultimately nonexistent. These two truths seem as different as night and day—being and nonbeing. But the import of 24: 18 and the doctrine we have been explicating is that their ultimate nonexistence and their conventional existence are the same thing—hence the deep identity of the Two Truths. And this is true because emptiness is not other than dependent-arising, and hence because emptiness is empty.

Furthermore, in order to see why chapter 1 is not only essential groundwork for this central argument but in fact anticipates it and applies its conclusion implicitly on the whole remainder of the text, we must note that this entire account depends upon the emptiness of dependent origination itself. To see this, suppose for a moment that one had the view that dependent arising were non-empty (not a crazy view, and not *obviously* incompatible with, and arguably en-tailed by, certain Buddhist doctrines). Then, from the identification of emptiness with dependent arising would follow the non-emptiness of emptiness. More-over, if conventional phenomena are empty, and dependent arising itself is non-empty and is identified with emptiness, than the Two Truths are indeed two in every sense. Emptiness-dependent arising is self-existent, while ordinary phenom-ena are not, and one gets a strongly dualistic, ontological version of an appear-ance-reality distinction. So the argument for the emptiness of emptiness in Chapter 24 and the identity of the Two Truths with which it is bound, depend critically on the argument for the emptiness of dependent origination developed in chapter 1.

SIMPLE EMPTINESS VERSUS THE EMPTINESS OF EMPTINESS

We can now see why positing real causation, in the fully reified cement-of-the-universe sense as the instantiation of the relation between *explanans* and *explan-anda*, could never be justifiable from the Madhyamaka standpoint. For though that would at first glance leave phenomena themselves empty of inherent exis-tence, it would retain a non-empty feature of the phenomenal world and lose the emptiness of emptiness itself. Moreover, a bit of reflection should lead us to recognize the deep tension in this metaphysics: if the causal powers of things are ultimately real, it is hard to see how one could maintain the merely conventional status of the things themselves. For they could always be individuated as the bearers of those ultimately real causal powers, and the entire doctrine of the emptiness of phenomena would collapse.

Substituting conditions for causes solves this problem. For as we have seen, by shifting the account in this way, we come to understand the relation between conditions and the conditioned as obtaining by virtue of regularity and explanatory utility. And both of these determinants of the relation are firmly rooted in convention rather than in any extraconventional facts. Regularity is always regularity-under-a-description, and descriptions are, as Nāgārjuna puts it, "verbal designations." Explanatory utility is always relative to human purposes and theoretical frameworks. Dependent origination is hence, on this model, a thoroughly conventional and hence empty alternative to a reified causal model, which nonetheless permits all of the explanatory moves of which a theory committed to causation is capable. For every causal link one might posit, an equivalent conditional relation can be posited. But the otiose and ultimately incoherent posit of causal power is dispensed with on Nāgārjuna's formulation.

But if the foregoing interpretation is correct, we can make a more radical interpretative claim regarding the structure of *Mūlamadhyamakakārikā*: the entire doctrine of the emptiness of emptiness and the unity of the Two Truths developed in chapter 24 is already implicit in chapter I. Recall the structure of the argument so far, as we have traced the complex doctrinal web Nāgārjuna spins: the central thesis of chapter 1 as we have characterized it is that there is no inherently existent causal nexus. The link between conditions and the phenomena dependent upon them is empty. To be empty is, however, to be dependent. Emptiness itself is, hence, as is explicitly articulated in chapter 24, dependent arising. Hence the emptiness of dependent arising is the emptiness of emptiness. And the emptiness of emptiness, as we have seen, is equivalent to the deep identity between the Two Truths. So the entire central doctrine developed in the climactic chapter 24 is present in embryo in the first. And this is the reason that Nāgārjuna began with causation.

Now, to be sure, it is not apparent on first reading the opening chapter of *Mūlamadhyamakakārikā* that this is the import of the argument. The rhetorical structure of the text only makes this clear in retrospect when enough of the philosophical apparatus is set out to make the entire framework clear. But once we see this framework, a rereading of the text in light of this understanding of the opening chapter is instructive. For it is one thing to argue for the emptiness of some phenomenon *simpliciter* and quite another to argue for that emptiness with the emptiness of emptiness in mind. If we read the opening chapter in the first way, we are likely to miss the force of many of the particular analyses in the text the depth of which only emerges in light of the deeper thesis of the emptiness of emptiness. If one argues simply that a phenomenon is empty of inherent existence, one leaves open the possibility that this is in contrast to phenomena that are inherently existent, and hence that the force of this argument is that the phenomenon in question is not actually existent. If, on the other hand, one argues that a phenomenon is empty in the context of the emptiness of emptiness, one is explicitly committed to the view that its emptiness does not entail its nonactuality. Emptiness in this context is not nonexistence. The lack of inherent existence that is asserted is not the lack of a property possessed by some entities but not by others, or a property that an entity could be imagined to have, but rather the lack of an impossible attribute. This reorientation of the argument gives what might appear to be a series of starkly nihilistic analyses a remarkably positive tone.

Consider briefly one example of the difference this reading of chapter 1 induces in reading the subsequent text: the analysis of motion and rest in chapter 2. I will not provide a verse-by-verse commentary on the chapter here (see Garfield 1995 for that analysis). But note the following salient features of Nāgārjuna's analysis: the target of the argument is a view of motion according to which it is an entity, or at least a property with an existence independent of that of moving things, or according to which it is part of the nature of moving things. These are versions of what it would be to think of motion as non-empty. Nāgārjuna argues that from such a view a number of absurd consequences would follow: things not in motion but that were in motion in the past or that will be in the future would have to undergo substantial change, effectively becoming different things when they changed state from motion to rest or vice versa; a regress would ensue from the need for the entity motion itself to be in motion; motion would occur in the absence of moving things; the moment at which a thing begins or ceases motion would be indescribable. Nāgārjuna concludes that a reification of motion is incoherent. Motion is therefore empty.

So far so good. But then is motion nonexistent? Is the entire universe static according to Madhyamaka philosophy? If we simply read this chapter in isolation, that conclusion might indeed seem warranted. It would be hard to distinguish emptiness from complete nonexistence. We would be left with an illusory world of change and movement, behind which would lie a static ultimate reality. But such a reading would be problematic. For one thing, it would be absurd on its face. Things move and change. Second, it would contradict the doctrine of dependent origination and change that is the very basis of any Buddhist philosophical system, and that Nāgārjuna has already endorsed in the opening chapter. How, then, are we to read this discussion more positively? The answer is hermeneutically critical not only for an understanding of this chapter, but for a reading of the entire text, which, if not done carefully, can appear unrelentingly nihilistic. And on such a nihilistic reading, the appearance/reality distinction that is forced can only coincide with the conventional reality/emptiness distinction, resulting in a denial of reality to the mundane world and a reification of emptiness itself.

The positive account we seek emerges when we recall the emptiness of emptiness and read this second chapter in the context of the reinterpreted first chapter: emptiness itself, as we have seen, according to the analysis of dependent arising, is dependently arisen. It is nothing but the emptiness of conventional phenomena and is the fact of their being dependent and conventional. If emptiness itself is understood as non-empty, on the other hand, then for a phenomenon to be denominated empty is for it to be completely nonexistent. For then its merely conventional character would stand against the ultimate reality of emptiness itself. We have just seen how this would play out in the case of motion, and a moment's reflection would indicate that any other phenomenon subjected to this analysis would fare about as well. But consider, on the other hand, how we interpret the status of motion in light of the emptiness of its emptiness: the conclusion that motion is empty is then simply the conclusion that it is merely conventional and dependent, like the putatively moving entities themselves. Since there is no implicit, contrastive, inherently existent ultimate reality, this conclusion does not lead us to ascribe a "second class" or merely apparent existence to motion or to movers. Their nonexistence—their emptiness—is hence itself nonexistent in exactly the sense that they are. Existence—of a sort—is hence recovered exactly in the context of an absence of inherent existence.

But existence of what kind? Herein lies the clue to the positive construction of motion that emerges. The existence that emerges is a conventional and dependent existence. Motion does not exist as an entity on this account, but rather as a relation—as the relation between the positions of a body at distinct times, and hence as dependent upon that body and those positions. Moreover, it emerges as a conventional entity in the following critical sense: only to the extent that we make the decision to identify entities that differ from each other in position over time, but are in other respects quite similar, and that form causal chains of a particular sort, as the same entity can we say that the entity so identified moves. And this is a matter of choice. For we could decide to say that entities that differ in any respect are thereby distinct. If we did adopt that convention for individuation, an entity here now and one there then would ipso facto be distinct entities. And so no single entity could adopt different positions (or different properties) at different times, and so motion and change would be nonexistent. It is there dependencies of motion on the moved, of the status of things as moved on their motion, and of both on conventions of individuation that, on this account, constitute their emptiness. But this simply constitutes their conventional existence and provides an analysis of the means by which they so exist. The emptiness of motion is hence seen to be its existence as conventional and as dependent and hence as not other than its conventional existence. And this just is the emptiness of emptiness. But in understanding its emptiness in this way, we bring motion, change, and movable and changeable entities back from the brink of extinction.

It is thus that seeing Nāgārjuna's analysis of the emptiness of phenomena in the context of the emptiness of emptiness allows for a non-nihilistic, non-dualistic, constructive reading of the Madhyamaka dialectic, but a reading which for all of that is rich in its explication of the structure of reality and of our relation to it. But this reading is only accessible in the chapters analyzing particular phenomena if we already find it in chapter 1. And this, I have argued, is possible once we reread that initial chapter in light of the analysis in chapter 24. The Nāgārjuna who emerges is a subtle figure indeed.

THE IMPORTANCE OF CAUSATION

The analysis of causation can often look like a highly technical aside in philosophy. It might not seem at first glance to be one of the really "big" questions, like those concerning what entities there are; what the nature of mind is; what the highest good is. By contrast causation often appears to the outsider or to the beginner like one of those recherché corners of philosophy that one has to work one's way into. But of course even in the history of Western metaphysics and epistemology it has always been central. One has only to think of the role of a theory of causation for Hume, Kant, Schopenhauer, or Wittgenstein to see this. This study of *Mūlamadhyamakakārikā* shows why: a clear understanding of the nature of the causal relation is the key to understanding the nature of reality itself and of our relation to it. For causation is, as Hume, Kant, and Schopenhauer as well as Nāgārjuna emphasize, at the heart of our individuation of objects, of our ordering our experience of the world, and of our understanding of our own agency in the world. Without a clear view of causation, we can view nothing else clearly.

Nāgārjuna begins by examining the causal relation for this reason generally. But for Nāgārjuna there is a further, more specific reason, one without explicit parallel in the work of other systematic philosophers, though it is to be sure hinted at darkly in the work of those just mentioned. According to Nāgārjuna, by examining the nature of dependent arising, and by showing the emptiness of causation itself, we understand the nature of emptiness itself, and thereby push the Madhyamaka dialectic of emptiness to its conclusion. By showing causation to be empty, we show all things to be empty, even emptiness itself. Nāgārjuna begins with causation because by doing the important conclusions at which the text is aimed are accessible throughout the examination, even if they are not made explicit until much later.

ANTIMETAPHYSICAL PRAGMATISM IN BUDDHISM

When a Westerner first encounters *Mūlamadhyamakakārikā* or other Madhyamaka texts, the philosophical approach can appear highly metaphysical and downright weird. The unfamiliar philosophical vocabulary, the highly negative dialectic, and the cryptic verse form are indeed forbidding. Most bizarre of all, however, at first glance is the doctrine that all phenomena, including self and its objects, are empty. For indeed Nāgārjuna and his followers do argue that the entire everyday world is, from the ultimate standpoint, nonexistent. And that does indeed appear to stand just a bit deeper into philosophical left field than even Berkeley dares to play. But if the interpretation I have been urging is adopted, the real central thrust of Madhyamaka is the demystification of this apparently mystical conclusion. While it might appear that the mādhyamika argue that nothing really exists except a formless luminous void, in fact the entire phenomenal world, persons and all, are recovered within that emptiness.

And if what I have said is correct, the principal philosophical move in this demystification of emptiness is the attack on a reified view of causality. Nāgārjuna replaces the view shared by the metaphysician and the person-in-the-street, which presents itself as commonsense but is in fact deeply metaphysical, with an apparently paradoxical, thoroughly empty, but in the end commonsense view not only of causation, but of the entire phenomenal world.

Emptiness and Positionlessness

Do the Mādhyamika Relinquish All Views?

In THE FINAL VERSE of his major work, *Mūlamadhyamakakārikā*, Nāgārjuna writes:

> I prostrate to Gautama
> Who through compassion
> Taught the true doctrine,
> Which leads to the relinquishing of all views. (27: 30)

This verse echoes an earlier remark:

> The victorious ones have said
> That emptiness is the relinquishing of all views.
> For whomever emptiness is a view
> That one has accomplished nothing. (13: 8)

It is not at all clear how one is to understand such claims. One response, of course, would be to mutter either with reverence or with derision about the mystery, paradox, and irrationality or about the fantastic transcendence of rationality of the East. But either would be too facile. For one thing, it would be simply to shirk the hermeneutic burden of making sense of the text. But more compellingly, given the relentlessly rational, meticulously argued character of the text as a whole, and indeed of his entire corpus, such a reaction would be hard to justify with respect to Nāgārjuna. And finally, given the extensive commentarial tradition rooted in this text, beginning with Nāgārjuna's immediate disciple Āryadeva and continuing to the present day, with its different readings and interpretations, several competing understandings of the text are already available.

So we can't avoid the task of providing a coherent reading of these prima facie paradoxical verses, nor can we ignore their apparently paradoxical character. For Nāgārjuna is, throughout his philosophical corpus, in one straightforward sense, advancing a view, the Madhyamaka view that all phenomena are ultimately empty though conventionally real and dependently originated, and so on. And it is through adopting this view that Nāgārjuna holds that we can attain nirvāna—liberation from the suffering whose root lies in false views. Can Nāgārjuna be seriously suggesting that we relinquish *that* view? Would that not be self-defeating? Would that not be like saying out loud, "I am now silent"?

A long and highly influential line of commentators, beginning with rJe Tsong khapa, the founder of the dGe lugs school of Tibetan Buddhism, and his disciple mKhas grub rje, provide a straightforward solution to the hermeneutic problem these verses pose: they simply argue that when Nāgārjuna speaks of relinquishing "all views," he means "all false views," or "all views according to which things are inherently existent."

> Nowadays some who wish to be prāsaṅgika-mādhyamikas say: Our system even conventionally does not have any assertions based on the ultimate or the conventional. . . . Therefore there is no such thing as an own system for prāsaṅgikas since Nāgārjuna, Āryadeva, and Candrakīrti say that mād-hyamikas have no position and no thesis. As Nāgārjuna's refutation of Objections says:
>
>> 29 If I had any proposition (*pratijñā*) then this defect would be mine. I have, however, no proposition. Therefore there is no defect that is mine.
>
> Answer: If this which you propound is not the Madhyamaka system, then it is contradictory to establish it through citing passages from the superior Nāgārjuna and his spiritual sons. . . . If you say it is Madhyamaka and, from within that, the system of Candrakīrti, then it would contradict your assertion that mādhyamikas in general and Candrakīrti in particular do not have their own system . . . (LRCM 435 b in Hopkins 1983)
>
>> Since it would have to be that there was no correct view leading to the state of nirvāṇa, all the activities of hearing, thinking etc. . . . with respect to the Madhyamaka scriptures would be senseless. (TKP: LRCM 471 b5 in Napper 1993)

The text, they point out, is full of passages in which the assertions are subject to im-plicit qualification of this kind. So, for instance, when Nāgārjuna in chapter 2 says,

> So movement and motion
> And agent of motion are non-existent. (2: 25)

nobody thinks that he is denying that anything ever moves. Rather, all commen-tators agree that he is asserting that we can't think of motion, movers, or the act of moving as inherently existent or independent. The dGe lugs pa commentators emphasize that to do this, we read the word *nonexistent* as qualified implicitly by *inherently*—that is, as "not inherently existent."[1] So, given the fact that Madhyamaka hermeneutics regularly requires the interpretive insertion of such qualifiers, and given that the passages can be readily demystified with just such an insertion, there is strong reason to read them in this way.

But there is more. Emptiness, for a mādhyamika, is an ultimate truth. One *can* achieve a correct view—a view of things as they in fact are. Such a view surely should not be relinquished, for this would be to relinquish the soteriological goal of all of Buddhist practice. So, the dGe lugs pas argue, one must read Nāgārjuna as suggesting straightforwardly, rationally, and without even a hint of paradox, that one should relinquish all false views, and that for the one who views emptiness as inherently existent there is no hope.

Though this route has every hermeneutic virtue, it emerges in the fourteenth century as a response to an older and then prevalent view, expounded most forcefully in Tibet by Ngog blo ldan shes rab, whose own texts unfortunately do not survive except in fragments quoted in later works. This older view is dominant in the commentarial tradition of the Nying-ma school of Tibetan Buddhism. According to Ngog, Nāgārjuna means just what he says. The central teaching of Madhyamaka is that one should relinquish all views, and that if Madhyamaka becomes a philosophical view, one has fundamentally missed its point.[2] Scriptural evidence for Ngog's view includes this passage from Śāntideva's *Bodhicaryāvatāra*:

2   The conventional and the ultimate
        Are explained to be the two truths.
        The ultimate is not grasped as an object of thought;
        Thought is explained to be merely conventional.
                                (Śāntideva, *Bodhicaryāvatāra* 10)

This of course requires the correlative and equally challenging theses that one who knows emptiness has no view of anything—and hence has objectless knowledge, and that emptiness itself is not an object of knowledge, and not an entity. And Ngog and his Nying-ma followers do not shy away from these claims.[3] Making sense of these claims is not easy, but this is my intention in this chapter. For Nāgārjuna generally, the dGe lugs to the contrary notwithstanding, says what he means. And, in the verses in question, nothing forces the kinds of implicit qualifiers that often *are* contextually forced. Too much of the remainder of the text, as well as Nāgārjuna's reply in his *Vigrahavyāvartanī* (to be discussed later in this chapter), coheres with the straightforward literal reading of these verses.

Moreover, reading Nāgārjuna in this way highlights some of the intriguing parallels between Madhyamaka philosophical method and Western Pyrrhonism, as it is articulated in the tradition running from Pyrrho and Timon through Sextus Empiricus right up to Wittgenstein's *Tractatus* and *Philosophical Investigations*. While subjecting an Indian Buddhist text to a European procrustean bed is hardly by itself an argument for an interpretation, there are so many powerful affinities in method and in detail between Madhyamaka and Western skepticism that the appearance of a further parallel must be taken as at least suggestive. So when we consider remarks like the following, we are forced to ask ourselves how we in the West make coherent sense of them, and whether the same interpretive strategies might not be apposite in the case of Nāgārjuna:

We determine nothing.

All things are undetermined.

We must not say about any one thing that it is or that it is not or that it is and it is not or that it neither is nor is not. (Pyrrho)[4]

[T]he sceptic does not take the real existence of these formulae wholly for granted. As he understands them, the formula "All things are false," for example, asserts its own falsity together with that of other things. . . . (36)

[I]f dogma is defined as "assent to a non-evident thing," then we shall say that we have no system. But if one means by "system" a "discipline which, in accordance with appearance, follows a certain line of reasoning, indicating how it is possible to live rightly . . . we shall say that we do have a system." (37)

Non-assertion . . . is a disuse of assertion in which . . . both affirmation and denial are applied. . . . [W]e neither affirm nor deny anything. (81) (Sextus, in Hallie 1985)

6.54 My propositions serve as elucidations in the following way: anyone who understands me eventually recognizes them as nonsensical, when he has used them—as steps—to climb beyond them. (He must, so to speak, throw away the ladder after he has climbed up it.)

7 What we cannot speak about we must pass over in silence. Wittgenstein, (*Tractatus*, trans. B. F. McGuiness, 1922)

What these traditions share, at the broadest level of description, is the philosophical project of undermining essentialism. For Pyrrho and for Sextus, Wittgenstein, and Nāgārjuna, and for all of their skeptical followers, the fundamental philosophical error is to propose a characterization of the nature of things. This is so, from their perspective, not because the nature of things is elusive, but rather because there is no nature of things—because the very concept of an essence is itself incoherent. In reading Western skepticism, we must always be sensitive to the expository difficulties of this project: for essentialism is virtually built into the grammar of our language. That is why it is so seductive. To articulate the critique requires a careful account of how language works, and of how it is being used in the philosophical critique in question. And that account itself will be subject to the same misconstruals. But we *can* understand what it is to kick away the ladder, and we *can* question the primacy of assertion as a linguistic act. This kicking and questioning—this banging our heads against the walls of language—is essential to attaining clarity about the role of language and conception in ontology and in our mode of being in the world (see chapters 1 and 5 of this volume for more on this issue).

This questioning of the primacy of assertion and with it the realist semantics for natural language that undergirds this presupposition lies at the heart of the Madhyamaka critique of essentialist philosophy. Such probing also affirms the important affinities of this ancient Indian philosophical movement to much of the contemporary, postmodern philosophy of language and epistemology based on the critical work of Wittgenstein. The affinities extend, as one would expect, beyond the narrow confines of semantics, to indicate a general agreement regarding the inescapability of situatedness and perspective in knowledge. They also share a faith in the possibility of a recognition of that predicament and in the power of that recognition to liberate us from the tyranny of our particular perspective. My aim in this chapter is not only to defend one side of a recherché medieval Tibetan debate in Nāgārjuna interpretation, but also to illuminate these larger issues in the philosophy of language and epistemology. So let us work towards such an understanding of Nāgārjuna's claim to relinquish all views, with Pyrrhonism in the corner of our eye, and more of Nāgārjuna's enterprise in view. We begin with a survey of emptiness itself.

EMPTINESS

When Nāgārjuna and his followers assert that all phenomena are empty, it is important to ask just what phenomena are asserted to be empty *of*. For emptiness is not, of course, a monadic property. A room that is empty of elephants, such as the one in which I am now writing, may not be empty of people. The property of which Nāgārjuna asserts phenomena to be empty is most often referred to as "inherent existence," which denotes the putative property of existing simply per se, independent of any conditions or relations or other phenomena. But we can also say that it is to be empty of essence—empty of any intrinsic property or characteristic that makes an entity what it is, or to be empty of substantial existence—to be empty of being an entity distinct from and a basis of its attributes. A good deal of Madhyamaka philosophy is devoted to showing that these characterizations amount to the same things.

The assertion that all phenomena are empty is tightly bound up with the doctrine of the Two Truths—of a conventional truth and an ultimate truth, and of the complex relation between them. The ultimate truth about phenomena is their emptiness: their lack of essence, independence, and exist ultimately would be to exist substantiality substantially independently, by virtue of the possession of an essence. Nothing, the mādhyamika asserts, exists in this way. But that does not mean that all phenomena are completely nonexistent, that they are imaginary. Rather, argue Nāgārjuna and his followers, real phenomena are conventionally existent. To be conventionally existent is to exist dependently, to possess one's identity nominally, to be essenceless and impermanent. A thorough discussion of the doctrine of the emptiness of phenomena and of the connection between ultimate emptiness and conventional or nominal reality would take us far afield. For now, these remarks will have to suffice.[5]

It is crucial to realize that Nāgārjuna does not argue that all conventional phenomena are empty of essence only to posit emptiness itself as substantially existent. Instead emptiness itself, rather than existing as an absolute reality beyond the relative—as true existence as opposed to illusion—is no more than the emptiness of conventional phenomena. As such, it too, is dependently originated, merely conventionally existent, and hence empty of inherent existence. This doctrine of the emptiness of emptiness, and consequent refusal to ascribe inherent existence to anything—whether a conventional or an ultimate phenomenon—is common to all Madhyamaka schools.

Emptiness must hence be understood, in this philosophical context, neither as nonexistence nor as an independent reality lying behind a veil of illusion, but rather as the mode of existence of conventional phenomena, and at that a mode that exists in exactly the same way as any other conventional phenomenon.[6] Emptiness is, in short, nothing more than the fact that conventional dependent phenomena are conventional and dependent. It is simply the only way in which anything can exist. Rather than to assert that because phenomena are empty they are nonexistent, the mādhyamika asserts that because phenomena exist they are empty.

For this reason it is important not to move from the fact that all phenomena are empty of essence to the assertion that emptiness is the essence of all phenomena. That is, we do not want to turn essencelessness itself into an essence. For if it is correct to argue that all things are empty of essence, and if emptiness were an essence, it would paradoxically turn out that all things were nonempty, in which case they would have essences. This purely negative characterization of emptiness must be kept in mind as we examine the degree to which and sense in which emptiness can be an object of knowledge or an entity, and so the sense in which Madhyamaka philosophy must be understood as, in the end, positionless.[7] (See chapter 5 of this volume for an extended discussion of the paradoxes that lie in this neighbourhood.)

Emptiness and Meaning

Before moving more directly to the question that concerns us, I turn to a few points regarding Madhyamaka philosophy of language. For the question whether

Nāgārjuna really advocates relinquishing all views is in fact semantic: is it possible to understand the words that Nāgārjuna utters to claim that he is not expressing propositions? If not, either he is flatly self-contradictory, talking nonsense, or in fact means something else. If so, I will have identified a nonassertorial understanding of his words, according to which they are nonetheless true.

We have seen that, from the standpoint of Madhyamaka, there is no convention-independent reality correspondence with which could be truth-making. But that does not entail the impossibility of a correspondence theory of truth *tout court*. Indeed, the very emptiness of phenomena that makes correspondence with a convention-independent reality chimerical ensures the empirical existence of a world of conventional entities. And indeed, these entities are our referents when we use ordinary, or even philosophical, discourse. They are the domain of conventional truth. For Nāgārjuna and his followers, sentences are indeed conventionally true just in case the entities their referring terms designate in fact satisfy their predicates, where these terms are understood in the ordinary way.

But what about sentences that purport to characterize ultimates or to describe things from the standpoint of ultimate knowledge? Here things are a bit more delicate. The subject, now, remember, is sentences that make assertions about emptiness itself, sentences like "Emptiness is itself empty," or perhaps more interestingly, "Emptiness is without characteristics." In thinking about these sentences, one must also bear in mind that their status must be considered from two distinct vantage points. The first is that of the ordinary philosopher whose objects of direct apprehension are conventional entities, but who can inferentially realize their emptiness, and who, by extension, can be the subject of cognitive states such as beliefs whose direct object, via conception, is emptiness. The second is that of the arhat, who directly perceives emptiness as it is unmediated either by apprehension of (other) conventional entities or by conception.

First things first: given the Madhyamaka analysis of the emptiness of all phenomena, and especially given the particular working out within Madhyamaka philosophy of the identity of the Two Truths and of the emptiness of emptiness, even ultimates are empty of inherent existence, and hence dependently originated, and hence merely conventional. So when I say that emptiness is empty of inherent existence, if you were to ask about the ontological basis of the truth of that sentence, at one level, the story I can tell is just the same as the one that I tell regarding the ontological basis of the truth of my claim that snow is white. Emptiness, like snow, is ultimately empty but (and therefore) conventionally existent. Insofar as it is conventionally existent, we can ask about the nominal properties that conventional entities can be asserted to have, and among them is, in the case of emptiness, its emptiness, just as among the properties that we can say snow has is its whiteness. But in neither case do we suppose, in order to make sense of this ordinary discourse, either the substantial existence of the referent of the subject term, or the independent existence of the ascribed property, or anything besides the nominal truth of the sentence. That is what it means to hypostasize neither the substantiality of conventional entities nor of the lack thereof.

But things, as we shall see, are subtly different from the standpoint of one *directly* perceiving ultimates. To make this case completely and to spell out its contents in detail will take some time and require a few side trips through semantic and epistemological terrain. But to explain my motivation for these detours, I offer a preliminary sketch of the destination (a sort of soteriological postcard: having a great time; wish you were here!): for the arhat who directly realizes emptiness, nothing is present in consciousness but emptiness itself. For such a consciousness there literally is no object, since there is in such a consciousness no reification of the kind that gives rise to subject-object duality. Moreover, since such a consciousness is directed only toward what can be found ultimately to exist, and since nothing can be so found, there is literally nothing toward which such a consciousness can be directed. But this very fact is what is ostended by the dictum that emptiness is itself empty: That is the fact that emptiness is not *the real object* as opposed to the unreal object of ordinary perception; not the object that appears when false appearance is shed; that it, to the extent that it appears as an object at all, it does so as falsely as does any table. But then the semantic story told from this perspective is somewhat different. The best that can then be said is that from such a standpoint the words "Emptiness is empty" ascribe no property to any object at all: from that standpoint, they express no proposition. At that stage, there is no view to be expressed, where a view is something that can be given assertoric voice. Or so I will argue.

This is the point that I take Nāgārjuna to be seeking when in *Vigrahavyāvartanī* he writes:

29   If I had any proposition at all,
        Thereby I would have that fault.
        Since I don't have a proposition
        I don't have any fault at all.

> If I had even one proposition thereby it would be just as you have said. Though if I had a proposition with the characteristic that you described, I would have that fault, I have no proposition at all. Thus, since all phenomena are empty, at peace, by nature isolated, how could there be a proposition? How can there be a characteristic of a proposition? And how can there be a fault arising from the characteristic of a proposition? Thus, the statement, "through the characteristic of your proposition you come to acquire the fault" is not true.

And so let us now take some time to examine this locus classicus for textual support for the position I now defend. There is a persuasive strain of dGe lugs pa and dGe lugs-inspired Western scholarship that urges the insertion of some qualifiers here—that Nāgārjuna really wishes to renounce only inherently existent propositions, or propositions that ascribe inherent existence to their objects. This interpretation derives some support from one contextual dimension. Consider, the dGe lugs say, the opponent's charge in the verse to which verse 29 responds:

4   If you say it is like the negation of a negation,
       If you maintain that, that won't do any good.
       Seeing it that way, your proposition will thus
       Have a defective characteristic, not mine.

If we pay attention merely to this dialectical move, the dGe lugs' construal is quite natural. The substantialist opponent charges Nāgārjuna with using an assertion (that all phenomena are empty) that he must, in order to be consistent, regard as itself empty. Now, for the opponent, emptiness is nonexistence. So the opponent charges Nāgārjuna with the self-refuting assertion that everything is nonexistent, including that very assertion. And she[8] points out that the same charge does not apply to anyone asserting the negation of the proposition—that all things are non-empty—that is, that phenomena in fact exist in some way, since for one making that assertion, the very assertion counts as evidence of its truth.

So on this reading, Nāgārjuna is only replying to a criticism that misconstrues the nature of emptiness and asserting that on a proper construal the alleged logical error is not committed. But consider the auto-commentary on the opponent's move:

> It may appear to you that a negation of a negation is impossible in this way. If so, your statement negating the negation of the statement that all things have essence would thus also be impossible. To this we reply: That won't do any good! This follows because the objection applies to *you* in virtue of the character of *your* proposition; since mine doesn't have that character, to say that the negation of a negation is not possible doesn't make any sense.

This subtle semantic remark requires close attention. It is important to bear in mind the Nyāya-influenced logico-semantic context in which these debates originate. The dominant view of the nature of meaningful assertion (the one that Nāgārjuna questions) is one that from our perspective can best be characterized as a version of Fregean realism: Meaningful assertions are meaningful because they denote or express independently existent propositions.[9,10] A proposition is the pervasion of an individual entity or groups of entities by a real universal or sequence of universals.

Against this background, opponent can be seen as attacking Nāgārjuna at a deeper, more ontologically significant level: she anticipates that Nāgārjuna will charge *her* with what must be, *on her own terms*, a contradiction.[11] For the opponent has, one move earlier in the debate, argued that Nāgārjuna's words, if true, deny the existence of what could make them true, that is, language-independent entities and universals. Hence, she asserts, Nāgārjuna's words are nonsense.

But this, the opponent recognizes, presents *her* with a prima facie problem, by virtue of *her* presupposition of the existence of propositions as foundations of meaning: in leveling this charge of self-undermining against Nāgārjuna, she in fact asserts the *negation of Nāgārjuna's thesis*. But the negation of nonsense must itself be nonsense. Hence Nāgārjuna, in this sketch of her next move in the debate has *her* anticipating *his* objection that the negation of nonsense must, given the opponent's position, then itself be nonsense, with the consequence that the *opponent's position* would be self-refuting.[12] The opponent *then* replies that all *she* is doing is providing a *reductio* on Nāgārjuna's position, and not offering an independent thesis of her own. In the context of *Prāsaṅgika-Madhyamaka* methodology, the irony is palpable and the logic poignant.[13]

Now consider the auto-commentary on Nāgārjuna's reply:

> If I had even one proposition thereby it would be just as you have said. Though if I had a proposition with the characteristic that you described, I would have that fault, I have no proposition at all. Thus, since all phenomena are empty, at peace, by nature isolated, how could there be a proposition? How can there be a characteristic of a proposition? And how can there be a fault arising from the characteristic of a proposition? Thus, the statement, "through the characteristic of your proposition you come to acquire the fault" is not true.

Note that Nāgārjuna does *not* refer here to emptiness or to nonexistence, or to any supposed confusion between the two. He is worried about whether or not he is asserting a proposition,[14] and so he should be. For the opponent has tried to turn the ontological tables on him, presenting a *reductio* whose conclusion is not that Nāgārjuna's assertion that all things, including those very *words*, are *nonexistent* entails its own nonexistence, but rather that his words, if true, are *meaningless*, since *if* they are true no proposition corresponds to them. If Nāgārjuna shared with her the presupposition that meaning is to be analyzed in terms of relations of words to propositions, the *reductio* would hit the mark. So he must respond by denying the commitment to such an analysis.

And that, of course, is just what he does: it is characteristic of Madhyamaka rhetorical strategy, and particular trademark of Nāgārjuna, to refute an opponent's position by demonstrating that the uncomfortable consequence she attributes to the mādhyamika's position not only does not attach thereto but moreover is a presupposition of the opponent's position. Here Nāgārjuna, adopting that strategy, asserts that he is merely using words. Their emptiness amounts to their being merely conventional tools denoting nothing, and whose sense presupposes no language-independent denotation but rather derives merely from their utility in discourse. In exactly this sense he has no proposition, though he uses plenty of words. It is the opponent, who, by virtue of denying the emptiness of language, is committed to the existence of propositions as entities that ground meaning. But if she is so committed, then she has a problem, for she must then make sense of her own denial of Nāgārjuna's proposition. And that requires that she concede the coherence of Nāgārjuna's thesis. But to concede its coherence is to give up the *reductio*. Moreover, it is to concede that meaning does not presuppose the existence of propositions, but rather relocates the burden of proof squarely on the opponent to demonstrate the existence of an unobserved metaphysical fifth wheel, and one that even leads to paradox.

This reading of these crucial verses from *Vigrahavyāvartanī* establishes several important points that are essential for understanding the mādhyamika's claims to relinquish all views: (1) Nāgārjuna *does* sincerely claim to assert no proposition, not merely to assert no inherently existent proposition. (2) He does *not* thereby deny that he *uses words*. (3) The claim to assert no proposition is a semantic claim that is bound up with the claim that language, like all other phenomena, is empty. (4) Nāgārjuna does not disclaim the truth of his utterances, though he does disclaim a nonconventional ontological ground for that truth.

Emptiness as Knowable I: Can Emptiness Be an Object of Knowledge?

At this point, I return to epistemological terrain and ask about the nature of our knowledge about emptiness. For positionlessness must be characterized in such a way that it does not, self-refutingly, entail that we cannot have the knowledge that gives rise to it. Moreover, of course, it must come out that it is consistent with all of the rest of Nāgārjuna's assertions. So, to put the point most straightforwardly, it must come out true that things are empty, and this truth must be knowable. It will therefore be a constraint on our analysis that a mādhyamika philosopher can say these things and come to realize the truth of emptiness in such a way as to enable release from the delusions of *saṃsāra*.[15,16]

Nonetheless, despite this emphasis on the knowability of emptiness, no party to this dispute would argue that emptiness exists inherently, or ultimately. Emptiness, all agree, is a conventional existent. But, as we will see in the discussion that follows, what it is to be a conventional entity is not a straightforward matter.

Positive and Negative Tetralemmas

I now add one more piece to this philosophical jigsaw puzzle. Nāgārjuna, famously, uses the classical Buddhist *catuḥskoti*, or tetralemma, form of analysis, which considers with respect to any pair of contradictories not only the possibilities of each being true, but also those of both being true and neither. Interestingly, though, in *Mūlamadhyamakakārikā*, the tetralemma is deployed in two distinct ways, which we can call "positive tetralemmas" and "negative tetralemmas."

When the phenomena under discussion are conventional entities, Nāgārjuna deploys positive tetralemmas. Consider this example, for instance:

> Everything is real and is not real,
> Both real and not real,
> Neither real nor not real.
> This is Lord Buddha's teaching. (MK 18: 8)

This tetralemmic verse occurs in the context of the discussion of the nature of the self and of external entities, a discussion that emphasizes the conventional reality of phenomena on both sides of that divide, together with their ultimate nonexistence. Here, Nāgārjuna notes that each of the four branches of the tetralemma with regard to reality can be asserted, subject to appropriate ontological qualification: (1) Everything is conventionally real. (2) Everything is ultimately not real. (3) Everything is both conventionally real and ultimately not real. (4) Everything is neither ultimately real nor completely unreal. The important point here is not simply that these four assertions are all held to be consistent but rather that it is appropriate to make these assertions in the first place. As we shall see in our next examples, that is not always, according to Nāgārjuna, the case.

> "Empty" should not be asserted.
> "Non-empty" should not be asserted.
> Neither both nor neither should be asserted.
> They are only used nominally. (MK 22: 11)

> Having passed into nirvāṇa, the Victorious Conqueror
> Neither found existence evident
> Nor found non-existence.
> Nor both nor neither thus to be evident. (25: 17)

In the first of these two verses, Nāgārjuna is discussing the status of emptiness in the context of a discussion of the nature of the Buddha and of Buddhahood. In the second, he is explicitly discussing the problem of formulating ontology from the standpoint of nirvāna. In these cases, where the subjects regarding which we are tempted to make assertions are considered from the ultimate point of view—that is, from the epistemic standpoint of one who sees things as they are independently of conventions—rather than assert that all branches of the tetralemma can be asserted, Nāgārjuna explicitly *precludes* assertion of *any* of them. Each would be fundamentally misleading. We see here that Nāgārjuna is drawing a logical distinction between two epistemological standpoints: as long as we remain within the conventional standpoint, we can, providing that we are careful, say many things, mundane and philosophical. But once we transcend that standpoint, no matter what we try to say, and no matter now carefully we hew to a *via negativa*, we can say nothing at all consistent with the *via media* Nāgārjuna is determined to limn. This will provide a valuable clue to the sense in which Madhyamaka philosophy requires us to regard emptiness not as an entity, and to relinquish all views when we understand emptiness.

Views and Entities

It is now time to make explicit the link between these two points—that regarding the status of emptiness as an entity, and that regarding the possibility of holding a view once one has directly cognized emptiness. The metaphor of view must first be explicated and unpacked a bit. Note that the ocular metaphor represented by the English term *view* is mirrored in both the Tibetan and the Sanskrit terms it is used to translate. In Tibetan, the term is *lta ba*, literally "seen." In Sanskrit there are two terms, both translated by the same Tibetan term, and their difference will be important for us, since, as Ruegg (1977) notes, they differ systematically with respect to the issue at hand. Both are derived from the root dṛṣ, "to see." The first, the one used in the admonitions against holding views, is *dṛṣṭi*. The second, used when the cognitive relation to emptines that is the goal of mādhyamika analysis and practice is being characterized is *darśana*, best literally rendered as "direct awareness", or "coming face to face with." Neither Nāgārjuna nor his mādhyamika followers ever deny the value or possibility of *śūnyatā- darśana*, (view of emptiness) though they are critical of the very idea of *śūnyatā- dṛṣṭi*. So here, using "*śūnyatā- darśana*," Candrakīrti writes,

> The thorough extinguishment of attachment is the cause of attaining nirvāna, and, except for the view of the lack of inherent existence, there is no other doctrine which is a cause of thoroughly extinguishing such attachment. (*Prasannapadā* 116a)

Tibetan, as Ruegg notes, does not draw this terminological distinction. Nor does English.

The metaphorical content here is doing real philosophical work, even if covertly. For (bracketing for now the interpretation of *śūnyatā- darśana*) when we view something, there must be something that we view, and we must view it from some perspective, with awareness of it under some description.[17] And so a view is possible *if* there is something to view and some way in which it is viewed. Let us take the first entailment, the ontic, first: if it were possible to have a (true) view about emptiness, emptiness would have to be a thing, an object of awareness.

But if we supposed that it is, a dilemma emerges: emptiness must then exist either conventionally or ultimately. The latter, as we have seen, is impossible, since then it would fail itself to be empty, and not only would a central tenet of Madhyamaka philosophy be contradicted, but the remainder would be rendered incoherent as well. But positing emptiness as a conventional existent and as the object of a correct view is no better. For things that appear conventionally appear as entities—as phenomena that exist independently and substantially. And all such appearance is, from the standpoint of Madhyamaka, in an important sense, *false* appearance.

Now, there is an important sense in which much of conventional reality also appears to us truly—that is, truly in conventional terms. So, for instance, this paper is in fact white, and so it appears. But note that the sense in which "This paper is white" is literally true is this: the perspective from which this paper exists is the conventional perspective, and in that perspective it is in fact white. But it is not from that perspective—the conventional perspective—that emptiness exists. The perspective from which things are empty is not the conventional, but the ultimate perspective, and from that perspective, nothing exists, since nothing exists ultimately. To put this point another way, true predication is always predication from a perspective in which the subject of the predicate exists, and within which the predicate can be instantiated. For conventional entities, the conventional standpoint provides such a perspective. But for emptiness, neither the conventional nor the ultimate standpoint can do the job: from the conventional standpoint there is no emptiness; from the ultimate standpoint there are no entities at all.

Now let us consider the second entailment, concerning the *manner in which emptiness would need to be viewed*. Views are views of the things under description, and as having some nature. I view this paper as paper, as white, as a bearer of print, a product of a tree, and so forth.[18] And again, so long as I am characterizing a conventional entity as it is viewed from the conventional perspective, there is no problem here. But when we attempt to extend this analysis to emptiness itself, problems again arise. For the attribution of properties, descriptions under which things can be viewed, again requires the existence of the substrata and the possibility of their serving as property bearers—as well as the dualism between substratum and property this presupposes. The perspective from which this existence and this dualism are available is the conventional perspective, for only conventions bring ontology into play. But again, from that perspective, we find no emptiness: we find all kinds of entities, but we find them as *entities*. But from the perspective from which we find emptiness, we find no entities nor any characteristics, nor even emptiness itself or the fact of its emptiness. Hence again, since we cannot view emptiness even as empty, by virtue of its very emptiness, we cannot have a view of emptiness. This point is made pithily in a verse quoted by

Nāgārjuna in his autocommentary to the *Vigrahavyāvartanī:*[19] "By their nature, things are not determinate entities. For they have only one nature, i.e., no nature" (*Astasāhasrikā Prajñāpāramitā*).

CONVENTIONAL TRUTHS AND ULTIMATE TRUTHS

Up to this point, I have been relying heavily on the Madhyamaka distinction between the Two Truths, and on some standard Madhyamaka doctrine concerning each of them. It is now important in order to develop the positive characterization of our cognitive relation to emptiness and the coherence of positionlessness and the renunciation of all views to draw that distinction more explicitly. The distinction between the Two Truths is at its foundation a distinction between two kinds of objects of knowledge: The conventional truth has as its domain all entities, properties, and so on posited by ordinary, unreflective awareness, science, philosophy, and other human activities. Its ontology is determined by language and by conceptual activity. The things we say about these phenomena, to the extent that they are true by the standards of human convention, are conventionally true.

Ultimate truth, on the other hand, is truth independent of convention. Its domain is therefore the class of entities that exist independently of convention—of phenomena as they are independent of language or the ontology induced by language and thought. The fact that emptiness is what we find on such an analysis makes it legitimate to say that emptiness is an ultimate truth (indeed the only one) and the domain of ultimate truth.[20, 21]

Here it is necessary to pause a bit over the English terms "conventional entity/truth/existent" and distinguish and comment on the Sanskrit and Tibetan terms these phrases translate.[22] There are two Sanskrit phrases translated as "convention." The most common is *saṃvṛti*. This term enjoys one of the most delightful ambiguities of any philosophical term in any tradition. For it can literally mean "convention" in all of the senses that term has in English—"agreement," "coming together," "nominal," "ordinary," "everyday," and so on. But it can also mean *obscured, concealed, occluded, disguised.* Plays on this ambiguity are significant in Madhyamaka literature as it is emphasized that conventional entities conceal their nature—the fact that they are merely conventional, and hence empty—and masquerade as substantial entities. The other term is *vyavahāra*, which more accurately means "transactional," "linguistically determined." Unfortunately, though the latter term does not convey the ambiguity of the former, the former is often used in its "nominal" sense.

Tibetans also use two terms here, etymologically distinct from one another, reflecting the two meanings of *saṃvṛti*, though often, because they are used to translate this term, regarded as synonymous. The first, *tha snyad*, really means "nominal," the second, *kun rdzob*, means "concealer"—literally "costumed." The former is almost always used to translate *vyavahāra*, but both are used indiffer-

ently to translate *saṃvṛti*. Tibetan Madhyamaka texts also use two distinct com-
binations of each of these terms as adjectival with noun phrases: each can modify
either *yod pa*, "existent," or *bden pa*, "truth." So we can get phrases that mean
"concealer," "truth," a "concealing existent," "nominal truth of nomimal existent."

When we say that something is a *tha snyad yod pa*, we are saying that it is
something whose existence is entirely nominal, due to verbal conventions. We are
saying of it that its status as an entity, as an enduring thing, as a referent of
linguistic expression, derives entirely from the ontology induced by language and
conceptual thought. Absent these conventions, we are saying; "Nature presents
no joints at which to be carved, and a fortiori none by virtue of which this thing
must be served as a portion to experience." Nāgārjuna argues that we can say
this about anything. When we say of a thing that it is a *kun rdzob yod pa*, on the
other hand, we are saying (1) that it is a something that appears to exist for a
deluded consciousness (one that has not understood that in reality all phenomena
are empty) or (2) that it presents itself falsely as existing inherently. Analysis shows
that it does not exist in the manner that we instinctively posit it as existing.
Nāgārjuna would argue that all conventional entities have this character. These
two terms hence appear to be coextensive.

There is, however, one point at which they diverge in application, and that is
the point central for our discussion, that is, the status of emptiness itself. Emptiness is a *tha snyad yod pa*, but not a *kun rdzob yod pa*. First, why is it a *tha
snyad yod pa*? Simply because emptiness is always the emptiness of something—of
a table, of the parts of stages of a table, of the emptiness of that table, or if its
emptiness. Independent of empty phenomena, there is no emptiness.[23] The emptiness of emptiness just is *its* lacking inherent existence, and so existing nominally.
But second, it cannot be a *kun rdzob yod pa*. Why not? Just because emptiness,
when it is perceived by the kind of consciousness capable of *perceiving* it, as
opposed to *inferring* its presence, does not come in costume. It does not deceive
and is not apparent to a deceived consciousness. When we see emptiness, we see
what really is the nature of things; when we see things as empty, we shed delusion.
It is in this sense that emptiness is *not* a conventional entity. But that does not
contradict its status as conventional in the sense of being *merely nominal*. But
being merely nominal is a way of *not being an entity* despite *entering the field of
knowledge*. And this provides the key to a positive understanding of nonassertorial knowledge of the nature of things.

Emptiness as a Knowable II: Emptiness Need Not Be an Object of Knowledge

We are approaching the conclusion—one poised on the edge of paradox and
incoherence—that emptiness can be known but that it is not a possible object of

knowledge, that we can say true things about it, but that those assertions in some sense indicate no proposition. To make sense of this conclusion, it will be necessary to remain conscious of the Two Truths and the two perspectives they provide from which emptiness may be known. Let us begin with some remarks of Candrakīrti from his commentary on Nāgārjuna's *Mūlamadhyamak-akārikā*. He begins by considering the position that emptiness is an actual essence of all things:

> Since entities are said to be empty, the essencelessness of entities does not exist. So, on the basis of their emptiness, entities are said to have a nature. This is explained to make no sense:

7   If there were even a trifle nonempty,
     Emptiness itself would be but a trifle.
     But not even a trifle is nonempty.
     How could emptiness be an entity?

> If emptiness existed, then essences of things would exist as its basis, but it doesn't. This is because emptiness and selflessness themselves are the universal characteristics of all things. It should be understood that because of the nonexistence of any non-empty phenomenon and of the non-existence of emptiness, since there is no non-empty phenomenon, it follows that emptiness and existence do not exist. It is dependent upon its opposite, and without that, like a sky-flower-garland, emptiness along with existence are explained not to exist. Since emptiness does not exist, entities and existence do not exist as its basis . . . (83a)

8   The victorious ones have said
     That emptiness is the relinquishing of all views.
     For whomever emptiness is a view,
     That one will accomplish nothing.

> So here emptiness is the ceasing of the perception of all views and of the persistence of all attachment to them. And since this is so, the mere relinquishing of views is not even an existent. We will not debate with whoever insists on seeing emptiness as an entity. Therefore, if one opposes this presentation through conceptual elaboration, how will liberation be achieved?

> It is like this: Suppose a someone says to some one else "I have nothing" and he says in reply "I'll take that very nothing you say you have." If so, without anything there, by what means can we get him to understand that there is nothing there? In just this way, how can someone stop insisting on seeing emptiness as an entity through seeing emptiness as an entity? Therefore, the great doctors with great wisdom and realisation, who have

performed great medical deeds, understanding their illness pass by them and refuse to treat them.

As it is said in the great *Ratnakūṭa-sūtra*, "Things are not empty because of emptiness; to be a thing is to be empty. Things are not without defining characteristics through characteristiclessness; to be a thing is to be without a defining characteristic. Things are not without aspiration because of aspirationlessness; since to be a thing is to be without aspiration, whoever understands each things in this way, Kāśyapa, will understand perfectly how everything has been explained to be in the middle path. Kāśyapa whoever conceives of emptiness through objectifying it falls away from understanding it as it has been explained to be. Kāśyapa, it would be better to view the self as just as stable as Mt Meru than to view emptiness in this way. This is because, Kāśyapa, since emptiness is understood through the relinquishing of all views, whoever conceives of emptiness through a view, I have explained, will be incurable.

Kāśyapa, consider this example: If a doctor gives a patient medicine, and this medicine cures all of his illness, but stays in his stomach, do you think that suffering will not arise, Kāśyapa? Do you think this man will be relieved of the illness in his belly? No way, blessed one! If the medicine, having cured all of his illnesses, stays in his stomach, this man will certainly become seriously ill.

The Blessed one said, "Kāśyapa, you should see the insistence on any view in just this way. If emptiness is seen like that, Kāśyapa, whoever sees emptiness like that, will be incurable. I have said that it is like that. (83b–84a)

Candrakīrti makes two related points here. First, if emptiness were an entity, things would in fact have essences—namely the essence of being empty, which would contradict their very emptiness since that is defined as the absence of essence.[24] Second, if emptiness were an entity, its relation to empty things would be contingent. It would then be possible for there to be non-empty things. But analysis that shows all things to be empty precludes that.

But Candrakīrti, like Nāgārjuna, surely does not shy away from using the term *emptiness* or talking about emptiness itself. Conventionally, we can speak about anything, even emptiness. The question about such discourse that needs to be posed, however, is this: does the use of the term or the sense of that discourse implicate the existence of emptiness? The answer to this is a definite "yes and no."

From a conventional perspective, emptiness is an existent. That is, if we ask, in ordinary philosophical discourse, whether things are empty, the answer is, for a mādhyamika, "yes." Does this mean that they have the property of emptiness? Well, just as the conventionally true sentence that this paper is white entails that it has whiteness, this entailment seems perfectly good. This suggests that within the context of convention, emptiness is no more or no less real than other properties. They are conventionally existent and ultimately empty, and so is it. And this is exactly the observation that underlies mādhyamika's emphasis on the nonduality of the conventional and the ultimate, and the insistence on the part of the dGe lugs interpreters on the existence of emptiness.

But there is an important disanalogy that must not be overlooked: whiteness, like the paper, only appears at all from the conventional viewpoint. Seen from the ultimate standpoint, there is no paper, nor any whiteness. There is, from that standpoint, only their emptiness. So the fact that the paper is white is true from the very standpoint in the context of which the paper and its whiteness exist. To the extent that either is real, the assertion says correctly that the former is characterized by the latter.

But all assertion—explicit in language or silent in thought—is nominal and conventional, including the assertions that the paper is empty and that emptiness exists. And from the conventional perspective, while emptiness can be known inferentially, it does not appear as it is. It is rather from the ultimate perspective that emptiness actually appears as *emptiness*. This is a delicate point, so let us take some case in articulating it. Paper and whiteness appear as, and are, paper and whiteness conventionally. So, to the extent that one cognizes either in a manner appropriate and adequate to such objects, one's knowledge is conventional. But emptiness can be known in two ways—indirectly through inference, that is conventionally; or directly, through that direct insight into the nature of reality that is the goal of Mahāyāna Buddhist practice. It is in the latter kind of gnosis that emptiness is known *as emptiness*, just as it is in conventional cognition that paper and whiteness are known *as paper and as whiteness*. But in this direct apprehension, there is no object, no entity to be perceived. For even emptiness is perceived by such a perceiver as empty, and hence not as an entity. Now to be sure, the emptiness that is perceived in these two ways is the same emptiness. In the one case, it is perceived as an existent quality; in the second as a mere negation—a mere absence of any essence or nature. But insofar as emptiness is the ultimate nature of things, it is the latter perception that gives us emptiness as it is.

So there are certain respects in which emptiness is just like any other conventional existent—it can be the object of a conventional, conceptual consciousness and can be truly asserted to characterize conventional phenomena. Yet as such, it is merely nominal, dependently arisen, and hence empty of inherent existence. To say this is merely to say that, like paper and whiteness, it is a *tha snyad yod pa*. On the other hand, there is an important respect in which emptiness is wholly different: while conventional phenomena, even when apprehended correctly, are deceptive with regard to their ultimate nature, their emptiness, and hence are properly also characterized as *kun rdzob yod pa*, emptiness, when apprehended correctly, is not so deceptive. That is the sense in which it is an ultimate truth, even if not an ultimate existent. But for it to be nondeceptive in its appearance is for it to appear as a mere negation, and not as a positive object or an entity, and hence not as something that can serve as the subject of characterization—as the subject of proposition—or as the object of a view.

WHY ASSERTIONS OR REAL POSITIONS ABOUT EMPTINESS WOULD BE IMPOSSIBLE

Nonetheless, it must be possible to talk one's way into the ultimate perspective. The whole point of Madhyamaka philosophy is to do so. That is why Nāgārjuna, for instance, writes:

10   Without a foundation in the conventional truth
        The significance of the ultimate cannot be taught.
        Without understanding the significance of the ultimate,
        Liberation is not achieved. (MK 24)

Conventional truth, including the language and conceptual apparatus that mediates our experience and knowledge, the ontology they induce, and the objects and properties constituted within that ontology, form the ladder that allows us not only to comprehend the conventional world, but to comprehend its merely conventional character—that is, its ultimate emptiness. But that ladder must be kicked away. We cannot simultaneously remain within the conventional perspective and transcend it. But transcending it requires the transcendence of many things: we transcend the ontology of substance and attribute; the duality of subject and object; the commitment to the independent existence of objects of thought as well as that of thought. We enter into a vision of reality as an interdependent realm of essenceless relata. From such a perspective, insofar as the role of assertions is to predicate attributes of entities and to characterize objects of a subject's consciousness, language becomes curiously self-undermining. From that perspective, nothing can truly be said (at least not without contradiction).[25]

So, to say something about emptiness is necessarily to operate from the conventional perspective. And this is the perspective from which we must operate in order analytically to engender the cognition that allows such transcendence, but whose content, as Wittgenstein put it, can only be "shown" and "not said." That perspective contains rich descriptive and rhetorical resources. From it we can say true things about tables, elephants, and philosophical positions. And the true things we say can be useful not only in everyday transactions and philosophical debate, but also soteriologically: that is, they can be the very vehicles by means of which we show ourselves and others that which these assertions themselves assert the impossibility of ever asserting.

But the things we say from that perspective can't be true of emptiness. And that is simply because from that perspective we get to say things about things, and about their properties, and emptiness simply is not one of those, though by treating it as though it were, we can move ourselves toward an inexpressible understanding of it.[26] That is, to return to the language of positions and propositions: while we can correctly utter sentences that have "emptiness" in the subject (or predicate) position, for example, "Emptiness is empty," the analysis of the meaning of these sentences cannot involve the notion that an entity, *emptiness* is characterized by a property, *emptiness.* Hence, in the technical sense of *proposition* in the sense of *pratijñā,* these sentences assert no proposition.[27] Rather, they must be understood as pure denials—denials that phenomena, including emptiness, have any nature—showing the way that things are when seen *per impossibile, sub specie aeternitatis.*[28]

How to Understand Positionlessness as Non-Self-Refuting

In conclusion, I have emphasized the following features of Nāgārjuna's account: (1) To say that the mādhyamika is without position, asserts no proposition, has no view is neither to take a position, nor to assert a proposition, nor to have a view. That is, this is not a self-refuting position, because a position in the relevant sense is a position regarding the nature of things, a proposition is an extralinguistic entity that stands as the semantic value of a sentence, and a view is a view of an entity. And according to Nāgārjuna and his followers, the function of language is not to characterize the nature of things, because things have no nature; language is not meaningful because of a correspondence to language-independent phenomena, because there are none; and an exposition of emptiness is not the characterization of an entity because it is the exposition of the incoherence of the very notion of an entity. (2) All of this is closely bound up with the question of whether emptiness is to be conceived of as an entity—as a positive phenomenon or an object of knowledge. I have argued that it cannot be coherently so conceived and that Nāgārjuna never intends it to be so conceived. (3) This is not a mystical posit of an ineffable truth; it is a recognition of the inability to make assertions from a nonperspectival perspective, together with the recognition that perspectives are ontologically determinative. We can say that it is an anticipation of the doctrine of the hermeneutical predicament. Candrakīrti expresses the point this way:

> So here emptiness is the ceasing of the perception of all views and of the persistence of all attachment to them. And since this is so, the mere relinquishing of views is not even an existent. We will not debate with whoever insists on seeing emptiness as an entity. Therefore, if one opposes this

presentation through conceptual elaboration, how will liberation be achieved?

It is like this: Suppose a someone says to some one else "I have nothing" and he says in reply "I'll take that very nothing you say you have." If so, without anything there, by what means can we get him to understand that there is nothing there? In just this way, how can someone stop insisting on seeing emptiness is an entity through seeing emptiness as an entity? Therefore, the great doctors with great wisdom and realisation, who have performed great medical deeds, understanding their illness pass by them and refuse to treat them.

As it is said in the great *Ratnakūṭa-sūtra*, "Things are not empty because of emptiness; to be a thing is to be empty. Things are not without defining characteristics through characteristiclessness; to be a thing is to be without a defining characteristic. Things are not without aspiration because of as-pirationlessness; since to be a thing is to be without aspiration; whoever understands each things in this way, Kāśyapa, will understand perfectly how everything has been explained to be in the middle path. Kāśyapa whoever conceives of emptiness through objectifying it falls away from understanding it as it has been explained to be. Kāśyapa, it would be better to view the self as just as stable as Mt Meru than to view emptiness in this way. This is because, Kāśyapa, since emptiness is understood through the relinquishing of all views, whoever conceives of emptiness through a view, I have explained, will be incurable.

Kāśyapa, consider this example: If a doctor gives a patient medicine, and this medicine cures all of his illness, but stays in his stomach, do you think that suffering will not arise, Kāśyapa? Do you think this man will be re-lieved of the illness in his belly? No way, blessed one! If the medicine, having cured all of his illnesses stays in his stomach, this man will certainly become seriously ill.

The Blessed one said, "Kāśyapa, you should see the insistence on any view in just this way. If emptiness is seen like that, Kāśyapa, whoever sees emp-tiness like that, will be incurable. I have said that it is like that. (83b–84a)

To say that things are natureless can only be designation—a ladder to be kicked away once we have ascended it. Indeed, if an assertion of positionlessness were meant to be the claim that one says nothing, that no words were uttered, or even that nothing was intended by those words, it would be self-refuting. But this is not what Nāgārjuna intends—though nor does he mean merely that he has no false view, or that he ever says anything that is meant itself to be inherently

existent. The claim to positionlesssness is deeply significant and represents a compelling vision of the utility of necessarily perspectival language and thought as
well as of the limitations imposed by that perspectival character. That is, such
assertions are meant as pointers—and that is the only way that such fundamental
philosophical discourse can be understood—if we are to use it to get to, as Sellars
calls it, an *archē* beyond discourse, the relinquishing of all views (Sellars 1997).

4

Nāgārjuna's Theory of Causality

Implications Sacred and Profane

Nāgārjuna PROPERLY EMPHASIZES that one understands the fundamental nature of reality (or lack thereof, depending on one's perspective) if, and only if, one understands the nature of dependent origination.

> Whoever sees dependent arising
> Also sees suffering
> And its arising
> And its cessation as well as the path. (MMK 24: 40)

He devotes two important chapters of *Mūlamadhyamakakārikā* to the analysis of causality, per se, and of dependent arising more generally. The analysis developed in these chapters permeates the rest of the treatise. I have in the preceding portion of this book, discussed how Nāgārjuna's chapters are to be read and explored their role in Nāgārjuna's larger philosophical enterprise (chapters 1 and 2 of this volume and Garfield 1995). I will review that account only briefly here as a preliminary to some applications.

I think that Nāgārjuna is not only right about the fundamental importance of causality, and dependence more generally, to our understanding of reality and of human life but also that his own account of these matters is generally correct. Given these two premises, it follows that our conduct of natural science as well as the pursuit of our moral life should be informed by Nāgārjuna's account of these matters. Here I will develop some of those implications. I caution, however, that my development, at least in the case of ethics is—though, as I will argue absolutely orthodox Madhyamaka—heterodox within at least one major living tradition in which Madhyamaka is preserved and practiced: that of the dGe lugs pa school of Tibetan Buddhism. As a consequence, we will have reason to question both certain substantive claims made within that tradition about the necessary conditions of the cultivation of *bodhicitta* (the altruistic aspiration to attain enlightenment for the sake of all sentient beings) and the doxographic strategy of the tradition.

My claims about the philosophy of science, though less controversial, will nonetheless offend some. And that (on both counts) is as it should be. For the philosophy of science has been steadily maturing into a more Buddhist framework over the past few decades (even if most Western philosophers of science would not recognize that characterization). But there are residues of pre-Buddhist modernism in practice, and even those who opt for a more enlightened approach to these matters do not always see the big picture.

I will first sketch Nāgārjuna's view. The account will be straightforward, following my earlier discussions, and I will not defend my reading further here. I will then turn to the implications of that view for the philosophy of science, arguing that Nāgārjuna's account of interdependence shows how we can clearly understand the nature of scientific explanation and the relationship between distinct levels of theoretical analysis in sciences (with particular attention to cognitive science), and how we can sidestep difficulties in understanding the relations between apparently competing ontologies induced by levels of description or explanation supervening on one another.

Finally, I will examine rGyal tshab's exposition of Dharmakīrti's account in the *pramānasiddhi* chapter of *Pramāṇavarttika* on the necessity of a belief in rebirth for the cultivation of *bodhicitta*. This account is accepted in the dGe lugs tradition both as an accurate representation of Dharmakīrti's views and as authoritative regarding *bodhicitta* and the mahākaruṇā that is its necessary condition. But, I will argue, Dharmakīrti, rGyal tshab, and their followers are, by virtue of accepting this argument, neglecting Nāgārjuna's's account of dependent arising and consequently are implicated in what might be seen from a proper Prāsaṅgika-Madhyamaka point of view as the very subtlest form of self-grasping. I use Nāgārjuna's account to extirpate this final self-grasping, thus freeing the morally central notion of *bodhicitta* from unnecessary and perhaps implausible metaphysical and cosmological baggage. This also suggests some caution regarding a doxography that takes as axiomatic the consistency of Dharmakīrti's *pramānavāda* and Nāgārjuna's Madhyamaka. I will conclude with a few observations on common lessons emerging from these applications of Nāgārjuna's insights in two such radically different domains.

The Emptiness of Causality

Nāgārjuna is often erroneously understood as a nihilist with respect to causality and dependent arising. On this misreading he is taken to argue that in fact there are no relationships of mutual dependence among phenomena, and even that no phenomena in fact exist. Nothing could be farther from the truth. Nāgārjuna assiduously defends the correlativity of emptiness and dependent arising and insists that to say that all phenomena are empty is just to say that they are dependently arisen.

Whatever is dependently co-arisen
That is explained to be emptiness,
That, being a dependent designation,
Is itself the middle way.

Something that is not dependently arisen,
Such a thing does not exist.
Therefore a non-empty thing
Does not exist. (24: 18–19)

Since nobody—particularly nobody who would offer a nihilistic reading of Nāgārjuna with respect to the conventional world and *pratītya-samutpāda*—would seriously claim that Nāgārjuna denies the emptiness of all phenomena, nobody who reads *Mūlamadhyamakakārikā* through to the end could seriously defend the nihilistic reading.

Since one of the principal phenomena Nāgārjuna analyzes as empty is causation, it is not surprising that some read the first chapter of *Mūlamadhyamakakārikā* as an attack on the reality of causation. After all, in the very first verse he asserts

Neither from itself nor from another,
Nor from both,
Nor without a cause,
Does anything whatever, anywhere arise. (1: 1)

But again, given a correct middle path reading Nāgārjuna's program, we can see immediately that such a reading must be erroneous. Nāgārjuna's strategy throughout *Mūlamadhyamakakārikā* is to argue that phenomena we normally assume to be inherently existent, to have convention-independent natures, and to exist as they do precisely because of their natures are in fact empty of inherent existence, exist only conventionally, and exist precisely because of their emptiness and interdependence. To quote a favorite Tibetan *Prāsaṅgika-Madhyamaka* saying: We do not say that because things are empty they do not exist; we say that because things exist they are empty. The converse, of course, is equally assertible.

Now, as I have argued before, in the case of causation, in chapter 1 of *Mūlamadhyamakakārikā*, Nāgārjuna proceeds by distinguishing *hetu* (*rgyu*) from *pratyaya* (*kyen*). He uses the former term to denote the cause of the metaphysicians—an event capable of bringing another about by virtue of a power that is part of its nature. The latter denotes an event or phenomenon whose occurrence or existence is correlated with that of another—a condition.

These give rise to those,
So these are called conditions. (1: 5a,b)

"When this arises, so does that. When this ceases, so does that." Of course Nāgārjuna identifies four kinds of conditions, in rough harmony with standard Buddhist taxonomies of causality (for more detail, see Garfield 1995). Nāgārjuna argues that the midpoint between reification of causation, the adoption of a realistic view with respect to causal powers, and nihilism, the view of a random and inexplicable universe of independent events, is the acceptance of the reality of conditions, and a regularist account of explanation. On such a view, what counts as *explanans* and as *explanandum* depends on explanatory interests and conventions for individuation and classification. Hume is often read (properly in my view) in roughly this way. Such a view, hence far from nihilism, is instead a moderate, sensible approach to explanation and to understanding.

Nāgārjuna's reasons for rejecting causal powers anticipate the arguments of Hume and of Wittgenstein: causal powers are never observed; causal powers, if sufficient for explanation can never inhere in isolated events or things, which always require cooperating conditions; causal powers cannot be explanatory on pain of regress (what would explain the arising of the powers, or their giving rise to effects?); positing causal powers imposes implausible uniformity on the explanatory landscape. These arguments are by now familiar, if still controversial, and this analysis of the first chapter of *Mūlamadhyamakakārikā* is by now familiar, if still controversial. I have defended these positions elsewhere (in the first chapter of this book and more extensively in Garfield 1995) and merely recall them here in order to use them as a platform for extension.

Nāgārjuna's conventionalist regularism, when joined with his eclectic view about dimensions of explanation represented in the account of the four kinds of conditions (efficient, supporting, immediately preceding, and dominant), gives rise to a reasonably straightforward analysis of explanatory and predictive language: we explain a phenomenon when we identify it as of a kind; when we connect occurrences of things of that kind with the occurrence of other related phenomena; when we connect the macroscopic and easily observable with the microscopic and harder-to-observe; when we place it within a network of events, purposes, and connections that form patterns enabling rational action, prediction, and cognitive access to the world.

The serious causal realist (really a reificationist in Nāgārjuna's sense) can be expected to press against Nāgārjuna the obvious question for any such regularist:[1] what explains these regularities, if not genuine causal powers inhering in genuine causes? After all, anyone who is even as realistic as Nāgārjuna, and as committed to the enterprise of explanation as Nāgārjuna, must be committed to explaining why the *explanans* appealed to in any explanation in fact explains, and in the end, why the world is regular at all. Appeal to causes and their powers would do this; anything less leaves the entire structure mysterious.[2]

Nāgārjuna's reply in chapter 7 of *Mūlamadhyamakakārikā* is straightforward: each regularity, each pattern, each connection posited in any explanation must indeed be explicable. That is the content of *pratītya-samutpāda*. But each is explained by still further regularities, patterns, connections. Deeper understanding consists in the increasingly richer embedding of interdependence into larger, more articulated patterns of interdependence. And there simply is no explanation of why the entire universe is interdependent. There is no such well-defined totality to explain.

> The arisen, the non-arisen, and that which is arising
> Do not arise in any way at all.
> Thus they should be understood
> Just like the gone, the not-gone and the going. (7: 14)

> If another arising gives rise to this one,
> There would be an infinite regress. (7: 19ab)

That is the problem of the limits leading to the unanswerable questions. Explanatory questions are always local. Attempting transcendental explanations of the possibility of explanation is not only fruitless, it is meaningless: what could explain why explanation itself is possible? Certainly not powers. What would explain *them* or more deeply their explanatory potential, if not the patterns into which they are embedded?

We have then, in *Mūlamadhyamakakārikā* articulated principally in chapters 1 and 7, but supported in a myriad of ways throughout the text—an account of explanation and causation that, like Hume's, grounds ontology in the conventions that underlie our explanatory interests and the sortals we choose under which to collect entities, and not in a self-evident or self-presenting partition of nature into things, properties, and relations. This is, of course, an ancient view, developed and defended long before the rise of modern science. For all of that, it provides a natural and compelling guide to the landscape of the world as captured by the scientific image. Let us now turn to the important implications of this way of seeing things for contemporary science.

A MADHYAMAKA VIEW OF SCIENTIFIC EXPLANATION AND ONTOLOGY

If we survey the world as it is understood in contemporary science, and contemporary science as it develops in order to understand the world, we are immediately struck by the fact that whichever way we come at the enterprise—whether from the standpoint of theory or from that of the object(s) of theory—multiple levels of explanation or of ontology present themselves. Economics, sociology, anthropology, psychology, neuroscience, ecology, cell biology, physiology, chemistry, fluid dynamics, macrophysics, and quantum theory each proceed and indeed progress. Each develops a proprietary vocabulary, methodology, explanatory strategy, and ontology. We have become accustomed—or at least we had better become accustomed—not only to the peaceful coexistence of departments of each of these disciplines in our science faculties, but also to the peaceful coexistence of the phenomena they posit at their various levels of description and explanation. Not only do departments of economics and of theoretical physics both exist, but exchange rates and neutrinos both exist as well.

This multiplicity of kinds of theories and of things sets much of the agenda for the contemporary philosophy of science and metaphysics. For as soon as a categorial multiplicity is countenanced, there is an imperative either to reduce or to systematize it. Is the multiplicity real or only apparent? Is one level fundamental? Are the relations between the levels uniform? Are they ordered? What determines a level? And so on.

Ontology and methodology become even more vexed when a single phenomenon appears to be explicable on multiple, prima facie orthogonal axes of explanation: is a movement of my arm to be explained by appeal to muscle contractions, neuromuscular synaptic events, and a neurophysiological story? is it to be explained by reference to my beliefs and desires? by reference to the cultural practices of my fellows? or by reference to the need to greet a friend? If one level is to be privileged, which one and why? But if multiple levels, how can such mutually independent, individually complete accounts of the necessary and sufficient conditions of the same object be equally acceptable?

Now, as anyone who has even a passing familiarity with contemporary metaphysics and philosophy of science knows, debates about these issues quickly become baroque. But we can cut through the Gordian knot if we slice at the right angle, and here is where Nāgārjuna's analysis helps us, for all of these questions and puzzles can be sorted into two closely related, but nonetheless distinct classes: the ontological and the methodological. The first asks to which entities and properties we ought to commit ourselves. The second asks how we should understand the relationship between theories and explanations pitched at distinct levels of analysis.

A Madhyamaka answer to questions of the first kind is a straightforward catholic realism: accept the deficits of economics, the kinship relations of anthropology, the classes of sociology, the beliefs of psychology, the molecules of chemistry, the niches of ecology, and the quarks of physics. Nāgārjuna's version of the Quinean dictum that to be is to be the value of a bound variable is simply, "to exist is to exist conventionally, dependently." The relevant conventions here are those of scientific theory, and the relevant dependencies are given by the laws discovered by science. From this perspective there is motivation neither to disparage the "high"-level phenomena of the social or biological sciences in favor of an ontological primacy accorded to the "low"-level phenomena of the physical science (see Churchland 1978) nor to disparage the "unobservables" of the latter in favor of its manifest entities (van Fraassen 1980).

For our purposes, it is important to see that this ontological generosity emerges precisely from Nāgārjuna's analysis of causality and explanation. It is best to come at this through a *via negativa*, or as I should say in the present context, a *prāsaṅga*: the urge to privilege one level over another always emerges in science and in the philosophy of science as a consequence of some doctrine regarding the locus of genuine causation. We might, following Churchland (1978), argue that because genuine causation is physical causation, by virtue of real causal power inhering in subatomic particles only the physical is really real, and all phenomena described at higher levels are real only to the extent that they are reducible to the physical. Or, following Van Fraassen (1980), we might reject the unobservable because real causal laws connect observables.[3] In either case, we justify an ontological distinction based upon a claim about where causal powers are to be located, and this because the only genuine explanations, *explananda*, and *explanans* are those adverting to, deriving from, and possessing, respectively, causal powers. But once we free ourselves from the thrall of this image of explanation and its ground, the motivation for these distinctions crumbles. Then we can pay attention to *pratītya-samutpāda*—to interdependence, and its multiple, multidimensional, inter- and intra-level character—and let a thousand entities bloom, requiring of each only that it genuinely toil and spin, accomplishing some real explanatory work.[4]

Maintaining our focus on this notion of "explanatory work" as the bulwark against ontological profligacy, we can dispose quickly of the second class of puzzles noted above—those regarding not levels of ontology but levels of theory. Where competing explanations are offered, or where competing sciences vie to explain particular phenomena, which—other things being equal—should claim our theoretical allegiance? Of course if we seriously believed in the cement of the universe, the answer to this question would be easy: the theory or the science founded in that very cement. The rest of the puzzles would then properly be regarded as pretenders or "what to do until the real science comes alone." But if all that explanation tracks is regularity and the increasingly rich embedding of regularity as Nāgārjuna would have it, the answer to the query is equally simple: if other things are really equal, take them all. Again, this does not mean that we should accept just any conjecture or explanation, together with the ontology it implicates. All of the standard desiderata of good theories apply—economy, elegance, predictive power, confirmation, coherence with other theories, and so on. The point is rather that these desiderata are *all* that matter because beyond *pratītya-samutpāda* no occult causal powers lurk as the unique and genuine targets of our theoretical activity.

These issues are particularly sharp in cognitive science, where naturalistic, intentional explanations vie with eliminative and cognitive neuroscience, nonlinear dynamic theory, computational models, and so on. Now many of these debates are straightforwardly empirical debates about how best to understand a particular cognitive phenomenon, and about the success of a particular theory on its own terms. Neither Nāgārjuna nor any other philosopher of science has anything to contribute to these debates. This is as it should be. These are all issues to be settled in the laboratory.

But some (for example, Churchland 1978, Fodor 1987 among many others) would resolve these debates on a priori grounds, arguing that because, for example, naturalistically individuated states cannot have causal powers, they cannot explain anything, are not real psychological states, and so psychology must be individualistic; or that causation in the mind is ultimately a neural phenomenon and so that no phenomena other than those described in the language of neuroscience are psychologically real; hence only neuropsychology is possible. Others (Burge 1979) argue that since all psychological phenomena are intentional, and since they are causally active under intentional descriptions, they can only be individuated and explained naturalistically. To all of these, Nāgārjuna's analysis of *pratītya-samutpāda* should lead us to answer, using a Sanskrit technical term from *pramāṇa* theory, "fiddlesticks."

As many philosophers of cognitive science (Garfield 1988, Hardcastle 1996, von Eckardt 1995) have argued, many empirical domains comprise phenomena whose explanation must proceed simultaneously at distinct levels of description, using theories and vocabularies that are, while mutually consistent, methodologically orthogonal to one another. Such theories may be mutually irreducible, and their vocabularies often comprise terms indefinable in terms of theories at distinct levels. The only relations between such theories might be those of global supervenience. None of this, however, requires anything but robust realism regarding each level, and regarding the entities posited by each theory. Only a dogmatic ideology regarding the unity of science could lead one to any different conclusion.[5] Nāgārjuna would smile.

BODHICITTA AND REBIRTH: A HETERODOX MADHYAMAKA VIEW

So much for the profane. Now I return to Buddhist metaphysics and epistemology proper and note that even in that domain the full import of Nāgārjuna's views has not always been appreciated. I will argue in fact that a claim about the preconditions for the cultivation of *bodhicitta*, the most ethically and soteriologically significant motivational state in Mahāyāna Buddhist ethics, that is taken as well established in the dGe lugs pa tradition of Tibetan Buddhism, is in fact inconsistent with Nāgārjuna's account of dependent arising, involves a subtle form of self-grasping, and so, by the lights of the tradition itself, should be rejected. That claim is, the cultivation of *bodhicitta*—the altruistic aspiration for buddhahood for the sake of the liberation of all sentient beings from *saṃsāra*—requires the belief in rebirth.

There is a hermeneutic fallacy in Western philosophy I call "Farabi's fallacy" after its most spectacular exponent. It goes roughly like this: X was a really smart philosopher. Y was a really smart philosopher. Two such smart guys were undoubtedly both right. So even though their views may not appear to be consistent, they must be, and the task of a successful philosophical hermeneutics is to weld them together. Farabi tried to accomplish this for Plato and Aristotle. Aquinas, inspired by that noble failure, tried it in the case of God and Aristotle. In the Tibetan tradition the gold medal for Farabi's fallacy undoubtedly goes to the founder of the dGe lugs school, rJe Tsong khapa, who at some point said, "Nāgārjuna—what a smart guy! Dharmakīrti—what a smart guy! So, despite the fact that *sunyavāda* and *pramānavāda* might look like two *vādas* diverging in a yellow wood, they must be consistent." Tsong khapa (unlike Robert Frost) devoted much of the rest of his philosophical life to the task of demonstrating and working out the consequences of their consistency, trying to take both roads simultaneously. Now I have enormous admiration for Tsong khapa as a philosopher, and he is arguably the titan of the Tibetan philosophical tradition. But in this respect I find his influence less than salutary.

The locus classicus for the dGe lugs argument for the conclusion that belief in rebirth is a necessary condition of the cultivation of *bodhicitta* is Tsong khapa's student rGyal tshab's commentary on the *pramānasiddhi* chapter of Dharmakīrti's *Pramānavarttika*. On reading this chapter, one might well wonder why immediately after a discussion of *bodhicitta* Dharmakīrti sets out to prove the existence of past and future lives. rGyal tshab's commentary on this passage explains this juxtaposition by setting up a materialist argument against the establishment of rebirth and argues that such a view is inconsistent with the cultivation of *bodhicitta*. The argument is interesting from our point of view not only because it is spectacularly bad, but also because its error consists precisely in its failure to appreciate the import of Nāgārjuna's account of causality and its implications for the selflessness of the person. As a consequence we shall see Dharmakīrti and rGyal tshab caught up in what I think of as the subtlest form of self-grasping a Buddhist could imagine, but a self-grasping nonetheless.

> [252.2] When the one endowed with great compassion became a sage, that required precursors: First, having developed a compassionate desire to free beings from all their sufferings, it was necessary for him to familiarize himself with a method to thoroughly pacify the suffering in order become a teacher. With respect to great compassion: It is neither arisen causelessly nor from irrelevant causes. It arises from previous familiarity of things of the same kind. Great compassion itself is what establishes one on the beginning of the practice of the Mahāyāna path.

> [252.11] "It isn't accomplished through familiarity with various kinds of compassion, and it doesn't come from prior births. That is because since

the conceptual mind depends on the body, if the body is destroyed, the mind will be destroyed as well. For example, just as light comes from a lamp, it [mind]is the effect of a body, just as the ability to get drunk from beer is a characteristic of the body; just as a picture depends on the wall; through its very nature, it [mind] depends on it[body]."

[252.18] With respect to the conceptual mind: This body is neither its cause nor its supporting condition, and therefore the mind does not depend on it. This is because since that that [the body] is the basis [of the mind] can be refuted through reasoning, it will be rejected. Moreover, from giving reasons for the non-existence of past and future lives [253] it would follow that familiarity with the arising of the various compassions would not be appropriate. Since this is not the case, through refutational reasoning this will be rejected. Therefore, since through good reasoning past and future lives are established, it follows from this—and on the fruit to be discussed below—that it is clearly established that one can obtain a favorable rebirth in a future life. Having proven this, and thus having established the Four Noble Truths, in that way one proves the excellent consequences of aban-donment, of causes and effects, upon which beings of the three capacities should meditate in common. Thus [the practitioner] adorned with con-stantly increasing boundless compassion, through having achieved a com-plete realization of the Four Noble Truths, establishes the way to achieving omniscience.

[253.17]   With past and future lives having been well established
          And with their absence having been refuted
          Self is refuted and on that basis evil is abandoned.

The argument in outline runs like this: great compassion (*mahākaruṇā*, the highest level of compassion achieved by the *bodhisattva*, characterized as com-passion regarding sentient beings as empty of inherent existence) is essential to the enlightenment of a *bodhisattva*. It is also hard to achieve, requiring many rebirths in which one accumulates its causes, and in which one becomes familiar with compassion and with the view that underlies it. Now, *bodhicitta* is the altru-istic aspiration to gain enlightenment for the sake of other sentient beings, and a fortiori the aspiration to achieve this level of compassion. But that is only possible given many rebirths, so one cannot coherently develop this aspiration if one does not believe in the requisite rebirths. So even to develop *bodhicitta* one must believe in rebirth. This is the argument on which I want to focus, and note that it is independent of the preceding argument specifically for the existence of rebirth.

Think about the *bodhisattva* resolution in any of its standard formulations: I will attain enlightenment for the sake of all sentient beings; or Śantideva's more poetic

> For as long as space remains;
> For as long as transmigrators remain;
> So long will I myself remain, and thereby
> I will relieve all transmigrators' suffering.
>
> (*Bodhicaryāvatāra* 10:55)

But who, or what, is this "I"? And what is its role in the expression of *bodhicitta*, particularly in the context of a Buddhist doctrine of *anātman*? Now of course it is not intended to be a substantial self of the kind that all mādhyamikas reject. And we do not want simply to dismiss these formulae as confused or nonsensical as someone nihilistic about the self might. But just noting that it is the Madhyamaka's familiar, conventionally real but ultimately nonexistent "mere I" will also be too facile. For the argument we have just surveyed for the connection between belief in rebirth and the cultivation of *bodhicitta* hinges directly on the need to posit this "I" in past, present, and future lives as the basis of the causal continuum linking the extraordinarily many causes of Buddhahood and the effect. It is hence doing real metaphysical work, well above and beyond what any "mere," nominally posited "I" could ever do: it is functioning as the basis for a real causal relation. If it were not needed for this, there would be no bar to a far simpler account of the aspiration for the liberation of all sentient beings (the one I will shortly defend), according to which the relevant aspiration is just that someone will attain Buddhahood, and that lots of people will have to perform many tasks to make that possible. Those causes will cooperate over time to enable the requisite enlightenment, and the practitioner resolves to contribute to that accumulation of causes. The fact that this option is not even considered by Dharmakīrti or rGyal tshab suggests that another view of the relevant causal process is at work. Let us explore it in more detail.

rGyal tshab, following Dharmakīrti, takes himself to be responding directly to a materialist opponent who denies the reality of rebirth, arguing:

> It isn't accomplished through familiarity with various kinds of compassion, and it doesn't come from prior births. That is because since the conceptual mind depends on the body, if the body is destroyed, the mind will be destroyed as well. For example, just as light comes from a lamp, it [mind] is the effect of a body, just as the ability to get drunk from beer is a characteristic of the body; just as a picture depends on the wall; through its very nature, it [mind] depends on it[body].

rGyal tshab argues that there must be rebirth precisely because "[compassion] arises from previous familiarity of things of the same kind" and that "from giving reasons for the nonexistence of past and future lives it would follow that familiarity with the arising of the various compassions would not be appropriate." On the other hand, if, and only if, there is rebirth, he asserts that "adorned with constantly increasing boundless compassion, through having achieved a complete realization of the Four Noble Truths, [the practitioner] establishes the way to achieving omniscience. . . ." That is, only personal rebirth—here defined explicitly in terms of a single mental continuum independent of the body—for rGyal tshab (and Dharmakīrti) and the subsequent dGe lugs pa tradition makes Buddhahood possible, and so only belief in this possibility could ground *bodhicitta*, the resolution to achieve Buddhahood for the sake of sentient beings.

Note that this implicates two specific theses: one regarding causality and one regarding the content of compassion. Both, I will argue, are misguided from a Madhyamaka perspective. The first, especially, is inconsistent with Nāgārjuna's own account of causality. The second is implicated by it and is inconsistent with the doctrine of *anātman*.

A central claim in rGyal tshab's argument is that without rebirth there cannot be any causal connection between the accumulating causes of *bodhicitta* and *mahākaruṇā* (accumulation of merit and wisdom and familiarization with compassion and its objects) and the crucial effect. That is why rGyal tshab can say that "from giving reasons for the nonexistence of past and future lives, it would follow that familiarity with the arising of the various compassions would not be appropriate." And that is why he can say that the fact that there are past and future lives enables "the excellent consequences of abandonment, of causes and effects, [and] . . . constantly increasing boundless compassion, through having achieved a complete realization of the Four Noble Truths establish[ing] the way to achieving omniscience."

But why should rebirth be necessary to mediate this causal link? We [where "we" includes both Dharmakīrti and rGyal tshab] are quite familiar with causal chains in which important causes are present in one group of entities and the effect in others (a tinderbox and flint give rise to a fire that burns in a candle and is used to light a lamp; a teacher's words together with the text in a book give rise to understanding in the mind of a student, and so on). And this last provides a plausible alternative model for the accumulation of causes of *mahākaruṇā*, *bodhicitta*, and omniscience: the acts, insights, writings, and discoveries of one individual make possible deeper insights, more profound realizations, and more informative writings on the part of another. Knowledge and compassion deepen over the generations, and after a time, some individual attains Buddhahood as a consequence of the accumulation of causes by others. Call this the transpersonal model of attainment, as opposed to the intrapersonal model embraced by the dGe lugs pa tradition, following Dharmakīrti and rGyal tshab.

The questions we must ask then, are (1) Why does rGyal tshab embrace the intrapersonal rather than the transpersonal model? (2) Is his doing so consistent with Nāgārjuna's account of causation? I think that the answer to the first is obvious, and this is confirmed by the oral tradition:[6] Only an intrapersonal continuum could mediate the connections between the relevant causes and effects.

Remove this premise and the argument loses all plausibility. After all, given that it is reasonable to believe that Buddhahood is difficult to achieve, one could argue convincingly that *bodhicitta* requires a belief in the past and the future, but not in *one's own* past and future lives, unless one thought that the relevant causal chain could only be intrapersonal. But why would rGyal tshab believe that? The only reason I can conjure is that he thinks that causation requires a substantial basis, something in which the causal powers inhere. That basis, for rGyal tshab, would be the mental continuum or subtle consciousness that continues across rebirths.

That implausible view leads us to the next question: Is that consistent with Nāgārjuna's account of causation, which rGyal tshab and the dGe lugs tradition also endorse? No, of course not. For Nāgārjuna, insistence on the emptiness of causation in turn insists precisely on the absence of the need for any causal powers or for any substantial basis for causal chains. Causation is redescribed in his Madhyamaka analysis as a matter of explanatorily useful regularities, and the notion of explanatory utility is further unpacked in terms of the embedding of regularities in further regularities. None of this requires the genidentity of the objects participating in cause and effect. Nor should it, as countless counterexamples show. Here the Cārvāka opponent seems to interpret things correctly: "It isn't accomplished through familiarity with various kinds of compassion, and it doesn't come from prior births. That is because since the conceptual mind depends on the body, if the body is destroyed, the mind will be destroyed as well." Or at least it could be like that.

Moreover, returning to the second thesis central to rGyal tshab's account, concerning the content of compassion, it would be more in harmony with the Mahāyāna understanding of *anātman* (also defended forcefully by Nāgārjuna in *Mūlamadhyamakakārikā*) to see it that way. This brings us back to the status of the "I" in verses like Śāntideva's, and the real content of *bodhicitta* and the *mahākarunā* it comprises. The aim and the motivation of *bodhicitta* is the alleviation of the suffering of all sentient beings. That is beyond question. It also includes the view that only a buddha could accomplish that task, given its stupendous difficulty. Moreover, *bodhicitta* is more than a mere wish that a buddha arise and that thereby sentient beings be released from suffering; it is an altruistic aspiration to bring that about. And the notion of "bringing about" is, of course, ineliminably causal. One can see, then, how if one thought about causality in terms of substantial supporting bases of causal chains one would then be led to believe that the only way to bring about the arising of a buddha for the sake of other sentient beings is to set about becoming one oneself, and the only way rationally to adopt that objective would be to believe in past and future lives; then the rest follows.

But once we have shed the reified view of causality Nāgārjuna so forcefully criticizes, this argument crumbles. And once we accept something like the transmission of knowledge as an analogy for a transpersonal causal chain linking epistemic and moral causes with their soteriological effects, we can see that the "I" as a future-tense subject in the Bodhisattva resolution is gratuitous. I must develop an altruistic resolve to do something; that something—if we accept more Buddhist soteriological theory about the necessity of a buddha's capabilities for the task at hand—might be to bring about enlightenment (or at least to contribute to bringing it about); but that enlightenment need not be mine. And if it need not, there is no entailment at all between *bodhicitta* properly understood and rebirth.

Nor should there be. For now we can see that to confuse an altruistic impersonal aspiration for enlightenment for the sake of sentient beings with an aspiration for one's own enlightenment—to confuse a conviction that there is a future for the sake of which one should work with the view that it is one's own future—is a serious, though subtle form of *ātmanvāda* or even *ātmangrāha*. The reason is this: the "I" that is posited here is posited not merely as a conventionally designated continuum, but as a substratum for a causal process. My dGe lugs proponent at this point—accusing me of nihilism about the self—will protest that the 'I' so posited is a mere "I"(*"nga" tsam*) as opposed to a substantial self. But simply to say that this is what is going on does not make it so. Here is the difference: A mere "I" does no metaphysical work—it serves as a conventionally posited imputation with no convention-independent identity conditions, and no explanatory value. Candrakīrti (1989, 1994) as well as Nāgārjuna and later Tsong khapa (1984, 1997) make this point with great force. But the "I" posited here— the "I myself" (*bdag ni*) of Śantideva, the one that is reborn for rGyal tshab— has work to do. It explains causation, something that according to Nāgārjuna is neither in need of explanation nor capable of being explained. To posit such a substantial substrate and then to stake the meaning of one's moral life on its continuation through time is to fall back from a view of emptiness into a barely disguised substantialism about the self. Only by opting for a more impersonal *bodhicitta*, a more impersonally *bodhisattva* resolution can the Mahāyāna remain consistently Madhyamaka.

I have heard three further objections to this account from dGe lugs pa interlocutors. Let me rehearse and respond to each quickly before turning to my conclusion.

1. On your view, it does not matter what I do in this life—whether I am Hitler or Mother Theresa, and this for two reasons: (a) If I am not going to exist in the future, I have no moral incentive to be good; after all, I will neither reap the benefits of morally good action nor suffer the consequences of morally bad actions; (b) Either kind of life might lead to benefits in the future, so there is no intrinsic reason to prefer a good life to a bad one. The answer in each case in simple: to the first objection, if your only motivation for leading a good life is your own benefit in the future, your motivation is not that of a *bodhisattva* in the first place. We are considering the necessary conditions of *bodhicitta*, after all,

not of self-interest. In the case of the second objection, the reason for thinking that Mother Theresa's life will be more likely to lead to universal moral improvement and enlightenment that Hitler's is not intrinsic by anyone's reckoning: it is causal (and though fallible, plausible). We think that it is simply likely that lives like hers generate the relevant moral benefits far more than do lives like his. If we thought otherwise, altruism might require strange things of us.[7]

2. Others object that there are plenty of independent reasons to accept rebirth (Dharmakīrti and rGyal tshab would agree). Maybe so. Maybe not. It does not matter, I say, for present purposes. My question is this: Do you need to believe in rebirth in order to generate *bodhicitta*? Just as it is true that there are nine planets and unnecessary to believe that in order to cultivate *bodhicitta*, it may be true that there is rebirth. But even so, I have argued that it is unnecessary to believe that in order to cultivate *bodhicitta*. Only the entailment is at issue between rGyal tshab and me at this point.[8]

3. Finally, some of my dGe lugs pa colleagues ask, if there is no rebirth, how does anyone reach the point of Buddhahood, given its stupendous difficulty, or, indeed, the point of generating *bodhicitta*, given its still impressive difficulty? Here I give the same answer I would give to the question how Kant wrote the *Critique*, or Einstein discovered relativity: by taking advantage of the accomplishments of those who go before. (Note that this is also a plausible and attractive way of understanding refuge in Buddhist practice.) And that has been the burden of the foregoing argument.

John Powers (personal communication) argues that the real reason for requiring belief in past and future lives is the fact that since the *bodhisattva* vow requires one to work to attain Buddhahood for the sake of *all* sentient beings, and since many of those sentient beings, on my view, fail to exist now (they died), and since others will exist only far in the future, the vow would be incoherent. You cannot, he argues, save sentient beings who no longer exist from *anything* and a buddha who then dies cannot save future beings. In fact, he argues, if you do not believe in future lives, the best way to rescue all sentient beings from suffering is to kill them all, right now. These would be unacceptable consequences, of course. But they do not follow. Powers's charges, however, do force a careful examination of the content of the vow and of the aspiration as I must understand them. *Bodhicitta* must, on my view, be directed only to actual sentient beings, present and future. One cannot hope to do anything for the dead. That does, to be sure, reduce the scope of this moral aspiration, but only realistically. With regard to the future, things are less dreary. The buddha one strives to bring into the world, I would hope, would not only help her contemporaries, but also her successors, just as the discoveries of medicines and vaccines help those who follow (the epithet "the great doctor" is a common way of referring to Siddhartha Gautama and has just this connotation). Finally, while killing all sentient beings might indeed relieve suffering, it does not thereby bring about happiness, and *bodhicitta* surely is the aspiration to bring about happiness as well. "May all sentient beings be happy" is, after all, among the most common Mahāyāna colophons. I conclude that Powers's objections fail.

If I am right about this, the doctrine of rebirth is of considerably less importance to Buddhism—especially to Mahāyāna Buddhism—than it is generally taken to be.[9] I take this as confirmation of my view. That doctrine, after all, is imported from an ambient Hindu culture. Buddhism jettisons a great deal of the central ideology of that culture, including, prominently, the ideal of *ātman*; there is no reason to think that this part should survive, especially if it can be shown both to be inessential to the central moral theses definitive of the Mahāyāna and to be inconsistent with its central insights, *anātman and the emptiness of causation*.[10]

CONCLUSIONS

I have enumerated distinct sets of implications of Nāgārjuna's views on causation: those for the profane and those for the sacred. But I could easily have adopted a more traditional classification of consequences: those pertaining to the selflessness of phenomena and those pertaining to the selflessness of persons. In each case, Nāgārjuna draws our attention to the subtle and seductive reification that comes to us so naturally, and to the extent to which our thinking about causation is implicated in that reification.

It is almost impossible to resist the temptation to seek to go beyond the merely interdependent and to posit some hidden glue—some cement of the universe—that holds not only the external world but the self in place and ensures the regular transition from link to link. "Surely," we think, driven by our deepest cognitive instincts, "even if everything we encounter is merely interdependent, that interdependence itself must have some substantial basis." But that commitment, when seen from the opposite side of the Madhyamaka dialectic, becomes the more insidious "Surely, even if everything we encounter is empty, that emptiness must be truly existent." And once we commit that fallacy, we are set on the royal road to nihilism about the world in which we lead our lives, and to untenable realism about the transcendent. It then becomes impossible to make any sense at all of empirical reality or of its emptiness. So, tempting as the "glue view" is, it merely traps us in an inescapable web of metaphysical illusion.

Nāgārjuna's analysis is powerful not only because it dissolves the hidden glue we instinctively posit to give coherence to our world, but also because it demonstrates the pernicious consequences of positing that glue. While a theory about causation—even a pre-reflective theory—might seem to be but a recherché corner of metaphysics and the philosophy of science, it in fact infects and determines our view of everything else—from the philosophy of science to the philosophy of mind to cosmology to ethics. Comprehending the issue of causality is indeed a prerequisite to the comprehension of everything else; it is true that a world without inner and outer glue disintegrates. Nothing holds the self together; nothing holds causes to their effects. Raw interdependence is all we encounter, and there is no hope of an explanation to end all explanations. That is the manifestation, in the philosophy of science and in the existential understanding of the nature of self, of the abyss of emptiness into which Dōgen much later commands us to leap. But that leap is a leap into emptiness, and not into nihilism: Just as Dōgen reassures us that in facing interdependence in this way the self and all things are affirmed, we have seen that in facing the emptiness of interdependence, while the inefficacious occult cement of the universe vanishes, the empirical world and the possibility of meaningful life therein are affirmed, its mere interdependence providing all the coherence one could coherently desire.

5

Nāgārjuna and the Limits of Thought

with Graham Priest

If you know the nature of one thing, you know the nature of all things.

Khensur Yeshe Thubten

Whatever is dependently co-arisen,
That is explained to be emptiness.
That, being a dependent designation,
Is itself the middle way.

(MMK *24: 18*)

Nāgārjuna is surely one of the most difficult philosophers to interpret in any tradition. His texts are terse and cryptic. He does not shy away from paradox or apparent contradiction. He is coy about identifying his opponents. The commentarial traditions grounded in his texts present a plethora of interpretations of his view. Nonetheless, his influence in the Mahāyāna Buddhist world is not only unparalleled in that tradition but exceeds in that tradition the influence of any single Western philosopher. The degree to which he is taken seriously by so many eminent Indian, Chinese, Tibetan, Korean, Japanese, and Vietnamese philosophers, and lately by so many Western philosophers, alone justifies attention to his corpus. Even were he not such a titanic figure historically, the depth and beauty of his thought and the austere beauty of his philosophical poetry would justify that attention. While Nāgārjuna may perplex and often infuriate, and while his texts may initially defy exegesis, anyone who spends any time with Nāgārjuna's thought inevitably develops a deep respect for this master philosopher.

One of the reasons Nāgārjuna so perplexes many who come to his texts is his seeming willingness to embrace contradictions, on the one hand, while using classic *reductio* arguments, implicating his endorsement of the law of noncontradiction, on the other. Another reason is his apparent willingness to saw off the limbs on which he sits. He asserts that there are two truths, and that they are one; that everything both exists and does not exist; that nothing is existent or nonexistent; that he rejects all philosophical views including his own; that he asserts nothing. And he appears to mean every word of it. Making sense of all of this is sometimes difficult. Some interpreters of Nāgārjuna, indeed, succumb to the easy temptation to read him as a simple mystic or an irrationalist of some kind. But it is significant that none of the important commentarial traditions in Asia, however much they disagree in other respects, regard him in this light.[1] And indeed most recent scholarship is unanimous in this regard as well, again despite a wide range of divergence in interpretations in other respects. Nāgārjuna is simply too committed to rigorous analytical argument to be dismissed as a mystic.

Our interest here is neither historical nor in a systematic exegesis or assessment of any of Nāgārjuna's work. Instead, we are concerned with the possibility that Nāgārjuna, like many philosophers in the West, and indeed like many of his Buddhist successors—perhaps as a consequence of his influence—discovers and explores true contradictions arising at the limits of thought. If this is indeed the case, it would account for both sides of the interpretive tension just noted: Nāgārjuna might appear to be an irrationalist in that he embraces some contradictions—both to Western philosophers and to Nyaya interlocutors who see consistency as a necessary condition of rationality. But to those who share with us a dialetheist's comfort with the possibility of true contradictions commanding rational assent, for Nāgārjuna to endorse such contradictions would not *undermine* but instead would *confirm*, the impression that he is indeed a highly rational thinker.[2]

We are also interested in the possibility that these contradictions are structurally analogous to those arising in the Western tradition. But while discovering a parallel between Nāgārjuna's thought and those of other paraconsistent frontiersmen such as Kant and Hegel, Heidegger and Derrida, may help Western philosophers to understand Nāgārjuna's project better, or at least might be a philosophical curio, we think we can deliver more than that: We will argue that while Nāgārjuna's contradictions are structurally similar to those we find in the West, Nāgārjuna delivers a paradox as yet unknown in the West. This paradox, we will argue, brings us a new insight into ontology and into our cognitive access to the world. We should read Nāgārjuna then, not because in him we can see affirmed what we already knew, but because we can learn from him.

One last set of preliminary remarks is in order. In this chapter we will defend neither the reading of Nāgārjuna's texts we adopt here, nor the cogency of dialethic logic, nor the claim that true contradictions satisfying the Inclosure Schema in fact emerge at the limits of thought. We will sketch these views, but baldly, not because we take these positions to be self-evident, but because each of us has defended his respective bit of this background elsewhere. This chapter will be about bringing Nāgārjuna and dialetheism together. Finally, we do not claim that Nāgārjuna himself had explicit views about logic, or about the limits of thought. We do, however, think that if he did, he had the views we are about to sketch. This is, hence, not textual history but rational reconstruction.

INCLOSURES AND THE LIMITS OF THOUGHT

In the *Tractatus*, Wittgenstein takes on the project of delimiting what can be thought. He writes in the preface (trans. B. McGuiness, 1922, p. 3):

> Thus the aim of the book is to draw a limit to thought, or rather—not to thought, but to the expression of thoughts: for in order to be able to draw a limit to thought, we should have to find both sides thinkable (i.e., we should have to be able to think what cannot be thought). It will therefore be only in language that the limit can be drawn, and what lies on the other side of the limit will simply be nonsense.

Yet, even having reformulated the problem in terms of language, the enterprise still runs into contradiction. In particular, the account of what can be said has as a consequence that it itself, and other things like it, cannot be said. Hence, we get the famous penultimate proposition of the *Tractatus* (ibid., p. 74)

> My propositions serve as elucidations in the following way: anyone who understands me eventually recognizes them as nonsensical, when he has used them—as steps—to climb up beyond them. (He must, so to speak, throw away the ladder after he has climbed up it.)

Wittgenstein's predicament is serious. No matter that we throw away the ladder *after* we have climbed it: its rungs were nonsensical *while* we were using them as well. So how could it have successfully scaffolded our ascent? And if it did not, on what basis are we now to agree that all of that useful philosophy was nonsense all along? This predicament, however, is not peculiar to him. It is a quite general feature of theories that try to characterize the limits of our cognitive abilities to think, describe, grasp, that they end up implying that they themselves cannot be thought, described or grasped. Yet it would appear that they can be thought, described and grasped. Otherwise, what on earth is the theory doing?

Thus, for example, when Sextus claims in *Outlines of Pyrrhonism* that it is impossible to assert anything about things beyond appearances, he would seem to be asserting just such a thing; and when he argues that no assertion is justified, this must apply to his own assertion as well. When Kant says that it is impossible to know anything about, or apply any categories to, the noumenal realm, he would seem to be doing just what cannot be done. When Russell attempts to solve the paradoxes of self-reference by claiming that it is impossible to quantify over *all* objects, he does just that. And the list goes on. Anyone who disparages the philosophical traditions of the East on account of their supposed flirtation with paradox has a lot of the West to explain away.

Of course, the philosophers we just mentioned were well aware of the situation, and all of them tried to take steps to avoid the contradiction. Arguably, they were not successful. Even more striking: characteristically, such attempts seem to end up in other instances of the very contradictions they are trying to avoid. The recent literature surrounding the Liar Paradox provides a rich diet of such examples.[3]

Now, why does this striking pattern occur again and again? The simplest answer is that when people are driven to contradictions in charting the limits of thought, it is precisely because those limits are themselves contradictory. Hence, any theory of the limits that is anywhere near adequate will be inconsistent. The recurrence of the encounter with limit contradictions is therefore the basis of an argument for the best explanation of the inconsistent nature of the limits themselves. (It is not the only argument. But other arguments draw on details of the particular limits in question.[4])

The contradictions at the limits of thought have a general and bipartite structure. The first part is an argument to the effect that a certain view, usually about the nature of the limit in question, transcends that limit (cannot be conceived, described, and so on). This is *Transcendence*. The other is an argument to the effect that the view *is* within the limit—*Closure*. Often, this argument is practical, based on the fact that Closure is demonstrated in the very act of theorizing about the limits. At any rate, together, the pair describe a structure that can conveniently be called an *inclosure*: a totality, Ω, and an object, o, such that o both is and is not in Ω.

On closer analysis, inclosures can be found to have a more detailed structure. At its simplest, the structure is this. The inclosure comes with an operator, δ, which, when applied to any suitable subset of Ω gives *another* object that is in Ω (that is, one that is not in the subset in question, but is in Ω). Thus, for example, if we are talking about sets of ordinals, δ might apply to give us the least ordinal not in the set. If we are talking about a set of entities that have been thought about, δ might give us an entity of which we have not yet thought. The contradiction at the limit arises when δ is applied to the totality Ω itself. For then the application of δ gives an object that is both within and without Ω: the least ordinal greater than all ordinals, or the unthought object.

All of the above is catalogued in *Beyond the Limits of Thought*. The catalogue of limit contradictions there is not exhaustive, though. In particular, it draws only on Western philosophy. In this chapter, we will add to the list the contradictions at the limits of thought discovered by Nāgārjuna. As we will see, these, too, fit the familiar pattern. The fact that they do, although proceeding from a different tradition, shows that the pattern is even less parochial than one might have thought. This should not, of course, be surprising: if the limits of thought really are contradictory, then they should appear so from both east and west of the Euphrates.

One way in which he does differ from the philosophers we have so far mentioned, though, is that Nāgārjuna does not try to *avoid* the contradiction at the limits of thought. He both sees it clearly and endorses it. (In the Western tradition, few philosophers other than Hegel and some of his successors have done this.) Moreover, Nāgārjuna seems to have hit upon a limit contradiction unknown in the West, and to suggest connections between ontological and semantic contradictions worthy of attention.

CONVENTIONAL AND ULTIMATE REALITY

Central to Nāgārjuna's view is his doctrine of the two realities. There exist, according to Nāgārjuna, conventional reality and ultimate reality. Correspondingly, there are Two Truths: conventional truth, the truth about conventional reality; and ultimate truth, the truth about the ultimate reality—qua ultimate reality.[5] For this reason, discussion of Nāgārjuna's view is often phrased in terms of Two Truths, rather than two realities.

The things that are conventionally true are the truths concerning the empirical world. Nāgārjuna generally calls this class of truths *samvṛti-satya*, or occasionally *vyavahāra-satya*. The former is explained by Nāgārjuna's commentator Candrakīrti as ambiguous. The first sense, the one most properly translated into English as "conventional truth (reality)" (*tha snyad bden pa*), is itself three ways ambiguous: on the one hand, it can mean "ordinary," or "everyday." In this sense a conventional truth is a truth to which we would ordinarily assent, common sense augmented by good science. The second of these three meanings is "truth by agreement." In this sense, the decision in Australia to drive on the left establishes a conventional truth about the proper side of the road. A different decision in the United States establishes another. Conventional truth is, in this sense, often relative. (Candrakīrti argues that, in fact, the first sense it is also relative—relative to our sense organs, conceptual scheme, and so on. In this respect he would agree with such Pyrrhonian skeptics as Sextus.) The final sense of this cluster is "nominally true." To be true in this sense is to be true in virtue of a particular linguistic convention. So, for instance, the fact that shoes and boots are different kinds of things here but are both instances of one kind, *lham* in Tibetan, makes their co-specificity or lack thereof a nominal matter. We English speakers, on the other hand, regard sparrows and crows both as members of a single natural superordinate kind, *bird*. Native Tibetan speakers distinguish the *bya* (the full-sized avian) from the *bya'u* (the smaller relative). Again, relativism about truth in this sense lurks in the background.

But these three senses cluster as one family against which stands yet another principal meaning of *samvṛti*. It can also mean "concealing," "hiding," "obscuring," "occluding." In this sense (aptly captured by the Tibetan *kun rdzob bden pa*, literally, "costumed truth") a *samvṛti-satya* is something that conceals the truth, or its real nature, or as it is sometimes glossed in the tradition, something regarded as a truth by an obscured or a deluded mind. Now, the Madhyamaka tradition, following Candrakīrti, makes creative use of this ambiguity, noting that, for instance, what such truths conceal is precisely the fact that they are merely conventional (in any of the senses adumbrated above) or that an obscured mind is obscured precisely in its improper understanding of the role of convention in constituting truth, and so on.

This lexicography provides preparation for the exploration of Nāgārjuna's distinction between the conventional and the ultimate truth (reality), and between conventional and ultimate perspectives—the distinct stances Nāgārjuna distinguishes toward the world, taken by ordinary versus enlightened beings. We will thus understand the word *conventional* with this cluster of connotations, all present in Nāgārjuna's treatment. Our primary concern as we get to the heart of this exploration will be, however, with the notion of ultimate truth (reality) (*paramartha-satya*, literally, "truth of the highest meaning," or "truth of the highest object"). This we can define negatively as the way things are, considered independently of convention, or positively as the way things are, when understood by a fully enlightened being who does not mistake what is really conventional for something that belongs to the very nature of things.

What is ultimate truth/reality, according to Nāgārjuna? To understand this, we have to understand the notion of emptiness, which for Nāgārjuna is emphatically *not* nonexistence, but, rather, interdependent existence. For something to have an essence (Tibetan, *rang bzhin;* Sanskrit, *svabhāva*) is for it to be what it is, in and of itself, independently of all other things. (This entails, incidentally, that things that are essentially so are eternally so; for if they started to be, or ceased to be, then their so being would depend on other things, such as time.) To be empty is precisely to have no essence, in this sense.

The most important ultimate truth, according to Nāgārjuna, is that everything is empty. Much of the *Mūlamadhyamakakārikā* (henceforth *MMK*) consists, in fact, of an extended set of arguments to the effect that everything that one might take to be an essence is, in fact, not one—that everything is empty of essence and of independent identity. The arguments are interesting and varied, and we will not go into them here. But just to give an overview of them, a very general argument is to be found in *MMK* 5. Here, Nāgārjuna argues that the spatial properties (and by analogy, all properties) of an object cannot be essential. For it would be absurd to suppose that the spatial location of an object could exist without the object itself—or, conversely, that there could be an object without location. Hence, location and object are co-dependent.

> From this it follows that there is no characterized
> And no existing characteristic. (*MMK*, 5: 4 a, b)

The existence in question here is, of course, ultimate existence. Nāgārjuna is not denying the conventional existence of objects and their properties.

With arguments such as the preceding one, Nāgārjuna establishes that everything is empty, contingently dependent on other things—dependently co-arisen, as it is often put.

We must take the *everything* here very seriously, though. When Nāgārjuna claims that everything is empty, *everything* includes emptiness itself. The emptiness of something is itself a dependently co-arisen property of that thing. The emptiness of emptiness is perhaps one of the most central claims of the *MMK*.[6] Nāgārjuna devotes much of chapter 7 to this topic. In that chapter, using some of the more difficult arguments of the *MMK*, he reduces to absurdity the assumption that dependent co-arising is itself an (ultimately) existing property of things. We will not go into the argument here, but its consequences will concern us.

For Western philosophers, it is very tempting to adopt a Kantian understanding of Nāgārjuna (as is offered, for example, by Murti 1955). Identify conventional reality with the phenomenal realm, and ultimate reality with the noumenal, and there you have it. But this is not Nāgārjuna's view. The emptiness of emptiness means that ultimate reality cannot be thought of as a *Kantian* noumenal realm. For *ultimate* reality is just as empty as *conventional* reality. Ultimate reality is hence only conventionally real! The distinct realities are therefore identical. As the *Vimalakīrtinirdeṣa-sūtra* puts it, "To say this is conventional and this is ultimate is dualistic. To realize that there is no difference between the conventional and the ultimate is to enter the Dharma-door of nonduality," or as the *Heart Sūtra* puts it more famously, "Form is empty; emptiness is form; form is not different from emptiness; emptiness is not different from form." The identity of the Two Truths has profound soteriological implications for Nāgārjuna, such as the identity of nirvāna and *samsāra*.[7] But we will not go into these. We are now nearly in a position to address the first of Nāgārjuna's limit contradictions.

Nāgārjuna and the Law of Noncontradiction

One more preliminary matter remains: Nāgārjuna's attitude toward the law of noncontradiction in the domain of conventional truth. For to charge Nāgārjuna with irrationalism, or even with an extreme form of dialetheism according to which contradictions are as numerous as blackberries, is, in part, to charge him with thinking that contradictions are true in the standard conventional realm. Though this view is commonly urged (see, for example, Robinson 1957, Wood 1994), it is wrong. Though Nāgārjuna does endorse contradictions, they are not of a kind that concern conventional reality, qua conventional reality.

We can get at this point in two ways: first, we can observe that Nāgārjuna himself never asserts that there are true contradictions in this realm (or, more cautiously, that every apparent assertion of a contradiction concerning this domain, upon analysis, resolves itself into something else). Second, we can observe that Nāgārjuna takes *reductio* arguments to be decisive in this domain. We confess: Neither of these strategies is hermeneutically unproblematic. The first relies on careful and sometimes controversial readings of Nāgārjuna's dialectic. We will argue using a couple of cases that such readings are correct. Moreover, such readings are defended in the canonical tradition by some of the greatest Madhyamaka exegetes.

The second strategy is difficult because, typically, Nāgārjuna's arguments are directed ad hominem, against specific positions defended by his adversaries, each of whom would endorse the law of noncontradiction. If we argue that Nāgārjuna rejects the positions they defend by appealing to contradictory consequences of opponents' positions he regards as refutatory, it is always open to the irrationalist interpreter of Nāgārjuna to reply that for the argument to be successful one needs to regard these only as refutations *for the opponent*. That is, on this reading, Nāgārjuna could be taken not himself to find contradictory consequences as problematic, but to be presenting a consequence unacceptable to a consistent opponent, thereby forcing his opponent to relinquish the position on the opponent's own terms. And indeed such a reading is cogent. So if we are to give this line of argument any probative force, we will have to show that in particular cases Nāgārjuna *himself* rejects the contradiction and *endorses* the conventional claim whose negation entails the contradiction. We will present such examples.

Let us first consider the claim that Nāgārjuna himself freely asserts contradictions. One might think, for instance, that when Nāgārjuna writes:

> Therefore, space is not an entity.
> It is not a nonentity.
> Not characterized, not without character.
> The same is true of the other five elements. (*MMK* 5: 7)

he is endorsing the claim that space and the other fundamental elements have contradictory properties (existence and nonexistence, being characterized and being uncharacterized). But this reading would be possible only if one (as we have just done) lifts this verse out of context. The entire chapter in which it occurs is addressed to the problem of reification—to treating the elements as providing an ontological foundation for all of reality, that is, as essences. After all, he concludes in the very next verse:

> Fools and reificationists who perceive
> The existence and nonexistence
> Of objects
> Do not see the pacification of objectification. (*MMK* 5: 8)

It is then clear that Nāgārjuna is not *asserting* that space and the other elements have contradictory properties. Rather, he is rejecting a certain framework in which they play the role of ultimate foundations, or the role of ultimate property bearers.

Moreover, though Western and non-Buddhist Indian commentators have urged that such claims are contradictory, they are not even prima facie contradictions unless one presupposes both the law of the excluded middle and Nāgārjuna endorsement of that law. Otherwise there is no way of getting from a verse that explicitly rejects both members of the pair "Space is an entity" and "Space is a nonentity" to the claim that, in virtue of rejecting each, he is accepting its negation, and hence that he is asserting a contradiction. It is much better to read Nāgārjuna as rejecting excluded middle for the kind of assertion the opponent in question is making, packed as it is with what Nāgārjuna regards as illicit ontological presupposition (Garfield 1995).

To consider a second example: in his discussion of the aggregates, another context in which his concern is to dispose of the project of fundamental ontology, Nāgārjuna writes:

> The assertion that the effect and cause are similar
> Is not acceptable.
> The assertion that they are not similar
> Is also not acceptable. (*MMK* 4: 6)

Again, absent context, and granted the law of the excluded middle, this appears to be a bald contradiction. And again, context makes all the difference. The opponent in this chapter has been arguing that form itself (material substance) can be thought of as the cause of all psychophysical phenomena. In the previous verse Nāgārjuna has just admonished the opponent to "think about form, but / Do not construct theories about form." (5 cd) The point of this verse is just that form, per se, is neither a plausible explanation of the material world (this would beg the question) nor of the non-material world (it fails to explain psychophysical relations). We are not concerned here with whether Nāgārjuna is right or wrong in these cases. We want to point out only that in cases like this, where it might appear that Nāgārjuna does assert contradictions, it is invariably the case that a careful reading of the text undermines the straightforwardly contradictory reading. And once again, when read with logical circumspection what we have here, in any case, is only a rejection in a particular context of the law of the excluded middle, and no warrant for moving from that rejection to any rejection of noncontradiction.

We now turn to the fact that Nāgārjuna employs *reductio* arguments to refute positions he rejects, showing that at least with regard to standard conventional situations, the fact that a claim entails contradictions is good reason to reject it. In chapter 15 of *MMK*, Nāgārjuna considers the possibility that what it is to exist and what it is to have a particular identity is to be explained by appeal to essence. But he is able to conclude that

> Those who see essence and essential difference
> And entities and nonentities,
> They do not see
> The truth taught by the Buddha. (*MMK* 16: 6)

precisely on the grounds that

> If there is no essence,
> What could become other?
> If there is essence,
> What could become other? (*MMK* 15: 9)

In this argument, lines c and d—the rest of whose details, and the question of the soundness of which, we leave aside for present purposes—Nāgārjuna notes that an account of existence, change, and difference that appeals to essence leads to a contradiction. Things do "become other." That is a central thesis of the Buddhist doctrine of impermanence that Nāgārjuna defends in the text. But if they do, he argues, and if essence were explanatory of their existence, difference, and change, they would need both to have essence, to account for their existence, and to lack it, in that essences are eternal. Since this is contradictory, essence is to be rejected. And of course, as we have already noted, Nāgārjuna does reject essence. That is the central motivation of the text.

In chapter 17 Nāgārjuna responds to the opponent's suggestion that action may be something uncreated (23), a desperate ploy to save the idea that actions have essences. He responds that

> All conventions would then
> Be contradicted, without doubt.
> It would be impossible to draw a distinction
> Between virtue and evil (*MMK* 17: 24).

Again, neither the details of the argument nor its success concerns us here. Rather, we emphasize that, for Nāgārjuna, contradictory consequences of positions in the standard conventional realm are fatal to those positions.

As a final example, in chapter 18 Nāgārjuna concludes;

> Whatever comes into being dependent on another
> Is not identical to that thing.
> Nor is it different from it.
> Therefore it is neither nonexistent in time nor permanent. (*MMK* 18: 10)

Here Nāgārjuna notes that the contradiction (not identical/not different) follows from the disjunction "An entity is either nonexistent or permanent" and so opts for the claim that existent phenomena are impermanent. We conclude, then, that not only does Nāgārjuna not freely assert contradictions; but when he employs them, at least when discussing standard conventional truth, he does so as the conclusions of *reductio* arguments, whose point is to defend the negation of the claim he takes to entail those contradictions.

At this stage, then, we draw the following conclusions: Nāgārjuna is not an irrationalist. He is committed to the canons of rational argument and criticism. He is not a mystic. He believes that reasoned argument can lead to the abandonment of error and to knowledge. He is not of the view that the conventional world, however nominal it may be, is riddled with contradictions.[8] If Nāgārjuna is to assert contradictions, they will be elsewhere: defended rationally and asserted in the service of reasoned analysis.

The Ultimate Truth Is That There Is No Ultimate Truth

We are now in a position to examine Nāgārjuna's first limit contradiction. The centerpiece of Nāgārjuna's Madhyamaka, or "middle way" philosophy, is the thesis that everything is empty. This thesis has a profound consequence. Ultimate truths are those about ultimate reality. But since everything is empty, there is no ultimate reality. There are, therefore, no ultimate truths. We can get at the same conclusion another way. To express anything in language is to express truth that depends on language, and so this cannot be an expression of the way things are ultimately. All truths, then, are merely conventional.

Nāgārjuna enunciates this conclusion in the following passages:

> The Victorious ones have said
> That Emptiness is the relinquishing of all views.
> For whoever emptiness becomes a view
> That one will accomplish nothing (*MMK* 13: 8).

> I prostrate to Gautama
> Who, through compassion
> Taught the true doctrine
> Which leads to the relinquishing of all views. (*MMK* 27: 30)

Nāgārjuna is not saying here that one must be reduced to total silence. He himself certainly was not! The views that one must relinquish are views about the ultimate nature of reality. And there is no such thing as the ultimate nature of reality. That is what it is for all phenomena to be empty.

It might be thought that the rest is simply ineffable. Indeed, Nāgārjuna is sometimes interpreted in this way too (Gorampa 1990). But this, also, would be too simplistic a reading. There *are* ultimate truths. *MMK* is full of them. For example, when Nāgārjuna says (*MMK*: 24: 19):

> Something that is not dependently arisen
> Such a thing does not exist.
> Therefore a non-empty thing
> Does not exist.

he is telling us about the nature of ultimate reality. There are, therefore, ultimate truths. Indeed, that there is no ultimate reality is itself a truth about ultimate reality and is therefore an ultimate truth! This is Nāgārjuna's first limit contradiction.

There are various objections one might raise at this point in an attempt to save Nāgārjuna from (ultimate) inconsistency. Let us consider two. First, one might say that when Nāgārjuna appears to assert ultimate truths, he is not *really* asserting anything. His utterances have some other function. One might develop this point in at least two different ways. First, one may say that Nāgārjuna's speech acts are to be taken, not as acts of assertion, but as acts of denial. It is as though, whenever someone else makes a claim about ultimate reality, Nāgārjuna simply says "No!" This is to interpret Nāgārjuna as employing a relentless *via negativa*. Alternatively, one may say that in these utterances Nāgārjuna is not performing a speech act at all: he is merely uttering words with no illocutionary force. In the same way, one may interpret Sextus as claiming that he, also, never made assertions: he simply *uttered* words, which, when understood by his opponents, would cause them to give up their views.[9]

Whilst these strategies have some plausibility (and some ways of reading Bhavaviveka and Candrakīrti portray them as interpreting Nāgārjuna in just this way), in the end the text simply cannot sustain this reading. There are just too many important passages in the *MMK* in which Nāgārjuna is not simply denying what his opponents say, or saying things that will cause his opponents to retract, but stating positive views of his own. Consider, for example, the central verse of the *MMK*:

> Whatever is dependently co-arisen,
> That is explained to be emptiness.
> That, being a dependent designation,
> Is itself the middle way. (*MMK* 24: 18)

Or Nāgārjuna's assertion that nirvāna and *sāṃsara* are identical:

> Whatever is the limit of nirvāṇa,
> That is the limit of cyclic existence.
> There is not even the slightest difference between them,
> Or even the subtlest thing. (*MMK* 25: 20.)

These are telling it like it is.

The strategy of claiming that, in the relevant portions of the text, Nāgārjuna is not making assertions gains some exegetical plausibility from the fact that sometimes Nagarjuna can be interpreted as describing his own utterances in this way. The locus classicus is *Vigrahavyāvartanī* where Nāgārjuna responds to a Nyāya charge that he has undermined his own claim to the emptiness of all things through his own commitment to his assertions. In his autocommentary to verse 29, he writes:

> If I had even one proposition thereby it would be just as you have said. Though if I had a proposition with the characteristic that you described, I would have that fault, I have no proposition at all. Thus, since all phenomena are empty, at peace, by nature isolated, how could there be a proposition? How can there be a characteristic of a proposition? And how can there be a fault arising from the characteristic of a proposition? Thus, the statement, "through the characteristic of your proposition you come to acquire the fault" is not true.

But context and attention to the structure of the argument make all the hermeneutic difference here. The Nyāya interlocutor has charged Nāgārjuna not simply with *asserting things* but with a self-refutatory commitment to the existence of convention-independent truth-makers (propositions—*pratijñā*) for the things he says, on pain of abandoning claims to the truth of his own theory. Nāgārjuna's reply does not deny that he is asserting anything. How could he deny *that*? Rather, he *asserts* that his use of words does not commit him to the existence of any convention-independent phenomena (such as emptiness) to which those words refer. What he denies is a particular semantic theory, one he regards as incompatible with his doctrine of the emptiness of all things precisely because it is committed to the claim that things have natures (in chapter 3 of this book). Compare, in this context, Wittgenstein's rejection of the theory of meaning of the *Tractatus*, with its extralinguistic facts and propositions, in favor of the use-theory of the *Investigations*. We conclude that even the most promising textual evidence for this route to saving Nāgārjuna from inconsistency fails.

A second way one might save Nāgārjuna from inconsistency is to suggest that his assertions that appear to be statements of ultimate truth state merely conventional, and not ultimate, truths after all. One might defend this claim by pointing out that these truths can indeed be expressed, and inferring that they therefore *must* be conventional, for otherwise they would be ineffable. If this were so, then to say that there are no ultimate truths would simply be *true*, and *not* false. But this reading is also hard to sustain. For something to be an ultimate truth is for it to be the way a thing is found to be at the end of an analysis of its nature. When, for instance, a mādhyamika says that things are ultimately empty, he is saying that when we analyze that thing, looking for its essence, we literally come up empty. The analysis never terminates with anything that can stand as an essence. But another way of saying this is to say that the result of this ultimate analysis is the discovery that all things are empty, and that they can be no other way. This, hence, is an ultimate truth about them. We might point out that the Indo-Tibetan exegetical tradition, despite lots of other internecine disputes, is unanimous on this point.

There is, then, no escape. Nāgārjuna's view is contradictory,[10] clearly a paradox of expressibility. Nāgārjuna succeeds in saying the unsayable, just as much as the Wittgenstein of the *Tractatus*. We can think (and characterize) reality only subject to language, which is conventional, so the ontology of that reality is all conventional. It follows that the conventional objects of reality do not ultimately (nonconventionally) exist. It also follows that nothing we say of them is ultimately true. That is, all things are empty of ultimate existence; and this is their ultimate nature and is an ultimate truth about them. They hence cannot be thought to have that nature; nor can we say that they do. But we have just done so. As Mark Siderits (1989, p. 231) has put it, "The ultimate truth is that there is no ultimate truth."

POSITIVE AND NEGATIVE TETRALEMMAS; CONVENTIONAL AND ULTIMATE PERSPECTIVES

It may be useful to approach the contradiction at the limits of expressibility here by a different route: Nāgārjuna's unusual use of both positive and negative forms of the *catuḥskoti*, or classical Indian tetralemma. Classical Indian logic and rhetoric regards any proposition as defining a logical space involving four candidate positions, or corners (*koti*) in distinction to most Western logical traditions that consider only two—truth and falsity: the proposition may be true (and not false); false (and not true); both true and false; neither true nor false. As a consequence, Indian epistemology and metaphysics, including Buddhist epistemology and metaphysics, typically partitions each problem space defined by a property into four possibilities, not two.[11] So Nāgārjuna in *Mūlamadhyamakakārikā* considers the possibility that motion, for instance, is in the moving object, not in the moving object, both in and not in the moving object, and neither in nor not in the moving object. Each prima facie logical possibility needs analysis before rejection.

Nāgārjuna uses both the positive and negative tetralemmas and uses the distinction in mood to differentiate between the perspectives of the Two Truths. Positive tetralemmas, such as this, are asserted from the conventional perspective:

> That there is a self has been taught,
> And the doctrine of no-self,
> By the buddhas, as well as the
> Doctrine of neither self nor non-self. (*MMK* 18: 6)

Some, of course, interpret these as evidence for the irrationalist interpretation of Nāgārjuna defused in the preceding discussion. But if we are not on the lookout for contradictory readings of this, we can see Nāgārjuna explaining simply how the policy of Two Truths works in a particular case. Conventionally, he says, there is a self—the conventional selves we recognize as persisting from day to day, such as Jay and Graham, exist. But selves do not exist ultimately. They both exist conventionally and are empty and so fail to exist ultimately—indeed, these are exactly the same thing. This verse therefore records neither inconsistency nor incompleteness: rather, it affirms the Two Truths and demonstrates that we can talk coherently about both, and about their relationship—from the conventional perspective, of course.

The distinctively Nagarjunian negative tetralemmas are more interesting. Here Nāgārjuna seeks the limits of expressibility, and the contradictory situation at that limit, when we take the ultimate perspective:

> "Empty" should not be asserted.
> "Non-empty" should not be asserted.
> Neither both nor neither should be asserted.
> These are used only nominally. (*MMK* 22: 11)

The last line makes it clear (as does context in the text itself) that Nāgārjuna is discussing what cannot be said from the ultimate perspective—from a point of view transcendent of the conventional. And it turns out here that *nothing* can be said, even that all phenomena are empty, nor its negation. We can't even say that nothing can be said. But we just did. And we have thereby characterized the ultimate perspective, which, if we are correct in our characterization, cannot be done.

The relationship between these two kinds of tetralemma generates a higher order contradiction as well: they say the same thing. Each describes completely (though from different directions) the relationship between the Two Truths. The positive tetralemma asserts that conventional phenomena exist conventionally and can be characterized truly from that perspective, and that ultimately nothing exists or satisfies any description. In saying this, it in no way undermines its own cogency and in fact affirms and explains its own expressibility. The negative counterpart asserts the same thing: that existence and characterization make sense at, and only at, the conventional level; and that, at the ultimate level, nothing exists or satisfies any description. But in doing so it contradicts itself: if true, it asserts its own nonassertability. The identity of the prima facie opposite Two Truths is curiously mirrored in the opposition of the prima facie identical two tetralemmas.

ALL THINGS HAVE ONE NATURE, THAT IS, NO NATURE

We have examined the contradiction concerning the limits of expressibility for Nāgārjuna. But as it is probably clear already, another, and more fundamental, contradiction underlies this, the ontological contradiction concerning emptiness itself. All things, including emptiness itself, are, as we have seen, empty. As Nāgārjuna expresses this in a verse that is at the heart of the *MMK*:

> Whatever is dependently co-arisen,
> That is explained to be emptiness.
> That, being a dependent designation,
> Is itself the middle way. (*MMK* 24: 18)

Now, since all things are empty, all things lack any ultimate nature; and this is a characterization from the ultimate perspective. Thus, ultimately, things are empty. But emptiness is, by definition, the lack of any essence or ultimate nature. Nature, or essence, is just what empty things are empty of. Hence, ultimately, things must lack emptiness. To be ultimately empty is, ultimately, to lack emptiness. In other words, emptiness is the nature of all things; for this reason, they have no nature, not even emptiness. As Nāgārjuna expresses it in his autocommentary to *Vigrahavyāvartanī*, quoting lines from the *Astasahasrika-prajñāpāramitā-sūtra*: "All things have one nature, that is, no nature."

Nāgārjuna's enterprise is one of fundamental ontology, and his conclusion is that fundamental ontology is impossible. But that is a fundamentally ontological conclusion—and that is the paradox. There is no way that things are ultimately, not even that way. The Indo-Tibetan tradition, following the *Vimalakīrtinirdesa-sūtra*, hence repeatedly advises one to learn to "tolerate the groundlessness of things." The emptiness of emptiness is the fact that not even emptiness exists ultimately, that it is also dependent, conventional, nominal, and in the end, it is just the everydayness of the everyday. Penetrating to the depths of being, we find ourselves back on the surface of things and so discover that there is nothing, after all, beneath those deceptive surfaces. Moreover, what is deceptive about them is simply the fact that we assume ontological depths lurking just beneath.

There are, again, ways that one might attempt to avoid the ontological contradiction. One way is to say that Nāgārjuna's utterances about emptiness are not assertions at all. We have discussed this move in connection with the previous limit contradiction. Another way, in this context, is to argue that even though Nāgārjuna is asserting that everything is empty, the emptiness in question must be understood as an accident, and not an essence, to use Aristotelian jargon. Again, though this exegetical strategy may have some plausibility, it cannot be sustained. For things do not simply *happen* to be empty, as some things *happen* to be red. The arguments of *MMK* are designed to show that all things cannot but be empty, that there is no other mode of existence of which they are capable. Since emptiness is a necessary characteristic of things, it belongs to them essentially—it is part of the very nature of phenomena, per se. As Candrakīrti puts it, commenting on *MMK* 13: 8:

As it is said in the great Ratnakūṭa- sūtra, "Things are not empty because of emptiness; to be a thing is to be empty. Things are not without defining characteristics through characteristiclessness; to be a thing is to be without a defining characteristic. . . . [W]hoever understands things in this way, Kasyapa, will understand perfectly how everything has been explained to be in the middle path.

To be *is* to be empty. That is what it is to be. It is no accidental property; it is something's nature—though, being empty, it has no nature.

This paradox is deeply related to the first one that we discussed. One might fairly ask, as have many on both sides of this planet, just *why* paradoxes of expressibility arise. The most obvious explanations might appear to be semantic in character, adverting only to the nature of language. One enamored of Tarski's treatment of truth in a formal language might, for instance, take such a route. One might then regard limit paradoxes as indicating a limit*ation* of language, an inadequacy of a reality that must itself be consistent, and whose consistency would be mirrored in an *adequate* language. But Nāgārjuna's system provides an ontological explanation and a very different attitude toward these paradoxes, and hence to language. Reality has no nature. Ultimately, it is not in any way at all. So nothing can be said about it. Essencelessness thus induces noncharacterizability. But, on the other side of the street, emptiness is an ultimate character of things. And this fact can ground the (ultimate) truth of what we have just said. The paradoxical linguistic utterances are therefore grounded in the contradictory nature of reality.

We think that the Nāgārjuna's ontological insight is distinctive of the Madhyamaka; it is hard to find a parallel in the West prior to the work of Heidegger.[12] But even Heidegger does not follow Nāgārjuna all the way to the dramatic insistence on the identity of the two realities and the recovery of the authority of the conventional. This extirpation of the myth of the deep may be Nāgārjuna's greatest contribution to Western philosophy.

NĀGĀRJUNA AND INCLOSURE

Everything is real and is not real,
Both real and not real,
Neither real nor not real.
This is Lord Buddha's teaching. (*MMK* 18: 8)

Central to Nāgārjuna's understanding of emptiness as immanent in the conventional world is his doctrine of the emptiness of emptiness. That, we have seen, is what prevents the two truths from collapsing into an appearance/reality or phenomenon/noumenon distinction. But it is also what generates the contradictions characteristic of philosophy at the limits. We have encountered two of these and have seen that they are intimately connected. The first is a paradox of expressibility: linguistic expression and conceptualization can express only conventional truth; the ultimate truth is that which is inexpressible and that which transcends these limits. So it cannot be expressed or characterized. But we have just done so. The second is a paradox of ontology: all phenomena, Nāgārjuna argues, are empty and so ultimately have no nature. But emptiness is, therefore, the ultimate nature of things. So they both have and lack an ultimate nature.

That these paradoxes involve Transcendence should be clear. In the first case, there is an explicit claim that the ultimate truth transcends the limits of language and of thought. In the second case, Nāgārjuna claims that the character of ultimate reality transcends all natures. That they also involve Closure is also evident. In the first case, the truths are expressed and hence are within the limits of expressibility; and in the second case, the nature is given and hence is within the totality of all natures.

Now consider the Inclosure Schema, introduced earlier, in a bit more detail. It concerns properties, φ and ψ, and a function, δ, satisfying the following conditions:

(1) $\Omega=\{x: \varphi(x)\}$ exists, and $\psi(\Omega)$.
(2) For all $X \subseteq \Omega$ such that $\psi(X)$:
    (i) $\neg\delta(X)\varepsilon X$ (Transcendence)
    (ii) $\delta(X)\varepsilon\Omega$ (Closure)

Applying δ to Ω then gives $\delta(\Omega)\varepsilon\Omega$ and $\neg\delta(\Omega)\varepsilon\Omega$. In a picture, we may represent the situation thus:

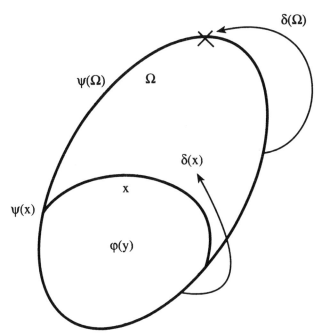

In Nāgārjuna's ontological contradiction, an inclosure is formed by taking

- φ(x) as "x is empty"
- φ(X) as "X is a set of things with some common nature"
- δ(X) as "the nature of things in X"

To establish that this is an inclosure, we first note that ψ(Ω). For Ω is the set of things that have the nature of being empty. Now assume that X⊆Ω and ψ(X), that is, that X is a set of things with some common nature. δ(X) is that nature, and δ(X)εΩ since all things are empty (Closure). It follows from this that δ(X) has no nature. Hence, ¬δ(X)εX, since X is a set of things with some nature (Transcendence). The limit contradiction is that the nature of all things (Ω)— viz. emptiness—both is and is not empty. Or to quote Nāgārjuna, quoting the Prajñāpāramitā, "All things have one nature, that is, no nature."

In Nāgārjuna's expressibility contradiction, an inclosure is formed by taking:

- φ(x) as "x is an ultimate truth"
- ψ(X) as "X is definable"
- δ(X) as the sentence "there is nothing which is in D," where "D" refers to X. (If X is definable, there is such a D.)

To establish that this is an inclosure, we first note that ψ(Ω). For "{x: x is an ultimate truth}" defines Ω.

Now assume that X⊆Ω and ψ(X), then δ(X) is a sentence that says that nothing is in X. Call this *s*. It is an ultimate truth that there are no ultimate truths, that is, that there is nothing in Ω; and, since X⊆Ω, it is an ultimate truth that there is nothing in X. That is, *s* is ultimately true: *s*εΩ (Closure). For Transcendence, suppose that *s*εX. Then *s*εΩ, that is, *s* is an ultimate truth, and so true, that is, nothing is in X. Hence, it is not the case that *s*εX. The limit contradiction is that δ(Ω), the claim that there are no ultimate truths, both is and is not an ultimate truth.

Thus, Nāgārjuna's paradoxes are both, precisely, inclosure contradictions. These contradictions are unavoidable once we see emptiness as Nāgārjuna characterizes it—as the lack of any determinate character. But this does not entail that Nāgārjuna is an irrationalist, a simple mystic, or crazy; on the contrary, he is prepared to go exactly where reason takes him: to the transconsistent.

NĀGĀRJUNA'S PARADOX AND OTHERS LIKE AND UNLIKE IT

Demonstrating that Nāgārjuna's two linked limit paradoxes satisfy a schema common to a number of well-known paradoxes in Western philosophy (the Liar, Mirimanoff's, the Burali-Forti, Russell's, the Knower, to name a few) goes further to normalize Nāgārjuna. We thus encounter him as a philosopher among familiar, respectable philosophers, as a fellow traveler at the limits of epistemology and metaphysics. The air of irrationalism and laissez faire mysticism is thus dissipated once and for all. If Nāgārjuna is beyond the pale, then so too are Kant, Hegel, Wittgenstein, and Heidegger.

This tool also allows comparison between Nāgārjuna's insights and those of his Western colleagues, and allows us to ask what, if anything, is distinctive about his results. We suggest the following: the paradox of expressibility, while interesting and important, and crucial to Nāgārjuna's philosophy of language (as well as to the development of Mahāyāna Buddhist philosophical practice throughout Central and East Asia), is not Nāgārjuna's unique contribution (though he may be the first to discover and to mobilize it, which is no mean distinction in the history of philosophy). It recurs in the West in the work of Wittgenstein, Heidegger, and Derrida, to name a few, and shares a structure with such paradoxes as that of the Liar. Discovering that Nāgārjuna shares this insight with many Western philosophers may help to motivate the study of Nāgārjuna by westerners, but it does not demonstrate that he has any special value to us.

The ontological paradox, on the other hand—which we hereby name Nāgārjuna's Paradox—though, as we have seen, intimately connected with a paradox of expressibility, is distinctive, and to our knowledge is found nowhere else. If Nāgārjuna is correct in his critique of essence, and if it hence turns out that all things lack fundamental natures, it turns out that they all have the same nature, that is, emptiness, and hence both have and lack that very nature. This is a direct consequence of the purely negative character of the property of emptiness, a property Nāgārjuna first fully characterizes, whose centrality to philosophy he first demonstrates. Most dramatically, Nāgārjuna demonstrates that the emptiness of emptiness permits the "collapse" of the distinction between the Two Truths, revealing the empty to be simply the everyday, and so saves his ontology from a simple-minded dualism. Nāgārjuna demonstrates that the profound limit contradiction he discovers sits harmlessly at the heart of all things. In traversing the limits of the conventional world, there is a twist, like that in a Möbius strip, and we find ourselves to have returned to it, now fully aware of the contradiction on which it rests.[13]

PART II

Yogācāra

6

Three Natures and Three Naturelessnesses

Comments Concerning Cittamātra
Conceptual Categories

You must not pay so much attention to the literal meanings of
these texts, but see how their meaning emerges in the context of
the commentaries.

The Ven Gen Lobsang Gyatso

GETTING IT BACKWARD

It took me a while, but I finally figured out the right place to assemble and from
which to begin to pick out the tangle of questions I had developed over the last
few years of reading Vasubandhu and his classical Indian, Tibetan, and twentieth
century commentators. I was perplexed about how one could move coherently
from the doctrine of three *natures* (*trisvabhāva, rang bzhin gsum*) so forcefully
and clearly articulated in *Trisvabhāvanirdeśa* (hereafter *TSN*), Triṃśika (hereafter
TK), and *Madhyāntavibhāgabhāsya* (hereafter *MVB/MV*) to the docrine of three
naturelessnesses (*trinisvabhāva, ngo bo nyid med gsum*) stressed so forcefully by
such Tibetan philosophers as rJe Tsong khapa and mKhas grub rje as the central
Cittamātra doctrine. These did not appear to be the same—or even consistent—
formulations, and the move to the second appeared philosophically questionable.
I was also perplexed both by the eschewal by Tibetan commentators of any discussion of the striking parallel between the opening stanza of *MV* and the central
verse 24:18 of *Mūlamādhyamakakārikā (hereafter MMK)* and by Nagao's (1991)
focus on it as an argument for the *continuity* of the system of Vasubandhu with
that of Nāgārjuna, despite the apparent challenge to the latter represented by the
MV verse and its commentary.

I think I have unraveled these tangles now and in the process have seen that
I erred by picking them up in the wrong place—with Vasubandhu himself—and
then wondering how he could be so understood. In fact, I should have, guided
by its name, started with the *Saṃdhinirmocana-sūtra* (hereafter *SNS*) and asked
how Vasubandhu used it as a platform for motivating his radical philosophical
program, and what the ramifications were for the reception of his thought given
that choice of scriptural basis. Then it all becomes clear, or so I will argue.

THE PROBLEM ABOUT CONTINUITY: NĀGĀRJUNA AND VASUBANDHU

Nāgārjuna in *MMK* 24:18 writes:

> Whatever is dependently co-arisen,
> That is explained to be emptiness.
> That, being a dependent designation
> Is itself the middle way. (1995)

Here Nāgārjuna emphasizes not only that all conventional phenomena are empty of essence, but also that emptiness and dependent arising are in fact the same property, and that emptiness itself is dependent, nominally established, and hence empty. The centrality of this verse to *MMK* as a whole cannot be overemphasized,[1] and its role in that text was surely well known to Vasubandhu when in *MV*1: 1,2 he writes[2]:

> There exists the imagination of the unreal.
> But emptiness exists in it, and also that (imagination) in it (emptiness).
> Therefore it is said that all entities are neither empty nor non-empty,
> Because of its [imagination's] existence, its [the object's] non-existence, and its [emptiness's] existence. This is the middle way.

Nagao (1991) notes correctly the striking formal parallel between these passages.[3] He exploits this parallel to argue for the continuity and compatibility of Madhyamaka and Yogācāra thought, claiming that this verse recapitulates and analyzes Nāgārjuna's. According to Nagao, the imagination of the unreal corresponds to dependent arising, and the existence of it in emptiness and vice versa recapitulates the identity of dependent arising and emptiness asserted by Nāgārjuna. He argues that the insistance by Vasubandhu on the existence of imagination, the nonexistence of the object, and the existence of emptiness provides an analysis of Nāgārjuna's doctrine that dependent arising, emptiness, and the relation between them are dependent-designations, existing in one way but not in another. Moreover, he argues, this verse indicates a thorough interpenetration of the ultimate nonexistence and convential existence of phenomena, mediated by dependent arising and conventional designation.

While Nagao's irenic syncretism has the great virtue of eliminating schism in the *sangha*, and while it provides an admirable foundation for later Chinese and Japanese attempts at reconciliation between these two principal Mahāyāna schools, I do not think that close attention to the texts sustains this interpretation. Much of the argument for the difference between Nāgārjuna's and Vasubandhu's respective projects will emerge implicitly throughout this chapter. But let me make a few central points now, as a springboard for a more direct investigation into Yogācāra and Cittamātra metaphysics and the evolution of its central doctines. First, note that Nāgārjuna, does *not* assert the *existence* of emptiness. Instead, he explicitly argues that predicates such as existence and nonexistence cannot be coherently applied to emptiness. Candrakīrti follows him in this position (see chapter 2, this volume). Second, Nāgārjuna is emphatic in his insistance that conventional phenomena such as the objects of perception *do* in fact exist conventionally. Third (and to explain why this is not incompatible with the first would take us far afield of this chapter, but see chapters 1, 3 and 5 in this volume and Garfield 1995), Nāgārjuna insists that the ontological status of emptiness is not fundamentally different from that of conventional phenomena. Both truths are conventionally real and ultimately empty, whereas for Vasubandhu external phenomena are completely nonexistent and their emptiness is ultimately real. Further differences will emerge as we explore the Yogācāra conception of emptiness in what follows. But this will have to suffice for now. On the other hand, there are other strking parallels and even continuities between Madhyamaka and Cittamātra thought that I will bring out, that explain how the latter can, as the Tibetan doxographers insist it must, be a springboard for the former.

So, what do we make of this striking (and, given Vasubandhu's dialectical proclivities, certainly intentional) parallel formulation? I suggest that Vasubandhu, renowned debater and keen sectarian that he was, is hurling a gauntlet at the feet of those followers of the Second Turning, the mādhyamika, both ostending and (in his view) correcting Nāgārjuna's most famous formulation of the character of emptiness and its relationship to conventional reality. Nagao is correct in noting the intentional parallel; he only mistakes the intention that motivates it.

Vasubandhu, I will argue, brings together two themes introduced in the *SNS*, and in doing so grounds the emerging Ciitamātra doctrine that all phenomena are ideal, due primarily to the work of his elder brother Asaṅga following on the *Lankāvatara-sūtra*, on a dual foundation. The first part of this foundation is the philosophical emphasis on the three natures (*trisvabhāva, rang bzhin gsum*) as an analysis of idealism itself. The second is the conjunction of the three natures with the three naturelessnesses (*trinisvabhāva, ngo bo nyid med gsum*) emphasized as an analysis of emptiness in *SNS*. Taken together, these allow Vasubandhu to argue that his interpretation of emptiness and his idealist ontology and phenomenology replaces Nāgārjuna's provisional and partial analysis. I will hence be portraying Vasubandhu as an innovator, drawing independent ideas from distinct earlier sources and synthesizing them into a new doctrine. But the consolidation of this synthesis, and its subsequent elision in the hermeneutic tradition, is due largely to Sthiramati, whose influential commentaries on Vasubandhu's principal works emphasize and extend the results of this synthesis through the assertion that the three natures and the three naturelessnesses are *identical*. To be sure, though, Sthiramati, as do all Indian Buddhist commentators, occludes the innovative character of this move. Sthiramati's commentaries became the standard entré into Vasubandhu's work for Tibetan scholars, following Tsong khapa's extensive use of them in his monumental *Legs bshad snying po,* which set the standard for subsequent dGe lugs pa doxography.[4]

CITTAMĀTRA AND YOGĀCĀRA: THE SNS AND VASUBANDHU

The terms *Cittamātra* and *Yogācāra* are often used interchangeably. This already represents an adoption of a later medieval Indo-Tibetan doxography. The first means "mind-only" and indicates a specific idealist doctrine about the nature of reality, elaborated through the three-nature theory I will be exploring below. The second indicates an adherence to an emphasis on certain meditational practices grounded in the metaphysics and practices set out in the *SNS* and related sūtras and an adherence to a "Third Turning" understanding of emptiness in terms of the three naturelessnesses. While the set of principal figures to whom these terms apply rapidly became coextensive, using the terms synonymously blurs distinctions useful in tracking the evolution of the philosophical system. In particular, it becomes impossible to ask the question that intrigues me: how did the Third Turning literature and its followers become implicated in idealism, and why the particular formulation of it provided by Vasubandhu? So, in what follows, I will use "Yogācāra" to refer to the literature, doctrines, and adherents to those doctrines associated with "Third Turning" sūtras such as the *SNS*. The term *Cittamātra* will apply to specifically idealistic texts and doctrines within that system, such as those espoused in the Laṅkāvatāra-sūtra, and in the works of Asaṅga and Vasubandhu.

While doxographically the *SNS* is, according to its own description and its subsequent use, a Third Turning text,[5] it is not therefore a Cittamātra text. In fact, in the entire sūtra, the term "mind-only" (*cittamātra sems tsam*) and its synonyms rarely occur, and when they do, not in an obviously idealist context. This sūtra has other projects, some hermeneutical—that is, establishing itself and related texts (some of which *are* Cittamātra in the apposite sense) as definitive and final teachings and, more important for our purposes, providing a new analysis of emptiness, in terms of three characteristics or three naturelessnesses.

Before turning to those two sets of three, however, let me emphasize that—while the *SNS* mentions (but does not analyze) the three natures—as we shall see later, it clearly holds them to be different from the three naturelessnesses. Vasubandhu, on the other hand, notes a relationship between them, but, with the exception of the third, does not identify them.

23   The naturelessness of all phenomena
      Has been explained with the understanding that

The three kinds of natures
Have the three kinds of naturelessness.

24   The first is natureless
With respect to characteristic.
The second through non-independence,
And the third is naturelessness. (*Trimśika*)

This is important for our present purposes because it highlights the fact that the eventual identification of these sets was not a mere noticing of what was already accepted doctrine as per these foundational sūtras but was rather a synthetic achievement. Moreover, we will see that this achievement is what makes possible the establishment of a doctrine that is simultaneously idealist and committed to the emptiness of all phenomena.

WHAT THE THREE NATURELESSNESSES ARE DOING

In the *SNS* we find frequent mention of the the three naturelessnesses or three characteristics of reality (*mtshan nyid*). The principal chapters to which we need attend are the *Paramārthasamudgata* chapter (7) and the *Maitreya*, chapter (9). Importantly, we find only two mentions of three natures (*ngo bo nyid*), and in one of those it is clear that the term is being used quite generically and in fact is merely designating a locus for the characteristics in question.[6] The other instance is in my view quite significant: in a list in the *Maitreya* chapter of those things a Boddhisattva must understand, we find the three naturelessnesses and the three natures listed separately. I will return to this point later.

The three naturelessnesses are introduced explicitly as an explanation of emptiness. Emptiness, by the time the Third Turning sūtras are being composed, is understood, following the Prajñāpāramitā and Madhyamaka literature, as naturelessness—as the fact that phemomena have no essence at all. The three naturelessnesses explicate this in greater detail. Indeed, this explication, as it stands, could be quite easily accepted by a mādhyamika, and in fact according to all standard Tibetan sources, is held in common by Madhyamaka schools, in that it was never specifically attacked by later mādhyamikas.[7] The text merely asserts that things are without any characteristic that makes them the things they are (*rang mtshan; svalakṣaṇa*);[8] that phenomena are empty of being independent, in being causally produced and depending upon conditions for their existence; and that upon ultimate analysis pheomena are not found to exist. That is, significantly, that they have no essence.

> P: I ask the Lord about the meaning of his saying, "All phenomena are natureless (*ngo bo nyid ma mchis pa*) . . ."
> B: *Paramārthasamudgata*, thinking of three types of naturelessness—na-

turelessness in terms of characteristic, naturelessness in terms of production, and ultimate naturelessness . . .

P, if you ask, "What is the naturelessness with respect to the characteristic of phenomena, it is the imputational character. Why? It is thus:
that is a character posited by nominal terms and does not abide through
its own characteristic. Therefore, it is said to be naturelessness with respect
to characteristic.

P, if you ask, "What is the naturelessness with respect to production
of phenomena, it is that of the dependent nature of phenomena. Why? It
is thus: those arise through the power of other conditions and not by
themselves. Therefore, they are said to be natureless with respect to production.

P, if you ask, what is the ultimate naturelessness of phenomena, it is
thus: those dependently arisen phenomena that are natureless due to being
natureless with respect to production are also natureless with respect to
the ultimate. Why? P, I explicitly teach that that which is the object of
observation for purification in phenomena is the ultimate. Since the dependent nature is not the object of observation for purification, it is said
to be natureless with respect to the ultimate.

P, that which is the thoroughly established character of phenomena is
also called the ultimate naturelessness. Why? P, that which in phenomena
is the selflessness of phenomena is called their naturelessness. It is the
ultimate, and since the ultimate is thoroughly distinguished as the naturelessness of all phenomena, it is called ultimate naturelessness.

P, with respect to that, it is thus: instances of naturelessness with respect to characteristic are to be viewed as sky-flowers. P, with respect to
that, it is also thus: instances of naturelessness with respect to production
are to be viewed as magical creations. (*SNSc.* 7, 98–102)

Note that it is made explicit that the three naturelessnesses are introduced as
an analysis of emptiness, for no other reason. They have nothing to do with any
idealistic program. Moreover, they are not, *as introduced*, incompatible with the
Madhyamaka in any way.

The three characteristics (*mtshan nyid; lakṣaṇa*) possessed by all phenomena
are just these three facets of emptiness. Speaking now of those who regard Second
Turning teachings as definitive, a view regarded here as dangerously nihilistic, the
Buddha later in this chapter says:

Even though they believe that doctrine they—with respect to the literal
meaning of all these doctrines—adhere to the terms as only literal: All
these phenomena are only natureless. All these phenomena are only un-
produced, only unceasing, only quiescent from the start, only naturally
passed beyond suffering. On that basis, they acquire the view that *character*

does not exist. Also, having acquired the view of nihilism and the view of the non-existence of chacteristic, deprecating all phenomena in terms of the characteristics, they also deprecate the imagined characteristic of phenomena, the dependent characteristic of phenomena and the characteristic of phenomena.

Why, P? It is thus: if the dependent characteristic and the consummate characteristic exist, then the imputational characteristic can also be known. However, those who perceive the dependent characteristic and the consummate characteristic as non-existent also deprecate the imputational characteristic. Therefore, those are said to deprecate all three aspects of characteristics. (*SNS*, c. 7, 118–20, following Powers 1995)

The three naturelessnesses and the three characters are thus one and the same. The characteristics in question are simply those of being natureless in each of the three senses adumbrated. To claim that in virtue of being natureless, things are entirely nondifferentiable and unknowable, the sūtra contends, is unwarranted nihilism. In the final paragraph just quoted, the point is made that that if one is completely nihilistic, one cannot even make sense of the reality of delusion. But a thorough analysis of delusion and its relation to truth requires all three characteristics. Note again that at this point in the dialectic while this account has amplified the Madhyamaka view, it has not in any way controvened it; note also that except in a very loose, colloquial sense of *nature*, it has imputed no nature at all to phenomena: quite the contrary, it has asserted in three different ways that nature is exactly what all phenomena lack. Nor at this point has it made the slightest move toward an idealist doctrine. All of what has transpired is compatible with the decidedly anti-idealist doctrine of Nāgārjuna and of the *Prajñāpāramitā-sūtras*.

Moreover, the *SNS* itself seems to urge that while there is a doctrine of three natures to be understood, those are *different* from the three naturelessness/three characteristics it has adumbrated. Consider this important passage, from the ninth (the *Avalokiteśvara*) chapter. The Buddha is enumerating the objects of a Bodhisattva's wisdom:

They also thoroughly and correctly know, just as it is, the meaning of nature, with respect to the three natures: (1) the imagined nature; (2) the dependent nature; (3) the consummate nature. They also thoroughly and correctly know, just as it is, the meaning of naturelessness, with respect to the three naturelessnesses: (1) naturelessness with respect to characteristic; (2) naturelessness with respect to production; (3) ultimate naturelessness. (*SNS* c. 9, Powers, 1995, 254–56)

If, as Sthiramati and the dGe lugs tradition would have it, the Yogācāra are committed to the identity of the three natures and the three naturelessness, it would be, to say the least, odd for them to appear as two separate entries on a single list, as distinct objects of a Bodhisattva's knowledge. Moreover, it would be odd for the language in which they are presented to be so explicitly contrastive— "imagined" (*kun brtags*) versus "characteristic" (*mtshan nyid*); "dependent" (*gzhan dbang*) versus "production" (*skye ba*); "consummate" (*yong su grub pa*) versus "ultimate" (*don dam*). The distinctions being indicated are at least as compelling as the parallel in formulation (*ngo bo nyid / ngo bo nyid med pa*). The question, then, is, How do we get from two different, and perhaps problematically related sets of three to a single set of three natures/naturelessnesses? and why? To answer these questions, we turn to Vasubandhu.

VASUBANDHU'S CITTAMĀTRA USE OF THREE NATURES

While the *Lankāvatara-sūtra* espouses the doctrine known as mind-only, and while Asaṅga articulates the phenomenology and the doctrine of the *ālaya-vijñāna* that figures so largely in the evolution of and subsequent debates about the doctrine as well as the doctrine of the three naturelessnesses, it is in the hands of Vasubandhu that the most thorough exploration of the ontological and phenomenological structure of idealism takes place, and in the course of this investigation the three natures take center stage. The discussion is sharpest in what is probably Vasubandhu's final, best and least read text—the *Trisvabhāvanirdeśa*, or *Treatise on the Three Natures*. But the most explicit discussion of emptiness, which is where the three naturelessnesses figure, is in the *Madhyāntavibhāgabhāṣya*, or *Commentary on the Separation of the Middle from the Extremes*. So, despite the fact that the latter was composed well before the former, I will begin with an examination of Vasubandhu's most mature articulation of his *trisvabhāva* theory. I will then turn to Vasubandhu's crucial remarks on the relationship between these two triads in *Triṃśikākārikā*.

Trisvabhāvanirdeśa introduces the fundamental doctrine of Buddhist idealism and clarifies its relations to the other principal doctrines of that school. The central topic of the text, a creative union of ontology and phenomenology, is the exposition of how this idealism entails the view that *every object of experience is characterized by three distinct but interdependent natures*. Not only does Vasubandhu argue that we can only make sense of objects if we ascribe to them these three natures, but also that a complete account of experience requires an account of three distinct kinds of subjectivity, which are related to one another as are the three natures themselves. Here Vasubandhu explicitly asserts the fundamental *trisvabhāva* thesis. Every phenomenon, according to Vasubandhu, has all three of these natures. The three are necessarily co-present in every phenomenon, and are, though distinct, mutually implicative, just as are the three naturelessnesses:

1   The imagined, the other-dependent and
         The consummate.
         These are the three natures
         Which should be deeply understood.

On the one hand, Vasubandhu characterizes what it is to be a phenomenon. On the other hand, he thereby characterizes the relation of the subject to the phenomenon, or the character of the subjectivity that constitutes the representation of the phenomenon. This is not surprising, for this is an idealistic treatise. As far as Vasubandhu is concerned, to be a phenomenon is to be an object of a mind, and this treatise is an exploration of what it is to be an object so conceived. So questions about subjectivity and questions concerning the ontology of the object are closely intertwined.

"Imagined" translates the Tibetan *brtags* or Sanskrit *parikalpita*. The terms connote construction by the mind, more than they do nonexistence, more akin to hallucination than fiction. But this simile can be misleading. To be imagined in this sense is not to be hallucinatory as opposed to being real—it is to be constructed as the object that it is by the operation of the mind. "Other-dependent" translates *gzhan gyi dbang*, or *paratantra*. Something that is other-dependent in this sense exists only in and through dependence on another thing. In this case, the emphasis will be that phenomena exist in dependence upon the mind and its processes, and not in the first instance, as in causal naturelessness, in dependence on external causes and conditions.

I use "consummate" to translate *yong su grub pa*, or *pariniṣpanna*. This is the most difficult of these three terms to translate. Others have used "perfect," "perfected," "thoroughly established," "thoroughly existent," "completed," and "ultimate." Each of these choices has merit, and the variety of options illustrates the range of associations the term has in Tibetan or Sanskrit. When affixed to *nature*, it connotes on the objective side the nature an object has when it is thoroughly understood. On the subjective side, it connotes the nature apparent to one who is fully accomplished intellectually and meditatively. It represents the highest and most complete understanding of a phenomenon. All phenomena have all three natures. Each nature is real in an appropriate sense; each must be understood to understand the nature of things; each subjective relation to things is present in a full understanding of a phenomenon.

2   Arising through dependence on conditions and
         Existing through being imagined,
         It is therefore called other-dependent
         And is said to be merely imaginary.

Any phenomenon comes into existence in dependence upon various causes and conditions. But Vasubandhu here calls attention to a special dimension of this dependence. For anything to exist as an object, its objective existence depends upon mental causes and conditions. But whatever is so dependent, and is hence when seen from this standpoint the content of a mental act, is nonetheless represented *as* an independent existent. No matter how thoroughgoing an idealist I may be in my philosophical moods, ordinary perception delivers me not imaginary objects seen as imaginary, but rather objects seen as *external*. But they do not, from this philosophical standpoint, exist in that way. In fact, they are merely dependent on and, transcendentally, internal to, my mind. For this reason I can say that the content of my mental, seen *as content*, is other-dependent, in its dependence on my mind; but seen *as it is experienced*, it is imaginary, since considered in the way it appears to exist, it is in fact nonexistent.

3   The eternal nonexistence
        Of what appears in the way it appears,
        Since it is never otherwise,
        Is known as the nature of the consummate.

This verse emphasizes that the way things appear to us is as independently existent. But the fact is that given their actual mind-dependent status, of which we can be aware through careful philosophical reflection or through extensive meditative accomplishment, we can say that these are only *apparent things*. What exists in their place are states of mind masquerading as independent phenomena. *That* nonexistence—the nonexistence of the apparent reality—is the consummate nature that all phenomena have.

The coexistence of subject-object duality in the first two natures with nonduality in the consummate is a consequence of this negative characterization of the consummate nature:

4   If anything appears, it is imagined.
        The way it appears is as duality.
        What is the consequence of its nonexistence?
        The fact of nonduality!

Whatever appears to us as an object, we have seen, does so in its imagined nature. In any such appearance, the fact that the object is presented to the mind *as independent* entails the fact that it is presented as wholly other than the mind that apprehends it.

23   The imagined is entirely conventional.
        The other-dependent is conventionally useful.
        The consummate, cutting convention,
        Is said to be of a different nature.

The imagined nature is the way that ordinary, unreflective persons represent things. The other-dependent, while constituting a more sophisticated view of things, remains at a conventional level. It, however, has real soteriological use, starting the process of freeing the mind from the tyranny of convention and fundamental ignorance, and providing a bridge to a more transcendent view. Finally, awareness of the consummate nature allows the move to a fully awakened view of reality.

25 Then one enters the consummate.
    Its nature is the nonexistence of duality.
    Therefore it is explained
    To be both existent and nonexistent.

Moreover, once one has thoroughly understood both of the merely conventional natures, including their apparent dualities, but the unreality of each duality, one sees that all phenomena are both apparently dual and ultimately nondual. That is their consummate nature. Realizing this nature is the consequence of a complete understanding of the other two.[9] Now, moving back to the *MVB*, we can ask how this analysis of things as having these three natures connects to the doctrine that things are natureless in three ways. While Vasubandhu never mentions the three naturelessnesses, in this text he is concerned to articulate a Yogācāra analysis of emptiness consistent with his understanding of the ontological demands of Cittamātra.

> Thus having explained the completely conceptual construction of that which is absolutely nonexistent, how should emptiness be known? To explain this, the text continues:

7 Emptiness, in brief
    Since, through its characteristics, categories,
    Meaning, classifications,
    Is completely established, it should thus be known.

How should its characteristics be known?

1 The nonexistence of duality and the existence of that nonexistence
    Is the characteristic of emptiness, (*MVB*, ab)

> The nonexistence of the duality—that of subject and object—and the existence of that nonexistence is the characteristic of emptiness. In this way, it has been thoroughly explained that the characteristic of emptiness has the nature of nonexistence. Since it has the nature of nonexistence, together with its existence, neither lacking existence nor nonexistence, it is said to exist and not to exist and thus is the nonexistence of that duality.

> So it is said neither to exist nor not to exist. (*MVB*, c)

How is it not nonexistence? Because the existence of the nonexistence of duality is the characteristic of emptiness. Since it is, the completely conceptual construction of what is absolutely nonexistent is

[w]ithout characteristic, neither the same nor different. (*MV*, d)

If they were different, the nondifference of a thing and its characteristic wouldn't make sense, like impermanence and suffering. If they were the same, the object of knowledge and its universal wouldn't be different. (*MVB*, 4a)

Emptiness, Vasubabdhu argues, is emptiness not of essence, but of subject-object duality. Moreover, emptiness, far from being a mere absence of essence, a purely negative phenomenon, is the existence of the nonexistence of that duality. And finally, that emptiness is the absence of the conceptually constructed character in things (the emptiness of dependent phenomena of the imagined nature, as it is often put). It is hence not difference in entity from empty phenomena (as impermanence is not different in entity from impermanent phenomena, and suffering is not different in entity from suffering phenomena). But nor is emptiness for Vasubandhu the same object of knowledge as a dependent phenomenon; otherwise to be aware of an entity would be to apprehend emptiness, and it manifestly is not, just as to be aware of a star is not to understand nuclear fusion.

In these verses and their commentary, we see Vasubandhu's understanding of emptiness, and how different it is from Nāgārjuna's. This is where the opening verses considered by Nagao are actually cashed out. Emptiness for Vasubandhu is emphatically not the lack of any essence. How could it be, when he assigns three distinct essences to all things? Rather, it is the absence of subject-object duality in the consummate nature. Moreover, that absence for Vasubandu, again in contrast to Nāgārjuna, is emphatically a positive, existent entity, and in fact an ultimately existent entity. For this reason Vasubandhu can say that emptiness is nonbeing and being. It is precisely the existence of the nonexistence of the duality posited in the imagined and dependent natures.

But it is important to note that nowhere in this analysis of emptiness—by far his most explicit discussion of this topic—does Vasubandu mention the three naturelessnesses. And here, as we saw above, they would naturally come into play if they were tools of analysis Vasubandu chose to use. I must conclude, I think, that while Vasubandhu was clearly aware of analyses of emptiness in terms of the three characteristics or three naturelesses (after all, he writes about them in *Triṃśikākārikā*), he systematically eschews recourse to such analyses in favor of an analysis in terms of the absence of subject-object duality, at odds both with Nāgārjuna and with the Saṃdhinirmocana-Mahāyāna-Sūtra.

On the other hand, as we have seen, Vasubandhu does think that the three naturelessnesses have a role, and a systematic relation to the three natures. Recall the passage from *Triṃśikākārikā*:

23   The naturelessness of all phenomena
         Has been explained with the understanding that
         The three kinds of natures
         Have the three kinds of naturelessness.

24   The first is natureless
         With respect to characteristic.
         The second through nonindependence,
         And the third is naturelessness.

Here Vasubandhu subordinates the naturelessnesses to the natures pedagogically and describes them as characteristics of, but not (except for the third, to
which I will come in a moment) *identical to* the three natures. Let us examine
the second of these two crucial verses carefully. Vasubandhu asserts that the imagined nature is natureless with respect to characteristic. That is, things as imagined
fail to have essences through characteristics that inhere in them. My coffee cup
experienced as an independent external object, when examined carefully, fails to
have any essence that makes it what it is, and fails to have any of the characteristics (externality, physicality, roundness, and so on I experience it to have—that
is why it is empty with respect to characteristic. Things considered as other-
dependent fail to have essences in that they depend on other phenomena for their
existence. My coffee cup fails to exist inherently because upon examination it
depends upon its parts, upon potters, upon my not dropping it, and so on, and
in particular, upon my mind for its existence as a phenomenon. The consummate
nature of my coffee cup is its nonexistence as imagined—the ultimate nonexistence of the thing I took to be real and hence of the attendant subject/object
duality, and that indeed is its ultimate naturelessness. Or alternately, it is the
emptiness of the imagined of the other-dependent. The mental episode mistaken
for a coffee cup is empty of the imagined coffee cup.

Now, one might be led by this coincidence of verbal formulation in the case
of consummate nature and ultimate naturelessness to assert an identity between
the two. And Vasubandhu's way of putting the point in the last line of verse 24
(quoted previously) lends aid and comfort to this strategy. But that would be
overhasty. For the sharp formulation and the economy of language so characteristic of Vasubandhu's philosophical verse creates an ambiguity: the *is* in question
could be, instead of an *is* of identity, an *is* of predication. In its striking use of
parallelism in this text a a whole, and in this verse in particular, a reading of this
line as parallel in structure to the assertions regarding the other natures/nature-
lessnesses seems warranted. If we so read it, we find Vasubandhu asserting that
the cup as understood from the standpoint of the consummate, is ultimately
empty—is empty of any subject-object duality and any externality.

This is important simply because these verses are cited by Sthiramati, by Tsong
khapa, and by mKhas grub, and recur in the oral tradition as indications that

from the earliest stages of Cittamātra thought the three natures and three naturelessnesses were identified. The crucial lines are from Sthiramati's commentary
on verse 24, cited by Tsong khapa and his followers in all discussions of this
matter:

> It is explained that this is how the ultimate nature of things is: First is
> the imagined nature. It is said to be naturelessness with respect to char-
> acteristic because its characteristics are merely imputed. (*dang po ni kun
> brtags pa'i ngo bo nyid de/de ni mtsham nyid kyis ngo bo nyid med pa ste/
> de'i mtshan nyid ni brtags pa'i phyir ro/*). For instance, one might say,
> the characteristic of form is in form itself. Or one might say that the
> characteristic of feeling is to be perceived, etc. Since these things lack
> their own nature, they are like a sky-flower in being without their own
> nature.

> The second one mentioned is the other-dependent nature. Since it is
> illusion-like, in virtue of depending on other things, it is without its own
> nature. Thus, since it appears in this way, it is uncaused. That is why it is
> said to be causal naturelessness. (*Gzhan pa yang zhes bya ba ni gzhan gyi
> dbang gi ngo bo nyid do/de ni sgyu ma bzhin de rkyen gzhan kyis rten pa'i
> phyir rang gi gngos po med do/ 'di ltar yang ji ltar snang b de bzhin du de
> la skye ba med do/de'i phyir skye ba ngo bo nyid med pa zhes bya'o/* It is
> explained that this is how the ultimate nature of things is. So it is said.

> The ultimate is what is known by the unexcelled supramundane wisdom.
> This is what "ultimate" means. To put it another way, since, like the sky,
> all things (from this perspective) are of the same flavor and are odorless
> and unarisen, [the nature of] things as consummate is said to be the ul-
> timate. Therefore, the consummate nature is the dependent nature of all
> things seem as it is ultimately. Since that is its nature, it follows that the
> consummate nature is naturelessness. (*'Di ltar yongs su grub pa'i ngo bo
> nyid de ni gzhan gyi dbang gi bdag nyid chos thams cad kyi don dam ste/
> de'i chos nyid yin pas de'i phyir yongs su grub pa'i ngo bo nyid med pa ste/
> yongs su grub pa ni dngos po med pa'i ngo bo nyid kyis phyir ro/*)
> (*Triṃśātikā-bhāsya*, Sde dge edition)

Sthiramati takes these predications as identity statements. He does not so much
argue for this interpretation but takes it as obvious. And he is followed in that
view by those who take him as authoritative. But a close reading, I suggest, shows
that they do not support this interpretation. At best, they would support the case
for the third members of each triad. But even there, the support is at least highly
questionable.

THE INDEPENDENCE OF THREE NATURES AND
THREE NATURELESSNESSES

The three natures and the three naturelessnesses are, rather than being inter-changeable formulations of the same philosophical framework, conceptually inde-pendent of one another. I have shown that this is true historically: in the *SNS* we find the three naturelessnesses emphasized, and the three natures receiving only passing comment, and indeed explicitly enumerated as distinct objects of knowl-edge. In Vasubandhu's work, we find the three natures emphasized, eschewed in his analysis of emptiness, which is the very context of the three naturelessnesses in the *SNS* and relegates them to a pedagogical role as explications of the compatibil-ity of the emptiness of all phenomena with the doctrine of the three natures.

But the point can be made philosophically as well: these two trinities do com-pletely different philosophical work, and there are consistent positions in all four cells their acceptance and rejection implicate. The three naturelessnesses provide an account of emptiness. The three natures are part of an account of idealism. One could be an idealist, endorsing the three natures, and yet advance a different account of emptiness than that advanced in the *SNS*. Indeed Vasubandu, we have seen, does just that. Or one could be such an idealist and think that emptiness is tripartite as per the *SNS*. Sthiramati holds this view, and it is the official Cit-tamātra view as per dGe lugs pa doxography. On the other hand, one could reject idealism and yet hold that the *SNS* provides a fine analysis of emptiness. Many contemporary dGe lugs scholars hold this view,[10] and, as we have seen, it is a perfectly reasonable extension of the explicitly nonidealistic Madhyamaka philo-sophical system. On the other hand, one could neither accept this analysis of emptiness nor accept the idealism Vasubandu defends. And of course both ma-terialists and many mādhyamikas fall into this cell. Now I have not defended the coherence of each of these four positions. But I think that there is strong prima facie reason to think that each is coherent as it stands, and that the difference of domain of these two distinctions grounds their independence.

The next question is, How, given this independence in content and in origin, did these two sets become joined, and to what end? In order to answer this question, I turn to the commentaries of Sthiramati and the agenda of Tsong khapa in accepting them. Answering this question will lead us to Nagao's correctness in noting continuities between Yogācāra and Madhyamaka, even though he locates these continuities in the wrong place.

DOXOGRAPHY AND SYNTHESIS: STHIRAMATI
AND TSONG KHAPA

It is impossible to understand the evolution of doctrine within the tradition with-out an appreciation of the hermeneutic imperatives internal to the tradition. Sev-

eral of my dGe lugs pa colleagues have remarked that the entire project of examining the *evolution* of interpretation of these texts strikes them as bizarre: after
all, the texts in question are either the word of the Buddha, or of *āryas* who
canonically expound that word. Third Turning texts are all of the same meaning
and have been since the day of the First Turning. The meaning was settled from
the beginning.[11] This remark itself reveals an important hermeneutic strategy—
the doxographic imperative to homogenize a tradition, an imperative that reaches
a kind of zenith in Tibetan scholastic philosophy. mKhas grub writes in this
regard:

> The first two wheels are said to be of provisional meaning and the last one
> of definitive meaning. Asaṅga and his brother make it quite clear in [their
> texts] and commentaries that their method of interpretation is the same
> as that of the *SNS*. . . . (sTong thun chen mo, trans. Cabezón 1992, pp. 39–
> 40)

Once we realize that any *apparent* difference in meaning, regardless of how
dramatic or nuanced, is merely *apparent*, the task of interpretation becomes one
of resolving apparent differences. Subsequent to their satisfactory resolution, texts
can be read back through the commentarial tradition, and the differences vanish
from sight, and Mutatis mutandis for apparent similarities between texts apparently similar in meaning but assigned by the interpretive tradition to distinct
schools.

Tsong khapa does not even take it as incumbent upon himself to *argue* for
the identity of the two triads. Sthiramati, whose commentaries on Third Turning
texts he endorses as authoritative, has done that work for him. He does not even
need to note that it is a problem that has been solved. There simply is no issue.

But we can allow ourselves to ask what, granted the context of the doxocographic imperative, the philosophical content is, and what the philosophical motivation might be of a merging of these two sets of distinctions. The answers to
these questions show how such a doxocographic project can result in a deeper,
more systematic articulation of a theory, and how Yogācāra evolves to its highly
sophisticated Tibetan formulation.

One leading cue, of course, might be Vasubandhu's ambiguous remark in verse
24 of *Triṃśikākārikā*, which can surely be read as an identification of the consummate with ultimate naturelessness. But that is an insufficient peg on which
to hang so large a hat. Recall that we argued that the three naturelessnesses were
introduced as a distinctive understanding of emptiness—one not so apparently
nihilistic as that of the mādhyamikas. They each provide a perspective in which
things are empty of nature, but one that leaves room for some ultimate, substantial reality. Things may lack essential characteristcs, independence, and reality
as they are conceived. But what?

Well, if the idea is to provide an account that allays nihilistic concerns about Madhyamaka, the "but" is this: those things can be characterized not only negatively, but positively as well. They may not have any distinguishing characteristics, *but they are so imagined*, and the fact that they are so imagined is the positive side of the coin whose negative side is that since they are *only* so imagined, those characteristics are *unreal*. Things might lack independence, *but they are dependent*, and the fact that they are is the positive side of the coin whose negative side is that since they are *only* so dependent, their imagined independence is *unreal*. Things might lack ultimate reality as they are perceived—as dually related to subjectivity—*but they are ultimately empty of that duality*.

From this perspective, the three natures and the three naturelessnesses can be seen as distinct perspectives on the same ontology—different in intention, but not in extension. One provides a negative account of phenomena; the other the positive side it implicates. There is a further elegance to this synthesis: it provides a perfectly natural and deep synthesis of the two strands we have seen in Yogācāra philosophy: the Cittamātra insistence on the ideal character of phenomena as developed in *trisvabhāva* theory, and the Yogācāra insistence on the *trinisvabhāva* qualification of the thesis of the emptiness of all phenomena. On the surface, these two theses appear at least independent, and at worst incompatible. But the demand for their reconciliation, motivated by a doxocographic unification of a prima facie disunified set of texts and theses, provides us with an account whereby they in fact articulate from different perspectives the same underlying ontology. So while the hermeneutic strategy of the tradition may elide certain apparent textual differences, its philosophical payoff is considerable—a subtler understanding of how idealism is possible within the general framework of Mahāyāna ontology.

MĀDHYAMAKA AND YOGĀCĀRA: NAGAO'S PUZZLE REVISITED

I concurred with Nagao at the outset of this chapter that *MVB* I: 1–2 is intentionally parallel with *MMK* 24: 18. On the other hand, I disagreed with him in his contention that this demonstrates or even indicates a continuity between Madhyamaka and Yogācāra with respect to their accounts of emptiness. Rather, I argued, Vasubandhu self-consciously uses that parallel to indicate his radical departure *from* Madhyamaka in his account, demonstrating that while the form of expression adopted by Nāgārjuna might be adopted by a Cittamātra, the content that fills that form is entirely different.

On the other hand, once we take into account the later developments of Vasubandhu's position and the hermeneutical project of its reconciliation with the position of the *SNS*, we are in a position to see a deep parallel that emerges between the position so reinterpreted and Madhyamaka, a parallel acknowledged in the dGe lugs pa oral tradition, and held there to account for the fact that Cittamātra can be an important philosophical stepping stone on the way to a Madhyamaka view.[12]

A central theme in Tsong khapa and mKhas grub's exposition of Cittamātra, following Asaṅga and Sthiramati, is their insistence that *both* the other-dependent and the consummate nature are established through their own characteristics (*rang gi mtshan nyid kyis grub pa*), This reading makes sense of Ciitamātra insistence that the dependent nature is the basis of both the imagined nature (it is what is imagined to exist externally) and of the consummate (it is that which is empty of that which it is imagined to be). Tsong khapa goes to considerable lengths in *LSNP* to resolve the apparent contradiction between Yogācāra pronouncements that the dependent nature is not so established and others that it is in favor of this reading. The arguments on this score are complex, some straighforwardly hermeneutical, some turning on issues in the philosophy of language (see Meyers 1995), and others turning on the need to grant a robust reality to causality for soteriological purposes.[13] When we see the position so reconstructed, the following interesting continuity emerges as a kind of doxocographic dividend.

It is possible to map the other-dependent and the consummate nature neatly now onto the conventional (*samvṛti, vyavahāra satya/ tha snyad, kun rdzob bden pa*) truth and the ultimate (*paramārtha-satya/ don dam bden pa*) truth, respectively. Just as in Madhyamaka metaphysics these truths represent distinct and equally *true* perspectives on reality, on Tsong khapa's reconstruction of Cittamātra metaphysics, these two natures are equally established as real. And just as in Madhyamaka metaphysics objects when seen as conventional are seen to be dependent upon external causes and conditions, part-whole composition, and conceptual imputation, in the dependent nature that is exactly how things are seen. For the Mādhyamīka, in the ultimate truth there is only emptiness; for the reconstructed Cittamātrika, the consummate nature just is the emptiness of the dependent nature of the imagined and hence of subject-object duality.

But what of the imagined nature? Here is the beauty of this story: the imagined nature, on Tsong khapa's reconstruction, is, unlike the other two natures, entirely false and deceptive. It is not established on its own but rather is perceived only through the force of delusion. Taking it seriously means *not* seeing the other-dependent or the consummate natures. This is the perspective of primal ignorance. Again—though they have no name for it—this is a perspective recognized by the mādhyamika. For on their view, to see things as dependently arising is already an achievement, a recognition of the conventional *truth*. Our naïve attitude toward the world—the one that gets us mired in *saṃsara*—is to consider phenomena as independent and as substantially existent. Once we see their interdependence, the fact of *pratītya-samutpāda*, we are onto the truth, and on our way to understanding emptiness. Just so, says the Tibetan cittamātrika: as long as we see only the imagined nature, we see falsely. Only once we see the dependent nature are we onto the truth of things and so can come to see that that dependent nature is empty of the imagined, empty of all duality, and so come to see the consummate nature. And finally, for the mādhyamika, just as once one sees the ultimate truth, one sees its deep identity with the convential truth, for the Tibetan cittamātrika, once one sees the consummate nature, one sees that it is only the dependent nature, properly understood, and one ceases entirely to see objects at all.

It is thus that the Cittamātra position, as reconstructed, is seen by the Tibetan tradition as the penultimate step on the philosopher's progress to Madhyamaka, and only subtly different from it. The continuities are real and are taken seriously. But importantly—and this is precisely why it can only be a *penultimate* step— when we get to the most important component of each theory, that is, its analysis of emptiness, the components are, *pace* Nagao, utterly discontinuous. (see also chapter 9 of this volume for more discussion of the difference between Madhyamaka and Yogācāra interpretations of emptiness.)

This construction of Cittamātra as even this proximate to Madhyamaka is itself very much a *construction*. This view, though attributed to the Third Turning sūtras and to Vasubandhu, was held by neither of them. Bits were held by each; other bits by neither. Only through a careful reworking of the central doctrines of the three natures and the three naturelessnesses were Sthiramati and his Tibetan followers able to construct the position I first encountered as Cittamātra.

7

Vasubandhu's Treatise on the Three Natures

A Translation and Commentary

THE TEXT *TRISVABHĀVANIRDEŚA* (*Rang bzhin gsum nges par bstan pa*) is one of Vasubandhu's short treatises (the others being the *Treatise in Twenty Stanzas* [*Viṃsatikā*] and the *Treatise in Thirty Stanzas* [*Triṃsikaikākārikā*]) expounding his Cittamātra, or mind-only philosophy. Vasubandhu and his older brother Asaṅga are regarded as the founders and principal exponents of this Buddhist idealist school, developing in the fourth or fifth century C.E. as the major philosophical rival within the Mahāyāna Buddhist tradition to the older Madhyamaka tradition. The latter school, founded by Nāgārjuna, urges the emptiness—the lack of essence or substantial, independent reality—of all things, including both external phenomena and mind.[1] Vasubandhu, however, reinterprets the emptiness of the object as being its lack of *external* reality, and its purely mind-dependent, or ideal status.[2] At the same time, however, he argues that the foundational mind is non-empty since it truly exists as the substratum of the apparent reality represented in our experience. The position is hence akin to the idealisms defended by such Western philosophers as Berkeley, Kant, and Schopenhauer.[3]

While *Trisvabhāvanirdeśa* is arguably the most philosophically detailed and comprehensive of the three short works on this topic composed by Vasubandhu, as well as the clearest, it is almost never read or taught in contemporary traditional Buddhist cultures or centers of learning. The reason may be simply that this is the only one of Vasubandhu's root texts for which no autocommentary exists.[4] For this reason, none of Vasubandhu's students composed commentaries in the text and there is hence no recognized lineage of transmission for the text. So nobody within the Tibetan tradition (the only extant Mahāyāna monastic scholarly tradition) could consider him or herself authorized to teach the text. It is therefore simply not studied, a great pity. It is a beautiful and deep philosophical essay and an unparalleled introduction to the Cittamātra system.

The text introduces the fundamental doctrine of Buddhist idealism and clarifies in remarkably short compass its relations to the other principal doctrines of that school—that all external appearances are merely ideal and originate from potentials for experience carried in the mind. The central topic of the text is the exposition of how this view entails the Cittamātra theory of the three natures, the view that every object of experience is characterized by three distinct but interdependent natures. Vasubandhu's idealism is distinctive in its insistence that a coherent idealism requires the positing of these three natures, and in its subtle analysis of the complex relations between the natures themselves, involving the thesis of their surface diversity but deep unity.[5]

This text also presents a creative union of ontology and phenomenology. Vasubandhu's characterization of the status of the objects of experience is at the same time self-consciously a characterization of the character of subjectivity itself. Not only will Vasubandhu argue that we can only make sense of objects if we ascribe to them these three triune natures, but he will argue that a complete account of experience—especially of the experience of a sophisticated and accomplished philosopher or meditator—requires an account of three distinct kinds of subjectivity, which are related to one another as are the three natures themselves. This phenomenology is crucial to the soteriological purport of the system. For this is not speculative philosophy for its own sake, but a philosophical system designed to guide a practitioner to Buddhahood in order that she or he can work to alleviate the suffering of all sentient beings.

Trisvabhāvanirdeśa is unique in its exposition of idealism as involving the doctrine of the three natures, in its detailed analysis of the natures themselves, and in its exploration of their relations to one another. In *Vimsatikā-kārikā* Vasubandhu clearly defends idealism against a series of objections but does not explicitly articulate the roles of the three natures in his idealistic theory or expound its structure. In *Trimsikākārikā* Vasubandhu explores the relation between the three natures and the three naturelessnesses (naturelessness with respect to characteristic [*laksana-nihsvabhāvatā, mtshan nyid ngo bo nyid med*], naturelessness with respect to production [*utpatti-nihsvabhāvatā, skye ba ngo bo nyid med*], and ultimate naturelessness [*paramārtha-nihsvabhāvatā, don dam pa'i ngo bo nyid med*]) adumbrated in the *Samdhinirmocana-sūtra* but does not explore their relation to idealism, per se, or their relations to one another. Only in the present text does he explicitly analyze idealism as implicating the three natures and explain in detail how they are interconnected.

Sthiramati, in his commentary on *Trimsikākārikā* (*Trimsikābhāsya*) argues that the three natures and the three naturelessnesses are equivalent. His understanding of the three natures as equivalent to the three naturelessnesses of the *Samdhinirmocana-sūtra* is adopted uncritically by such Tibetan doxographers as Tsong khapa[6] and mKhas grub.[7] The adoption of this commentarial tradition, which emphasises the homogeneity of the *Samdhinirmocana-sūtra* with Vasubandhu's and Asanga's thought, along with the exposition of the three natures as presented in *Trimsikākārikā* and *Vimsatikā* reinforces the elision of this more mature and explicit articulation of Vasubandhu's theory from subsequent developments of Yogācāra. The emphasis of the dominant Madhyamaka school on naturelessness as a fundamental metaphysical tenet, and its need to see Yogācāra as the penultimate step to its own standpoint lends further impetus to this tendency to assimilate these two doctrines.[8] Of all of the mādhyamika, only Candrakīrti really takes the trisvabhāva doctrine itself seriously as a target for critique (*dBu ma la jugs pa/Madhyamakāvatāra*.[9]

The thirty-eight verses of the text divide neatly into six sections. In the first six verses, Vasubandhu introduces the three natures and provides a preliminary characterization of each. In verses 7 through 9 he sketches two schemata for thinking about the character of mind from the standpoint of Three Nature theory. Verses 10 through 21 develop a dialectically complex and elegant discussion of how to view the polar pairs of existence / nonexistence, duality / unity, and affliction / nonaffliction in relation to each of the Three Natures, culminating in a discussion of the senses in which the natures are identical to one another and the senses in which they are different. Verses 22 through 25 present the natures hierarchically from the standpoint of pedagogy and soteriology. Vasubandhu presents the famous simile of the hallucinatory elephant conjured by the stage magician in verses 26 through 34. This is probably the most famous and oft-cited moment in this text. In a vivid and simple image, Vasubandhu presents a way of understanding the Three Natures, their relation to one another, to idealism, and the phenomenology they suggest to Buddhist soteriology. The concluding four verses are devoted to the soteriological implications of the text.

Trisvabhāvanirdeśa is not only a philosophically subtle text. It is also a considerable literary and poetic achievement. (Much of the elegance of Vasubandhu's Sanskrit is preserved in the Tibetan translation. I have found it difficult to produce a translation that does proper justice to the poetic value of the text while remaining faithful to the philosophical ideas and rhetorical structure.) The doctrine it expounds is packed with dynamic tension born of constantly impending paradox and of the need continuously to balance several levels of discourse. The poetic text that develops this doctrine mirrors that tension in its constant shifting of level; in its frequent double entendre allowing claims to be made at two or more levels simultaneously; and in its multileveled discourse in which claims that appear contradictory are reconciled, albeit often in startling and revealing ways. The poem is full of unexpected rhetorical and philosophical turns and is structured so as to reflect the ontological and phenomenological theory it articulates. The language is as spare and vibrant as the radiant mind-only ontology it presents.[10]

The Text of *Trisvabhāvanirdeśa*

1   The imagined, the other-dependent and
       The consummate.

These are the Three Natures
Which should be deeply understood.

2   Arising through dependence on conditions and
Existing through being imagined,
It is therefore called other-dependent
And is said to be merely imaginary.

3   The eternal nonexistence
Of what appears in the way it appears,
Since it is never otherwise,
Is known as the nature of the consummate.

4   If anything appears, it is imagined.
The way it appears is as duality.
What is the consequence of its nonexistence?
The fact of nonduality!

5   What is the imagination of the nonexistent?
Since what is imagined absolutely never
Exists in the way it is imagined,
It is mind that constructs that illusion.

6   Because it is a cause and an effect,
The mind has two aspects.
As the foundation consciousness it creates thought;
Known as the emerged consciousness it has seven aspects.

7   The first, because it collects the seeds
Of suffering is called "mind."
The second, because of the constant emergence
Of the various aspects of things is so called.

8   One should think of the illusory nonexistent
As threefold:
Completely ripened, grasped as other,
And as appearance.

9   The first, because it itself ripens,
Is the root consciousness.
The others are emergent consciousness,
Having emerged from the conceptualization of seer and seen.

10   Existence and nonexistence, duality and unity;
Freedom from affliction and afflicted;
Through characteristics, and through distinctions,
These natures are known to be profound.

11   Since it appears as existent
        Though it is nonexistent,
        The imagined nature
        Is said to have the characteristics of existence and noncxistence.

12   Since it exists as an illusory entity
        And is nonexistent in the way it appears
        The other-dependent nature
        Is said to have the characteristics of existence and nonexistence.

13   Since it is the nonexistence of duality
        And exists as nonduality
        The consummate nature
        Is said to have the characteristics of existence and nonexistence.

14   Moreover, since as imagined there are two aspects,
        But existence and nonexistence are unitary,
        The nature imagined by the ignorant
        Is said to be both dual and unitary.

15   Since as an object of thought it is dual,
        But as a mere appearance it is unitary,
        The other-dependent nature
        Is said to be both dual and unitary.

16   Since it is the essence of dual entities
        And is a unitary nonduality,
        The consummate nature
        Is said to be both dual and unitary.

17   The imagined and the other-dependent
        Are said to be characterized by misery (due to ignorant craving).
        The consummate is free of
        The characteristic of desire.

18   Since the former has the nature of a false duality
        And the latter is the nonexistence of that nature,
        The imagined and the consummate
        Are said not to be different in characteristic.

19   Since the former has the nature of nonduality,
        And the latter has the nature of nonexistent duality,
        The consummate and the imagined
        Are said not to be different in characteristic.

20   Since the former is deceptive in the way it appears,
And the latter has the nature of its not being that way,
The other-dependent and the consummate
Are said not to be different in characteristic.

21   Since the former has the nature of a nonexistent duality,
And the latter is its nonexistence in the way it appears,
The other-dependent and the consummate
Are said not to be different in characteristic.

22   But conventionally,
The natures are explained in order and
Based on that one enters them
In a particular order, it is said.

23   The imagined is entirely conventional.
The other-dependent is attached to convention.
The consummate, cutting convention,
Is said to be of a different nature.

24   Having first entered into the nonexistence of duality
Which is the dependent, one understands
The nonexistent duality
Which is the imagined.

25   Then one enters the consummate.
Its nature is the nonexistence of duality.
Therefore it is explained
To be both existent and nonexistent.

26   These Three Natures
Have the characteristics of being noncognizable and nondual.
One is completely nonexistent; the second is therefore nonexistent.
The third has the nature of that nonexistence.

27   Like an elephant that appears
Through the power of a magician's mantra—
Only the percept appears,
The elephant is completely nonexistent.

28   The imagined nature is the elephant;
The other-dependent nature is the visual percept;
The nonexistence of the elephant therein
Is explained to be the consummate.

29   Through the root consciousness
      The nonexistent duality appears.
      But since the duality is completely nonexistent,
      There is only a percept.

30   The root consciousness is like the mantra.
      Reality can be compared to the wood.
      Imagination is like the perception of the elephant.
      Duality can be seen as the elephant.

31   When one understands how things are,
      Perfect knowledge, abandonment,
      And accomplishment—
      These three characteristics are simultaneously achieved.

32   Knowledge is nonperception;
      Abandonment is nonappearance;
      Attainment is accomplished through nondual perception.
      That is direct manifestation.

33   Through the nonperception of the elephant,
      The vanishing of its percept occurs;
      And so does the perception of the piece of wood.
      This is how it is in the magic show.

34   In the same way through the nonperception of duality
      There is the vanishing of duality.
      When it vanishes completely,
      Nondual awareness arises.

35   Through perceiving correctly,
      Through seeing the nonreferentiality of mental states,
      Through following the Three Wisdoms,
      One will effortlessly attain liberation.

36   Through the perception of mind-only
      One achieves the nonperception of objects;
      Through the nonperception of objects
      There is also the nonperception of mind.

37   Through the nonduality of perception,
      Arises the perception of the fundamental nature of reality.
      Through the perception of the fundamental nature of reality
      Arises the perception of the radiant.

38   Through the perception of the radiant,
        And through achieving the three supreme Buddha-bodies,
        And through possessing Bodhi:
        Having achieved this, the sage will benefit him or herself and others.

THE TEXT WITH COMMENTARY

1   The imagined, the other-dependent and
        The consummate.
        These are the Three Natures
        Which should be deeply understood.

Every phenomenon, according to Cittamātra metaphysics, has all three of these natures—three ways of being. It is not the case that some have one nature and some have others; nor that phenomena appear to have one or another of the three, but in fact have another. The three are necessarily co-present in every phenomenon, and are, though distinct, mutually implicative.

Let us pause for a moment over the three terms themselves, whose translation into English is no straightforward matter. Each is a *nature* (*svabhāva, rang bzhin*). So each is part of what it is to be a thing—not an accidental attribute that a thing might have. But each of the three qualifiers added to this term to denote one of the three natures creates a subtly ambiguous compound, and plays on this ambiguity form part of the structure of Vasubandhu's ingenious verse treatise. On the one hand, each characterizes the nature itself—part of what it is to be a phenomenon. On the other hand, each characterizes the relation of the subject to the phenomenon, or the character of the subjectivity that constitutes the representation of the phenomenon. This duality is not surprising, for this is an idealistic treatise. As far as Vasubandhu is concerned, to be a phenomenon is to be an object of a mind, and this treatise is an exploration of what it is to be an object so conceived. So questions about subjectivity and questions concerning the ontology of the object are closely intertwined.

"Imagined" translates the Sanskrit *parikalpita* or Tibetan *kun brtags*. The terms connote construction by the mind, more than they do nonexistence—more akin to hallucination than fiction. But this simile can be misleading. To be imagined in this sense is not to be hallucinatory as opposed to being real—it is to be constructed as the object that it is by the operation of the mind. "Other-dependent" translates *paratantra* or *gzhan gyi dbang*. Something that is other-dependent in this sense exists only in and through dependence on another thing. In this case, the emphasis will be that phenomena exist in dependence upon the mind and its processes.[11]

I use "consummate" to translate *yong su grub pa* or *pariniṣpanna*. This is the most difficult of these three terms to translate. Others have used "perfect," "per-

fected," "thoroughly established," "thoroughly existent," "completed," and "ultimate."¹² Each of these choices has merit, and the variety of options illustrates the
range of associations the term has in Sanskrit or Tibetan. When affixed to "nature" it connotes on the objective side an object's nature when it is thoroughly
understood. On the subjective side, it connotes the nature apparent to one who
is fully accomplished intellectually and meditatively. It represents the highest and
most complete understanding of a phenomenon. It is important, however, not to
misinterpret this term to connote the *real* nature as opposed to the *unreal* natures
denoted by the terms *imaginary* and *other-dependent*, or the *ultimate*, as opposed
to the *conventional* nature of things. Ultimately, all phenomena have all three
natures. Each is real; each must be understood to understand the nature of things;
each subjective relation if one is to things is present in a full understanding of a
phenomenon.¹³

2   Arising through dependence on conditions and
         Existing through being imagined,
         It is therefore called other-dependent
         And is said to be merely imaginary.

Vasubandhu begins by sketching in the second and third verses the outlines of
the relation between the three natures. In the second verse he focuses on the
relation between the first two. Any phenomenon comes into existence in dependence upon various causes and conditions. But Vasubandhu here calls attention
to a special dimension of this dependence. For anything to exist as an object, its
objective existence depends upon mental causes and conditions. This is a straightforwardly Kantian point, that there are conditions on the side of the subject that
make it possible for anything to exist as an object.

But whatever is so dependent, and hence, when seen from this standpoint, the
content of a mental act, is nonetheless represented *as* an independent existent.
Consider, for example, my perceptual representation of the screen on which these
words appear as I type. I see it not *as* my representation, but rather *as* something
that exists independent of, external to, and standing against my mind and perceptual faculties. No matter how thoroughgoing an idealist I may be in my philosophical moods, ordinary perception delivers me not imaginary objects seen as
imaginary, but rather objects seen *as external*. But they do not, from this philosophical standpoint, exist in that way. In fact they are merely dependent on and,
transcendentally, internal to, my mind. For this reason it is appropriate to say
that the content of my mental acts, seen *as content*, is other-dependent, in virtue
of its dependence on my mind: but seen *as it is experienced*, it is imaginary, since
considered in the way it appears to exist, it is in fact nonexistent.

3   The eternal nonexistence
         Of what appears in the way it appears,

Since it is never otherwise,
Is known as the nature of the consummate.

The third verse emphasizes this last point and uses it to connect these first two natures to the consummate nature: things appear to us as independently existent. They do so in virtue of their dependence upon other such things and upon our minds (which—in an important sense to be discussed later—do share these three natures). But given their actual mind-dependent status, of which we can be aware through careful philosophical reflection or through extensive meditative accomplishment, we can say that these *apparent things*—independently existent computers, camels, and coffee cups—are always nonexistent. What exists in their place are states of mind masquerading as independent phenomena. *That* nonexistence—the nonexistence of the apparent reality—is the consummate nature of all phenomena.

The next two verses examine two consequences of this negative characterization of the consummate nature: the coexistence of subject-object duality in the first two natures with nonduality in the consummate, and the mind-dependence of the imagined nature:

4   If anything appears, it is imagined.
       The way it appears is as duality.
       What is the consequence of its nonexistence?
       The fact of nonduality!

Whatever appears to us as an object, we have seen, does so in its imagined nature. In any such appearance, the fact that the object is presented to us *as independent* entails the fact that it is presented as wholly other than the mind that apprehends it. Kant makes this point against Berkeley when he urges in the "Refutation of Idealism" that even though in a transcendental sense all appearances are in us, in an empirical sense, for anything to appear to us in space, it appears to us as outside us.[14] Schopenhauer hones this point and wields it against Kant himself when he points out that any account of the genesis of representation that harmonizes with a coherent transcendental idealist account of the ontology of representation must grant phenomena a genuine independent empirical reality in order to account for their causal impact upon us that is responsible for our cognitive apprehension of them.[15] But, he argues, such an idealism must also grant them a status as mere representations when we consider them as they appear to us. This point is made on the way to an account of a third nature of which Schopenhauer charges Kant of being unaware—their status as noumena, or will, in which all subject-object duality disappears.[16,17]

5   What is the imagination of the nonexistent?
       Since what is imagined absolutely never

Exists in the way it is imagined,
It is mind that constructs that illusion.

Vasubandhu here simply repeats the tight connection between the account offered of the status of phenomena as imagined and their mind-dependence. Since the imagined nature is in fact totally imaginary, it does not arise from the side of the thing that appears. Rather, it is an artifact of the operation of the mind.

The next four verses sketch two alternative ways of presenting the nature of mind in Vasubandhu's idealistic system. In (6) and (7), he presents a division that distinguishes the mind in its role as subject from the mind in its role as object:

6   Because it is a cause and an effect,
        The mind has two aspects.
        As the foundation consciousness it creates thought;
        Known as the emerged consciousness it has seven aspects.

Vasubandhu, in another move prescient of Kant,[18] distinguishes the mind in its role as transcendental subject from its role as object, as it appears to itself. In the first aspect, to which Vasubandhu refers as the "foundation consciousness" (*ālaya-vijñāna, kun gzhi*), the mind functions as the condition of the appearance of phenomena, and hence as the ground of the possibility of the imagined and other-dependent natures. But in its second aspect—the "emerged consciousness" (*pavṛtti-vijñāna, jug pa'i shes pa*)—the mind exists as the object of introspection and is conditioned both by external phenomena that appear in perception and by its own phenomena. Hence it constantly evolves and emerges in new states as a consequence of experience. The "seven aspects" to which Vasubandhu alludes are the five sensory consciousnesses, the introspective consciousness apprehending the self as object, and the reflective consciousness of the transcendental subject of experience. These aspects are hence distinguished by their proper objects or spheres of operation.

7   The first, because it collects the seeds
        Of suffering, is called "mind."
        The second, because of the constant emergence
        Of the various aspects of things, is so called.

Vasubandhu is making a tendentious etymological claim about the Sanskrit term translated here as "mind" (*citta*). On one etymology, he claims, the term is derived from *cita*, which means "piled up" or "accumulated." Hence, he argues, *mind* can be thought of as indicating a storehouse of seeds of experience or mental potentials. In this sense it can also be thought of as the location of the seeds of future experiences. The second etymology, Vasubandhu contends, connects *citta* to the Sanskrit term *citra*, meaning "various" or "manifold." This suggests the role of mind as a constantly emerging developing phenomenon. Hence,

Vasubandhu suggests, the very etymology of the term connotes its two parallel roles.[19]

The next two verses develop a threefold account of the aspectual character of mind. These are not intended to compete with one another, but rather as alternate, compossible, ways to understand the multiple roles played by mind in experience.

8   One should think of the illusory nonexistent
        As threefold:
        Completely ripened, grasped as other,
        And as appearance.

Here Vasubandhu notes three prima facie characteristics of the mind in our experience, all on the side of its role as object of inner sense: first, insofar as mind is an object, and hence an empirical phenomenon, it is a ripened potential—the fruit of a seed of experience heretofore dormant in the foundation consciousness. Second, and perhaps most paradoxically, since it appears as an object, it appears as other than the self to which it appears. Here Vasubandhu is emphasizing that even in apperception there is a duality between subject and object: a self that appears to us appears as distinct from the ego to which it appears. Third, the self is an appearance—not as a continuing, stable, or independent phenomenon, but rather as a series of moments of awareness, each an evanescent ripening of a potential for consciousness, and so like all external objects, with its apparent unity a matter of construction, not of discovery in some independently given noumenon.[20]

9   The first, because it itself ripens,
        Is the root consciousness.
        The others are emergent consciousness,
        Having emerged from the conceptualization of seer and seen.

Nonetheless, Vasubandhu argues, the first of these three aspects has a particular connection to the subject side of the self, as per the first division, while the second and third aspects of this threefold division are better aligned with the second side of the first division: the root (*mūla, rtsa ba*), "consciousness" (the same as the foundation consciousness), is not only the subject of all experience. It is also the repository of all of the latencies, or potentials, more often called the *seeds*, which, when actualized or "ripened," become actual phenomena—objects of experience. On the other hand, when the self is represented as an object of experience in introspection, it stands over and against the root consciousness of which it is an object. It is hence in this sense emergent from the root consciousness and is "grasped as other than the self." In being so grasped, it is grasped as a series of evanescent moments of experience. These latter two aspects hence emerge as aspects of the self considered as object; the first as an aspect of self considered as subject, or as storehouse of latencies.

The next eleven verses develop a delicate and logically acrobatic dialectic concerning the interplay of three pairs of contradictories and their relation to the three natures: existence and non-existence; duality and unity; freedom from afflictions and affliction. Vasubandhu will argue that each of the three natures is characterised by both members of each of these contraries. He then argues that these natures are each both identical to and distinct from one another. While it might be tempting and facile to think that here Vasubandhu is simply trading in paradox or irony, this would be a mistake. This important section of the treatise is concerned with the alternation in voices and perspectives represented by the Three Natures: they have a phenomenological side, representing not only the tripartite ontological dimension Vasubandhu sees in all phenomena, but also the three phenomenological perspectives that together constitute the complex subjectivity Vasubandhu envisions.

10   Existence and nonexistence, duality and unity;
       Freedom from affliction and afflicted;
       Through characteristics, and through distinctions,
       These natures are known to be profound.

Existence and *non-existence* are understood here in a perfectly ordinary sense, though of course within the framework of idealism generally. Given this context, it will always be possible to ask about the standpoint of an assertion regarding existence, Is it subjective—that is, an empirical, objective claim? Or is it transcendental? Moreover, we can always ask whether, when a thing is asserted to exist, we mean that it exists in the way in which it is apprehended, or whether it exists *simpliciter*. So, for instance, if I ask whether the "water" I see on a hot highway on a December day exists, one must be careful: the *mirage* exists. No *water* does. The percept to which I refer as "water" exists, but not in the manner in which it is apprehended. (And, of course, if I am an idealist, from a transcendental perspective neither the water nor the mirage can be said to exist at all. Both are merely appearances.)

The duality/unity pair concerns subject/object duality. To assert that there is, from a specific standpoint, a duality in this sense is to assert that from that standpoint there is a real distinction between subject and object. To assert a unity or a nonduality is to deny such a duality. The important thing to bear in mind regarding this pair as one approaches Vasubandhu is that questions about duality and nonduality can always be posed in both a metaphysical and a phenomenological voice. So we can ask of each of the natures in what sense it implicates such a duality as part of the structure of the object of experience. But we can also ask the question regarding the nature of the corresponding aspect of subjectivity itself. So in each case we can ask whether, or in what sense, in a subject considering things *as other-dependent*, and so on, there is such a duality, as well as asking whether, or in what sense, each nature implicates such a duality in the structure of the object.

The third pair—affliction/freedom from affliction—introduces specifically Buddhist soteriological concerns. Again, the concerns in play are both ontological and phenomenological. The afflictions are those associated with the suffering of *saṃsāra*, or cyclic existence. Those include not only physical and psychological suffering themselves but also the craving and grasping that are their proximal causes and, most importantly in this context, the primal ignorance regarding the nature of things that takes the phenomena of experience and the self to be in-herently, or substantially existent, as opposed to empty of substance. So we can say either that a mind apprehending an object is afflicted in that it regards that object as inherently existent or that the object as perceived is an afflicted object. In the latter case we are saying that the object itself, through of one or more of its natures, is constituted in a manner essentially implicating the afflictions.[21] Vasubandhu begins by arguing that the imagined nature involves both existence and nonexistence.

11   Since it appears as existent
        Though it is nonexistent,
        The imagined nature
        Is said to have the characteristics of existence and nonexistence.

Let us work through these verses with an ordinary example in mind. Let us consider a teacup on your desk. Consider its imagined nature. As imagined, it is an existent—indeed independently, substantially existent—teacup entirely distinct from and independent from your mind and mental processes. It endures through time and has a nature all its own. Hence existence, in a very strong sense, is part of its imagined nature. On the other hand, when we move up one level in the dialectic and see that this is merely an imagined nature, merely the way the cup appears to a consciousness, we see that the cup that so appears—the imagined cup itself—does not exist at all, just as no water exists in the mirage. In this sense, the very fact that the cup-as-imagined *is only imagined* means that *though it is imagined as existent, in fact it is nonexistent.* Insofar as we simply imagine the cup, we imagine an existent cup. Insofar as we become reflexively aware of that act of imagination, the cup we imagine disappears.

12   Since it exists as an illusory entity
        And is nonexistent in the way it appears,
        The other-dependent nature
        Is said to have the characteristics of existence and nonexistence.

Now, consider the same teacup from the standpoint of its other-dependent nature: From this standpoint, the cup exists as an entity dependent upon the mind. The cup so considered certainly exists, as a mental phenomenon, a representation. On the other hand, we can ask what the objective character[22] of that representation is. Then the answer is simple and takes us back to the imagined nature: the cup considered objectively is the old, real, independent cup, which, when we understand it from the standpoint of the dependent nature, does not exist at all, simply because from this standpoint it is dependent. So, from the perspective of the dependent nature, the cup—the dependent mental phenomenon we mistake for a real cup—like the refraction pattern we mistake for water, exists. But that real cup that is the content of that mental episode does not.

13   Since it is the nonexistence of duality
        And exists as nonduality
        The consummate nature
        Is said to have the characteristics of existence and nonexistence.

Now we come to the consummate nature of our cup. The cup we have been considering all along, whether from the standpoint of the imagined or the dependent nature, is, in an important and common sense, dual in nature. In its imagined nature it is an independent object of mind and so is distinct from the subject that apprehends it. But in its dependent nature, as an episode of mind, it is still, as a mere episode or mental act, distinct from the mind that is its agent or subject. In the consummate nature, this duality vanishes. For the consummate nature of the cup is the very fact of its illusory status—that it is nothing other than an aspect of mind. Hence the apparent, dual, cup is, in its consummate nature (or, equivalently, from the point of view of one of consummate attainment) utterly nonexistent. *But that nonduality really exists.* That *is* the final nature of the cup.[23] And in this sense, the consummate nature embraces both existence and nonexistence—the nonexistence of the cup as dual is its true existence as nondually related to the mind apprehending it. This consideration of duality and nonduality as the mediators of existence and nonexistence in the consummate forms the bridge to the consideration of duality and nonduality per se in the three natures.

14   Moreover, since as imagined there are two aspects,
        But existence and nonexistence are unitary,
        The nature imagined by the ignorant
        Is said to be both dual and unitary.

For a thing *to exist as imagined,* and for it *not to exist in the way it appears,* are both diametrically opposed and identical, depending on how one conceives them. For on the one hand, they represent existence and nonexistence, the most opposed of properties. In that sense, the imagined nature is thoroughly dual, encompassing both of these in virtue of the more fundamental subject-object duality it represents. That more fundamental duality gives rise both to the imagined existence of the object of experience, and, when seen for what it is, a mere illusion, the nonexistence of that object in the way that it appears. On the other hand, to exist *as imagined* just is *not to exist in the way a thing appears.* In this sense the mode of existence and the mode of nonexistence of the imagined nature—of a thing as it is imagined—are the same, and are nondually related. And this nonduality is rooted in the more fundamental nonduality that emerges when we see from a higher standpoint that a thing as imagined is merely mental, and hence not distinct from mind. Hence the imagined nature is both dual and unitary, depending on how it is conceived. And the object as imagined is experienced dually in a nonreflective consciousness, but nondually by a more accomplished consciousness reflecting on that experience.

15   Since as an object of thought it is dual,
      But as a mere appearance it is unitary,
      The other-dependent nature
      Is said to be both dual and unitary.

We can say just about the same thing of the other-dependent nature. A phenomenon understood as other-dependent is both dependent upon the mind that represents it and is also a mere appearance of, and content of, that consciousness. In that sense the object is no different from that consciousness. Hence this nature, too, is both dual and unitary, depending on how it is conceived.

16   Since it is the essence of dual entities
      And is a unitary nonduality,
      The consummate nature
      Is said to be both dual and unitary.

The unity of duality and nonduality is perhaps a bit less compelling in the consummate nature. For the consummate nature is virtually defined by its nonduality and by the fact that from its perspective all duality is erased. But Vasubandhu is concerned to argue that it, too, in a sense, participates in duality, and this for two reasons. The first, and least interesting, is his obvious drive for poetic symmetry in the exposition. The second reason is a bit more philosophically interesting: the pair duality/unity is itself a duality and so should, from the standpoint of the consummate, be overcome. So to say that the consummate nature is nondual, or unitary *as opposed to being dual* would be self-defeating. So Vasubandhu needs to achieve a kind of sublation of duality and nonduality in the consummate. And he achieves this by noting that while the consummate nature itself may be nondual, it is nonetheless the nature of dual entities—entities that appear in their imagined nature, in virtue of their other-dependent nature. Inasmuch as it is a nature of dual entities, then, the consummate nature can be said to be dual.

17   The imagined and the other-dependent
      Are said to be characterized by misery.
      The consummate is free of
      The characteristic of desire.

This verse introduces the discussion in stanzas 17 through 21 of the sense in which the three Natures are identical to one another despite *their* apparent differences. Vasubandhu begins by emphasizing the prima facie ontological and soteriological gulf separating the imagined and the other-dependent from the consummate: the former are on the side of *saṃsāra*; the latter is on the side of nirvāna. The former two represent the aspects of phenomena apparent to a mind beset by primal ignorance, and hence by the suffering it engenders; therefore also the aspects responsible for the perpetuation of that ignorance and craving on the vicious circle of ignorance, grasping, and suffering that constitutes cyclic existence. The third, on the other hand, represents that aspect of phenomena apparent to a mind that has transcended all of that, and the aspect that conduces to the alleviation of suffering.[24] But, as we shall see, this prima facie ontological, epistemological, and phenomenological gulf will be obliterated in the final union of the Three Natures.

18   Since the former has the nature of a false duality
      And the latter is the nonexistence of that nature,
      The imagined and the consummate
      Are said not to be different in characteristic.

Vasubandhu now begins the task of unifying the Three Natures as three mutually implicative aspects of a single reality. He begins with the relation between the imagined and the consummate: the imagined nature is essentially dualistic, in that it involves an ontic distinction between subject and object; but seen *as imagined*, that duality is in fact seen to be nonexistent. But the nonexistence of that duality is exactly what the consummate nature is. The imagined nature and the consummate nature are hence, from an ontological perspective, not different from one another. The difference is only apparent, representing a difference in perspective, rather than one of reality. The next verse makes the same point in the reverse direction.

19   Since the former has the nature of nonduality,
      And the latter has the nature of nonexistent duality,
      The consummate and the imagined
      Are said not to be different in characteristic.

20   Since the former is deceptive in the way it appears,
      And the latter has the nature of its not being that way,
      The other-dependent and the consummate
      Are said not to be different in characteristic.

Verses 20 and 21 are devoted to establishing the identity of the consummate and the other-dependent natures. The point in (20) is parallel to that made with respect to the imagined nature. The dependent nature is deceptive, in that phenomena that are so dependent appear to be distinct from—although dependent upon—the subject. But when that nature is seen, from a higher perspective, to be not only dependent, but to be the fact of being merely mental, and hence nondifferent from the mind on which the phenomena depend, that understanding is the understanding of the consummate nature of things. Again, the difference between the natures is revealed to be not ontological in character, but merely perspectival.

21   Since the former has the nature of a nonexistent duality,
        And the latter is its nonexistence in the way it appears,
        The other-dependent and the consummate
        Are said not to be different in characteristic.

The parallel to the relation between the imagined and the consummate natures is emphasized in (21). The other-dependent, like the imagined, is dualistic in character. But when things experienced in their other-dependent nature are seen to be so experienced, the duality vanishes, and the nonexistence of that duality is the consummate nature itself. The apparent difference between the natures is hence, for Vasubandhu, a difference not in the object—in the ontological character of phenomena, but rather in the subject, and hence not a difference in nature, but a difference in experience of a single triune nature.

22   But conventionally,
        The natures are explained in order and,
        Based on that, one enters them
        In a particular order, it is said.

Nonetheless, though the three natures are at a deeper level a unity, pedagogically they form a hierarchy. There is an order in which they must be presented for the sake of clarity and soteriological efficacy. This is the topic of stanzas 22 through 25.

23   The imagined is entirely conventional.
        The other-dependent is attached to convention.
        The consummate, cutting convention,
        Is said to be of a different nature.

The imagined nature is the easiest to present first. It is the way that ordinary, unreflective persons represent things. The other-dependent, while constituting a more sophisticated view of things, remains at a conventional level. It, however, has real soteriological use, starting the process of freeing the mind from the tyranny of convention and fundamental ignorance, and providing a bridge to a

more transcendent view. Finally, awareness of the consummate nature allows the
move to a fully awakened view of reality.

24   Having first entered into the non-existence of duality
        Which is the dependent, one understands
        The nonexistent duality
        Which is the imagined.

On the other hand, Vasubandhu claims, the order of understanding the nondual characters of the two conventional natures is reversed. It is easier to see that
the dependent nature is nondual. For once one has ascended to an awareness of
this nature, and hence of the multiplicity of the natures of phenomena and of
their mind-dependence, it is possible to see phenomena as nondually related to
mind. One can then reflect on the imagined nature—initially experienced as a
dualistic relation to appearances—and see it, too, as nondual in character, in
virtue of the identity in ontic status between subject and object in that nature.
One must bear in mind that the point being made in this and the surrounding
verses is pedagogical: as long as one experiences only the imagined nature, it is
hard to see things nondualistically. That ability is made possible by the understanding represented by awareness of the other-dependent nature and then reflectively applies to the other-dependent.

25   Then one enters the consummate.
        Its nature is the nonexistence of duality.
        Therefore it is explained
        To be both existent and nonexistent.

Moreover, once one has thoroughly understood both of the merely conventional natures, including their apparent dualities, but the unreality of each duality,
one sees that all phenomena are both apparently dual and ultimately nondual.
That is their consummate nature. Realizing this nature is the consequence of a
complete understanding of the other two.

26   These three natures
        Have the characteristics of being noncognizable and nondual.
        One is completely nonexistent; the second is therefore nonexistent.
        The third has the nature of that nonexistence.

This verse sums up the result of the previous two discussions: going "from
top to bottom," the consummate nature is noncognizable because all cognition,
as discursive, is inescapably dualistic; the other two natures are nondual when
seen from that perspective, despite the duality engendered from within the perspective of each. But going the other way, the nature that is imagined is completely
nonexistent from any higher perspective. Therefore, the other-dependent nature,
being the dependence of a nonexistent entity on the mind, is also nonexistent,

when seen from the standpoint of the consummate. And the consummate is just the fact of the nonexistence of the first two. Thus, Vasubandhu concludes, despite the vast difference in the phenomenological character of the three perspectives from which phenomena have these three natures, the natures themselves are identical, joined in the object in virtue of its ideality.

The next section of the text develops the famous simile of the illusory elephant conjured by the stage magician. This is in fact the only portion of this text regularly cited in later polemical and hermeneutic discussions of Cittamātra philosophy by Tibetan commentators:[25]

27   Like an elephant that appears
        Through the power of a magician's mantra—
        Only the percept appears,
        The elephant is completely nonexistent.

The magician, allegedly using a mantra, causes the astonished audience to see an apparition of an elephant. But, we are assured, there really is no elephant. The illusion is engendered purely by the skill of the magician and the gullibility of the audience.

28   The imagined nature is the elephant;
        The other-dependent nature is the visual percept;
        The nonexistence of the elephant therein
        Is explained to be the consummate.

Now we can see the diverse aspects of subjectivity marked by the Three Natures as well as the ontological unity of the natures in the object (or putative object) they characterize. The nonexistent elephant—the apparent object of perception—is the elephant. The deluded audience believes it to exist, due to decidedly non-pachidermic causes and their own deluded ignorance. But nothing in fact exists in the way the elephant appears. But there is indeed a percept—not a living, breathing elephant—but a psychological episode brought into and sustained in existence in dependent on numerous conditions. This corresponds to the dependent nature. And the fact that there is no elephant in this percept—that the elephant is completely nonexistent and the percept is purely mental—is the consummate nature.

Note that this is a simile, and not a literal model of perception. It is crucial that to a naive observer, the hallucinated elephant appears as real and independent. To one "in the know," there is a real percept, but one that is decidedly not an independent elephant, and whose existence is entirely dependent on the state of mind of the member of the audience. And finally, the full story is that there simply is no elephant at all—not even one in perception—only a hallucination that is purely mental and entirely in the mind of the audience member. Just as the imagined nature of my teacup is that it is an independent object; the dependent nature is that it is my mental representation and not an independent external object; and its consummate nature is its complete nonexistence from a transcendental point of view.

29   Through the root consciousness
        The nonexistent duality appears.
        But since the duality is completely nonexistent,
        There is only a percept.

Just as through the force of the magician's incantations and manipulations the illusory elephant appears, through the force of our own mental predispositions the percept appears. But just as the elephant is purely hallucinatory, the percept is purely mental.

30   The root consciousness is like the mantra.
        Reality can be compared to the wood.
        Imagination is like the perception of the elephant.
        Duality can be seen as the elephant.

The psychological basis of appearances, for Vasubandhu and his Cittamātra followers, is the root consciousness and the potentials it contains for experiences. The mantra, the magician's incantation, is the basis, or cause, of the hallucination of the elephant. But the magician, in this analogy, has a prop—a piece of wood. (How this trick is actually performed is utterly mysterious at this point.) So what appears to be an elephant is actually a piece of wood, transformed by the magician into an apparitional elephant. Likewise, in experience, what appears to be an independent object is in fact a mere mental episode, caused by the actualization of latencies in the root consciousness to appear as independent. "Reality," (*tattva, de bzhin nyid*) in this context, refers to the dependent nature, since that nature gives us the perceived object *as a mere percept* as opposed to *as the object it appears to be*. The imagined nature, on the other hand, is analogous to the hallucinated elephant, and the nonexistent duality is like the intentional object of that hallucination, the nonexistent elephant.

The concluding verses of the text are devoted to its soteriological implications. For Cittamātra philosophy, like any Buddhist system, is soteriological in intent. The point of the system is to gain liberation from the delusions, attachments, and suffering of *saṃsāra* in order to be able to assist other sentient beings in accomplishing the same. From the Cittamātra point of view, the root delusion is to interpret the imagined nature of things to be their reality, and to fail to appreciate the other two natures and the identity of the Three Natures, and hence to fail to achieve the viewpoint represented by the consummate nature that reveals the world as it is.

31   When one understands how things are,
        Perfect knowledge, abandonment,
        And accomplishment—
        These three characteristics are simultaneously achieved.

To understand how things are is to understand all Three Natures simultaneously and in their correct relations to one another. This amounts to perfect knowledge of the ontology of the world and of the character of one's own subjectivity. That in turn means to abandon attachment to the imagined phenomena craved by one who believes them to be real as they appear in imagination, and that is to accomplish the goal of perfect insight into the nature of things and consequent freedom from the craving that is the necessary condition of ignorance and afflicted action.

32   Knowledge is nonperception;
        Abandonment is nonappearance;
        Attainment is accomplished through nondual perception.
        That is direct manifestation.

Perfect knowledge of this kind is nonperception in the sense that it is objectless, for the objects of ordinary perception are seen to be illusory, and the duality of perceiver and perceived that structures perception is transcended. Abandonment of commitment and attachment to imagined phenomena is achieved through the transcendence of instinctive assent to the imagined nature. The attainment of freedom is accomplished through the direct, immediate understanding of the unity of the Three Natures, and hence the nondual awareness of all phenomena in their consummate nature. For one who has attained this kind of knowledge, Vasubandhu claims, this cognitive relation to things is direct, intuitive, and immediate—not the consequence of constant philosophical analysis—but the primary way of taking up with the world, albeit through long analysis and practice.

33   Through the nonperception of the elephant,
        The vanishing of its percept occurs;
        And so does the perception of the piece of wood.
        This is how it is in the magic show.

Here Vasubandhu returns to the analogy in order to explain the structure of this accomplishment. When one sees through the trick—when one stops being taken in by the show—one stops seeing the elephant, and the percept vanishes. One no longer sees the piece of wood as an elephant at all. All of the illusion ceases.

34   In the same way through the nonperception of duality
        There is the vanishing of duality.

> When it vanishes completely,
> Nondual awareness arises.

Similarly, through an accomplished perception of things in accord with the Three-Nature theory, one stops seeing the dualistically represented phenomena. Those things, *as they are seen by an ordinary, deluded consciousness,* completely disappear. One sees through the show of ordinary experience, and the illusion ceases. One sees things simply as they are, without duality, without ascribing to them independent reality, as having all of the Triune Natures, each understood fully from the standpoint of the consummate.

35   Through perceiving correctly,
      Through seeing the nonreferentiality of mental states,
      Through following the three wisdoms,
      One will effortlessly attain liberation.

This understanding has, Vasubandhu here announces, soteriological consequences. Through understanding that one's mental states do not represent an independent reality, and through understanding fully the Three Natures and their relations to one another, attachment to objects as genuinely real and as legitimate objects of craving ceases. They are only dream-objects, nothing to take seriously, including both objects perceived as external, and one's self as it appears to oneself. The attendant cessation of grasping and of attachment is precisely the cessation denominated by the term *nirvāna*.

36   Through the perception of mind-only
      One achieves the nonperception of objects;
      Through the nonperception of objects
      There is also the nonperception of mind.

This verse emphasizes the connection between the release from attachment to external objects and the release from attachment to self. One begins the Cittamātra analysis by seeing all phenomena as purely mental. This dissipates the view that external phenomena are real. But with this realization comes the realization that the mind we experience—the self we cherish—is every bit as much an object for us (albeit of inner and not outer sense) and so is every bit as unreal as the outer objects to which it is so easy to become attached. Our self-attachment is hence revealed by this analysis to be every bit as much the product of ontological delusion as is our attachment to external phenomena.

37   Through the nonduality of perception,
      Arises the perception of the fundamental nature of reality.
      Through the perception of the fundamental nature of reality
      Arises the perception of the radiant.

This realization is the full understanding of the Three Nature theory and its implications. The fundamental nature of reality is its threefold character, and the unity of this threefold character in the ultimate nonduality of all that appears as dual. The experience of the world in this way is, Vasubandhu claims, a radiant, or totally illuminating gnosis.

38   Through the perception of the radiant,
        And through achieving the three supreme Buddha-bodies,
        And through possessing Bodhi:
        Having achieved this, the sage will benefit him or herself and others.

The deep insight embodied in this gnosis, coupled with the altruistic aspiration to attain liberation for the sake of other sentient beings, enables the practitioner, through physical acts (the use of the form-body), through the blissful detachment from suffering that enables one to take the welfare of others fully into account (the fruits of the enjoyment-body) and through thorough understanding (the truth-body) to be maximally effective on behalf of others.

This brief text hence articulates all of the principal features of Cittamātra philosophy: its thoroughgoing idealism; the three nature theory of the ontology of representation and of the phenomenology entailed by that idealism; the understanding of nonduality and emptiness in which that theory issues; and the soteriological consequences both of the Three Nature ontology and of the full understanding of the theory itself.[26] There certainly are briefer as well as, more detailed expositions of this system in the classical literature, but perhaps none so elegant and perspicuous.

8

Western Idealism through Indian Eyes

A Cittamātra Reading of Berkeley, Kant, and Schopenhauer

Metahermeneutic Preliminaries

This is an essay in metaphilosophy, in which I use one philosophical tradition as a lens through which to examine another. So it is already at one level an abstraction from the already-rarefied plane of metaphysics. But the principal agenda is yet one level more abstract: what I really aim to accomplish in this discussion is a reconception of the range of possibilities and the methodology of comparative philosophy and cross-cultural hermeneutics—a kind of meta-meta-metaphysics, if you will. So I begin with a discussion of the nature of and problems associated with cross-cultural hermeneutics and comparative philosophy in particular, and then I will explore a number of more fundamental levels.

Comparative philosophy has acquired a deservedly bad reputation of late (see, for exmaple, Klein 1995, Tuck 1990, Larson and Deutsch 1989). It has been noted that it too often functions as an arm of Orientalism in the most pejorative sense of that term, as an appropriation of expertise on non-Western traditions by Western scholars, with a consequent disempowerment of their non-Western colleagues. Moreover, it has been noted, comparative philosophy often imports hermeneutical and philosophical methods to the study of non-Western texts that succeed in distorting or simply missing the significance of those texts or the meaningfulness of their claims and arguments in the context of their home cultures. In addition it has been noted that the interpretive lens privileged in most comparative philosophy is distinctively Western, assuming a horizon of interpretation that itself should be a matter for contention in comparing multiple traditions. As a closely related matter, it has been charged that in comparing philosophical texts and views, the Western texts, views, and arguments are typically taken as the standards against which non-Western texts are compared and with respect to which are inevitably found either wanting, or, in the most generous case, found to approximate—the latter serving as the highest (and most patronizing) accolade vindicating the comparativist's attention to a tradition beyond his or her own (see also chapter 13 in this volume for a more extensive discussion of these issues).

All of these charges are, of course, overly broad, tarring with a single brush a wide range of philosophical activity. Nonetheless, there is enough truth in each of them, and truth in each case with respect to enough of the literature subsumed under this rubric to take them all seriously. I argue in chapter 13 that the enterprise of cross-cultural interpretation, and, inter alia, comparative philosophy as a wing of that enterprise, is in need of a new model of scholarship—a conversational model based not on the interpretation of fixed canonical texts by readers, but rather on discussion of texts-in-being-read by colleagues, in which active interchange between scholars with shared concerns and presumed comparable authority addresses questions of mutual interest. In such a conversation, neither party can take his or her tradition, texts, or conceptual framework for granted as providing a privileged or Archimedean standpoint from which to approach the other. The goals of such interchange are then not simply to *compare* texts for the sake of comparison, but rather to further understanding to the benefit of participants in each tradition, and perhaps to erode the boundaries between traditions in a nonhegemonic fashion.

But such conversations require more than good faith, shared interests and mutual respect. They require the willingness of each participant to take seriously—as a moment in the dialectic, though not as its endpoint—the possibility of interpreting his or her own tradition and texts from the standpoint of the other. For even though the goal of conversational cross-cultural interpretation is the displacement of both text and tradition as the fundamental units of analysis in favor of scholarly interactions, and the abandonment of particular traditions as privileged contexts for those interactions, that is a goal to be achieved, and not a situation to be presupposed at the outset of hermeneutic practice. We must begin where we find ourselves, and that is in a situation in which Western scholars have succeeded in taking their own tradition as privileged and have avoided the task of providing access to that tradition to their non-Western interlocutors, thus doubly impeding collegial progress. We must therefore strive to make our texts available on terms accessible to our cross-cultural colleagues, and strive self-consciously to see these texts from a distant point of view, the better to problematize them in the larger context we seek to create.[1]

It is therefore necessary first not entirely to *abandon* comparative philosophy, but to *use it*, in a way that, albeit self-undermining, will at the same time provide remedial equity to traditions too often placed in the object position under the comparative subjective lens and provide the kind of window into both the Western tradition and its hermeneutic practice for at least some of our non-Western colleagues. I therefore propose to take up the challenge implicit in this set of charges and to subject a slice of Western philosophy to the comparative method from the standpoint of an Indian tradition. I will take the Indian analysis for granted as the standard against which to measure the Western tradition; I will, insofar as it is possible, adopt an Indo-Tibetan standard of interpretation and doxography as I approach the Western texts; and I will self-consciously adopt readings of the Indian text I use derived from the Indo-Tibetan doxographic/philosophical tradition.

Now, I cannot altogether shed my identity as a Western philosopher; I can pretend neither to the same distance from my target texts nor the same proximity to my lens presumed in ordinary comparative philosophy. And I come to the task with a self-conscious metaphilosophical agenda that inevitably distorts the ground-level project. The real philosophical activity I await will require practitioners of a non-Western tradition to analyze ours themselves, as a prelude to an open dialogue among equals. Some of this is already happening, with interesting results (Chakrabarti 1996 is a good example). I believe—and I hope that this exercise will demonstrate—that we can learn a great deal about our own tradition and can prepare ourselves for such an open conversation by seeing our tradition from the vantage-point of another. Comparative philosophy, when pursued properly, can still be genuinely revelatory to all parties to the dialogue and can assist in bringing together the resources of all traditions in preparation for a future in which such comparative exercises will be passé and a plurality of traditions, each conscious of its own history and of the histories of those with which it comes into contact, can interact through collective activity.

My case study will involve the examination of a fragment of the history of Western transcendental idealism, namely, the development of the account of representation beginning with Berkeley, proceeding through Kant, and concluding with Schopenhauer. The lens through which I intend to examine this history, and the framework in which I propose to reconstruct the story of this evolution is provided by the metaphysical account of phenomena developed by Vasubandhu in *Trisvabhāvanirdeśa*—that is, the doctrine of the Three Natures that forms the basis of the doctrine that came to be called Cittamātra, or "mind-only" (sometimes also referred to as *vijñānavāda* or *vijñāptimātra*, "the way of consciousness," or "consciousness-only"). I will argue that when we examine Western idealism (or this slice of it) from this classical Indian vantage point, we can discern a definite and somewhat surprising progressivity in the Western tradition, a progressivity invisible without that lens, and one that reveals this episode in the history of our tradition as a progressive approximation of Vasubandhu's own analysis.

In order to launch this venture, I must first defend what was once a noncontroversial claim—that Cittamātra in Vasubandhu's formulation is in fact a Buddhist idealism. I will then briefly sketch the outlines of Vasubandhu's own formulation of that idealism, emphasizing his analysis of phenomena as three-natured. With this framework in hand, I will argue that Berkeley's idealism respects the *parikalpita-svabhāva*; that Kant adds to this an appreciation of the importance of *paratantra-svabhāva*, and that Schopenhauer completes the tradition by emphasizing the importance not only of these two natures, but of the *pariniṣpanna-svabhāva* as well. Hence we will be able to see, through this Indian lens, the respect in which the Western tradition can be seen as progressive. I hope we will then see both the value of privileging non-Western as well as Western traditions for the purposes of cross-cultural analysis, and the possibility of reading texts from very different traditions together, despite their disparate contexts.

CITTAMĀTRA IS IDEALISM

It has become something of a fashion lately to argue that Cittamātra is not idealist (Kalupahana 1987, Kochumuttom 1982, Dunne 1996, Lusthaus 1996a, b, Powers 1996a, b). Some argue that it is a form of pragmatism; others, that it is a neutral monism; still others, that it is completely continuous with Madhyamaka, as a doctrine of the emptiness of all phenomena. While simply saying that "all this is mind only" is not by itself, in a Buddhist context, enough to indict a school as idealist, given the plethora of metaphorical or qualified readings available for such formulae, I think that there are absolutely compelling internal and doxographic arguments for reading Vasubandhu and his fellow travelers as idealists in a strong sense of that term.

First let us be clear about what idealism in the relevant sense is, so that we do not find ourselves merely quibbling about terms. Idealism is a contrastive ontology: it is the assignment to the mind and to mental phenomena of a fundamental reality independent of that of external objects, while denying it to apparently external phenomena and assigning them a merely dependent status, a second-class existence as objects of and wholly dependent upon mind. Now there are different grades of idealism. As we shall see, Berkeley, Kant, and Schopenhauer, for instance, diverge dramatically on points of detail, and if we were to add Hegel, Fichte, Bradley, and the early Wittgenstein to the discussion still more divergence among idealists would be apparent. But these figures are unanimous in urging that the mind, or the transcendental subject, exists prior to and independently of any of its objects, and that its objects exist only as its objects, and insofar as they are characterized as objects, exist in no way external to consciousness.

When Kochumuttom, Anacker, Kalupahana, Lusthaus, and Powers deny that Vasubandhu or Asaṅga are idealists, they intend to deny them precisely this view—that objects of consciousness have a special, lower-grade existence, while mind has a high-grade existence, is a necessary condition for the existence of those objects and is independent of their existence. Consider these remarks:

It [Yogācāra] is *not* idealism. The mind is not the only "reality" according to them . . .

Unfortunately the standard "interpretation" of Yogācāra (especially of the Vimsatikā) treats it as a form of idealism, which then renders all of the Yogacarin arguments silly. . . . [T]heir ontological position is neither materialist nor idealist, but rather ontological silence . . . (Lusthaus 1996a)

I have never read a Yogācārin text that ever made the claim that mind creates physical things . . .

The point of refuting "objects" is to eliminate the appropriative consciousness that generates them qua appropriational goals. It is not to deny the objects in order to reify the consciousness. If Tibetan commentators say otherwise, they need to go back to school. (Lusthaus 1996b)

Tibetan commentators do in fact commonly characterize Yogācāra writers as holding a view that everything exists in the mind, but Asaṇga, Vasubandhu et al. never say this, as far as I'm aware. . . . [I]n my opinion their [Tibetan doxographers'] presentation of Yogācāra creates a view with which the proponents of the system would not agree. (Powers 1996b)[2]

There are indeed passages in the Yogācāra literature which apparently support an idealistic monism. But I maintain that the entire system, when understood in terms of realistic pluralism, makes better sense and that, therefore, even those passages which apparently support idealist monism, have to be reinterpreted in accordance with realistic pluralism. . . . It positively holds that individuals are real as well as mutually independent beings. (Kochumuttom 1982, p. 3)

There was a time when one could simply take it for granted that the Cittamātra or Yogācāra school (I will use the terms interchangeably here despite good doxographic reasons for distinguishing both their intension and extension[3]) is the school of Buddhist idealism. However, academic fashions and imperatives are such that once a position is regarded as obvious, attacking it becomes mandatory. And so now we must defend the obvious. Taking John Dunne's (1996) and John Powers's (1996a) point, and following with various points made in chapter 6 of this volume, I refrain from ascribing a common philosophical position to all of those referred to in Indo-Tibetan doxographies as Yogācārins. Here I restrict my gaze to Vasubandhu, and more particularly to the position he articulates and defends in *Viṃsatikā* and *Trisvabhāvanirdeśa*. These, probably his last two works, present the most articulate and explicit statement of his ontology. I will also allude to *Madhyāntavibhāgabhāṣya*, which presents the most complete elaboration of his ontology and epistemology. I argue in chapters 6 and 9 that Vasubandhu's idealism is shared by Sthiramati, and is accurately characterized by Candrakīrti, Tsong khapa, and mKhas grub, among others. Consider the following verses:

1   All this is appearance only
        Because of the appearance of the nonexistent.
        Just someone with cataracts
        Sees hairs, the moon and other nonexistents.

16   Perception is like a dream, etc . . .
        That is, when it occurs
        The object it distinguishes does not appear.
        So, how can one call this perception? (*Vimsatika*)[4]

Vasubandhu in this text explicitly asserts that the entire phenomenal world is in fact "consciousness only" and that the objects that appear to us are "nonexistent" like the hairs seen by the proverbial cataract patient. What is apparently the perception of external objects is actually more like a dream—the confusion of mere phantoms of the mind with physical objects.

20   Whatever is an object
        Of conceptual thought,
        That is thoroughly imaginary.
        Without any entity, it does not exist. (*Trimśikākārikā*)

5   What is the imagination of the nonexistent?
        Since what is imagined absolutely never
        Exists in the way it is imagined,
        It is mind that constructs that illusion.

36   Through the perception of mind-only
        One achieves the nonperception of objects;
        Through the nonperception of objects
        There is also the nonperception of mind. (*Trisvabhāvanirdeśa*)

In *Trisvabhāvanirdeśa* as well, Vasubandhu emphasizes the illusory character of external objects and the reality of the mind as the source of that illusion. He further emphasizes that the mind as it appears in introspection is no more real than external objects. It, too, is merely a phantom object of pure subjectivity that is the only reality.[5] This emphasis on the reality of consciousness and the unreality of its objects runs throughout to *Madhyāntavibhāgabhāṣya* as well.[6] The following verse and its commentary is apposite:

I:3   Consciousness is the appearance of
        Objects, sentient beings, self and representation.
        Arising entirely this way, it is without object.
        Being without that, it itself is nonexistent. (sDedge vol. Bi, 4b–c)

Here, when an object appears it appears as form, etc. When a sentient being appears it appears as sense powers in one's own and in others' mental continua. When the self appears, it appears as an afflicted mind, etc, and is like that because of having afflictions. The appearances of representations are the six consciousnesses. It says, "It is without object," since when objects and sentient beings appear they are all nonexistent, and when self and representations appear they appear falsely. Since it is without object, the grasping consciousness is nonexistent. (Bi, 4c–e)

I:4   Since it exists as the construction
        Of the completely nonexistent,
        It is thus not existent, yet not completely nonexistent. (Bi, 4e)

So, how has appearance arisen, since it is nonexistent—It is only illusion, but it is not completely nonexistent. Therefore though it does not entirely exist, it gives rise to desire. So, (Bi 4e)

I:4d   Through eliminating it, one can expect liberation. (Bi, 4e–f).

Note that Vasubandhu specifically asserts in these remarks and in many other points in these texts that the mind is real and persists even from the standpoint of nirvāna—that is, in its guise as *ālaya-vijñāna* the mind exists per se and not as an illusion. Moreover, he asserts that the nature of all apparently external phenomena, when they are correctly understood is seen to be mental—that they are purely appearances to the mind. He also asserts that while the mind is a necessary condition for the appearance of phenomena, the mind exists anterior to, and will exist in a purified state posterior to, the appearance of objects:

27   Even the thought, "All this is appearance only,"
        Involves an object.
        And anything that places something in front of it
        Is not grounded in this-only.

28   When no object is apprehended
        By consciousness,
        Then grounded in appearance-only
        With no object there is no grasping subject.

29   Then with no mind and no object
        With supramundane knowledge,[7]
        It is transformation of the basis,
        And the end of the two adversities.

30   It is uncontaminated,
        An inconceivable and stable sphere.
        It is blissful, the liberation body,
        And is called the Accomplished One's dharma body.

This position is as idealist as one can imagine. Indeed it is hard to imagine Vasubandhu being read in any other way. I emphasize here that this does not rely on any second- or third-hand authority of later doxographers (though to be sure it is in agreement with the unanimous verdict of both critics and followers of Vasubandhu in the Indo-Tibetan tradition). I am simply reading the texts themselves and taking Vasubandhu at face value.[8]

VASUBANDHU'S CITTAMĀTRA IDEALISM

While it is easy to clinch the argument in favor of construing Vasubandhu as an idealist, that does not tell us precisely what variety of idealist he is. For idealism comes in many varieties determined by the precise characterization of phenomena and of their relation to the mind representing them. We will see this variety played out in the history of Western idealism in a moment. But let me first quickly present the distinctive features of Vasubandhu's own presentation. Here I rely on the precise articulation of *Trisvabhāvanirdeśa*.

I will not here present a complete exegesis of this complex work but simply note the features of the idealism Vasubandhu presents that will be crucial for our comparative task. In this text Vasubandhu articulates his view of what it is for a phenomenon to be ideal. He argues that each phenomenon has three distinct natures, each of which is implicated by ideality.

First, each such object has an imagined nature (*parikalpita-svabhāva/kun btags kyi rang bzhin*). To have such a nature is to be merely imaginary. More precisely, for Vasubandhu insofar as any phenomenon is ideal, its status as an external object is merely imagined. We see physical objects, and even our mind as an object of introspection, as existing external to us. But that status is illusory. These things therefore, conceived as external to the mind, are imaginary.

Second, each phenomenon is asserted by Vasubandhu to have an other-dependent (*paratantra-svabhāva/gzhan dbang gi rang bzhin*) nature. That is, for an object to be ideal is for it to exist in dependence upon the mind. If a thing were independent of mind, it would fail to be ideal in the requisite sense. This aspect of Vasubandhu's idealism emphasizes the fact that while an object of consciousness may be imaginary qua external, independent object, it is a *real* object of consciousness and has a kind of existence. It exists as a mental act, or as the intentional—though not distinct and independent—object of a mental act, even though it fails to have the kind of existence it may be naively thought to have— that is, external, independent existence.[9]

Third, each object of consciousness has a consummate nature (*paranispanna-svabhāva/yong su grub pa'i rang bzhin*). This is the nature a thing is seen to have when it and its ideal status are completely understood. The consummate nature is the absence of the imagined nature; it is the fact of a thing's not existing as distinct from mind and the fact that even though a thing appears to exist in dependence upon mind, even the duality and distinction suggested by the relation of dependence is illusory. Phenomena are not, when seen from this final perspective, as much *dependent upon* mind, as they are *aspects* of it. One way to sharpen this point is to say that the other-dependent nature from one standpoint distinguishes mind and object as mutually *other* (hence its name). That very distinction preserves part of the perspective of the imagined nature, namely, its duality of subject and object. But from the standpoint of the consummate nature, it reveals the nondifference of object from mind, by virtue of its nonexternality. The consummate nature hence reflects a complete understanding of objects qua ideal and an abandonment of the subject-object duality apparent in the imagined.[10]

I pause at this point for some clarifications and amplifications. First, while Vasubandhu presents these as three distinct natures that all phenomena have by virtue of their ideality, they are not presented as *independent*, but rather, mutually implicative. It would be impossible to have one of them and not the others. They are, as it were, three aspects of ideality, which together make sense of that notion and are explained by it. Second, they are as much epistemological as they are ontological. This is not surprising in view of the tightly intertwined relation between epistemology and ontology in the Buddhist philosophical tradition, a feature characteristic of idealistic philosophy generally, including the idealism of the West to which I will turn in a moment (see chapter 7 for a more complete exposition).

So when I say that the consummate nature is the nature a thing is seen to have when it is completely understood, I use an epistemological entrée into an ontological insight—things as they *really are* are empty of the subject-object duality and are empty of any real distinction from the mind through which they are imagined. Likewise, when we characterize the ontology of the imagined nature, we approach it through consideration of the way things appear to consciousness. This interpenetration of epistemological and ontological concerns is unavoidable in this context and may be partially responsible for the erroneous view that there is no ontological import whatever in Cittamātra.[11]

Third, I emphasize that for Vasubandhu the central ontological-epistemological claim of *trisvabhāva* theory is not that all phenomena are ideal; that is almost assumed by this point (though it is defended at greater length in *Viṃsatikā* and its commentary); rather, the claim is that *what it is to be ideal is to be characterized by the Three Natures.* *Trisvabhāvanirdeśa* is an exploration of the structure of idealism itself. Let us now use that exploration as a guide to the history of Western idealism and see what we can learn about our own traditions.

BERKELEY AND *PARIKALPITĀ-SVABHĀVA*

The history of modern Western idealism properly begins with Berkeley, and the locus classicus for the articulation of his brand of that doctrine, which we might, following Kant, call "dogmatic idealism," is the *Three Dialogues between Hylas and Philonous*. There, Berkeley famously argues that "there is no such thing as matter" (1954 p. 12) and that nothing exists but minds and the contents of those minds (1954, pp. 77ff). In the dialogues Berkeley castigates two doctrines: First that we could have any knowledge of external phenomena and second, that the conception of external phenomena is even coherent. All of this is mobilized as a defense of idealism, the details of which can be left to one side for the moment and for the purposes of this investigation. For what concerns me is not so much the arguments Berkeley marshals for his ontological-epistemological position, or their success, but the structure of the position itself, and its historical relation to that which displaced it.

Berkeley's idealism is characterized by the following central principles:

1. Ideas are immediately perceived by the mind, and like the mind themselves in which they reside, they are real. (1954, pp. 45ff)
2. Nothing external to a mind is ever perceived, and no such thing is even possible. (ibid.)
3. Space and spatiality, and externality quite generally, though they may be thought to characterize the objects of our perception, are entirely illusory, and necessarily so. (ibid., pp. 55ff)

A crucial tenet that emerges from this cursory summary of Berkeley's views is the claim that to the extent that we represent the objects of our awareness as existing outside of us, in any sense, we are necessarily wrong. To put the point in Vasubandhu's terms, the externality of phenomena, in virtue of their ideality, is an imagined nature. Kant criticizes Berkeley on just this point, referring to Berkeley as "degrading bodies to mere illusion" (1965, §B71) and arguing that he "regards things in space as merely imaginary entities" (1965, §B274) It is important for our purposes to note that whatever the merits of Berkeley's idealism, Kant is correct in pointing out that it goes no farther than this. Even if we grant Berkeley the conclusion that all phenomena are ideal, we see that his analysis of what it is to be ideal is unidimensional: he argues that for an apparent material object to be ideal is for it to be merely imaginary. From the standpoint of Vasubandhu, this first stab at idealism in the West is a good start, but only one-third of the story.

KANT AND *PARATANTRA-SVABHĀVA*

Kant, as I have already noted, criticizes precisely this inadequacy in Berkeley's theory. With both Descartes's primitive representational realism (which he calls misleadingly "problematic idealism") and Berkeley's primitive dogmatic idealism in view, Kant sets out self-consciously to develop an idealism more sophisticated than either, which he calls "transcendental idealism." In the *Critique of Pure Rea-*

son, Kant argues that when we characterize a thing as a representation, and hence as an object for subjectivity, we must represent it both as empirically real and as transcendentally ideal.

It would be folly in work of this scope to attempt to sketch even the vaguest outlines of Kant's entire system of transcendental idealism, or even of that part articulated in the transcendental aesthetic and transcendental analytic, which is most relevant to present concerns. Instead, I will make the necessary exegetical claims quickly and dogmatically: in recognizing the compatibility—and indeed the mutual entailment between—transcendental ideality and empirical reality, Kant is acknowledging that any coherent account of representations must assign them at least (and in his case at most) a dual status. Kant emphasizes that from one standpoint, our representations of objects in space and time (including our representations of ourselves in inner sense) must be thought of as empirically real. They are genuinely *outside* of us qua objects of representation. Yet at the same time, qua representations, they are, from the transcendental perspective, *in* us. Kant emphasizes this *twofold* nature of representation in the Transcendental Aesthetic, and it is a central theme in his transcendental idealism:

> Our exposition therefore establishes the *reality*, that is, the objective valid-
> ity, of space in respect of whatever can be presented to us outwardly as
> object, but also at the same time the *ideality* of space in respect of things
> when they are considered in themselves through reason. . . . We assert,
> then, the *empirical reality* of space, as regards all possible outer experience;
> and yet at the same time we assert its *transcendental ideality*—in other
> words that it is nothing at all, immediately we withdraw the above con-
> dition . . . (§A28/B44, trans. N. Kemp-Smith, 1965)

> What we are maintaining is . . . the *empirical reality* of time, that is, its
> objective validity in respect of all objects which allow of ever being given
> to our senses. . . . On the other hand, we deny to time all claim to absolute
> reality. . . . This, then, is what constitutes the *transcendental ideality* of time.
> What we mean by this phrase is that if we abstract from the subjective
> conditions of sensible intuition, time is nothing . . . (§A35–36/B52, trans.
> N. Kemp-Smith, 1965)

The focus of Kant's complaint against Berkeley can be seen from this perspective as a charge that Berkeley simply fails to note this dual character of
representations and so develops what from Kant's perspective can only be seen
as a deficient, one-sided idealism. Kant takes himself to be the first to emphasize
both sides of the coin of an idealist theory of representation: whereas things
considered as they appear to us, when seen from a transcendental perspective,
are, as Berkeley correctly noted, completely nonexistent, Berkeley, according to
Kant, failed to note the corollary of this truth, namely, that things, as seen from

the point of view of subjectivity, are empirically real, and that their empirical reality and transcendental ideality are mutually implicative.

The two natures Kant distinguishes—empirical reality and transcendental ideality—are quite naturally mapped on to the imagined and the other-dependent nature as these are articulated by Vasubandhu. The empirical reality of objects as characterized by Kant, and hence the reality of space and time themselves, is a merely represented reality and no part of the objects themselves. When seen from a transcendental point of view—a God's-eye view, as Kant himself would put it, and hence from the standpoint of omniscience—such objects and space and time themselves are "nothing at all." On the other hand, the kind of reality they *do* have for Kant is reality qua representation, and that gives them a kind of "objective validity." That is, as objects of the mind, as things dependent upon us, they are in fact real. Even God would assent to that. But *that* reality does not guarantee that the reality they *appear to have* is in fact actual. Hence, for Kant, their dependent nature is a deeper fact about phenomena than their imagined nature.

Moreover, the relation between these two natures as it is sketched in the First *Critique* maps rather neatly onto the relations between these two natures as it is presented in *Trisvabhāvanirdeśa*. Vasubandhu emphasizes that the imagined nature simply is the other-dependent nature as it appears to naive consciousness, and that when it is correctly understood, the appearance of things as they are imagined is seen to be merely illusory—that things when properly understood from a vantage point abstracting from the afflictions that determine ordinary subjectivity are completely devoid of the characteristics they are imagined to possess. Nonetheless, he also emphasizes that to be a phenomenon for an ordinary human consciousness simply is, inter alia, to appear through the imagined nature, and to do so in a way *dependent upon* the structure of the human mind. Hence the imagined nature is the dependent nature become appearance. And so it is for Kant. Things appear to us in space and time in dependence upon the structure of human consciousness. So appearing as a real empirical object to consciousness is part and parcel of what it is to be an object of knowledge for a human being. This is what it is for something that is *in fact* a mere mental episode—and so, *as phenomenon*, to exist only in dependence upon mind—to appear to us in space and time. But that appearance—though in one sense real *as appearance*, is in another sense completely illusory. *Parikalpitā* and *paratantra svabhvāva*s are two sides of the coin of appearance for Vasubandhu. Empirical reality and transcendental ideality are two sides of the same coin for Kant.

Though for Berkeley things qua appearance have only imagined reality, and though I have lined up Kant's empirical reality with Vasubandhu's imagined reality, I cannot infer through transitivity that Berkeley and Kant agree that objects of experience are empirically real, as Kant himself emphasizes. But that is not surprising. It is not as accurate to say that Berkeley's primitive form of idealism *omits* one of (at least) two characteristics that idealism forces us to ascribe to objects as it is to say that Berkeley *conflates* two characteristics, and in doing so fails to articulate the dependent reality that phenomena in fact have *as a characteristic of those phenomena*. We can hence see Kant as developing a very Vasubhandan critique of Berkeley—forcing a distinction between mutually implicative characteristics, while emphasizing their nonduality in the very context of that distinction.[12]

Now a reader of Kant might be impatient at this point with the fact that I have not yet discussed Kant's doctrine of the thing-in-itself. For Kant argues that the phenomena we see have yet another nature, one hidden to us, and independent of their status as objects of experience—a noumenal nature as *Ding an sich*. And a reader of Kant familiar with Vasubandhu might impatiently argue that this noumenal character hints at *paranispanna-svabhāva*. Such a reader would be correct, as far as that goes.

However, I deliberately refrain from ascribing to Kant a doctrine of *trisvabhāva* for two reasons. First, Kant himself is inconsistent on this point. Sometimes, consistent with the remainder of the critical theory, he asserts that the thing-in-itself is unknowable and uncharacterizable, not even subject to categories such as unity, plurality, or existence:

> The true correlate of sensibility, the thing in itself, is not known, and cannot be known, through these representations; and in experience no question is ever asked in regard to it. (1965, pp. A30, B45)

> [N]othing whatsoever can be asserted of the thing in itself ... (ibid., pp. A49, B66)

> We cannot define any [category] in any real fashion, that is, make the possibility of their object understandable, without at once descending to the conditions of sensibility, and so to the form of appearances—to which, as their sole objects, they must consequently be limited. For if this condition be removed, all meaning ... falls away. (ibid., pp. A241, B300)

> The pure categories, apart from formal conditions of sensibility, have only transcendental meaning; nevertheless they may not be employed transcendentally, such employment being in itself impossible, inasmuch as all condition of any employment in judgments are lacking to them, namely the formal conditions of the subsumption of any ostensible object under these concepts. (ibid., pp. A248, B305, trans. N. Kemp-Smith *passim*)

At other times he asserts that things-in-themselves exist, and that each phenomenon is an appearance of a thing-in-itself, in manifest contradiction to the framework of the *Critique:*

But our further contention must be duly borne in mind, namely that though we cannot *know* these objects as things-in-themselves, we must yet be in a position to *think* them as things-in-themselves; otherwise we should be landed in the absurd conclusion that there can be appearance without anything that appears (ibid., p. Bxxvi)

Tracing, explaining and untangling Kant's unclarity on this point would take us far afield. But the most charitable reading of Kant takes the Transcendental Deduction seriously and hence eschews *any* theorizing regarding things-in-themselves.[13]

Second, even if one does take seriously Kant's confused discussions of things-in-themselves, it is clear that this account plays no role in Kant's account of what it is to be an object of experience, and in particular no role in the discussion of the empirical reality of things or of their relationship to consciousness.[14] But for Vasubandhu this is precisely a central role that each of the Three Natures must play. For the Three Natures are each aspects of what it is to be an object in the context of idealism. Just as Kant criticizes Berkeley for ignoring the empirical reality of phenomena, we will see that Schopenhauer criticizes Kant for failing to properly appreciate the reality and role of the thing-in-itself. In encountering Schopenhauer's account, we will see what it is for Western idealism to live up to Vasubandhu's demands in this regard.

Schopenhauer and *Paranispanna-svabhāva*

Schopenhauer adopts and extends Kant's transcendental idealism, most notably by bringing the thing-in-itself into the field of knowledge, defending a fundamental nonduality of subject and object from a transcendental point of view, and arguing that that nonduality appears as a subject-object duality only at the level of universal illusion. The appearance of that duality, he argues, reflects only our illusion about the truly nondual nature of reality; the appearance of representations *as* representations is a consequence of that cognitive process grounded in fundamental ontological ignorance. Vasubandhu would be proud.

I begin by noting Schopenhauer's thoroughgoing commitment to a Kantian idealism as a foundation for his more ambitious ontology and epistemology. Schopenhauer in fact explicitly (albeit a bit confusedly) connects this idealism with Indian views:[15]

That which knows all things and is known by none is the *subject*. It is accordingly the supporter of the world, the universal condition of all that appears, of all objects, and it is always presupposed; for whatever exists, exists only for the subject. (1969, vol. 1, p. 5, trans. E.F.J. Payne)

[T]hese two halves [subject and object] are inseparable even in thought, for each of the two has meaning and existence only through and for the other ... (ibid., vol. 1, p. 5)

Past and future ... are as empty and unreal as any dream; but the present is only the boundary between the two, having neither extension nor duration. In just the same way, we shall also recognize the same emptiness in all the other forms of the principle of sufficient reason, and shall see that, like time, space also, and like this, everything that exists ... has only a relative existence ... ; it is Māya, the veil of deception, which covers the eyes of mortals, and causes them to see a world of which one cannot say either that it is or that it is not; for it is like a dream, like the sunshine on the sand which the raveler from a distance takes to be water, or like the piece of rope on the ground which he regards as a snake. (ibid., vol. 1, pp. 7–8)

Schopenhauer emphasizes the two natures adumbrated by Kant and indeed emphasizes even more explicitly than does Kant their distinctness and mutual implication. He argues that while all representation, in being given as real and external, is illusory, *qua representation* all that we experience (at least veridically) is indeed real:

Only [through the] understanding ... does the world stand out as perception extended in space. (ibid., vol. 1, p. 12)

The whole world of objects is and remains representation, and is for this reason wholly and forever conditioned by the subject; in other words it has transcendental ideality. But it is not on that account falsehood or illusion; it presents itself as what is, as representation ... (ibid., vol. 1, p. 15)

But whereas Kant stopped in his analysis of the character of representations with these two natures, Schopenhauer explicitly asserts not only the necessity of positing in thought the thing-in-itself,[16] but also its reality, and indeed *the more complete and genuine reality* of the thing-in-itself. Moreover, Schopenhauer, unlike Kant but like Vasubandhu, regards this noumenal reality as essential to phenomena conceived as representations. This point must be put delicately: it is not that *qua phenomenon* a thing is represented *as thing-in-itself*. Rather, for Schopenhauer, in providing a full account of what it is to be a phenomenon, we must include its character as it is in itself, and not merely negatively. That noumenal nature is, of course, Will.

Phenomenon means representation and nothing more. All representation, be it of whatever kind it may, all *object* is *phenomenon*. But only the *will* is *thing-in-itself* ... It is that of which all representation, all object, is the phenomenon, the visibility, the *objectivity*. It is the innermost essence, the kernel, of every particular thing and also of the whole . . . (ibid., vol. 1, p. 110)

To present Schopenhauer's entire metaphysics of the will would take us far afield. But I can say this much. For Schopenhauer will is far more than personal or psychological. It is an unconscious and undifferentiated force[17]—itself unitary or at least not plural—which in its multiple manifestations becomes phenomenon. These manifestations include not only objects represented as external, but also the empirical selves we know. Schopenhauer, then, unlike Berkeley for whom our own minds are fundamental subjects, agrees with Vasubandhu that the evolving consciousness is itself as much representation as any of the phenomena it knows as exterior to itself. Ultimate reality is foundational to both empirical subject and empirical object and is free of that merely apparent duality. Indeed, for Schopenhauer, as for Vasubandhu—and unlike either Berkeley or Kant—the distinction between duality and nonduality marks the distinction between appearance and ultimate reality.

> [The Will] is free from all *plurality*, although its phenomena in time and space are innumerable. It itself is one, yet not as an object is it one, for the unity of an object is known only in contrast to possible plurality. (ibid., vol. 1, p. 113)

We can hence see that the will for Schopenhauer is indeed the consummate reality of (or at least *behind*) all phenomena. Indeed, in a paraphrase of Vasubandhu not at all unfaithful to the spirit of *The World as Will and Representation*, we can say that will is what a representation is when its illusory character as external and independent phenomenon is discounted. That is, it is the dependent nature, emptied of the imagined. In Schopenhauer, then, we see idealism in the West in its fully evolved form. All three natures are present and are related to one another in precisely the way Vasubandhu argues that they must be. They are represented as distinct but mutually implicative, and the signal characteristic of the most real, the most fundamental, is the absence of all duality and plurality, and the absence of any external object of consciousness.[18]

THE PROGRESSIVE CHARACTER OF WESTERN IDEALISM

I have told the story of Western idealism not as it is told in Western histories of philosophy, but as it would be told by a Cittamātra philosopher, or perhaps as it would be told *to* a Cittamātra philosopher, or perhaps more realistically to a philosopher whose entrée into idealist thought was through Cittamātra. My aim in telling the story this way is not simply to demonstrate the possibility of *alternative* perspectives on our own tradition or to show that turnabout can be fair play. Rather, I think that telling the story in this way is in fact illuminating. It shows that Western philosophy is progressive and how it is so revealing a dynamic at work in this strand of our intellectual history that may have been invisible to us.

The invisibility to which I allude is traceable to two sources: first, proximity and custom. We are simply so close to our own tradition, and so accustomed to the hermeneutic story internal to it that we do not countenance the need for or the possibility of an alternative reading of our history. This is not unique to us, of course. Our Tibetan colleagues also inhabit a philosophical tradition that develops and understands itself through its own hermeneutic, a hermeneutic that we often challenge when we come as Westerners to the history of Buddhist philosophy. The point is simply that traditions do not problematize their own self-understanding until they come into dialogue not so much with other *ideas* but with other *ways of reading*. (See chapter 13 of this volume for more discussion of this phenomenon.)

Second, and at a more straightforwardly philosophical level, the construct that reveals this particular progressive dynamic is not thematized within our own tradition. We do not develop *trisvabhāva* theory as such. For that reason, lacking a vocabulary in which to distinguish theories in this way, we fail to see the distinction and so miss a crucial dimension of our own increasing sophistication. It is in this sense that the alternative way of reading Vasubandhu offer us is not simply an *alternative*, but a *better* way of seeing our own history. We should not react to such a comparative exercise with shame at our own blindness but with a certain pleasure in the discovery of a deeper dimension to our own heritage than we might hitherto have suspected and the hope that we can contribute similar insights to our interlocutors if we tread with care on contested ground.

COMPARATIVE PHILOSOPHY AS A ROAD TO CONVERSATION

I hope that this has been an example of comparative philosophy done right—providing a reading that sheds light from one tradition upon another. But a crucial component of "doing the right thing," as far as I am concerned, is the motivation, the intended next step. For if the enterprise stops here, not enough has been accomplished to make it all worthwhile. We note a surprising relationship between two traditions; we discover a way of conceptualizing our own not hitherto considered; we are on the way to understanding idealism itself more deeply. Not bad. The real dividend, however, is the philosophical progress this understanding makes possible. For up to this point, our gaze has been in the direction of the past—that of a historian or a curator of dead traditions. Philosophy is, however, a live enterprise, both in the West and in the East, and if cross-cultural philosophy is to mean anything and to contribute anything to philosophical progress, it must do so with a view toward ideas and their development.

To that end, I urge that the kind of exercise in which I have been engaging be seen as a prolegomenon. It is a stage in, to borrow a Gadamerian phrase, the fusion of horizons. The task is to provide a common horizon that can be a background for genuine collaboration and conversation in a joint philosophical venture. The possibilities for such a venture are enormous. The enlargement of the world scholarly community and the range of texts and resources on which it can draw portends a greater philosophical depth and rate of progress. But the condition of the possibility of such progress and of such a future is the establishment of genuine collegiality and conversation, as opposed to contact and the interrogation of informants. And the condition of the possibility of conversation is taking seriously the standpoint and hermeneutic method of one's interlocutor as well as his or her ideas themselves, and taking seriously one's own tradition not as a lens through which to view another's, but also as specimen under one's colleague's lens at particular moments in the dialectic. That is the point of the present examination and the value of comparative philosophy when it is conceived not as an activity in itself, but rather as a moment in a dialogical dialectic whose apogee is reached at the point where these previous moments are transcended in the collegiality they make possible.

Of course, in any intercultural dialogue, and particularly at explicitly comparative moments in the dialectic, one must be alert to the dangers of procrustean beds. One can abuse the comparative method—and the cases of such abuse are legion and are the basis of the bad name comparative philosophy has earned of late. Such abuse leads to dramatic distortion of alien traditions through the imposition of hermeneutic and doxographic frameworks, or philosophical problematics or presuppositions entirely foreign to the traditions themselves. But the danger of abuse is not an argument against careful use. I have urged here that such careful use is not only possible, but desirable. In part this is true because of the essential role of comparative philosophy as a rung in a ladder to be discarded by our descendants, whose interlocution it may some day be seen to have enabled.

9

Sounds of Silence

Ineffability and the Limits of Language in Madhyamaka and Yogācāra

The Silence of Śāriputra

The *Vimalakīrtinirdesa-sūtra* offers us two dramatic and contrasting moments of silence. The first of these, the silence of Śāriputra, sets the problem for this chapter: when, and how, can silence be articulate? About what can silence inform? And what can it tell us? We will see that the two principal Mahāyāna schools—or at least prominent protagonists of each—disagree dramatically with regard to the answers they provide to this set of questions, and that this divergence reflects and illuminates their differences with regard to the status of emptiness and the nature of our knowledge thereof. But let us begin with Śāriputra's predicament:

> Then the venerable Śāriputra said to the goddess, "Goddess, how long have you been in this house?"
>
> The goddess replied, "I have been here as long as the elder has been in liberation."
>
> Śāriputra said, "Then you have been in this house for quite some time?"
>
> The goddess said, "Has the elder been in liberation for quite some time?"
>
> At that the elder Śāriputra fell silent.
>
> The goddess continued, "Elder, you are 'foremost of the wise!' Why do you not speak? Now, when it is your turn, you do not answer the question."
>
> Śāriputra: Since liberation is inexpressible, goddess, I do not know what to say.
>
> Goddess: All the syllables pronounced by the elder have the nature of liberation. Why? Liberation is neither internal nor external, nor can it be

apprehended apart from them ... Therefore, reverend Śariputra, do not
point to liberation by abandoning speech!

(1984, p. 59, trans R. Thurman)

Poor Śariputra! Not only has he discovered that he has been in a house with
a goddess in the closet, with all of the implications for *vināya* that suggests, but
she turns out to be a clever goddess. And when he tries to wriggle out of a
dialectical corner into which she backs him with what looks like a profound
manoeuvre, she calls his bluff and humiliates him. This should be a lesson to us
all: never appear as a *hinayāna* character in a Mahāyāna sūtra![1] Śariputra aban-
dons speech too quickly, after all. He has been asked a question in a particular
context, in which very little scaffolding is available, in which we begin an investigation almost from scratch. To refuse to speak at such a point is neither an
indication of wisdom, nor a means of imparting wisdom, but at best a refusal to
make progress. Even if the proverbial raft is eventually to be abandoned, we need
it to cross the river. Śariputra would have us swim and possibly drown. Language
is not, according to any Mahāyāna school, to be abandoned at the outset; it is
not, whatever its limitations, a useless or a wholly misleading cognitive vehicle.
To adopt an aphasia or cognitive quietism from the start would be pointless, and,
as the Goddess notes, contrary to the practice of the Buddha himself, who uttered
an enormous number of words during his career.

But of course the episode gets its point precisely from the fact that Buddhist
literature is replete with a rhetoric of silence—with episodes of especially significant silence—and indeed, as we discover a mere two chapters later in this very
sūtra, Śariputra's failed silence is but a contrastive prelude to Vimalakīrti's far
more articulate silence. This forces us to confront the question, Just when is
silence articulate, and just when is nonsilent language required? And this question
in turn suggests two deeper ones: What explains the possibility of articulate silence, and what determines the limits of articulate speech? We will see that the
answers to these last questions differ between Madhyamaka and Yogācāra schools,
and that the difference is grounded in their account of the epistemology and
ontology of emptiness.

Emptiness and Positionlessness in Madhyamaka

Madhyamaka philosophers—I will be concerned primarily with Nāgārjuna, but
also with Candrakīrti and Śantideva, whose positions on these matters I take to
accord in all major respects with Nāgārjuna's—distinguish between two truths:
the conventional truth of the world as it appears to ordinary consciousness and
as it is constituted by our conventions and practices, including prominently our
linguistic and cognitive practices, and the ultimate truth, which is the emptiness
of all phenomena. That emptiness, for these philosophers, is not to be understood

as nonexistence, but rather as a lack of essence or independence; more positively it is understood as being interdependent, and as having identity constituted by our conventions, prominently including linguistic and cognitive conventions for more on the nature of emptiness and its relation to the Two truths see chapters 1 through 4 of this volume, Garfield 1995, Newland 1992, Napper 1989, Huntington and Wangchen 1989, Rabten and Batchelor 1983). Śantideva puts the point this way:

2   The conventional and the ultimate
       Are explained to be the Two Truths.
       The ultimate is not grasped as an object of thought;
       Thought is explained to be merely conventional.
                       (Śantideva, *Bodhicaryāvatāra* 10)

Here Śantideva explicitly draws the connection between the conventional character of the conventional world and the fact that it can be characterized by language and grasped by thought. This contrasts with the cognitive and linguistic inaccessibility of the ultimate. It, being the way things are independent of convention, is therefore uncharacterizable, unconceptualizable, precisely because all characterization and conception is convention-dependent and implicates ontologies that can only be conventionally constituted. Śantideva follows Nāgārjuna, who writes in *Mūlamadhyamakakārikā*:

7   What language expresses is nonexistent.
       The sphere of thought is nonexistent.
       Unarisen and unceased, like nirvāna
       Is the nature of things. (*MMK* 8)

In this stanza, Nāgārjuna sharply contrasts the character of things as they present themselves in conventional reality with the way they are ultimately and connects expressibility and conventional reality, inexpressibility and ultimate reality: language and thought indeed grasp and characterize phenomena (ab); those phenomena, however, do not ultimately exist. The true nature of things, by contrast (cd), is not graspable by thought, expressible by language, which can only comprehend things that arise and cease. Nāgārjuna develops this theme further in this important and oft-quoted verse:

8   The victorious ones have said
       That emptiness is the relinquishing of all views.
       For whomever emptiness is a view,
       That one has accomplished nothing. (*MMK* 13)

Views, of course, are philosophical theories, and so of necessity conceptual and expressible. Emptiness, the ultimate reality of things, cannot be the subject of any such view precisely because it is inexpressible, unconceptualizable. The limits of thought and expression are coextensive with the limits of conventional truth. Candrakīrti, in commenting on this verse, writes:

> So here emptiness is the ceasing of the perception of all views and of the persistence of all attachment to them. And since this is so, the mere relinquishing of views is not even an existent. We will not debate with whoever insists on seeing emptiness as an entity. Therefore, if one opposes this presentation through conceptual elaboration, how will liberation be achieved?

> It is like this: Suppose a someone says to someone else, "I have nothing" and he says in reply, "I'll take that very nothing you say you have." If so, without anything there, by what means can we get him to understand that there is nothing there? In just this way, how can someone stop insisting on seeing emptiness is an entity through seeing emptiness as an entity? Therefore, the great doctors with great wisdom and realization, who have performed great medical deeds, understanding their illness, pass by them and refuse to treat them.

> As it is said in the great *Ratnakūta sūtra*, "Things are not empty because of emptiness; to be a thing is to be empty. Things are not without defining characteristics through characteristiclessness; to be a thing is to be without a defining characteristic. Things are not without aspiration because of as-pirationlessness; since to be a thing is to be without aspiration, whoever understands each thing in this way, Kāśyapa, will understand perfectly how everything has been explained to be in the middle path. Kāśyapa whoever conceives of emptiness through objectifying it falls away from understanding it as it has been explained to be. Kāśyapa, it would be better to view the self as just as stable as Mt. Meru than to view emptiness in this way. This is because, Kāśyapa, since emptiness is understood through the relinquishing of all views, whoever conceives of emptiness through a view, I have explained, will be incurable.

> Kāśyapa, consider this example: If a doctor gives a patient medicine, and this medicine cures all of his illness, but stays in his stomach, do you think that suffering will not arise, Kāśyapa? Do you think this man will be relieved of the illness in his belly? No way, blessed one! If the medicine, having cured all of his illnesses, stays in his stomach, this man will certainly become seriously ill.

> The Blessed one said, "Kāśyapa, you should see the insistence on any view in just this way. If emptiness is seen like that, Kāśyapa, whoever sees emptiness like that, will be incurable. I have said that it is like that. (*Prasannapadā* 83b–84a)

These comments, of course, are about emptiness and its absolutely negative character and are aimed at forestalling any reification of emptiness. But they are apposite to the issue of expressibility as well. For if someone was to object to the claim that the ultimate truth is inexpressible by arguing that one had just managed to express something about it, the same reply is available: I have denied that there is any available adequate expression. To say that this expression is adequate is simply to fail to accept the claim of inexpressibility and to beg the question. The fact that the same analogy works so well as an explication of the negative character of the ultimate truth and of the impossibility of its expression is certainly at least suggestive of the deep link between them.

Nonetheless, this insistence on a domain of ineffable truth in Madhyamaka does not amount to a rejection of the utility of language, or even of a rejection of the utility of language as a means to come to know ultimate truth. And that, of course, is the point of the goddess's rebuke to Śāriputra. In the twenty-fourth chapter of *MMK*, Nāgārjuna addresses the relation between the conventional and the ultimate truth, and hence implicitly between the expressible and the inexpressible. He argues that the conventional and expressible is a necessary scaffolding for the ascent to knowledge of ultimate truth:

9   Without a foundation in the conventional truth,
       The significance of the ultimate cannot be taught.
       Without understanding the significance of the ultimate,
       Liberation is not achieved.

But perhaps more surprisingly, Nāgārjuna argues for an identity—a nonduality—between the conventional and the ultimate, and hence between the expressible and the inexpressible. In the central verse of *MMK* he writes:

18   Whatever is dependently co-arisen
       That is explained to be emptiness.
       That, being a dependent designation,
       Is itself the middle way.

Here Nāgārjuna claims that the ultimate and conventional truths are not different from one another, despite the fact that one lies with the sphere of thought and language and one does not. This forces us to think hard about how the limits of expression are to be understood in Madhyamaka: how could it be that the same reality could be comprehensible through language and conception and at the same time be incomprehensible through those same media? The answer, we shall see, lies not in the character of reality, but in the distinction between conventional and ultimate perspectives on that reality. At the end of *MMK* Nāgārjuna writes:

30   I prostrate to Gautama
        Who through compassion
        Taught the true doctrine,
        Which leads to the relinquishing of all views.

                                        (27)

The goal of Madhyamaka philosophy is the abandonment not of reality, but of a way of taking up with reality, and that way turns out to be inexpressible precisely because of the character of language and thought—always reificatory; always imposing a conventional grid. And against the charge that even to say this—even to express the true thought that truth is inexpressible—is to engage in self-refutation, Nāgārjuna responds:

29   If I had any proposition at all,
        Thereby I would have that fault.
        Since I don't have a proposition
        I don't have any fault at all.
                (Vigrahavyāvartanī)

That is, the language through which the bounds of expression are approached is itself to be understood by those who have transcended them as merely instrumental, as merely the scaffold to be used only so long as it is useful in climbing, or in assisting others to climb to that level where the language is no longer necessary.

Language and thought, for Nāgārjuna and those who would follow him, then, are adequate to the conventional truth precisely because it is conventional and nominal. The fact that language and thought are constitutive of our ontology explains the fact that they also characterize it. The ultimate truth, on the other hand, is purely negative—it is the emptiness of all phenomena of inherent existence, of all convention-independent existence. For this reason it is also the way things are independent of the conventions embedded in language and conception and for that reason cannot be captured by them. The moment they are employed, they impose the ontology with which they are saturated.

But we have also seen that language can be used to convey ultimate reality in two senses: first, it presents the necessary scaffolding by means of which the nature of reality, and hence its emptiness can be explained. Second, given the emptiness of emptiness and the ultimate identity of the Two Truths, truth as expressed by language and thought—then properly understood as merely conventional—shows, but cannot say, the ultimate nature of reality. Hence the inexpressibility of ultimate reality for Madhyamaka is limited—it is inexpressible from one side only, albeit the most important one—and rests on its purely negative character as compared to the positive character of conception and language, and so finally its relation to its expressibility in another sense is grounded on the emptiness of emptiness and the identity of the Two Truths.

EMPTINESS AND MIND ONLY IN YOGĀCĀRA

When we turn to central Yogācāra texts,[2] the account of emptiness we discover is subtly different and underpins an idealism contrasting sharply with the more homogenous ontology of Madhyamaka: mind is accorded a fundamental onto-logical status, and the existence of external objects is denied altogether. Emptiness must then be reinterpreted if all is to come out empty. For if emptiness were to be understood in this system as the mere absence of inherent existence, mind could not be regarded in this way, and if emptiness were understood as equivalent to conventional reality, external objects could not be regarded as empty. The opening verses of *Madhyāntavibhāga,* a text attributed to Maitreya and delivered by Asaṅga, sum things up nicely:

1   There is the construction of the nonexistent
       In that there is no duality.
       There is emptiness there.
       It exists in that very thing.

2   Thus all things are taught to be
       Neither empty nor non-empty
       Because of existence, nonexistence and existence.
       This is the middle path.

External objects are nonexistent. But their conceptual construction by the mind is real. That construction, being itself purely mental, is not dual: it does not resolve into subject and object simply because there is nothing to be found on the object side—there is only the conceptual activity of the subject, which is mistaken for an independent object. Now, whereas for the Madhyamaka we saw that emptiness is a purely negative phenomenon, emptiness appears more posi-tively on this view: "There is emptiness there." The emptiness in question is the absence of subject-object duality, not the lack of essence or inherent existence. That, to be sure, is negative—it is, after all, an absence—but it is not a *pure* negation. It is an absence of *something* (like Pierre's absence from the café), but it is not an absence of essence, and in fact this emptiness turns out to be an essential characteristic of things. So while the mādhyamika's emptiness is itself empty, and leaves things benefit of nature, even the nature of being empty, the Yogācārin's emptiness is precisely the nature of things.

So we find in the second verse that things are *not* empty of *all* essence, though they *are* empty of subject-object duality, precisely because of the actual existence of conceptual construction, the complete nonexistence of that which is constructed (the external world) and the existence of the emptiness of subject-object duality as the nature of these phenomena. Instead of Nāgārjuna's middle path, regarding emptiness and dependent arising as identical, and emptiness as empty as everything else, we have a middle path regarding emptiness as ultimately real, and the dependently arisen as absolutely nonexistent, its nonexistence—not its dependent existence—being precisely the ultimate reality.

Just as Madhyamaka philosophers adopt a rhetoric of ineffability regarding the ultimate, Yogācāra philosophers argue that ultimate reality as they conceive it is ineffable. In order to explore that claim and its connection to their account of emptiness, I would like to take a tour through Sthiramati's commentary to the last ten verses of Vasubandhu's *Trimsikākārikā, Trimsikābhāsya*. We will occasionally turn as well to Vinitadeva's subcommentary:

21   The other dependent nature is conceptual:
        It arises from conditions.
        The consummate is
        The eternal nonexistence of the former in that.

> Since it is unchanging it is called "the consummate." The "that" is the other-dependent, and "the former" is the imagined. With respect to the conceptual, the imagined has the nature of subject and object, and therefore with respect to it, given the absence of subject and object as it is imagined, it is imaginary. The complete, permanent and eternal separation of subject and object from the other dependent is the consummate nature.

This text explores the Three Natures and the implications of *trisvabhāva* theory for the nature of our knowledge of ultimate reality—of fully enlightened consciousness. One of the principal issues Vasubandhu and Sthiramati explore in this text and commentary is the implication of the complete nonexistence of objects of consciousness for the character of enlightened consciousness itself. Just what is objectless knowledge? And of course it turns out that such knowledge will also be inexpressible and unconceptualizable. In the commentary to (21) Sthiramati emphasizes that the consummate nature of all things—the way the world is understood when it is understood perfectly—is free from all subject-object duality, and that all objects distinct from subjectivity are purely imaginary.

22   Therefore it itself is neither
        The same as nor different from the other-dependent. (a, b)

> Since the other-dependent is without subject and object, then, you might ask, "How do you know that it exists, grasping where there is no grasping?" He therefore says,

23   Without seeing that it is not seen. (d)

> He says "without seeing that," meaning the consummate. He says, "[T]hat
> is not seen," meaning the other-dependent. "Without seeing" means nei-
> ther apprehending nor realizing the consummate nature, which is the ob-
> ject seen by transcendental wisdom.

When the other-dependent nature is seen, we are seeing our experience of
external objects as dependent upon the mind and mental processes. The other-
dependent is Janus-faced: when seen from the standpoint of delusion, these subjective episodes are seen as external objects and as objectified mind—as objects
for a perceiving or apperceiving subject. When seen from the standpoint of enlightenment, on the other hand ... And here is where the problem begins. For
since there is nothing for the mind to grasp in the consummate, the question
arises, What kind of cognitive state is this? And why call it knowledge in the first
place? Sthiramati first explains that the other-dependent nature is not really understood at all until one has apprehended the consummate. But then, since the
apprehension of the consummate is nonconceptual and since the understanding
of the other-dependent must be conceptual, how is this supposed to work? Sthiramati answers:

> In the subsequent pure knowledge, since it is within both the spheres of
> mundane and transcendental knowledge, another consciousness appre-
> hends the other dependent. Therefore, without seeing the consummate, the
> other-dependent is not seen; the non-seen is not seen by the wisdom sub-
> sequent to the transcendental wisdom.

So here is the story: the initial apprehension of the consummate, wholly within
the sphere of transcendental knowledge, is objectless, nonconceptual, uncharacterizable, ineffable. But it is also not knowledge of the other-dependent per se
and so cannot by itself be efficacious in ordinary life. On leaving meditative
equipoise, however, the "subsequent pure knowledge" arises. This is a conceptual
cognitive state, which takes as its object not the consummate nature but the
transcendental awareness of the consummate achieved in meditation. The knowledge this apprehension enables allows one to see the dependent nature—and
hence the totality of dependently arisen phenomena—for what it is: an illusion,
a dream, a mirage. But all of this is an enlightened apprehension of the conventional world, and not an apprehension of the ultimate. It is hence within the
sphere of conception and thought. Sthiramati expresses it this way:

> As the *Avikalpapravesadharāni* says, "through that subsequent wisdom all
> things are seen as illusions, mirages, dreams, spectres, echoes and moons
> in the water and apparitions." (337) Here, things denotes all things having
> the dependent nature. Now he talks about the consummate: It is wisdom

always of one taste. As it says, "Through this nonconceptual wisdom, all things are seen as the vault of the sky." Through the dependent nature, the bare quiddity of things is seen.

26   As long as the understanding
          Is not grounded in mind only (ab)

"As long as the understanding is not grounded" means for as long as the appearance of subject and object is there; "in mind only" means in the nature of mind. The two graspings are the grasping of subject and the grasping of object . . .

By the words "not eliminated" he means this: For as long as the yogi's mind does not come to be grounded in the nondual characteristic of mind only, the two graspings will not be eliminated. Hence, having taught that if the external appearance is not eliminated, the internal one is not eliminated either, one might think, "I grasp form, etc through my eyes, etc." There one is an answer to this: When there is the appearance of objectless mind only, is that what it is to be grounded in the nature of mind? No way!

Sthiramati emphasizes here the sharp distinction between the nondual transcendental awareness of emptiness—of the fact that only mind is real—and any awareness of subjects and objects, including any conceptual awareness of ultimate reality. If objectless mind appears as an object of awareness, he argues, we do not have a real awareness of ultimate reality, precisely because there is an object of such an awareness. Vasubandhu develops this in the next verse, on which Vinitadeva offers a perceptive gloss:

27   Even the thought "All this is appearance only"
          Involves an object.
          And anything that places something in front of it
          Is not grounded in this-only.

That is not how it is to be grounded in the nature of mind. The reason is: Whoever thinks, "This is the pure representation-only," since that appearance has arisen, there is thereby an object in front of him. As long as there is something in front of him his is not grounded in mind only. Thus, only through the elimination of all other objects will mind only itself become apparent. . . . (Vinitadeva, *Triṃsikatīkā* 117c–e)

Any conceptual content, any object of awareness indicates a cognitive state directed in the first instance on the conventional, and at best—if it is causally connected to and directed subsequently on a transcendental awareness—indirectly on the ultimate. Sthiramati continues:

For instance, if some conceited fellow, just by hearing would think, "I am grounded in pure appearance only," in order to eliminate that grasping, it says "Even the thought, 'All this is appearance only' involves an object," etc. The word "object" is used to indicate that though he says he is without an external object there is grasping and labelling.

The grasping and labeling is precisely grasping on to the content "all this is appearance only," to *all this*, and to the concept *appearance only*. And the medium through which these are grasped by the mind is conceptual and hence, for Vasubandhu and Sthiramati, adequate only to the conventional, and in the end, entirely deceptive.

28   When no object is apprehended
        By consciousness,
        Then grounded in appearance-only
        With no object there is no grasping subject.

Consciousness directed on the ultimate, by contrast, has no object and involves no apperceptive subjective consciousness, no conceptual content or medium, and hence nothing expressible.

When consciousness does not objectify these as external to mind; doesn't see them; doesn't grasp them; doesn't posit them, then it perfectly sees the pure meaning. At that time, no longer like a blind person, having eliminated the grasping of consciousness, it is grounded in the nature of mind itself. This is because "With no object there is no grasping subject." Where there is an object, there is a grasper. Where there is no object, there is none. Where there is no object, there is a subjectless realisation, not just an objectless one. So, conceiving of neither the constructed object nor the constructor of the object, the equanimous transcendental wisdom is attained. The remnants of subject and object are eliminated and the mind becomes grounded in its own nature. When the mind is grounded in mind only itself, what is it like?

29   Then with no mind and no object
        With supramundane knowledge,
        It is transformation of the basis,
        And the end of the two adversities.

This verse is taken, of course, by Sthiramati, to be an answer to the question we have all been dying to ask, "What is it like?" Well, what *is* it like? Neither Vasubandhu nor Sthiramati, nor Vinitadeva can say. And the reason, of course, is that at this point we have transcended the realm of expression. But, as we shall see, while these Yogācāra philosophers, like their Madhyamaka interlocutors, distinguish an inexpressible ultimate from a characterizable conventional, the ultimate so characterized is different, the apprehension is of a different epistemic order, and the explanation of silence differs as well.

The Limits of Thought and Language in Yogācāra

It is now time to draw together the threads spun by the text we have been examining, to present a more direct account of the limits of thought and language as presented in Yogācāra. Our ordinary language and our conceptual thought are shot through with subject-object dualism and commitment to the reality of external objects. Even though, as Berkeley was to put it a millennium later, all we ever perceive are our perceptions, we cannot help, as Hume was then to point out, but to take these perceptions as external objects. Our language presupposes external referents and properties. Without them, our words have no meaning, and it is impossible to assert anything about anything.

Sadly, however, these innate and conventional commitments to an external reality and even to a phenomenal mind are entirely false. There are no such things in the world, and to one perceiving the world as it is, these things do not appear. Hence thought and language, however adequate they may be to the world of illusion—the imaginatively constructed world—are entirely inadequate to anything true.

But it is possible to know the world as it is, and to attain that knowledge through reasoning supplemented by special meditative awareness. That, after all, is the entire point of Yogācāra practice and the subject matter of the text whose end we have just been examining. The meditative awareness in question is of a very special kind. It is a transcendental awareness free from all subject-object duality, and is directed upon an ultimate reality free from any such duality. It is hence nonconceptualizable and inexpressible and unattainable through ordinary cognitive processes. These states of awareness enter the ordinary epistemic domain only through their causal impact on subsequent, more ordinary states that then take the transcendental states as their objects, transforming the way we experience the ordinary world, by infusing that ordinary experience with an understanding that all we experience is illusory.

The limits of language and thought are thus defined in this system by the boundaries between appearance and reality. Language is adequate only to appearance—and hence only to what is entirely false and illusory. Reality is inexpressible, beyond conception, and accessible only through nonconceptual, nondual trance states.

Madhyamaka versus Yogācāra

With respect to the two truths, Yogācāra differs from Madhyamaka in at least three respects important for our purposes:

1. Emptiness in the Yogācāra system we have been examining is *not* the emptiness of inherent existence but rather the emptiness of subject-

object duality, or, in other words, the fact that the dependent is empty of the imagined. As a consequence, the fact that all phenomena are ultimately empty entails very different consequences for Nāgārjuna and Candrakīrti than it does for Vasubandhu and Sthiramati. For the mādhyamika, it entails that nothing, including emptiness, lacks inherent existence and that all phenomena are on the same ontological footing. For the Yogācārins, on the other hand, it entails that all objects of consciousness are completely nonexistent and merely imaginary, while the mind itself and the absence of duality are truly existent.

2. Ultimate reality as understood by Vasubandhu and Sthiramati is *not* purely negative: it is a positive entity characterized as mind-only. Emptiness is hence not, as it is in Madhyamaka, a pure negation of inherent existence and an affirmation of interdependence, but involves a positive characterization of an alternative mode of inherent existence, albeit an inexpressible one.

3. As a consequence, whereas for Nāgārjuna the Two Truths are in the end identical, characterizing the same reality from distinct perspectives, and emptiness ends up affirming conventional reality as conventional, for Vasubandhu ultimate reality and conventional reality are not in any sense identical (though they share an ontological basis in the dependent and though the perception of ultimate reality does alter one's subsequent perception of the conventional). Conventional reality is entirely nonexistent; ultimate reality truly exists; conventional reality is always dualistic; ultimate reality is free from dualism. When one sees conventional reality, one does not see ultimate reality; when one sees ultimate reality, one does not see conventional reality at all.

So, whereas for Nāgārjuna and his followers, the limits of language and thought are reached because of the inability to express a convention-independent perspective on *the ordinary world*, for Yogācāra, the limits are reached because of the existence of *another* world, *toto genere* different from the conventional world, a world whose character defies expressibility. For Nāgārjuna ultimate reality is an ineffable characteristic of conventional reality, but a character that is nonetheless apprehensible as one apprehends conventional reality; for Sthiramati and Vasubandhu, perceiving ultimate reality precludes seeing conventional reality. For Nāgārjuna we can express genuine truths through language and can understand reality conceptually. For Vasubandhu neither is possible.

Madhyamaka hence provides a non-mystical, immanent characterization of the nature of reality, of the limits of thought and language, and of the nature of our knowledge of Two *Truths* about *one reality*. Yogācāra epistemology and metaphysics, on the other hand, require for genuine knowledge, for access to truth, a mystical intuition of a transcendent realm, and not only a special kind of awareness, but a special kind of nonobjective object of knowledge. It hence implicates a strong ontological version of an appearance/reality distinction. Madhyamaka silence reflects the impossibility of expressing the truth about the conventional world. Yogācāra silence reflects the intuition that there is none.

> When the Bodhisattvas had all given their explanations, they all addressed the crown prince Mañjusrī: "Mañjusrī, what is the Bodhisattva's entrance into nonduality?"

> Mañjusrī replied, "Good sirs, you have all spoken well. Nevertheless, all your explanations are themselves dualistic. To know no one teaching, to express nothing, to say nothing, to explain nothing, to announce nothing, to indicate nothing, and to designate nothing—that is the entrance into nonduality."

> Then the crown prince Mañjusrōi said to the Liccavi Vimalakīrti, "We have given our teachings, noble sir. Now may you elucidate the teaching of the entrance into the principle of nonduality!"

> Thereupon the Liccavi Vimalakīrti kept his silence, saying nothing at all.

> The crown prince Mañjusrī applauded the Liccavi Vimalakīrti: "Excellent, noble sir! This is indeed the entrance into the nonduality of the Bodhisattvas. Here there is no use for syllables, sounds and ideas." (trans. R. Thurman 1984, pp. 76–77)

PART III

Ethics and Hermeneutics

10

Human Rights and Compassion

Toward a Unified Moral Framework

A compassionate mind, nondualistic awareness and
The aspiration for enlightenment are the causes of the
    Bodhisattvas.

However, chief among all of these is compassion.
Like nurturing a seed with water, in time
It ripens the causes of the victors.
So I praise compassion above all else.

          (Candrakīrti, Madhyamakāvatāra, 1: 1cd, 2)

HIS HOLINESS THE DALAI LAMA has been a tireless advocate for human rights in a global context. Some leaders and moral theorists of non-Western cultures—and some contemporary Western moral and political theorists—have argued that the assertion of fundamental human rights is merely an accidental feature of the moral outlook of modern Western moral and political theory. The extension or imposition of this moral framework and its demands on non-Western cultures, they argue, is an instance of cultural imperialism and hegemony, incompatible with and disruptive of those cultures. Some in the West have even argued that this framework has outlived its usefulness even in Western cultures and that the overcoming of modernism should include the abandonment of a moral and political discourse grounded in rights. His Holiness has consistently rejected this view and has urged in his public statements and in his writings on morality and politics that the demand for the recognition of human rights is indeed universal in scope, and that to the extent that a culture deprives its citizenry of fundamental human rights, that culture is morally deficient. It follows from such a view that to demand of a society that it respect some fundamental set of such rights is not an instance of illegitimate cultural imperialism but one of mandatory moral criticism, even if it is not so experienced by those to whom such an effort is directed at the time.

On the other hand, His Holiness, grounded in and advancing with considerable eloquence the tradition of Buddhist moral theory rooted in the teachings of the

Buddha, as transmitted through texts such as Āryadeva's *Catuḥśataka* and Śān-tideva's *Bodhicaryāvatāra*, has been a consistent exponent of the view that moral life is grounded in the cultivation and exercise of compassion. He has urged in many public religious teachings, addresses, and numerous writings that the most important moral quality to cultivate is compassion, and that compassion, skill in its exercise, and insight into the nature of reality are jointly necessary and sufficient for human moral perfection.[1] This view, is of course, not original with His Holiness. It is the essence of Buddhist moral theory. On the other hand, His Holiness is certainly the most eloquent exponent and advocate of this moral position of our time, and his application of this moral vision to public life and to international relations is highly original and of the first importance, justly recognized by the the Nobel Peace Prize, which was awarded to him in 1989. For instance, in one recent discussion His Holiness writes:

> To me it is clear that a genuine sense of responsibility can result only if we develop compassion. Only a spontaneous feeling of empathy for others can really motivate us to act on their behalf.

> . . .

> [D]emocracy is [the system] which is closest to humanity's essential nature. Hence those of us who enjoy it must continue to fight for all people's right to do so. . . . [W]e must respect the right of all peoples and nations to maintain their own distinctive characters and values. (1992, pp. 6–7)

Now at first glance, there is nothing surprising about this pair of commitments—that to the universality of human rights and that to the cultivation and exercise of compassion as the foundation of morality. Both seem laudable. Both seem to be prima facie noble moral commitments. But a second look may raise deep and difficult questions. A number of influential moral theorists[2] have recently argued persuasively that moral theories grounded in rights (to which I will henceforth refer as *liberal* theories) and moral theories grounded in compassion are fundamentally incompatible with one another. Moreover, they have argued that liberal theories are critically deficient—that they fail to account for, and to provide guidance in, our morally most important circumstances—matters of interpersonal relations where sentiments, attitudes, and behaviors are of moral significance, but where questions concerning the rights and duties of those involved are at best beside the point. If these critics of liberal moral theory are correct, focusing on rights and duties impoverishes our moral discourse and distorts our moral vision and is to be abandoned in favor of a morality grounded exclusively in compassion and attention to interpersonal relations.

Importantly, responses to this view have typically defended liberal theories against compassion theories, arguing that the former are indeed adequate to the full range of moral questions, and that compassion theories, to the extent that they are accurate, are no more than restatements of liberal theories.[3] The significance of this response is not its degree of success, but its concession to the compassion-theorist of the most important point, that rights and compassion are in tension with one another. And if that point, on which the parties to this debate concur, is correct, then His Holiness's advocacy of *both* of these approaches to morality would turn out to be incoherent. On the other hand, if his moral vision is, as I will argue, both coherent and compelling; the argument will require some clarification of the precise relation between compassion and rights.

In this essay in honor of His Holiness and his ceaseless campaign to keep morality and its demands at the center of public discourse, I will first explore the prima facie tension between liberal and compassion-based approaches to morality. I will then argue that these approaches are in fact *not* incompatible, but that fusing them into a coherent whole requires a particular ordering: compassion must be taken as fundamental. Rights can be coherently formulated and advanced in the context of a moral vision incorporating compassion only if they are grounded in compassion. It is when we attempt to subordinate compassion to rights and duties, or to give these considerations equal status that incoherence looms. This essay hence defends the fundamental Buddhist insight that compassion is the foundation of moral life as well as the liberal vision of human rights as universal and hence defends His Holiness's moral teaching against both liberal and compassionate critics.

WHAT WE WANT FROM RIGHTS

In coming to an understanding of just what rights are, it is instructive to first ask what work they do, question that is best answered by noting when they are asserted. That, of course, is when they are violated or threatened with violation. When individuals or groups are threatened with abuse or actually abused, rights are asserted—when people are hurt physically, deprived of opportunities for expression of views, opportunities to practice religion, to move about, and so on. . . . We then speak of a right being violated. Rights can be hence seen as fundamentally *protective*. They protect individuals against interference. Rights such as this can be called "negative rights." The right to life is such a right. It is a right *not to be killed*. Fundamental rights typically have this character.[4]

To be sure, some rights have a more positive character. For instance, in many countries a child has a right to receive an education. But two kinds of considerations mitigate this observation: first, positive rights such as this require the active construction of the obligations or institutions concerned. A right to a primary education requires the establishment of an educational system and the enactment of appropriate legislation, just as one's right to the repayment of a debt by a borrower requires the occurrence of the loan and the promise to repay it.

Contrast this with the right to free exercise of religion. A nation that does not recognize such a right has not simply failed to confer it; in failing to do so, it violates a right that is more fundamental than any legislative authority. This is what makes possible the liberal moral critique of institutions, as opposed to the mere bland comparison of democracy with tyranny as two interesting alternatives for ordering society. Second, positive rights such as these are always specific to particular actions by particular individuals or institutions. Fundamental negative rights are rights against *everybody*. My child's right to an education is a right that the local school system admit him to school. The shopkeeper on the corner is irrelevant to this right. He can neither satisfy nor violate it. But my right to life is satisfied by all who do not kill me and can be violated by any assailant.[5]

We can identify three more specific functions that rights serve, which are central to defining the liberal moral outlook: they create a domain of free expression; they establish clarity regarding life expectations; they enable moral criticism. Each of these functions is complex and deserves examination.

Human flourishing—both at the individual and at the social level—requires the freedom of expression must be realized in a number of ways. For an individual to experience him or herself as creative, as responsible, as a being whose views matter, who is taken seriously, who can interact spontaneously and genuinely with those with whom he or she lives, it is essential that he or she be able to express his or her views without fear of persecution. Moreover, for a human society to flourish, it is essential that as many voices be heard as possible, and that no views be suppressed. The suppression of free speech harms not only the individual whose voice is silenced but also the community deprived of what might have been the correct view of a crucial matter, or the beauty of a work of art never created. And of course a society of individuals who fear to express their views is miserable. Social and individual flourishing hence require enforcement of the right to free speech.

But of course not all speech is protected absolutely. Speech may be slanderous. Speech may be used to menace or to deceive. So it becomes important to demarcate the domain of speech to be protected. This is notoriously difficult and almost certainly cannot be accomplished explicitly by any clear set of general principles. But, given the general motivations just sketched for the protection of speech, there are central cases of speech that merits protection: speech critical for individual self-development, such as that related to scholarship, art, or the development of bonds of friendship of family is clearly to be so protected. Moreover, speech related to the political process, to debates regarding social policy, and to the pursuit of religious practice is also to be protected. In short, for those domains central to individual and collective flourishing, to contribute to those goals, there must be domains in which one can advance views free of the fear of censorship. This is the definition of the freedom of speech.

But rights protect not only discourse and discursive practices such as the creation of art and the practice of religion. They also allow us to organize our lives rationally, and to plan our lives with the confidence that our plans have some chance of success. That is, rights ensure a relative clarity of expectations. That others will respect our rights to property, for instance, allows us to plan to use that property. That others will respect our right to move freely allows us to plan travel, and to plan a career or course of action that will involve travel. And it is of course the recognition of these rights and their instantiation in a set of institutions enforcing them that allows this confidence necessary for rationally lived lives, free from the terror of the unexpected crushing of legitimate expectations.

Rights have yet another central role in our moral lives. They enable moral criticism.[6] Among our most ethically significant activities is our criticism of ourselves, our fellows, and of alien practices. The role of rights is most central in the latter case, in that we often encounter practices that we find morally abhorrent and wish to condemn and even to extirpate. And we often find that those engaged in those practices not only show reluctance to abandon them but defend them as morally acceptable. And to make matters more disturbing, the participants in these practices may urge that our condemnation represents an illicit—even culturally imperialist—universalization of the parochial moral prejudices of our own culture to their very different context. They argue that just as they do not interfere with our moral practices, we should leave their very different culture intact and mind our own business.

A case in point is the rejoinder of the government of the People's Republic of China against pressure from Western governments and from nongovernment human rights advocacy groups, as well as the statements made by representatives of this government at the 1994 Conference on Human Rights in Asia. In these statements this government asserted that such putative fundamental rights free speech, freedom of emigration, freedom to practice religion, and indeed the entire framework of individual human rights are artifacts of Western liberalism, and that any attempt to impose respect for such a set of rights on Asian cultures is simply a new version of imperialism.

Now, leaving aside how the debate between the Chinese leadership and its critics *ought to* turn out, let us notice what the liberal discourse of rights accomplishes for its exponents in this debate: To put the matter simply, it makes the criticism of these practices possible in the first place. For absent the liberal framework, the most that we can do is notice that the Chinese government adopts different practices from our own, and comment that we, given our preferences, would prefer to live under our system than under theirs, and perhaps even that so would many of the Chinese and colonial subjects of that government. But that fact does not allow us, as outsiders, to intervene in that system, or even, with any justification, to *criticize* it in a way that its practicioners should take seriously any more than our noting *culinary* differences between us and the Chinese, any more than our preference for *our* food would justify *criticism* of Chinese gastronomy. For they can respond to us in a parallel fashion: they could note that we liberals have a different system. They could remark that they, the Chinese, would prefer not to live in it, and prefer their own. However, they could remark, they acknowledge that they have no grounds on which to *criticize* our system, and ask that just as they refrain from doing so, we do likewise with respect to them. What makes moral criticism possible for the liberal is that the discourse of rights presents itself as a *universal* discourse in an important sense. It makes claims that transcend cultural difference. The rights posited are not *American* rights, *Tibetan* rights, or *Buddhist* rights, *Western* rights, or *men's* rights, and so on. They are precisely *human rights,* which are self-evidently possessed by any person. A social structure that abrogates them is not, on this view, simply different from our own in that respect: it is morally wrong in that respect.[7] And to the extent that we can make the liberal framework precise—and that turns out to be a very great extent[8]—we can specify precise ways in which such a system in wrong and in which it must reform or be reformed.

Rights, Duties, and Privacy

Rights entail duties on the part of others. Where I have a right to something, you have a duty to respect that right. Moreover, duties toward specific persons entail rights on the part of those to whom duties accrue. If you—say as a consequence of a loan—have a duty to pay me a sum of money, I have a right that you do so. If I have a right to practice my religion, you have a duty not to interfere with that practice. Since, as we have noted, rights divide into positive and negative rights, duties similarly divide into positive and negative duties. Negative rights and duties are those liberals regard as universal. And all of the fundamental rights I have noted are of this character. Positive rights are accorded by particular kinds of institutions, such as government structures, laws, employment contracts, or voluntary agreements or associations. These last may be more conventional, less universal, and as such are generally justified on pragmatic grounds or on grounds of mutual agreement, rather than on universal moral grounds.

The important consequence of this mutual entailment between rights and duties for present purposes is that any moral theory that takes rights as foundational ipso facto takes duties as foundational. To the extent that our collective moral landscape is defined by our human rights, it is equally well defined by our duties. While this may seem like a trivial restatement, it raises a problem: I will argue below that compassion has as a defining characteristic an intention and aspiration to benefit even those to whom we have no particular duties, and who have no particular rights against us. We act compassionately, I will argue, precisely when we act not from duty, and precisely when we do not simply respect the rights of others, but when we positively benefit or refrain from harming where there are no rights and duties. Moreover, as I will show, compassion governs our interactions in a private sphere where talk about rights would seem bizarre, for example, relations between parents and children.[9] To the extent that we define the moral landscape by rights and duties, we appear not to define it through compassion.[10] Liberalism and Buddhism are apparently at odds.

We can sharpen this point by attending to the deep connection between the liberal conception of the private/public distinction and the liberal discourse of rights and duties, and the consequent centrality of this distinction and of the demarcation of a specifically private sphere to liberal moral theory. This point is conceptual but can be usefully illuminated through attention to the history of liberal theory. Modern liberal moral theory has its origins in the work of the Western philosophers Locke and Kant (as well as Hobbes and Rousseau). Each was concerned in his own way to defend the rights of individuals against hegemonic powers that militated against individual liberty—in the case of Locke, the British Crown that threatened the development of constitutional democracy and mercantile capitalism, and in the case of Kant ecclesiastical authority that threatened academic freedom and the development of science. Each saw it necessary to demarcate that sphere of life in which one's liberty is properly limited by legitimate public authority from that in which one is properly is regarded as autonomous, and so to demarcate a private sphere. For Kant the most important domain to protect as private is that of thought, and as such he is properly seen as the earliest forceful exponent of a fundamental right to freedom of thought and expression.[11] But for Locke, his philosophical predecessor, the original private domain is the home, and the most important right to privacy is the right to property, and to the noninterference with one's use of one's property and conduct in one's home.[12]

Both strains of privacy theory are influential in the contemporary world's most influential articulation of liberal moral and political theory, the Constitution of the United States of America. The constitutional protection of the right to privacy has been forcefully articulated in a series of interpretively important decisions in the past century according to which the boundaries of the private sphere are demarcated by rights against self-incrimination, against the intrusion of the state into one's home and documents, against religious coercion, against the abridgment of speech, and so on . . . , and against the dictation of one's decisions regarding one's family size and structure.[13] These have been summed up by one U.S. Supreme Court justice in the famous epigram, "The most important right is the right to be let alone."[14]

This epigram in a certain sense simply sums up liberal moral theory. Liberalism is predicated on the demarcation of a private sphere in which one is free to articulate one's ideology, daily life, and vision of the good as one sees fit. What one does there may be the subject of comment by others, but not of moral criticism. One's duties concern what one does in the public sphere. Restrictions of one's prerogatives in the private sphere are always prima facie violations of rights.[15] I may be obligated to pay my taxes (a public matter), but I cannot be required to give money to my temple (a private matter); and if I do so, it is not out of any duty (unless I have established one through a promise). Failing to come to work on time is a breach of duty to my employer (a public matter), but failing to go to bed at a reasonable hour is a private matter—perhaps stupid, but nobody's business but my own. Or so liberal theory would have it. Liberal theory, in sum, adumbrates the goods for us earlier—security of thought and conscience, security in planning our lives, access to the good ideas and beautiful works of others, and a platform for moral criticism—simply by restricting the zone of such criticism to the public and establishing the sanctity of the private.[16]

Now to a certain degree, I have overstated my case. For liberal moral theory does not in fact ignore moral phenomena other than rights completely, and indeed the most prominent liberal moral theorists often have a great deal to say about character and about virtue. To do justice to all of the nuances of the liberal tradition would take us far beyond the scope of this discussion. For now, these few remarks will have to suffice to emphasize the contrast to which I wish to draw attention: first, while liberal *moral* theory is indeed richer than one might believe were one to focus solely on its discussion of rights, liberal *political* theory is very much concerned to articulate a framework of rights as an exclusive characterization of the moral structure of the public sphere. (Indeed, the separation of the moral from the political is another respect in which liberalism diverges from compassion-based moral theory.) Second, even within the moral domain, there is a preoccupation in liberal theory with an articulation of rights which often obscures other moral concerns, and a preoccupation within liberal theory generally with the articulation of the political dimension of our moral lives to the detriment of attention to the private sphere, a preoccupation explained by the demarcation of that sphere within liberalism in the first place. Third, even when liberal moral theory *does* turn its attention to matters of character and virtue, the account of these phenomena is often grounded in a primary account of rights and duties.[17]

THE LIMITS OF RIGHTS IN MORAL DISCOURSE

We are now in more of a position to see what is problematic about liberal theory if we want compassion to have an important place in our moral life. When rights are taken to be fundamental, too much emerges as morally permissible. Since, for instance, a person with whom I have no particular contractual arrangement has no right to my generosity, I am in no way obligated to be generous. Since no one has a claim on my concern, I need not be concerned for anyone else.

Compassion is, hence, on this view, strictly optional—one of the many permissible ways to address the world.[18]

This highlights the most important limitation of liberal moral discourse: it is in an important sense silent about character. Since a person's character—his or her fundamental values and set of virtues, vices, dispositions, and attitudes—is a private matter, and the first principal of liberal moral theory is to protect individual liberty in the private sphere, liberal theory can in no way by itself recommend or condemn any particular qualities of character.[19] To the extent that we find character to be a morally significant phenomenon, this is deeply problematic. In particular, to the extent that the cultivation of compassion is of genuine moral significance—and for any Buddhist moral theorist it must be—then liberalism is at least deficient in its neglect of this attribute and at worst wrong-headed in characterizing it as optional.[20]

But yet another difficulty afflicts the foundation of liberal theory, one that is indeed acknowledged by the social contract tradition, but that is never satisfactorily resolved: the general duty to respect the rights of others requires a justification. Or, to look at the other side of the coin, the claim that persons have natural rights at all must be justified, antecedent to the task that often occupies most of a liberal's attention, that of specifying exactly what our rights and duties are. And of course one cannot simply appeal to a right to have one's rights respected, or a duty to do one's duty, on pain of infinite regress.

The social contract tradition adopts one of two strategies: theorists in this tradition sometimes argue that the sanction of the rights and duties we recognize lies in an explicit or implicit original agreement to which we are all either tacit parties or heirs.[21] Aside from the odd historical problems this raises, and the problems with the status of implicit or inherited contracts, there is a stunning logical problem with this kind of reasoning. For the original agreement to be in any sense binding, there must already be duties to keep one's word and to be bound by agreements presupposed, and correlatively rights that others abide by their agreements. The regress just adumbrated is merely ignored by talk of social contracts as binding.

The second strategy is to argue that it is in each of our self-interests to abide by the hypothesized or hypostasized right-establishing contract—that the alternative is a social disintegration that benefits none of us. There are at least two problems with this form of reasoning, though: first, for most of us most of the time, it is simply false. It is often, in fact, in terms of the kind of narrow self-interest to which morality is supposed to be a countervailing force, precisely in our self-interest to shirk our duties, and to violate the rights of others. This is not surprising. It is one of the reasons for the prevalence of evil. But more deeply, even were this true, it would be the *wrong kind* of justification for a structure of rights and duties. For it would then be the case that our having rights and duties would be contingent upon the supposed fact that it is in others' and our own self-interest to respect them. And again, the very point of rights and duties is to *restrain* action that, while justified from the standpoint of narrow self-interest, is morally wrong. Such restraint clearly demands independent justification.

Now of course the demonstration of the inadequacy of *these* routes to the justification of liberalism as a foundation for morality does not show that *no* route will succeed. But if some route is to succeed, it will require a lot of argument to show how. And it does appear that the reasons for the failure to provide a truly adequate foundation for liberalism are principled. Valuable as rights are, they are not self-justifying, and broad as their scope is, it is not broad enough to encompass all that is morally significant. It is therefore appropriate to look for a broader foundation for our moral life, and to hope that such a foundation will allow us to preserve what goods rights promise, while giving us moral guidance in those areas where rights fail us. It is with such hopes in mind that I turn to an examination of compassion.

Why Is Compassion Morally Significant?

The first thing to notice about a discourse grounded in compassion is that it allows us to address moral life in what the liberal regards as the private domain.[22] That is, we can assess relations between parents and children; between spouses; between friends and siblings with regard to whether the interactions in question are compassionate or not, and with regard to whether they are of a kind conducive to the cultivation and encouragement of compassion. This is important not only because so much of moral life focuses on precisely these domains, and because liberalism is so problematically silent about these domains, but also because our moral sensibilities, even though they are often played out on a more public stage, are cultivated in these domains. The importance of attending to the nature of our "private" affairs hence transcends the already great moment of those affairs themselves in our lives.[23]

Moreover, regarding our moral life in this way allows us to talk about a broad range of our choices regarding morally significant behavior about which liberalism is silent simply because of its focus on rights and duties. So my choice to give or not to give to a beggar or to a temple, or my choice to treat my fellows with patience or courtesy become matters—as they ought to be—of moral evaluation. In short, speaking in terms of compassion significantly broadens the sphere of morality to encompass more of what we pretheoretically place in that domain, and more of what is recognizably foundational even to issues that liberalism locates at center stage.[24]

In addition, we can make greater sense of moral development from the standpoint of compassion than we can from the standpoint of liberalism. There is a certain mystery about moral development as seen by the liberal: how do we come to be good persons? Since for the liberal to be a good person is for him or her to respect rights and discharge duties, moral education would seem to require and to comprise exactly education regarding duties and rights and training in discharging and respecting them. But if we actually examine what kind of upbringing in fact leads to the development of morally admirable persons, it just does not conform to this pattern. Loving families, close relationships, and exposure to kindness seem as a matter of fact to be the necessary conditions for satisfactory moral development. This makes little sense if moral development is *liberal* moral development but makes perfect sense if to develop morally is to develop compassion. For children learn modes of interaction and attitudes to which they are exposed in childhood. Those brought up compassionately learn to be compassionate. And it is these children who grow to moral maturity by any standards. They are precisely the individuals who respect the rights of others and who discharge their duties. Grounding that moral maturity in their compassion makes moral development comprehensible.

Grounding moral theory in compassion has an interesting consequence: the public/private distinction so fundamental to liberal moral theory vanishes. That divide is, as I discussed earlier, that between what is of moral concern—one's public life—and what is a matter of personal taste—one's attitudes and values. Liberalism constructs that divide because of its essential concern with the right to privacy as the fundamental moral good to be protected. But when we take compassion as the primary object of moral concern, there is no basis for the primacy of such a divide. The concerns of morality are, from this standpoint, both broad and uniform. The same questions can be asked about my behavior in my home that can be asked about my behavior in the street. The same standards of evaluation apply to my business and political relations that apply to my fundamental values or religious commitments.[25] This represents a very different view of the moral landscape. Again, we must ask just how this view can be reconciled with the view embodied in liberalism. They cannot simply be joined. Moral life cannot be both heterogeneous and homogenous. And yet, there is something, as we have seen, of great value and truth in both.

Before reconciling these divergent perspectives, I will note another way in which compassion and liberalism differ as perspectives on ethics: moral criticism must be seen differently. When a liberal criticizes a social practice or institution on moral grounds, she or he argues that it violates of certain fundamental human rights. When one criticizes a social practice or institution from the standpoint of compassion, on the other hand, the grounds of such criticism are equally universalist, but somewhat different and more straightforward: institutions and practices are not deemed wrong because they violate some right (though, as we shall see, this might often be the case, and might often be derivative grounds for such criticism) but rather simply because they are harm people; because they are not expressive of individual or collective compassion, and because they do not foster it among the citizens exposed to those institutions.[26] From the standpoint of liberal moral theory, this is an inadequate basis for *moral* criticism, simply because the individuals harmed or denied benefits may have no particular *rights* against those harms or to those benefits. But from the standpoint of compassion, that is irrelevant to the question of the immorality of such institutions.[27]

RIGHTS WITHIN COMPASSION

Having scouted the principal differences in outlook between liberalism and compassion-based moral theory, I now return to the central problem this chapter aims to resolve: given that these two approaches to moral theory—which at first glance appear so harmonious—turn out upon inspection to be very much in tension with one another, is it possible to join them in any way? That is, is the recurrent plea of His Holiness the Dalai Lama on behalf of both human rights and compassion coherent? If so, how?

Given our accounts of these two frameworks, it should be apparent that if liberalism is taken as foundational, this task is hopeless. For central to liberalism is the protection of the private, and central to that protection is the protection of individuals from obligations to undertake any particular attitudes or visions of the good life. And compassion is nothing if not a very particular moral attitude, and an embodiment of a very particular vision of the good life. Liberalism essentially makes compassion optional.[28]

But what happens if we adopt compassion as the foundation of our moral outlook and try to reconstruct what we can of a liberal account of rights and duties upon that foundation? There is more hope in this direction. Moreover, not only can we construct a unified moral framework in such a way, but also some of the outstanding problems concerning rights insoluble within the framework of liberalism admit of solution within the framework provided by compassion. In particular, the problem of the sanction of rights and duties will turn out to have a straightforward resolution.

To begin from compassion is to begin by taking the good of others as one's own motive for action.[29] This happens quite naturally within the family and the circle of one's intimate friends and associates, when those relationships are healthy and intact. Hume remarks: " '[T] rare to meet with one, in whom all the kind affections, taken together, do not over-balance all the selfish . . . [T]here are few that do not bestow the largest part of their fortunes on the pleasure of their wives, and the education of their children, reserving the smallest portion for their own proper use and entertainment" (1978, p. 487).

But compassion, like the gravitational force to which in local social life it is so analogous, obeys something like an inverse square law and so will end up being counterproductive on a large scale: the related to us a person or other less sentient being is, the less natural compassion we feel for his or her suffering, and the easier it is to be indifferent or even hostile. Were this phenomenon to persist unchecked in human affairs, the sentient universe would, as a consequence of the operation of this essentially local force, come to resemble the physical universe, shaped as it is by the essentially local force of gravitation: we would find ourselves living in small, internally tightly bound but mutually hostile bands, each one of us bound to our immediate fellows, and intensely loyal to members of our clans at the expense of the interests of others, like tiny planets floating in sterile isolation in the frigid vastness of space:

> But tho' this generosity must be acknowledg'd to the honour of human nature, we may at the same time remark that so noble an affection, instead of fitting men for large societies, is almost as contrary to them, as the most narrow selfishness. For while each person loves himself better than any other single person, and in his love to others bears the greatest affection to his relation and acquaintance, this must necessarily produce an opposition of passions, and a consequent opposition of actions . . . (ibid.)

This would of course be a profoundly unsatisfactory state of affairs. For one thing, it runs against even the narrow self-interest of all concerned. We deprive not only others of the benefits to be derived from interaction with us, but also ourselves the benefits to be derived from interactions with them. Moreover, we perpetuate an unstable and dangerous hostility that keeps us all in a state of peril. But moreover, it runs against both reason and another component of human nature—our capacity for imaginative exchange of our own situation for that of others. For reason urges that drawing distinctions in the absence of genuine difference is arbitrary, and that doing so in ways detrimental to the interests of all concerned is downright stupid.[30] And that is precisely what the narrow limitation of compassion does. For this reason compassion must be deliberately given a public, social face.

The construction of an edifice of rights can hence be seen, as Hume saw it, as a device for extending the reach of natural compassion and for securing the goods that compassion enables to all persons in a society. For, he saw, compassion is a natural endowment of the human being, present in each of us as the innate attitude toward those close to us—those for whom we care and those who care for us. Since we all require, as we have argued, the many goods that rights enable, including the ability to express ourselves, the security to plan and to conduct our lives, and the availability of a platform for moral criticism; and since we each benefit from a society in which all enjoy these goods, not only self-interest but regard for each other demands that we adopt a mechanism for enabling these goods. By a natural process of generalization, compassion extends to those in our larger family, and in our circle of friends, associates, and acquaintances. So while compassion is of the utmost moral significance, we need no moral theory or explicit social structure to ensure its operation in this intimate ambience. Human nature takes care of this (and even on an antiessentialist Buddhist view of the nature of persons, we can successfully appeal to contingent universal, and even innate facts about human psychology). But to extend it far enough to ensure necessary social goods, we need a mechanism, a human convention. Conferring rights is simply the best mechanism we have devised to this end. Hume expresses the idea this way:

> The remedy, then, is not deriv'd from nature, but from *artifice;* or more properly speaking, nature provides a remedy in the judgment and under-standing, for what is irregular and incommodious in the affections. For when men, from their early education in society, have become sensible to the infinite advantages that result from it, and have besides acquir'd a new affection to company and convention; and when they have observ'd, that the principal disturbance in society arises from the goods, which we call external, and from their looseness and easy transitions from one person to another; they must seek for a remedy by putting these goods, as far as possible, on the same footing with the fix'd and constant advantages of the mind and body. This can be done after no other manner, than by a convention enter'd into by all the members of the society to bestow sta-bility on the possession of these external goods, and leave everyone in the peaceable enjoyment of what he may acquire by his fortune and industry. (Hume 1978, p. 489)
>
> . . .
>
> After this convention . . . , there immediately arises the ideas of justice and injustice; as also those of *property, right,* and *obligation.* The latter are altogether unintelligible without understanding the former. (ibid., pp. 490–491)

Moreover, as we are all aware both as a consequence of our introspective evidence but also as a consequence of the evident ability of the media to stir the sympathy of millions for even those who are very distant physically, culturally, and circumstantially, we are endowed with an innate ability and propensity to imagine ourselves in the place of others and to be moved by their suffering and interests, even when these others are far from us on every relevant dimension of distance. We teach each other to cultivate this capacity, and it forms the basis of our ability to extend the bounds of our community of interests beyond our im-mediate circle of friends. It gives rise to sentiments of solidarity with those we recognize as like us: in its most limited form, petty nationalism or communalism (dangerous sentiments, perhaps, but better than egoism and steps on the way to something better); with greater scope, to nationalism; and finally, in those of the highest moral character, to universalism. In each case, the greater generalization is achieved by coming to see others as more like us, or like those to whom we already extend compassionate regard, and by imagining ourselves or those we already love in the circumstances of the other.[31]

But having extended the sentiment of compassion, we must then ask how to turn that sentiment into tangible goods for those to whom it is directed, as well as how to ensure that those goods are available even when imagination and instinctive human goodness fail, as they all too often do. And that is where rights come in. By extending either a basic set of general human rights to our fellow persons, or more particular rights of citizenship to those who share our vision of civic life and who participate with us in its institutions, we grant enforceable claims to the goods of life and against oppression. These provide the tools with which each individual can protect him or herself and achieve his or her own flourishing. These tools will be available even when our compassion or those of others fails and can even be used as rhetorical vehicles to reawaken that compassion.

This has been successfully demonstrated in the Indian independence movement, the American civil rights movement, the South African anti-apartheid movement, and, though sadly with less tangible success, in the Tibetan freedom movement. In each case, a double role can be discerned for rights: on the one hand rights are used as tools to fight against those who show a paucity of compassionate regard for the oppressed. They can be asserted in courts of law, in political processes, or in diplomatic channels in order to secure the goods that would ordinarily be available through fellowship. On the other hand, the very assertion of those rights makes a claim to humanity and hence a claim to compassionate regard. Mahatma Gandhi, the Rev. Dr. Martin Luther King, President Nelson Mandela, and of course His Holiness the Dalai Lama have, in strikingly similar ways, used the assertion of rights as part of a rhetorical demonstration of the humanity of those on whose behalf those rights are asserted. This demand to recognize humanity is at the same time a call to others to imagine themselves in the place of the oppressed, and so to generate compassion, and so to act on behalf of the oppressed.[32]

The important feature of such appeals for present purposes is this: in no case is it either necessary or helpful to take the rights to which appeal is made as constituting moral bedrock. To merely note that someone has a right is not to establish that that person has a claim on *me* to act. And in general, rights claims by themselves will be impotent to establish such obligations. No particular English person could have been shown to have an obligation to assist any particular Indian; no American stands under any definite obligation to liberate any particular Tibetan. What generates our sense of moral duty in such cases is the fact that we come to *care* about those in need, and that we see them as *our fellows*. And we treat our fellows in a way nicely captured by the rights we are called upon to recognize. In short, others' rights generate claims on us not because of the brute fact of rights-possession, but rather because of the brute fact that those others are seen *not* to be *other*, but rather as *our own*. And hence they have a claim on our feeling. Rights are on this account not insignificant: they have a central moral role in gaining recognition, in giving specificity to claims for action, and even as tools against those who withhold recognition. But without a foundation in the compassion that recognition facilitates, rights become pointless. And if there is an antecedent relation of compassion, rights are unnecessary. To quote Schopenhauer:

> If anyone were to ask me what he gets from giving alms, my answer in all conscience would be: "This, that the lot of that poor man is made so much the lighter; otherwise absolutely nothing. Now if this is of no use and no importance to you, then your wish was really not to give alms, but to make a purchase; and in that case you are defrauded of your money. If, however, it is a matter of importance to you that that man who is oppressed by want suffers less, then you have attained your object from the fact that he suffers less . . . (1965, p. 165, trans. E.F.J. Payne)

Neither rights nor incentives can motivate compassionate action. But compassion can certainly provide the motivation for constructing a system of rights, and for the creation of incentives to further compassionate action.

BEYOND PRIVACY

The foregoing discussion entails neither rejection of a central role of rights in moral and political discourse nor regarding them as morally fundamental. In its preservation of a role for rights, it recontextualizes them as a mode of expression of and as a call for the exercise of compassion, and as moral tools to ensure the personal and collective flourishing that is possible and valuable only in the context of compassionate interpersonal relationships and a compassionate attitude toward the world. Without such a context, a meaningful human life is not possible; meaningful accomplishments would not find their necessary conditions. And even if by some miracle these conditions were satisfied, and what would otherwise be meaningful accomplishments were achieved, they would have no larger significance absent a culture designed to enable them to benefit other beings and the world.

But we thus retain rights in a very different form than that recognized by that liberal moral theory responsible for their articulation. This is true because by taking compassion as our moral foundation we erase the fundamental divide between the public and the private spheres that grounds liberal theory and a liberal construal of rights. The reason for this is that once one regards one's character, attitudes, and relations to others as topics of moral discourse, one allows morality and moral criticism to intrude into the most intimate realm of personal life; once one subjects one's view of the good to moral evaluation, there is no sphere of thought and action protected from such scrutiny by a demarcation of a zone of privacy; and once one allows the same moral questions to be raised about one's behavior in the household and family as about one's behavior in the marketplace or in the international political arena, the very line between the public and the private domains whose demarcation is the point of liberalism and the task of rights is erased completely.

This erasure could be seen in one of two ways: negatively, it means that we open the boundaries of our private lives to intrusion to the demands of morality. We cannot say, as can the liberal, that our choice about what kind of person to be, and other such moral decisions are "nobody's business but our own."[33] On the other hand, it also means that the positive reach of morality, and its potential as a force for human development is extended from the marketplace and political arena into the family and into our most intimate deliberations.

But the erasure of this fundamental principled divide must not be seen as the rejection of the value of privacy *tout court*. For privacy is indeed a good, and, as we saw above, a good essential to many kinds of flourishing. Much of what we do in life requires the kinds of protection comprised by the general right to privacy—including freedom of speech, association, religious practice, and so forth. The security that allows us to order our lives, to develop our talents, and to express our views is a good deserving of protection, and its protection is a matter of primary concern to morality as it is articulated in public policy. But the very fact that privacy so understood, and the cluster of rights it comprises are such goods entails that they are goods that compassion leads us to grant to one another, and that a compassionate society grants to its citizens. The failure to do so would constitute a kind of cruelty. The privacy so granted, however, is different from the privacy understood by the liberal: it is a set of freedoms *to* pursue ends, *to* express views, and to develop talents. But it is not a freedom *from* moral constraint. Those ends, views, and talents are themselves understood as bound by our interrelations, and the freedom that is one aspect of privacy so understood is hence constrained by our moral bonds to one another. On this view, our mutual responsibility is fundamental, not our personal rights. Personal rights emerge only as goods we extend to one another as a consequence of our concern.[34]

Conclusion: Rights as Foundations versus Rights as Derivative

We can now sum this investigation up straightforwardly: human rights in the West have, for the past three centuries, been most frequently articulated within

a liberal moral framework. While there is a real conflict between such a framework and an outlook that grounds morality in compassion, there is nonetheless
no real conflict between seeing compassion as the fundamental moral phenomenon and recognizing and utilizing rights in moral criticism and in moral and
political discourse. The apparent conflict is resolved by grounding rights not in
the liberal theory of the public/private dichotomy, but rather in compassion itself. On such a view the purpose and sanction of rights derive exactly from their
role in extending natural compassion when it might not naturally be extended,
in eliciting compassion where it is tardy, and in articulating compassion skill-
fully. Rights are hence important at a number of levels, despite being morally
derivative.

Moreover, despite the erasure this entails of the principled boundary between
the public and the private, a morality based on compassion allows us to recognize
and to protect the fundamental values that are embodied in a right to privacy.
The very rights that liberals properly advance and protect so vigorously are reconstructed and protected with equal vigor on a new basis when they are
grounded not in individual autonomy but rather in collective mutual responsibility.

Taking rights and individual autonomy as foundational to morality does indeed
give us a great deal ethically and politically, and nobody who looks at the general
trend—albeit occasionally halting and marked by setbacks—toward greater freedom, democracy, and their ancillary human goods in the world can help but be
grateful to liberal moral theory for its significant role in facilitating this progress.
At the same time, however, we must recognize that this approach to morality
comes at a price, the essential individualism of liberal theory. And while that
individualism is a useful liberative tool against tyranny, it can also be an obstacle
to the development of mutual responsibility and to the extension of compassion
to others that moral life also demands. The development of these traits of character are, of course, on a Buddhist understanding, enabled precisely by the relinquishing of a sense of oneself as an isolated, integrated entity, and the tension
between the liberal commitment to the integrity and individuality of the self as
the foundation of morality and the Buddhist commitment to the anihilation of
precisely that conception as a condition of moral progress is the root of the
conflict between these two perspectives.

By instead starting from a perspective that takes our mutual responsibilities
and our moral sentiments as foundational, we can avoid paying the price of this
individualism, and can reconstruct, albeit on new foundations, many of the same
rights the liberal defends. We thus get a more far-reaching moral sensibility. To
be sure, we lose something the liberal values: the protection of our right not to
care about others, and to pursue our own vision of the good life in isolation. But
in a world characterized by the omnipresence of suffering, that is a right well
lost. Finally, we can now understand how it is possible, despite the vast difference

in theoretical outlook between liberal and Buddhist moral theory, for a moral advocate such as His Holiness the Dalai Lama simultaneously to advocate the cultivation of compassion as the most basic moral task and work toward the recognition of human rights. For properly conceived, the latter is but the social face of the former.

11

Buddhism and Democracy

WHAT IS THE RELATION between Buddhism and liberal democracy? Are they compatible frameworks for social value, which can somehow be joined to one another to gain a consistent whole? Or are they instead antagonistic, forcing those who would be Buddhist democrats into an uncomfortably choice between individually attractive but jointly unsatisfiable values? Or do they operate at entirely different levels of discourse so that questions regarding their relationship simply do not arise?

The question is important for several reasons: first, we indeed have in Buddhism and in liberal democratic theory two prima facie plausible frameworks for value, and their independent plausibility leads immediately to the question of their compatibility. Second, each framework has staked a claim to a central role in the global quest for human rights and justice, and indeed partisans of each have used the other in defense of their respective frameworks. Third, the Tibetan government in exile has formulated a national charter explicitly grounded in a Buddhist view of moral and social life and espousing a liberal democratic social ideology. It would be nice to know whether that vision is coherent. Fourth, the perennial debate between proponents of the universality of the liberal vision and those suggesting that liberalism is incompatible with "Asian values" might move forward if it turned out that at least one major Asian tradition is compatible with liberal democracy, or on the other hand that there is a fundamental incompatibility between these two systems.

In this essay I argue that not only are Buddhism and liberal democracy compatible, but that they are complementary in a deep sense: democracy, I argue, is strengthened by values drawn from Buddhist moral and social theory, and Buddhist moral and social theory gains concrete institutional and procedural specificity when it is articulated through the framework of liberal democratic theory.

The terms *Buddhism* and *liberal democracy* are each, to be sure, vague, and I will be painting throughout this essay with a broad brush. Nonetheless, I will explain how I understand these terms for present purposes. My conception of liberal democracy is that of the social contract tradition, and more particularly that of Locke, Kant, and Rawls. Its central tenets regarding the distinction between public and private and the centrality of individual rights are articulated in Mill's *On Liberty*, in Rawls's *A Theory of Justice*, and are enshrined in the United States Constitution. To be sure, these texts do not speak on all issues with a single voice, but they indicate a clear and coherent vision of the nature of justice, of the primacy of fundamental individual rights in justice, and of the primacy also of justice over any particular conception of the good. They also indicate a need for any just society to tolerate a plurality of conceptions of the good and of the responsibility of government to its populace.

The Buddhism I have in mind is the Mahāyāna tradition of moral theory, comprising and extending the Pali tradition of morality as expressed in the eight-fold path by the addition of the Bodhisattva ideal and the six perfections as providing an analysis of human moral perfection. More specifically, I have in mind that tradition as it is understood and expounded in medieval India and Tibet by such figures as Āryadeva, Śantideva, and Tsong khapa. But I will also draw on insights from contemporary scholars and activists in the so-called "Engaged Buddhist" movement, whose work is in the spirit of this tradition. Again, this tradition is not homogenous, but the conceptual space it marks out is coherent enough for present purposes. This is not so much an exercise in exegesis as it is in deploying the insights I find in these traditions. Indeed, given the contemporary context of the problematic with which I am concerned, it will often be the case that the implications I draw from the Buddhist tradition would not have been considered by classical scholars.

THE DIVISION OF THEORETICAL LABOR

I first note that in a strictly formal sense, Buddhism and democracy are mutually independent. Buddhism neither precludes nor entails liberal democracy; liberal democracy neither precludes nor entails Buddhism. Buddhism—and by this term I understand the doctrine presented in the *suttas* of the Pali canon and developed in the Indian Mahāyāna *śastras*, insofar as this doctrine can be relatively uncontroversially identified—is generally silent about social institutions and forms of government. In the first instance it is a doctrine about the good life for the individual and about the values, practices, traits of character, states of mind, and view of reality that conduce to the liberation of the individual from suffering. Though this is elaborated in the Mahāyāna into an altruistic doctrine, Buddhist theory for the most part remains resolutely a theory about individual life and practice.

There are two classes of exceptions to this generalization, one of which will turn out to be important for our project. First, there is the *vinaya-pitaka*, devoted in good measure to the elaboration of the social and administrative structures for the Buddhist *sangha*, or monastic community. While this might appear to be the right place to begin an inquiry into the relation between Buddhism and democracy, inasmuch as the *vinaya-pitaka* comprises the most explicitly sociopolitical of all Buddhist scriptures, here we find discussion of the method of choice of leaders of the assembly, of the method for deciding community membership, of resolving disputes, and so on. But there are compelling reasons for *not* starting here as well: the *vinaya* is a code formulated explicitly and solely for the governance of a voluntary, celibate, ideologically homogenous monastic community. Liberal democracy gets its very point from the presumption of heterogeneity, and from the need to adjudicate disputes and to formulate institutions and policies in circumstances where the option of removal from the community is not present. If Buddhism and liberal democracy are to be joined or compared, it must be on this more secular terrain.

This brings us to the second body of literature, considerably smaller in size: the corpus of Buddhist advice to rulers, of which Nāgārjuna's "Letter to a Friend" and "*Ratnāvalī*" are the best examples. Here we find direct advice grounded in Buddhist moral values regarding the ruling of a state. And from this literature two general salient points emerge (as well as a number of more specific points with which we will be concerned later): first, Buddhism has *nothing* to say about the appropriate *form* of government. Nāgārjuna's letters are addressed to *kings.* But in these letters we find neither a conservative royalist defense of monarchy nor a revolutionary tract calling for a democratic order. Nāgārjuna is silent about these matters, focusing instead on the goods the state must deliver: hospitals, roadside resthouses, good water supply, care for animals, schools, and so on. Buddhism emerges in these texts as a theory about the good, silent about procedures, except for the general implicit proviso that only procedures capable of facilitating the pursuit of that good are legitimate. But with respect to the good, Buddhism has a lot to say: the goal of any social order, on a Buddhist view, is the maximization of happiness, the minimization of suffering, the provision for the least advantaged and the cultivation of traits of character such as compassion, patience, generosity, and wisdom. If a monarchy can do this, fine. If a democracy can accomplish that, fine, too.

Liberal democratic theory—that is, the democratic theory of the social contract tradition as handed down from Locke through Jefferson to Mill to Rawls—is, by contrast, relatively silent about the good, but quite articulate and specific about social institutions and procedures. Indeed, liberal democracy—while to be sure embodying some specific values relative to social good, values that I will discuss later in this chapter—is self-consciously minimalist with respect to such commitments. This, indeed, is one of its strengths, and part of the genius of the liberal democratic tradition is the insight that procedures themselves can be legitimized independently of many nonprocedural values and that legitimate procedures can legitimate both institutions and conceptions of the good.

Now, the contrast between Buddhism and liberalism on this score can easily be overstated, and it is important to be careful here. It is neither true that Buddhism is devoid of procedural ideas nor that liberalism is bereft of specific values or conceptions of the good life or the good social order. Each tradition embodies commitments of both types, and indeed it would be a conceptual impossibility for a moral framework to be either entirely substantive or entirely procedural in content. Procedures reflect substantive values and vice versa. And indeed these values at the extremes must be mutually constraining. This is evident, for example, in constitutional protections of some values against ready change, however democratic the procedure.

The contrast, however, is real, and can be properly emphasized in two ways: first, the respective orders of legitimation for the two traditions are *toto genere* distinct. Liberal democratic theory legitimates its goods on procedural grounds; Buddhism legitimates any procedures on the grounds that they produce appropriate goods. Second, and related, procedures of particular kinds are constitutive of liberal democracy, whereas commitments to particular social goods are constitutive of Buddhist societies in very deep ways: whereas liberal democratic societies may differ widely (or one may change wildly over time) with respect to some particular vision of the good (say free education, universal health care, or a minimum wage) and remain recognizably democratic, any society that abandoned election, open access to offices, or transparency of the judicial process would ipso facto no longer count as a liberal democracy. (There is, however, also a sense in which a specific conception of the good is built into most Western liberal democracies beyond the necessary implication of some minimal conception of the good by the procedural commitments and by the initial presuppositions of the contractual situation: most liberals—whether they acknowledge it or not—tacitly supplement democratic principles with a heavy dose of Judeo-Christian values, including the presumption of human dominion over the earth, of the sanctity of individual property, of the primacy of individuals over collectives, of the legitimacy of violence in the service of a legitimate cause, among others, which are called upon [sometimes in suitably secularized language, sometimes in the original] in policymaking or in the adjudication of institutions to fill in the gaps left by liberal theory. A Tibetan student once asked in a class on Locke's political philosophy, "Do you have to be a Christian to take this theory of property and natural rights seriously?" Maybe.)

Similarly, while some Buddhist societies might be monarchies and others democratic, or the same one might change its form of government over time and remain recognizably Buddhist, any society that abandoned commitment to nonviolence, to maintaining the welfare of the least advantaged, to providing health care and education to all its citizens, and to facilitating spiritual practice for those who aspire thereto would cease to be recognizably Buddhist.

For these reasons we can treat Buddhism and liberal democracy as diametrically opposed on one issue, namely, the direction of legitimation as between procedure and conception of the good. But this does not entail that they are therefore incapable of fusion. Legitimation, after all, might not in the end have a foundational structure: it might well be that procedures and conceptions of the good are mutually reinforcing. In fact this is a picture we will suggest. But these observations suggest more by way of a strategy for social and political philosophy—a division of theoretical labor: a Buddhist democratic theory needs, after all, a theory both of the good and of the political institutions capable of and appropriate to realizing that good. Why not, then, turn to Buddhism for the former task, and liberal democratic theory for the latter? I propose to do just that, allowing each body of theory to do what it does best, with the hope that we will end up with a consistent set of institutions and social objectives that lend normative support to each other. As we shall see, however, it will not be enough simply to spell out independently the demands and content of each theory and to join them by the word *and*. To show their deep theoretical connection and affinity, I will turn to the explicitly Buddhist notion of *upāya*—of skilful means—as a mediating concept.

Buddhist Ideals for a Society

From the fundamentals of Buddhist moral theory as articulated in the sūtras and *śastras* we can distill several specific components of a theory of social good: first, social institutions should aim at maximizing happiness and minimizing suffering for all members of society. In particular, given Buddhist egalitarian concerns and given the content of compassion, social institutions should aim at equity in distribution and opportunity and especially at the minimization of suffering for the least advantaged.

The Buddhist doctrine of the *pancśila,* or five ethical precepts for laypersons, adds to the Buddhist conception of social institutions and conceptions of the good: these precepts enjoin refraining from killing, stealing, lying, sexual misconduct, and intoxication. Put together and viewed in a social context, they together constitute advice against violence and actions likely to sow discord and favor openness and integrity. These more general values can inform the development of social institutions. If we were to read them too narrowly and apply them crudely as instruments of social policy, it might seem that they require not only the criminalization of homicide, theft, and perjury, but also the prohibition of alcohol and a strict code of sexual conduct. But this would be far too narrow a reading and in any case fail to see the values that underlie this moral code and their relevance to social theory.

What do killing, theft, intoxication, sexual misconduct, and lying have in common that they should be brought together as *the* five things any person is admonished to forswear? Just this: all are either directly violent or are seeds of violence. The fundamental value thus reflected in this code is nonviolence, and the obvious application to social philosophy is that political institutions and policies should themselves be nonviolent and directed primarily to the eradication of violence in society.[1] Spelling out the content of this prescription is, of course, not a trivial task and must remain outside the scope of this chapter. But the sense of the fundamental value should be clear.

Buddhist moral literature distinguishes a number of important human virtues or perfections of character. Given that we are asking from Buddhism a conception of social good, and given that for Buddhism society can only be seen instrumentally as a mechanism for ensuring the good of individuals, it follows that social institutions should, from a Buddhist perspective, encourage, develop, and foster these virtues. A brief list of these would include prominently generosity, patience, wisdom, moderation, and nonattachment. Buddhist moral theory can best be characterized as a concern with certain *vastus*—areas of importance in conduct, traits of character, and ranges of behavior on which one should focus in worrying about one's moral development, and not as a set of imperatives or specific prescriptions. Now since Buddhist literature is so sparse when it comes to very specific advice on social institutions or policies, I—simply spelling out the way that Buddhist and democratic theory can be joined—will allow myself to be even more reserved. That is, I will not venture here a specific set of recommendations for how political arrangements might encourage, develop, and foster these virtues. But I can say a few things to indicate the direction that such an account might take.

Social structures and institutions that reflect ideals build consensus regarding the probity of those ideals. Protection of the freedom of speech, for instance, not only reflects the view that speech should be free but encourages that value in those who dwell in societies with such policies. Generous social programs and programs conducive to equity will not only reflect but encourage values such as generosity and moderation. Policies creating shared public goods and enabling their enjoyment without the amassing of private wealth will generate nonattachment. The facilitation of education will encourage the development of wisdom. Public disarmament will conduce to private nonviolence and so forth.

Moreover, since the Buddhist ideals I here take seriously include those of the Mahāyāna, Buddhist social institutions and political arrangements should presume and cultivate a sense of responsibility for others. This requirement would most obviously find expression in the requirement for extensive health and welfare services as the primary brief of government but would extend to the establishment of service agencies involving substantial numbers of citizens, perhaps involving a civil service force in which all or most would serve at some time.

THE FORMAL PROMISE OF LIBERAL DEMOCRACY

We have seen that Buddhism provides a rich positive conception of social goods and of the values a political system ought to reflect and encourage. What does liberal democratic theory bring to the table? A lot, of course: it demands a respect for a basic set of universal human rights, prominently including the right to vote for those who will hold significant government offices; the right to free speech and expression broadly conceived; the right to free religious expression and against the imposition of religious beliefs or practices; freedom from torture or unwarranted imprisonment or restriction of movement; the right to informational privacy and allied rights. All of these can be summed up as the right to participate without fetter in an open public sphere, and to be free from unwarranted interference in the private sphere.

To continue in the same vein, liberal democracy requires that institutions preserve and reflect the equal liberty of the citizens of the state and the rule of law and that all offices be open and all processes transparent. That is, special privileges or restrictions on citizens should result from fair allocation procedures; positions of authority should in principle be open to any citizen, and their occupants should be fairly chosen; all political and legal processes should be open to scrutiny and assessment, be fair, and have consensual support.

Also, pluralism is fundamental to the liberalism of any liberal democracy. Aside from the minimal set of values adumbrated above (perhaps plus or minus a few), liberalism is committed to impartiality among conceptions of the good and to providing each citizens with the liberty to pursue his or her own conception of the good, so long as that commitment does not trammel the rights of others. A consequence of this is that a liberal democracy will be committed to allowing the flourishing of a number of ideologically and axiologically distinct communities as part of a body politic, without either assisting or hampering in special ways any of these in its independent activities.

This brief outline of the central commitments of these two frameworks reinforces the sense that while they are not directly contradictory to one another, there is no obvious point of intersection between the two. If we were to leave the analysis at this point, it might then seem that while a Buddhist democratic theory is not impossible, it would at least be a peculiar accident and in no way conceptually motivated either by Buddhism or by liberal democracy. I now turn to a construct from within Buddhism that, I argue, provides the necessary link, that motivates specifically an attempt to forge Buddhist democratic theory.

UPĀYA AS A CONCEPTUAL BRIDGE

An important and insufficiently noticed conceptual construct in Buddhist theory is that of *upāya*, or skilful means. From a Buddhist perspective, skill is necessary to cultivate because enlightenment is difficult to achieve and to facilitate, and because the Buddhist virtues—and this is true both of individual and social virtues—require not simply intention but success. It is not enough to form a desire, even a sincere desire, to be generous. Without the successful completion of generous acts, generosity is not realized. Even an act motivated by generosity, if it does not succeed in benefiting its target, fails, on a Buddhist analysis, to be a fully generous act. The road to hell, one might say, is paved with good intentions; the road to Buddhahood, with good realizations. This is not, of course, to say that such an act is thereby vicious, or bereft of moral worth, but only to recognize that complete virtue requires more than just good intention. (The parallels to Aristotle's argument for the need for practical wisdom in moral life are intriguing here. But a full comparison would take us far afield.) What goes for generosity goes as well, mutatis mutandis, for patience, wisdom, effort, concentration, compassion and the rest. The injunction to any virtue is always, in Buddhism, *ipso facto* an injunction to cultivate the *upāya* necessary for its realization.

Moral skill is necessary for the expression and development of Buddhist virtues and for the attainment of the good as seen from the Buddhist standpoint. But the other side of this coin is that such skills are therefore valued not for their own sake, but rather simply as *means* to goods that are antecedently regarded as valuable (and these, too, instrumentally valuable—because they conduce to enlightenment). And any skill or method that conduces to Buddhist virtues or goods is, simply in virtue of that fact, worthy of cultivation. This is not to say that other considerations might not weigh against the use of any particular means: Buddhism is resolutely multivariate and nonabsolute in its assessment of actions and institutions and admits an indefinite range of moral quality between the irredeemably wicked and the morally perfect, depending on the complex admixture of motives and consequences involved. The centrality of this category of instrumental good, however, allows for a distinctively Buddhist justification and interpretation of democracy.

The route to such a justification and interpretation should be clear: given the conception of the collective, social good to which we have seen Buddhism is committed, if it turns out that liberal democracy is the best means to achieve those goods, it follows straightforwardly from Buddhist principles and from the theory of *upāya* that liberal democracy is the preferred Buddhist social framework. Moreover, considerations of *upāya* would then determine the precise shape of those democratic institutions and the social ends toward which they are to be directed. From this standpoint the intuition with which I began this discussion reappears: that democratic theory could provide the institutional and procedural framework for a social order whose conception of the good is rooted in Buddhism as potentially vindicated through this mediating concept. The important question to ask, then, is this: Is liberal democracy plausibly construed as the best means for realizing the social goods Buddhism seeks? It is to this question I now turn.

The Empirical Argument from Efficacy

The argument at this point becomes empirical, if only in the broadest sense of that term. For if *upāya* is what counts, the question regarding whether Buddhism permits or even demands a liberal democratic political order boils down to the question, "Does liberal democracy represent the best method for maximizing happiness, for minimizing suffering, for realizing equity, for achieving nonviolence, and for cultivating virtues such as patience, generosity, wisdom, and commitment to others?" If it does, we are home free. If not, perhaps we should be seeking a different sociopolitical order.

If this is the question, the answer appears to be too easy. A quick glance around the world's nation-states reveals that on any reasonable index of social utility the world's liberal democracies lead their more totalitarian rivals. This is so whether we look at straightforward economic indicators such as median income, percentage of population living in poverty, equity or distribution, and the like, basic welfare indicators such as access to medical care, housing, nutrition, or schooling, or softer indicators such as level of social unrest or satisfaction with government. There is no doubt that on hierarchizing of the world's nations on these parameters the liberal democracies rise to the top. Neither can doubt exist about the empirical evidence that liberal democracy tends to reduce of suffering and engender happiness.

What about the violence/nonviolence dimension? Here is one striking fact: in the last two-hundred years, one democratic country has never waged war against another. Democracy, one might say, as Kant argued, is the best inoculation against war. At the level of personal violence, the story is more equivocal. There are indeed some notably violent democracies (such as the United States) and some notably peaceful autocracies (Singapore). But these exceptions aside, the trend still evidently favors democracies even at this level.

We have seen that the Buddhist conception of the social good also includes an account of the virtues to be encouraged, cultivated and supported by a social order. This is a harder desideratum with respect to which to make the requisite empirical claim. There may be good plausibility arguments on both sides, and there are no obvious data, whether rigorous or intuitive, to which to appeal. I can at least say that on this dimension liberal democracy is *no worse*, as far as I know, than its alternatives.

This brief empirical argument is hardly conclusive. It is at best a good motivator. I have not appealed to any hard data. Nor would the generalizations I defend based on these intuitive characterizations lack exceptions. Nonetheless, I feel confident in saying that empirical considerations at least favor the hypothesis that liberal democracy is most likely the best political means for achieving the kind of society that Buddhist moral theory recommends. I turn now to some more theoretical considerations to suggest that the central feature of liberal democracy, the articulation and protection of fundamental human rights, is the best way to promote a Buddhist conception of the good, and hence that such a framework is indicated from the standpoint of *upāya*.

The Argument for the Importance of Rights as a Facilitator

As we have seen, a straightforwardly empirical argument for liberal democracy as the best means to realize Buddhist social ideals is, while a bit tendentious, a good motivator. But in the absence of compelling empirical evidence either way, I turn to a more theoretical argument, asking whether there is good reason to believe that respect for the fundamental set of human rights and the correlative political institutions recognized in the liberal democratic tradition provides greater *promise* as a vehicle for the development of a society conforming to Buddhist ideals than do its competitors. The answer to this more forward-looking question, is more strongly positive.

Asking this question also gives us additional theoretical leverage. For by focusing on the more abstract connections between Buddhist and democratic ethics and politics, we can get some insight into the ways in which the two bodies of theory might mutually inform each other and into how a Buddhist democracy might actually look. That is, at the same time that we examine the degree to which these two systems are consistent or even axiologically complementary, we can determine the exact nature of that complementarity.

What are rights good for? From the standpoint of classical liberal theory, an important class of personal rights, which we might call "privacy rights," can be understood as constructing protective barriers against the intrusion of other individuals and state power into our private lives. Examples include rights to free speech and association, to freedom of religious expression, freedom against unwarranted search and seizure, and so on. First and foremost, these rights protect their bearers against gratuitous harms, whether inflicted by other individuals or by government, and, equally importance create a space—the private sphere—in which an individual or group can pursue and cultivate the good as they see it. Without a framework of such basic personal privacy rights, no one can be secure to pursue any particular vision of the good. Now, as I argued above, Buddhism is nothing if not a view about the good. It follows that if the protection of privacy rights is ipso facto a protection of the realization of such views, liberal democracy's commitment to such rights enables a Buddhist life, at least for individuals. But at this level of analysis, all that we are really saying is that the individual rights enshrined by liberal democracy provide protection for *any* set of values an individual might wish to pursue, and not that there is any special relationship between democracy and Buddhism. We can, however, go farther.

One important core value in Buddhist social morality is the minimization of the suffering of the disadvantaged. How can a social order best realize this value? One obvious answer is this: enshrine a fundamental civil right to a minimal standard of living and minimal access to such basic goods as medical care. Now, to be sure, these goods themselves can be provided by even the most totalitarian regime. But the only way to guarantee them effectively is to establish them as fundamental rights within a political order. And the institution of rights itself has its home only in the context of a liberal political order. The best way to realize this particular value, a core of the Buddhist conception of the good, is therefore to embed these specific rights in a liberal social order.

Similarly, we can ask what the best route is to the achievement of nonviolence in social institutions. I noted above that in general democracy is an excellent guarantee against the settling of major internal disputes through organized physical violence, such as civil war. That empirical argument counts of a lot. But violence comes in other, more implicit forms, such as institutional racism, oppression, coercive political and economic structures, and the like. Each of these forms necessarily rests on a foundation of either explicit or constantly threatened violence for its maintenance. Liberal democracy is of course the best way imaginable—both because of its universal enfranchisement and its respect for fundamental rights—to reduce and to eliminate the degree of violence present in a society. Many of the forms of institutional violence I have examined consist directly in the violation of recognized rights or the failure to recognize rights enshrined in liberal democratic institutions. Essential features of such political orders such as universal enfranchisement and the openness of political processes combine with principles generally acknowledged by citizens and enshrined in law concerning access to education and basic social welfare codes to dramatically reduce the level of such institutional violence in all liberal democratic societies, when this is compared with totalitarian neighbors.

Liberal democratic societies also cultivate a greater sense of mutual responsibility than do their totalitarian counterparts, simply because they offer their citizens a genuine voice and chance to participate in civic affairs. The sense of membership in a common venture this engenders cannot be underestimated, and the consequence is an increased commitment to the common good—after all, it is a good in which every citizen has a voice in determining.

Openness of government institutions has two other benefits that support Buddhist values: inasmuch as Buddhism is concerned first and foremost with soteriology and with the religious practices that support liberation, it has an interest in political regimes that permit the free exercise of religion and of course the privacy, and hence the protection of religious practice is a hallmark of liberal democratic theory and societies. But this openness also limits the possibilities for corruption and hence alleviates the suffering that corruption inevitably produces.

Now all of this is subject to innumerable objections to the contrary. There are many examples both of liberal democratic societies that fail to live up to these ideals or that fail despite living up to them to deliver all of the goods I have emumerated. And there are certainly plenty of examples of illiberal societies that do deliver at least some of these goods. I have not, though, and need not, to make the case for liberal democracy as *upāya*, to show that there is a clear line between liberal democratic societies and all others, with Buddhist goods realized in their entirety for all citizens on the one side and denied to all on the other. To claim that this is possible would be foolish. All that is necessary is to show that overall the social structures advanced by liberal democracy represent the best means to achieve the ends recommended by Buddhism. And this I have endeavored to do.

What Liberal Democracy Can Offer to Buddhism

Can Buddhism gain anything from attention to liberal democratic theory? I think so. It is a striking feature of Buddhist literature, as I noted previously, that despite the tremendous importance of the structure of a society and its institutions, including predominantly its political structures, in determining the conditions of human life and the possibilities for the attainment of both temporal and spiritual goods, there is very little—really nothing—in the Buddhist philosophical tradition by way of social or political theory. This must be regarded as a serious lacuna in a philosophical system that aims at characterizing the nature of suffering and of its elimination for a being who is ineliminably social.

On the other hand, as also noted, Buddhism demands of its practitioners the development of *upāya*, and this must include social and political *upāya*. If what I have said about the conceptual and empirical relationships between the Buddhist conception of the good and the deliverances of democracy is valid, liberal democratic theory might simply be the obvious body of theory with which to fill this gap. The Mahāyāna canon prides itself on its perpetual openness to new texts. Perhaps it is time to make space in canonical collections of such *mahapanditas* as Locke, Rousseau, Mill, Jefferson, Dewey, Rawls, and Habermas. And indeed in the democratization of the Tibetan exile government and in the discussions of Buddhist democratic institutions within that community, I see the beginnings of this process.

What Buddhism Can Offer to Liberal Democracy

But the benefits of intercultural fusion philosophy do not flow in one direction only. Liberal democratic theory and those formulating policy in liberal democratic societies can also benefit from an injection of Buddhist ideas. Again, attention to the development of Buddhist democratic institutions in the Tibetan exile community can be instructive—and not only, I emphasize, to Buddhists or members of Buddhist societies, but to secular theorists and policymakers.

There is a curious tension at the base of liberal democracy. When I examine the strategies by means of which it is legitimated—and I have in mind those of Hobbes, Locke, Rousseau, and Rawls—there is an essential appeal to practical reason in the following sense: it is argued that for arbitrarily chosen citizens, described in abstraction from their particular fortunes within society, it is rational to choose liberal democracy precisely because it offers the best chance for achieving personal happiness, or at least the best chance for avoiding the worst suffering. This is, of course, captured with the greatest clarity in Rawls's account of the original position and of the deliberations of the parties.

On the other hand, while liberal democracy offers this prospect precisely because it promises a government and set of social institutions that will not obstruct individual efforts to realize the good, it is deliberately minimalist in its promise to provide particular social goods, leaving such decisions either to contingent political processes or to individual enterprise. The reason for this is straightforward: democratic theory is resolutely both individualistic and pluralistic. The individualistic side leads to an emphasis on a broad zone of privacy and little positive social intervention for good or ill into the lives of individuals. The pluralism leads to a hesitancy to propose any but the most general and formal social goods as the objects of state action for fear that any more determinate commitment to a particular vision of the good will run roughshod over the rights and aspirations of those who do not share that vision.

But given the logic of legitimation that underlies this political framework, any enhancement of the basic stock of goods delivered to its citizens by a liberal democratic society would be chosen by initial contracting parties, so long as those goods are not parochial in nature—so long as they benefit the society generally and, as Rawls puts it, benefit the least advantaged, and hence protect citizens' vital interest in not falling too far in terms of total utility. That is, not only would a basic minimum of primary social goods be demanded by any rational contracting parties, but any rational parties would insist that as much as possible be available to as many as possible, and that avoidable poverty be avoided.

At this point Buddhism has something to contribute to the framework. First, the Buddhist goal of eliminating suffering enjoins a strong social welfare policy. That is, it enjoins the provision of basic education, health care, and a decent minimum standard of living for all citizens. Contracting parties who take this injunction seriously—who recognize both the universality of susceptibility to suffering and the possibility of its remediation—would think only briefly before rejecting an unbridled free market, for instance, and would insist on liberal social welfare programs. This is already an enrichment of the minimal conception of the good in most liberal theory.

But we can go farther. On any plausible contractarian story of the legitimation of and limits of government power, the parties to the initial contract know the general facts about human nature, though they may not know their specific circumstances, preferences, or positions. Knowledge of these general facts enables them to imagine the likely effects of any social order they contemplate establishing. Now it is overwhelmingly plausible that the set of virtues endorsed by Buddhist moral theory—patience, wisdom, nonviolence, generosity, and so on—in fact, when broadly realized, yield happier, stabler societies. Social institutions can be designed to encourage, reward, and foster these values or to discourage them. Parties to a social contract cognizant of these facts can be expected to agree to institutions that foster rather than discourage them. Again, this represents a substantial enrichment over a more value-neutral liberal framework.

We would therefore expect to find in a Buddhist democracy not armies but social service corps; not private health insurance schemes but a strong social welfare and health care system, egalitarian access to education, and significant incentives to charitable work. Institutions like this would take primacy over incentives to competition, to the concentration of wealth, and to the development of power differentials. This substantive account of the good stands in contrast to an emphasis on economic growth and the encouragement of private gain. But none of this is in any way incompatible with the democratic ideals of equality before the law, of participation in a public discourse, of open office and of a broad range of personal freedoms. In fact it is, one would argue, central to enabling these freedoms to make a real difference in the quality of human life. There is also no reason to think that Buddhist moral theory is *unique* in its ability to contribute a positive conception of the good to liberal democracy. Other substantive value systems may do as well. I only argue that it *can* make a contribution, and one that liberal democratic theory is in a position to reciprocate.

I hence conclude that while Buddhist values have typically been overlooked as valid considerations in the legitimation and design of social institutions in democratic theory and practice, this is both unnecessary and unjustified. A democratic society that draws on these principles in its social order and institutions has a greater prospect for success, and providing its citizenry with good lives and in fact greater claim to moral legitimacy than one that is neutral with respect to these principles. Buddhist democracy is thus not only not oxymoronic but is better democracy even when judged on the terms that the liberal tradition itself chooses and better Buddhism when judged on the terms that Buddhism itself chooses for moral evaluation. I conclude that these systems are—far from being antithetical—complementary, and that each is more compelling when adjoined to the other.

12

The "Satya" *in* Satyagraha

Samdhong Rinpoche's Approach to Nonviolence

THE MOST VEN. PROF. SAMDHONG RINPOCHE has been for the past decade the world's foremost theoretical exponent and practical advocate of a specifically Gandhian approach to nonviolence, both as a doctrine of political action and as a personal religious practice. From one perspective this is unsurprising: Ahimsa is central to Buddhism; the Tibetan exile has its center in India; His Holiness the Dalai Lama pays homage to the Mahatma's legacy. From another perspective, however, there is a surprise here: *Satyagraha* as it is theorized by Gandhi and as it is theorized by Samdhong Rinpoche is a specifically religious doctrine. But the religious contexts in which they each theorize are dramatically different, and in particular differ regarding the nature of *satya* itself and regarding the nature of the practitioner and the soteriology implicated by the practice of *satyagraha*. It would therefore be both facile and misleading to assume that *satyagraha* for Samdhong Rinpoche is the same *satyagraha* as it is for Gandhi.

In particular, to construct Samdhong Rinpoche's *satyagraha*, I must provide an account of *satya* appropriate to an atheistic Buddhist context, and an account of *agraha* and of *graha* that makes sense in the context of Buddhist practice and soteriology. It should be plain that this is necessary. For Gandhi's *satya* is grounded in the permanence of *ātman* and its centrality for action, in the union of the personal *ātman* with the godhead, and in the revealed truth of the Hindu scriptures. These truths are not available to a Buddhist *satyagrahi*. But this does not mean that Gandhi's central insight that grasping the nature of reality and insistence on truth is the foundation of all morally significant action and meaningful life. All that it means is that we need to understand what that truth could be for a Buddhist practitioner and what it is to grasp and to insist on it. When we do so, we will see that the core Gandhian commitment to nonviolence in body, speech, and mind as an organizing principle for personal and political life remains intact, but that this commitment is provided with a new foundation.

TRUTH, EXISTENCE, AND REALITY

Satya is most often translated into English, particularly in the context of *satyagraha* theory, as "truth." While this translation is perfectly good, it can mislead if we do not pay attention to the full semantic range of the term, which could as well be translated "reality" or "what is the case." This emphasisis is important because one might otherwise think that *satyagraha* is especially connected with some doctrine or set of theses—true sentences. It is not. While sometimes theses are the things on which the *satyagrahi* insists, or grasps, sometimes it is simply realities that are grasped or on the recogntion of which the *satyagrahi* insists.

The compound *satyāgraha* also poses interesting translational problems in its own right, even once we understand the meaning(s) of *satya*. For it could arise from conjoining *satya* with *graha*, and so mean "grasping the truth." Or it could result from conjoining *satya* with *āgraha* and so mean "insistence on the truth." Either reading can be appropriate, depending on context. So, *satyagraha* does involve a grasping, and an insistence on the truth of, and action reflecting the grasping and insistence upon, certain correct doctrines. Obviously, given the fact that this first meaning of *satya* is in play in *satyagraha* theory, we are going to have to understand Samdhong Rinpoche's *satyagraha* as involving the grasping and insistence upon certain Buddhist truths or on reality as it is seen from a Buddhist perspective. We will return to this issue later in this chapter. But while *satyagraha* is indeed always connected to certain doctrines or theses, to understand it in such purely declarative terms would be at best partial.

In the second sense of *satya*, *satyagraha* is action that reflects and is grounded in the nature of reality. In this sense *satyagraha* need not itself derive from any specific theory or doctrine but might reflect a spontaneous and direct awareness of how things stand and indeed might itself not so much derive from but represent truth, by demonstrating the nature of reality and appropriate engagement with that reality.

The third sense of *satya*, "what is the case," might appear to be indistinguishable from the second. The difference, however, is crucial if we are to understand the multilayered character of *satyagraha* and if we are to set it in a properly Buddhist context. Whereas in the second sense *satya* denotes the nature of reality, in the third it denotes what is the case in a particular circumstance, how things in fact contingently stand. Effective action requires not just (or perhaps not at all) a grasp of theory, not just a harmony of action with the fundamental nature of reality, but also awareness of the concrete details of the immediate context of action. A firm grasp of the details of the action-context and insistence on the particular facts against obfuscation or error is constitutive of *satyagraha*.

All of these senses of *satya* and correlatively of *satyagraha* are present in Gandhi's theory and practice, as well as in that of Samdhong Rinpoche. I will not be exploring the way they articulate in Gandhi's own account but rather explaining how to understand Samdhong Rinpoche's version of *satyagraha*, given his understanding of truth, reality, and action in accordance with reality and circumstances, grounded as it is in Buddhist action theory. I will also be concerned with *satyagraha* as a practice for ordinary human beings. Buddhas and highly realized bodhisattvas are necessarily *satyagrahis*. But I am not writing for them. They need neither a philosophical discussion of truth nor a discussion of the nature of a life lived in accordance with truth. *Satyagraha* must, if it is to be relevant to human political and personal life, be possible for ordinary beings like us, and it is to ordinary beings that the mahatma and Samdhong Rinpoche address themselves. Indeed, it may by Gandhi's deepest insight, and one with which Samdhong Rinpoche would undoubtedly agree, that *satyagraha* represents the only way that an ordinary human being can lead a fully human life. For this reason the analysis of truth, of action, of thought, and of speech I provide will be resolutely an analysis of these phenomena as they are experienced, enacted, and lived by ordinary human beings.

THE FOUR NOBLE TRUTHS AND THE FUNDAMENTAL NATURE OF REALITY

Let us first pay attention to reality. The reality in question is *human* reality, the world in which we find ourselves and in which we act. It is important to hold this fact in mind because otherwise we might confuse the reality with which we are concerned in action theory and in ordinary individual and political practice with the impersonal reality of the physicists. We might then be very puzzled about how even to understand the Four Noble Truths or the doctrine of the Two Truths so central to any Mahāyāna account of life and action. Or we might on the other hand confuse that reality with which we are concerned with that experienced by a buddha, and so be perplexed regarding the degree to which reality is characterized in a Buddhist framework as so problematic.

The reality of the physicist is impersonal in precisely the following sense: it is furnished indifferently with physical objects: some observable and some not; some sentient, some not; some alive, some not. And all are equally real whether they matter or not; whether they come to any consciousness or not. All equally *exist*. But none are *present*. None *matter*. None are *persons*. Such a universe is a universe of *things*, but not of *beings*. We, however, inhabit no such universe. We instead inhabit a *world*. And a world is populated by beings, which beings are *present* to us. These beings are heterogenous. Some are, like us, other persons. Others, while not persons, are nonetheless sentient. These *matter*. Others are *merely* matter and are of less account. But they are not for that reason of *no* account. For there are valuables and values that transcend persons and their concerns.

But persons and their concerns are nonetheless crucial to bringing a world and its beings into presence and hence into the reality that matters from the standpoint of action and morality. For things become present to us by virtue of our concerns and projects, and they become present to us as the things that they are, enmeshed in the networks of interdependence in which they figure, by virtue of our projects, concerns, and the way of seeing the world they induce. These projects and concerns are conditioned, to be sure, by the projects and concerns of the other persons with whom we (not necessarily willingly) share, and in (not necessarily voluntary or conscious) collaboration with whom we construct our world.

Other persons present themselves to us *as* persons because we *care* about persons; sentient beings are present to us *as* sentient beings because sentience matters; tools emerge from the physical totality as tools, and as tools of specific kinds—computers, swords, or ploughshares—precisely because of our purposes and their suitability to and design for those purposes. To live in a world is hence to live in an organized and interdependent structure of objects whose existence in that world and whose place in that ordered totality is determined by our patterns of concern and care, by our projects and intentions. We are, of course, inextricably embedded in and constituted by that world. It and its beings reciprocally determined our patterns of care and concern, our projects, possibilities of action and plans, and hence our very being. To be a person is hence both to determine and to be determined by a world.

Though I have expressed this point in the language of Western existential phenomenology, my point is perfectly Buddhist, just another way of insisting on the special role of mind in determining the ontology of the world, a role always limited by the corporeal. It is another way of explaining how all objects of consciousness are conventional and lack existence from their own side. It is another way of explaining *pratītya-samutpāda*. It is another way of expressing the principle that the world we live in is determined by our karma—our actions, including those of body, speech, and mind. Finally, it is another way of expressing the first two of the Four Noble Truths and of grounding the second two and so provides a way of addressing the question regarding both the nature of the *satya* and the nature of the *agraha* in *satyāgraha*.

To say that our care and our concerns structure the world in which we find ourselves is not to adopt a mystic idealism—far from it. It is rather to say that what emerges out of the background as an object of potential engagement is determined by what we care about, what we are ready to perceive, by our human purposes, and by what we are prepared to recognize. That is why it is fair to say with the Madhyamaka tradition that the phenomena we encounter—those comprised by our world—are conventional, and that their existence is only an existence relative to our distinctive consciousness. That is why the world we inhabit is a function of our activity.

The Four Noble Truths are truths about our world, not about the abstract reality of the physicist. The truth of dependent arising, and the Two Truths, likewise, are pre-eminently truths about the world we humans inhabit. Let us explore just how to understand these truths in the context of praxis and hence in the domain of *satyagraha*. All *this* is suffering. All of *what*? All that emerges from our care and concern. How so? First, and most obviously, to care about something is to be vulnerable to the inevitable fact that that about which one cares is inevitably impermanent, imperiled, and less than one might have hoped it would be. This is true whether the object of care is a loved one, a possession, the welfare of distant others, or even a cherished ideology, political program, or theory. It is a deep fact about the human predicament, and one of the Buddha's greatest insights, that for anything to be an object for us is for it to come into presence and hence into being for us through suffering, and to be an endless cause of suffering. The only alternative is the depersonalization of reality and ceasing to inhabit a human world. But that is no help. From a Mahāyāna viewpoint, and that is the moral perspective of Samdhong Rinpoche, to cease to inhabit a human world—even were that possible—would be a far greater suffering for beings like us. (And again, the care with which we are concerned is ordinary human care, nothing supramundane—a care sufficient to generate a world, sufficient to recognize and to ground suffering, and sufficient to motivate its alleviation.

Second, though, and from the standpoint of social action, of equal importance: this is all suffering because it comprises countless sentient beings, and countless sentient beings are suffering in countless ways. If the world were simply a collection, simply a heap of unrelated things, it would hardly follow from this fact that *all* this is suffering. But given that our world is constituted as an interconnected whole and not as a collection of atomic points, the fact of suffering anywhere inevitably means that the whole must be thought of as suffering. It is an inevitable fact that we will be aware of the suffering of others. Our choices are two: to be moved by that suffering to suffer alongside, or to remain indifferent. In the first case, of course, we suffer. In the second case, however, we suffer even more, by virtue of our diminished humanity and our alienation from that world that alone can give our lives meaning. Any suffering is hence omnipresent. (And this, we might add, is as true for the Boddhisattva as it is for the ordinary person.)

Suffering has a cause, and that, globally and transcendentally, is attachment. We have seen why this is so. The very fact that we are enmeshed in a world structured by our concerns, attached to others through bonds of community and care, and connected to other points in space and time by projects, plans, and memories guarantees that we are vulnerable to pain, to death, to impermanence in all its guises and to the unpredictable and uncontrollable slings and arrows of outrageous fortune. And even were it, *per impossibile,* an option, as we have seen, detachment would be useless. Furthermore, each mundane instance of suffering has a cause. Wars do not just happen. They are waged. Starvation comes about not through random meteorological events, but through a failure to distribute food adequately. Poverty is a consequence not of privation but of economic injustice. And so on and on. The particular causes of suffering are as innumerable as are its instances, and the root is as universal as the phenomenon is universal.

So there is a release from suffering. We must understand this release in at leat two ways: first, the suffering we encounter in the world can be alleviated, and indeed it can be alleviated through our efforts. We can comfort and sometimes cure the sick. We can calm the dying. We can prevent war and violence. We can promote economic justice and reconciliation. We cannot be guaranteed success in any of these ventures, but neither is failure a certainty. And progress requires only effort. Second, a release from suffering is possible through one's own practice, through the alleviation of what the Buddhist tradition calls "primal ignorance." That is ignorance about the fundamental nature of reality. Understood within this framework, such ignorance is embodied in the delusion that we are atomic, that our fate is independent of that of others, and that our world is not of our making. So long as we see ourselves, our fate, and our world in this way, it is inconceivable that anything could give our lives meaning, simply because we thereby cut ourselves off from everything meaningful, and everything in which our lives could be reflected. To extirpate this ignorance is not to transcend the web of interconnection and care that constitutes suffering, but to live in it with sufficient understanding, hope, and purpose that that suffering itself gains meaning and that our lives gain purpose. This mundane release from suffering is thus not an escape from the world in which suffering is omnipresent, but an engagement in that world in a way that transforms suffering into purposive action.

The eightfold Buddhist path then offers a solid commonsense approach to achieving that purpose, to living a life of careful interdependent action aimed at the alleviation of suffering, a life in which physical action, the livelihood that organizes one's productive life, thought, and speech are directed to issues that merit concern. The Fourth Noble Truth is the simple fact that only a life lived in authentic awareness of and response to our existential situation is a life worth living. To fall from this standard is necessarily to fail to grasp the nature of existence, to fail to face up to reality, and ultimately to fail to insist on the truth as the guiding principle of one's life. In short, it is to lead a life guided by delusion and devoid of real significance, "a tale told by a fool, full of sound and fury, signifying nothing."

The Four Noble Truths are, of course, grounded in interdependence, and this grounding, I hope, has emerged in this existential analysis, as it emerges in that of the Buddha and in that of Nāgārjuna. But they are also, as Nāgārjuna properly emphasizes, grounded in the Two Truths—the conventional truth of the reality and interdependence of phenomena and the ultimate truth of their emptiness of inherent existence. If there is an advantage to the existential understanding of the Four Noble Truths as truths about the lived world of human existence, it is that it is so plain on this account just how the Two Truths ground the Four: the emptiness of all phenomena is simply the fact that the beings of our world have no being independent of our care, our projects, our consciousness, and our lives; the emptiness of the person is the fact that to be a human being is to project oneself into a world with such cares, projects, and consciousness of others, and that absent these, we and the world are literally nothing.

The conventional truth of things is the fact that despite being nothing in abstraction from this context of concern, the being we bring to things through such engagement is indeed being in the fullest possible sense, not some counterfeit or second-class being. Moreover, such a conventionally constituted world is—not despite, but because of its conventional character—worthy of our effort and care. There simply is no more real, more important place in which to expend our efforts or to live our lives. And the unity of the Two Truths that is the foundation of the Madhyamaka and the wellspring of compassion is the fact that being can *only* be being-in-the-world, and that being-in-the-world can only be conventional in precisely this sense and therefore can only be empty, precisely in this sense.

This is the truth, the reality, and the existence on which it makes sense, from a Buddhist perspective, to insist, which it makes sense to face, and which must be grasped in order for effective action and meaningful life to be possible. We now consider what it is to actualize this truth and our insistence on it in the practice of *satyagraha* so understood.

GRASPING REALITY AND INSISTING ON THE TRUTH

What is it to face up to what is, to grasp reality and to insist on the truth? First of all, to face up to what is, is to acknowledge frankly the omnipresence of suffering, the fact that the causes of suffering are concrete, adventitious, and often actions for which human beings typically bear causal and moral responsibility. This is no mean feat. It is easy to avert one's gaze, to lose oneself in contemplation and enjoyment of the good things in life, and to treat suffering either as unreal, distant, or as an unavoidable part of the background against which we live. It might appear that by living in denial of suffering we live more happily. But a central insight of *satyagraha* is that the reverse is in fact true. For alienation from all that is significant cannot be a source of genuine happiness, and to deny suffering is to alienate oneself from the world and all that it comprises. That is to lead a life both lonely and meaningless, and to anticipate a death at which one will have no option but to look back over a wasted and pointless existence, that of the "poor player who frets and struts his hour upon the stage and then is heard no more. . . ."

To face authentically what is, is to take seriously the fact one can be an agent for the alleviation of suffering and that to fail to act is to be complicit in the causation of suffering. Again, it is easy not to face up to this fact, but not to do so is to turn one's back and so to live in bad faith. And finally, to face up to what is, is to take seriously the fact that specific courses of action, specific ways of thinking, and the participation in particular discourses are necessary tools in the alleviation of suffering and become morally mandatory for anyone who takes life seriously. That is, *satyagraha* determines a course of action, and that course of action is roughly specified in the eightfold path.

All of this is at the level of concrete, conventional truth, and all of this reflects the simple consequences of taking the empirical facts of the human condition seriously together with taking one's own humanity seriously. But what is it to grasp reality at a somewhat deeper level—the second dimension of Buddhist *satyagraha?* To grasp reality in this sense is to grasp the truth of interdependence, or one's own situatededness in a world in which bonds of causation and care connect one to all others situated in that world. It is to grasp the fact that all suffering is inevitably one's own, and so to cultivate not merely sympathy but compassion, the great compassion that inevitably leads to engagement and action. It is to grasp the fact that in participating in the constitution of the world we inhabit we are therefore responsible for that world. To grasp reality in this sense is hence to grasp the fact that the bodhisattva path is not simply the *supreme* human moral path, but the *only* truly human life. And to grasp that reality is therefore to embark upon that path.

To *insist* on the truth is to proceed one step farther. In the language of the evangelical Christian tradition, it is to "testify." For this reason *satyagraha* is necessarily a public life. *Satyagraha* in this sense is pedagogical, publicly calling attention to the truth and demanding attention. This insistence may be verbal. But effective *satyagraha* is always more than that. The actions of the *satyagrahi* are themselves, as Alomes (1998) has eloquently argued, representational, and this representational character is as important as their more direct effects, as they force broad attention to the situations toward which they are directed and to *satyagraha* itself. They simultaneously engage with reality and publicly demonstrate uncomfortable facts and the duties those facts impose. When the Mahatma led the salt march, the public character of that act demonstrated the immorality of the Salt Act, of British repression in India, of the possibility of nonviolent resistance, of the right to make salt, and of the right to *svaraj* and, most important, of the duty injustice imposes to resist openly and nonviolently. To make salt in secret would indeed to have been to make salt but would have been literally an insignificant act, failing utterly to engage the moral issues simply because without the public dimension there can be no representational content to the act. The Rev. Dr. Martin Luther King, Jr., urged a public boycott of the Montgomery, Alabama, buses. It was important not simply that African-Americans not ride segregated buses, but that they be *seen* not to do so, and that their being seen not to do so was articulate, ostending an injustice, a just alternative, and a non-violent method for obtaining justice.

This representational character of *satyagraha* imposes the greatest duties on the *satyagrahi*. His or her every action is not only an engagement, but a demonstration and an assertion. Hence to misstep is also to mislead and to deceive. An act either of violence or of cowardice, however unintentional, could be read by the audience of the action as indicating the justice of such an action. Insistence, hence, requires supreme effort and supreme mindfulness. For the same reason that mindfulness is at the foundation of the eightfold path and of all Buddhist practice, it lies at the heart of *satyagraha*.

I have been characterizing a Buddhist *satyagraha* by grounding practice on a Buddhist conception of truth in an effort to understand the most Ven. Prof. Samdhong Rinpoche's appropriation of Gandhi's ideas and approaches in a Buddhist context. It is perhaps not at all surprising that the account of the practice of *satyagraha* that emerges is no different from what Gandhi himself would have articulated, despite the vast difference in the account of truth and in the relation of practice to that truth. For each account is grounded in a common insight: political action is not incompatible with spiritual practice. It can, in fact, be the highest form of spiritual practice. For to live an authentic life is to live in recognition of interdependence and to honor one's commitment to the world of which one is a part, living so that one's own being is a public reflection of reality. Retreating from the public sphere when public action is necessary is a betrayal. Any truth worthy of articulation is too important to betray.

Temporality and Alterity: Dimensions of Hermeneutic Distance

Snapshots from a Philosopher's Travel Album

If Western philosophers don't think that philosophy can lead to liberation from cyclic existence, why do they do it?

> *A question asked by dozens of Tibetan colleagues and students*

But of course the point of all of this is to attain enlightenment. Otherwise philosophy would be just for fun.

> *rJe Tsong khapa, Drang nge legs bshad snying po, commenting on the motivation for philosophical analysis*

I am worried that these students are just getting religious indoctrination. I mean, they are learning Buddhism, right. And aren't most of the teachers monks?

> *A dean of a small Western secular college at which the works of Aquinas, Augustine, Farabi, and Maimonides are taught in philosophy classes, in response to a proposal that students have an opportunity to study Buddhist philosophy at a Tibetan university*

I can understand why you have come to India to study Buddhist philosophy. For our tradition is indeed deep and vast. But I frankly don't see what we have to learn from you. For Western philosophy is very superficial and addresses no important questions.

> *The Ven. Gen Lobzang Gyatso, director of the Institute of Buddhist Dialectics, in response to an offer of lectures on Western philosophy at his college*

How can an authentic commentary criticize the root text? . . . For a commentary to be authentic, the person writing the commentary has to have the lineage of the root text and permission to expound it. For that reason I could never write an authentic commentary on a Western text. When I read a commentary by a Western scholar, the first question I ask is "Who was this person's teacher?" Then, "Is this person commenting from the perspective of that lineage?"

The Ven. Geshe Ngawang Samten, Director and Vice-Chancellor, Central Institute of Higher Tibetan Studies

Locke talks a lot about how God gives us natural rights, and about how society has to respect those rights. If you don't have a religion with a God does this make any sense?

"Endowed by the Creator with certain inalienable rights . . .": Is this really secular or do you have to be Christian to accept this?

Isn't Mill forgetting that an individual has only the purpose to benefit his society? How can you have complete individual liberty if your society needs you? What would the point of existing be?

A sampler of questions asked by Tibetan students studying Western political philosophy

Hermeneutic theory is always concerned with historicity and with the horizons, prejudices, and purposes that determine and give urgency to the act of interpretation. So let me begin with a few remarks about the situation in which I find myself, and which leads me to this tentative and open-ended query of my own philosophical activity. I have spent most of the last decade and a half working on cross-cultural philosophy. The work I have in mind includes the translation of and the composition of commentaries on texts from Asia for Euro-American audiences, and the translation of and composition of commentaries on texts from Europe for Asian audiences as well as a range of activities subsumed by the rubric "intercultural academic exchange." All of this is, I will argue, of a piece. It must be part and parcel of a single intercultural philosophical venture.

But such enterprises are, despite the present trendiness of multiculturalism in the academy and in the culture at large, deeply problematic. In order to arrive at an understanding of an instance of such interchange, one must inquire into the historical conditions under which it takes place; into the respective characters of each of the textual traditions brought thereby into contact; into the relations they bear to one another; into the nature and the very possibility of the linguistic and cultural translation such interchange involves; and finally into the very possibility of reading a text in a tradition that is not one's own.

All of these questions are fraught with real political significance. We operate in the shadow of colonialism and its intellectual wing, orientalism. This history conditions the way we read the literature and respond to the scholars of non-Western cultures, the way they read our literature and respond to us, and even our very conception of what a textual tradition is, and of what constitutes a boundary across which traditions confront one another. Moreover, Euro-American academics meet Tibetan or Indian academics on terms of unequal power. The power differential is manifested concretely in economic and academic terms: in terms of access to university posts; to grants; to libraries, journals, and presses; and even the ability to obtain that indispensable tool of the academic trade, the laptop computer—in short, the issue is access to the seals of authenticity and to positions from which those seals can be conferred or withheld. More subtly, but no less significantly, the languages in which we interact encode power relations. It is no accident that many more philosophical texts are translated from Tibetan into English than the other way around, and that most of the professional literature on Tibetan philosophy is published in English, Italian, or German, languages that many of the most distinguished Tibetan philosophers neither read nor speak. One cannot engage in cross-cultural scholarship and interpretation without becoming implicated in these political problems. To ignore them is only to be implicated unreflectively. Moreover, to the extent to which hermeneutic activity is essentially historical—and that is a very great extent—and to the extent to which political facts are central to the historical character of any moment— also a very great extent—this political dimension is part and parcel of the character of cross-cultural hermeneutics today. It defies bracketing, however desirable such bracketing might appear.

So why advance on such difficult ground, particularly when to advance might involve one, however inadvertently, as a philosophical mercenary in a strange, late-colonial proxy war? The answers here are simple, and, to me at least, utterly compelling: first, it turns out that the West has no monopoly on good philosophical ideas. So to treat *philosophy* as denoting something the Greeks and their German descendants did, and therefore as comprising nothing Asian, commits one to two grave errors: either one presumes falsely that no Asian ever did what the Greeks and Germans did (think reflectively about the nature of things) or one presumes that there is something terribly special about such reflection when done in Athens or Freiburg. Just what could that be? So if one wants to study philosophy, restriction of one's purview to the European tradition is both arbitrary and imprudent.[1]

The second reason is this: the world is increasingly one of close interconnection. Whereas only a few decades ago we could ignore Tibetan philosophy and the Tibetans could ignore ours simply because Tibet and its intellectual community remained more or less hermetically sealed behind the Himalayas, just as a few centuries ago European and Indian pandits could safely ignore one another, this is true no longer.[2] Maybe cultural purity was a good idea. Maybe it was not. But whether or not it was, it is history (if that). As Dan Quayle put it with characteristic eloquence, "We live in a global world." It hence becomes increasingly difficult, even if one wants to, to avoid contact with other philosophical traditions. People who look different, who understand their intellectual lives differently, and who read different books in strange languages often move into the next office! or enter your classroom! And when they do, strange things happen. I direct your attention to the collection of curios at the beginning of this essay. These collectively can be taken to pose or to indicate a problem: how is it possible, given the apparent substantive and methodological gulfs we find between ourselves and those with whom we wish to be colleagues, to interact productively—to become genuine colleagues? Reflect on these snapshots as you read. This chapter attempts to understand them and the broader phenomena they indicate and hence to elucidate both the possibility and the value of cross-cultural interpretation.

How to understand the recent acceleration of intercultural contact is a complicated matter. On the one hand, one might say that what we are seeing at this turn of the century is a rapidly progressing intercultural dialogue or fusion of cultures, with each contributing to the ferment. But that optimistic view of the situation is surely too naive. It ignores the tremendous disparity between the resources and power of Western culture and those with which it comes into contact. If we reflect on this disparity, and on the reality of such contact, it might be more accurate to say that we are currently witnessing the erasure of the world's other cultures by the West. But this is also too simple a view. For the erasure is not complete, and not simply for lack of effort or success. Rather even if (a big *if*) one sees a looming Western global culture, it will be a changed culture, in view of its incorporation of much from those it has subsumed. Or one might see this subsumption not as a process of erasure, but of recontextualization of other traditions in relation to the West. I take no position on this matter here. However one understands this situation, it sets a philosophical problem: to the extent to which we consider traditions to be radically distinct from one another, it is hard to see how productive cross-cultural interpretation can take place at all. For if we take this strong notion of tradition seriously, each tradition—each temporally extended set of texts, written and oral, musical and artistic—comes with its own hermeneutic method. Inasmuch as such a method is internal to a tradition, and concerned primarily with the relation of texts and interpreters to very particular traditions, these hermeneutic theories will be ill suited to reading texts of alien traditions.[3]

I started thinking hard about this problem when I embarked upon a translation of and commentary on an Indian Buddhist philosophical text (Garfield 1995). The task of presenting to Westerners a polivalent text in English, without erasing its available readings in its home tradition yet allowing it a life of new possibilities in English, became both urgent and apparently theoretically impossible: urgent because of the force and clarity of the philosophical vision I encountered and what I saw as its potential value to Western philosophers; impossible because of the inappropriateness of a importing the hermeneutic theory of the Western tradition of the task, and because of the inevitably self-defeating character of exporting the Buddhist hermeneutic method to the West in order to clarify a Buddhist text to Western readers.

So I have decided that we need a more general hermeneutic approach for global scholarship, not a context-free Archimedean principle of universal interpretation—that is chimerical—but a practical guide to talking across borders with the purpose of achieving some mutual understanding. We need nothing transcendent, just a useful guide to productive interchange between persons of good will.

This remark about talking—about conversation between persons—as opposed to the interrogation of text, is self-conscious and is central to my project here. I will argue that a model of understanding and interpretation that takes traditions or their texts as primitive and takes the recovery of meaning from texts as the goal of hermeneutic activity lacks the resources to explicate intercultural exchange. However, we can achieve a measure of understanding of this activity if we take a more pragmatic approach to the activity. That is, I will urge, crosscultural interpretation can only be understood to the extent that we conceive of ourselves as engaged with interlocutors in a common purpose, and that the texts with which we engage are texts—in-being-read, or in-being-explained.

The problem for the cross-cultural scholar is not simply that understanding is difficult to achieve, but rather that it is not clear whether understanding across truly distinct cultural traditions is *possible*, or even that we can have a clear notion of what such understanding would *be*. This is true because understanding as a hermeneutic notion has been most clearly explicated as having an essentially temporal structure, involving a historical orientation of the reader with respect to the text read and with respect to the tradition comprising both text and reader. This linear structure imputed by such theorists as Heidegger and Gadamer to reading and to understanding is neither arbitrary nor parochial. The Buddhist hermeneutic tradition, for instance, despite the fact that in detail it is different from European hermeneutic theory, agrees about this fundamentally temporal structure of the hermeneutic task.

Writing, reading and speaking are communicative deeds that are always enacted incompletely. Each succeeds only by presupposing an indefinite background, a structure of prejudice, and a horizon capable of rendering determinate a set of essentially indeterminate signs. Absent such a context, a text is so much elaborately distributed ink; a conversation, an abstract design in sound. Meaning enters the knots of Indra's net only from the infinite distance marked by each cord. What could constitute an appropriate context for cross-cultural understanding, and how are we to create such a context?[4] In general, hermeneutic context is provided by the history of calls and responses that together constitute a tradition. Calls may find responses in unexpected places; responses may be for a time ignored and may re-emerge. In the end this improvisational, conversational activity is the source of the essentially temporal character of human existence. Our cognitive episodes gain content from our history and anticipate a future whose context they themselves construct. Our individuality mirrors, even as it constitutes, our collective intellectual history. J. L. Mehta expresses the point this way:

> [Husserl, Heidegger, and Merleau-Ponty] . . . reflect on the basis of [the Occidental] tradition, so that the questions they raise and seek to answer have a necessary reference to that tradition. They also exhibit a relatively novel concern within philosophy for this fact itself as being integral to that quest for universality which is of the very essence of philosophical thinking. What we call progress in philosophy depends in large measure on the continued exposure and overcoming of our naiveté, of what is at any stage taken for granted and remains implicit. Philosophical claims to universality, not only in individual thinkers but also in entire traditions are themselves rooted in presupposed particularities of vision and what was once regarded as an obvious, straightforward and absolutely valid affirmation turns out to have been "rendered possible" by certain implicit presuppositions. A significant advance in present-day philosophical awareness consists in the growing sense of new sorts of questions engendered by this and in the quest of a wider generality of thought and utterance which is not yet unmindful of the particularities it seeks to transcend and of the fact that such transcendence always remains relative to the particulars which constitute its point of departure. (Mehta 1985b, pp. 135–36)

Mehta, despite his optimism regarding contemporary philosophy, indicates obliquely the problem we face: most contemporary hermeneutic theory presupposes the integrity and relative insularity of traditions, and, despite their historicity, the stability of texts as objects of interpretation. Without integral traditions, the background against which interpretation takes place is too indeterminate to yield understanding. It is through taking the text as a fundamental unit of analysis that we arrive at the notion of the evolving horizons of a text, and of a tradition as constituted by a series of texts.[5] But in addition, this hermeneutic standpoint presupposes that in reading we can know in which tradition(s) we and the text we read are to be located, and that that fact is determinate. For otherwise there would be no ability to access the relevant tradition in interpretation.

All three of these assumptions must be questioned. It is not clear that the world's intellectual traditions—when that term is used broadly enough not to yield insularity as a trivial consequence of its definition—ever were mutually insulated, and it is clear that they are not now so. It is not at all clear that in thinking about the goal of scholarship and of reading, especially in a cross-cultural context, the exegesis of particular texts is the central phenomenon in understanding. And it is far from clear that we can unproblematically locate ourselves or the texts we read in these contexts in one tradition or the other, and it would seem undesirable in this context to do so in any case.

To question the integrity and the unidimensionality of traditions, is also to rethink the role of hermeneutic distance. Temporal distance—the distance most often discussed in this context—can be an impediment to understanding. Time can distance readers from the idiom, concerns, or presuppositions of a text and render what would be familiar to an author's contemporaries obscure and curious. But temporal distance is also essential to the possibility of genuine understanding and of progress in a tradition—that is, of the possibility of intellectual *history*.[6] Without distance, what is presupposed at one moment could never become questioned at another. Understanding, always an interplay of prejudice at work and prejudice revealed, is only possible when we are far enough from our object to see it more completely and so to reveal that which it conceals from anyone in its neighborhood.

This double-edged character of distance is intriguing in the cross-cultural context. For while barriers of language and culture can conceal that which is known to the other—just as temporal distance can make mysterious what would be commonplace in proximity—one would think that just as temporal distance also reveals what is hidden in proximity, cultural distance can make salient for a somewhat alien interpreter what is hidden to the denizen of a culture.[7] Perhaps just as we read Plato with greater understanding than Plato himself ever could, Tibetans, or Tutsis, can read Plato—and especially Quine—with greater understanding than we ever could.

This sets the present task. I intend to inquire into the possibility of cross-cultural understanding, and into the relationship that such an understanding would indicate between readers and texts separated by alterity as well as by time, and between interlocutors from distinct traditions. I inquire in a spirit of optimism, born only of my own sense of the benefits already achieved from such interactions when undertaken in good faith, and I hope to come to understand a little better the difference between distances found on these distinct hermeneutic axes.

I will begin by setting out a few commonplaces of hermeneutic theory—at least as I find it in my home tradition. With these tools, I will turn to a survey of temporality and alterity as axes of difference. At the end I will try to develop a picture of the kind of conversation I hope will become possible.

HERMENEUTIC CIRCLES

It has become commonplace since Heidegger's account of understanding in *Being and Time* (Heidegger 1962) to note the circular character of the hermeneutic enterprise. But merely noting the reality of the hermeneutic circle is insufficient to characterize the complexity of the labyrinth of interpretation. For in any interpretative situation there are circles within circles. First of all we can note the circle constituted by the relation between any account of the meaning of an entire text and an account of the meaning of its parts. Any theory of the meaning of an entire text is built upon an interpretation of its components. But at the same time, any hypothesis about the meaning of any component of a text—of a word, a phrase, or even a chapter can be justified only by reference to an account of its role in the text as a whole, and of its relation to the remainder of the text. This constitutes the first hermeneutic circle.[8]

This circle has its image in a far larger and, for present purposes, a far more important hermeneutic circle: just as part and whole are reciprocally related in the understanding of a text, they are reciprocally related in our understanding of a tradition. A text makes sense only as a response to its predecessors, only in light of its consequences for future texts, and in the end only as seen through subsequent commentary. Imagine reading or writing a serious commentary on the *Critique* in isolation from the *Meditations,* the *Treatise,* or the *Essay.* Imagine explaining its significance without mentioning Hegel or Schopenhauer, or Heidegger, Sellars, or Quine. Imagine understanding *Mūlamadhyamakakārikā* as a text from Mars, out of the context set for it by Abidharma debates, or the *Prajñāpāramitā* literature. Better yet, imagine explaining its significance without mentioning Buddhapālita, Bhāviveka, or Candrakīrti. These eminent texts, to use Gadamer's apt phrase, derive their significance and eminence from their roles in the traditions in which they are located. But at the same time the very traditions that determine the significance of these texts themselves comprise precisely the texts they make possible. This second hermeneutic circle hence has the same structure, on a grander historical scale, as the first circle noted.

This third circle—the one Heidegger emphasizes most forcefully—involves the relationship between the reader and the text in the context of interpretation itself. A text is not a mere splash of ink on paper, or an agitation of the atmosphere. A text is constituted as such by its meaning, and hence by being understood. Its character and identity are hence determined by a history of encounters with readers. Each encounter transforms its meaning, and hence its identity. This is a central expression of the historicity of any text. But nor is a reader a biological organism, at least not qua reader, embodied though she or he may be. A reader is a structure of prejudices, anticipations, and views: an occupant of a horizon whose interaction with that of the text constitutes the phenomenon of understanding. For a text to be understood is, however, for the horizon of the reader to be altered thereby, and for her attendant prejudices, questions, and sensibilities to change. That is, in understanding a text, the reader becomes a different reader. Any two apparent encounters of an individual scholar with a single text are really distinct first encounters—in each instance a new reader encounters a new text. This third hermeneutic circle is also constitutive of the temporal and interactive dimensions of personhood. It brings us to the centrality to scholarship of the actual encounter with the text—with the practice of reading. It is easy to think of intellectual traditions as constituted by abstract texts read by disembodied minds. But to think of them thus is to ignore the heart of the matter. A tradition is a tradition of acts and activities. These include acts of reading, of writing, and especially of talking. By focusing more directly on the praxis of understanding, I hope that we will see our way more clearly to a legitimate cross-cultural intellectual enterprise.

These three hermeneutic circles are mutually implicative. None can be realized without the others. Together they constitute both what it is to be a text, what it is to be a tradition, and what it is to be a reader. Each issues in an endless spiral of textual evolution, and of the reconstruction both of content and of context through the interplay and evolution of the horizons of text, tradition, and interpreter. This interplay constantly modifies each participant. Every serious text is composed, and every serious reading undertaken, with this historical dimension in view. The encounters that constitute this history are easily overlooked, though, in discussions of traditions themselves, even by those—such as Gadamer and Heidegger—who have done so much to bring them to our attention in their accounts of the hermeneutic circles. One then thinks of the tradition itself as a collection of texts, and the hermeneutic practice as merely a means by which those texts are read and extended. I want to reverse figure and ground here and urge that we attend to the *act* of interpretation, and to the *act* of discussion as central constitutive components of traditions, and to focus on texts not as independent objects of study, but rather as texts-being-read; and to consider our interactions with our colleagues and students as central to our intellectual life. Only by taking this radically pragmatic turn can we understand the possibility of intercultural dialogue.

A strictly Gadamerian-Heideggerian account of the circular and temporal structure of understanding and of writing presupposes the integrity and the unidimensionality of a tradition. The tradition is, on this view, the context that makes textual meaning and its understanding possible, and that gives point both to writing and to reading. If this picture is correct, there is no way to understand the possibility of crossing traditions. It then behooves us, before turning to the problematic situations that occur when distinct traditions encounter each other, to examine more closely the concept of tradition itself.

THE ROLE OF TRADITION

Traditions make understanding possible. But this possibility is also always achieved through occlusion. When we understand a text, we exploit its anaphoric relation to its predecessors, as well as our background of cultural prejudices. These considerations apply mutatis mutandis to conversational interactions. Locating a text as an object of analysis involves making salient particular features of that text while suppressing others, privileging certain intertextual relationships over others, and selecting among commentarial traditions. Interrogating a text is always interrogation with interest. A decontextualized text is impossible to read; a decontextualized interchange is impossible to follow, just because of the essentially intertextual character of any text. But all of this means that in *selecting,* and in *foregrounding,* we unavoidably select *against,* and *background.* Understanding hence involves, as part of its very structure, *blindness.*[9]

A principal role of tradition is to provide the material for this horizon—to supply the intertextual context and the background of prejudices that makes reading and talking possible. They thus provide the context in which revelation of meaning and the composition of a meaningful text become possible. But at the same time traditions conceal the prejudices they comprise, as well as alternative readings and possible significances of the texts whose readings they enable. And once again, just as the hermeneutic task implicates the possibility of bringing to the foreground its own horizons, every tradition implicates the possibility of foregrounding its own historical horizons.

Traditions, according both to Gadamerian and to Mahāyāna Buddhist hermeneutic theory, have an additional crucial role in the hermeneutic enterprise: they are a repository not only of context but also of commentary. Commentary provides an explicit reading of a root text or set of texts, or of a previous commentary. Sets of commentaries define ranges of possibilities. And even when taken to be erroneous, or at least unsuccessful, a commentary demands response and recognition. In an articulated tradition, such as the philosophical, musical, artistic, or literary traditions of the West, of South/Central Asia or of East Asia, a large volume of textual material consists of commentary and subcommentary, and these commentaries provide constraints on subsequent discussions of texts. Attending to the role of commentary at a time when I was simultaneously writing a commentary on an Asian text for a Western audience and on a series of Western texts for a Tibetan audience has in fact led me to my own questions about the possibility and nature of cross-cultural exchange. It is in commentarial literature that the temporal dimension of a tradition is most salient, and also there that traditions may appear to be the most insular and unified. But these appearances can be deceiving: interpenetrations are apparent—sometimes acknowledged (as in the case of Schopenhauer or Dharmakīrti); sometimes alleged (Pyrrho or Ngog blo ldan shes rab). And as translation, interaction, exchange, and dialogue occur, intertextual relations multiply. Deutsch presents what we might call the "standard" version of a commentarial tradition, in his account of South Asian textual traditions:

> A tradition text has . . . authoritative sources grounded in the oral transmission, its summaries, its ongoing written elaborations. The basic commentary (*bhāṣya*), or the shorter commentaries (*vrttis*), with the subcommentaries (*tikas*) and glosses (*varttikas*), form, hermeneutically, integral parts of a continuing argument or text. They are not so much appendages to an otherwise fixed and completed work (the *sùtra*) . . . as they contribute to a larger, developing work. The exegetical material expands, refines, modifies arguments and ideas, and presents new ones, usually with increasing precision . . . , seeking to bring greater systematic coherence to a body of ideas. The philosopher-commentator seeks to remain faithful to his authoritative sources, but on his own creative terms. It is thus that we can speak of his work, together with its authoritative sources, as a constituting a "tradition text." (Deutsch 1989, pp. 169–70)

But the problem such a picture presents should be evident: to the extent that traditions are this integral, and to the extent to which authors must select and situate themselves within a determinate tradition, the prospect for exchange between traditions is nil. For within each, understanding, writing, and talking require complete situation. And no one can be in two places at one time. This is doubly problematic: on the one hand it makes the actual porosity of traditions mysterious. On the other hand, it argues against any attempt at genuine interchange in the future. This last consequence is particularly troubling. For if the view Deutsch articulates is correct, it entails the possibility of coming to awareness of a multiplicity of traditions. The choice—or chance occupation—of any one hence becomes arbitrary. And just as no rational interpreter would privilege a particular historical moment as that at which interpretation should occur, none should privilege any particular tradition as that within which interpretation should occur. Just as temporality demands attention to texts as historical, alterity should demand attention to texts as cross-culturally significant. But if we accept the strong integrity and insularity thesis, this demand cannot be fulfilled. On the other hand, of course, there is much that is correct about Deutch's Gadamerian view of traditions. The task is to preserve these insights while extending the network of intertextual and interpersonal links available to us.

A tradition also determines a reader's proximity to a text and a discussant's proximity to an interlocutor. It is a determinant of sameness or difference, and of the possibility of functioning as a genuine interlocutor, as opposed to an intellectual stranger. Suppose a close colleague drops in on you in your office to ask your opinions about some matter of campus politics, or about a recent book. The ensuing conversation will reflect a shared background, purposes, sense of what is important and salient, dialogic strategies, and a mutual trust. The understanding you two achieve of each other's remarks, and of each other's own views, state, and situation are determined by this shared background. Now, suppose instead that a Tuvan anthropologist turns up, armed with her tape recorder, bush jacket, and solar topi, pursuing research on the anthropology of the American academy, asking the same questions, eliciting the same views regarding the same range of subjects. Your response to these superficially identical conversational gambits will be markedly different: indeed, they are not at any interesting level the *same* gambits. You are being interrogated by an alien. No shared background can be presupposed. How will your remarks be interpreted? How can she know what you mean, and to what unspoken resonances you respond in speaking? Can you trust her? Should she trust you? What is important from her perspective? How can you convey to her what is important from yours? What must be explicit? How is it appropriate to talk when one is an informant or an anthropologist, as opposed to a friend? How is it appropriate to listen? Hard questions. But whatever the answers, we can note two truisms: Much that will be apparent to you and your friend will be hidden from your Tuvan interrogator. Much of which she discerns about you will come to you and to your friend as a surprise—heretofore hidden just because of its proximity.

At stake here is the possibility of productive conversation. It is hard to speak with as much precision as one would like about these matters. But we can note an interesting tension along the dimension of alterity here: if we really occupy *toto genere* different worlds, the best we will get will be travelogue snapshots of each other. The folks back home will oooh and aaah, but nothing will be learned. If we are too much alike, not enough will come into relief to make the exercise more than a friendly chat. Think for a moment of our respective positions not as separated by walls but as distant in a continuous space. To occupy a position is to participate in a "form of life" in precisely Wittgenstein's sense.[10] That means that much of the background we exploit is tacit, comprising practical rather than theoretical wisdom. The ethnographer encodes some of that background in a more explicit form. But conversation presupposes a sharing of enough of that tacit background to make interchange possible—an overlap in cognitive and conversational abilities. How much? That will depend on many factors, and will vary from context to context. If there is to be an interchange, and not a study, we need enough proximity on certain dimensions to talk, and enough distance to see.

The same range of phenomena that determine distance and proximity in conversation determine our relations to texts with which one enters into dialogue. When one shares a great deal with a text, one approaches it with a familiarity that facilitates dialogue but at the same time masks all that one shares with it. When one encounters an alien text, much will be hidden that will be apparent to home-culture interpreters. But much of what they share with it, though hidden to them, will be apparent to the alien reader. Our understanding of this phenomenon depends on our understanding of the traditions themselves. If we conceive of them too rigidly, they end up partitioning the world into insiders and outsiders, and boundary-crossing becomes mysterious. If we rethink them as marking locations in a more continuous space, this dual role of distance is comprehensible.

THE ROLE OF DISTANCE

The space in which hermeneutic distance is delimited is not obviously isotropic. Let us note some special features of temporal distance. First, texts mature over time. A sequence of commentaries, replies, apologies, and influences changes a text. This point is especially clear if we understand texts pragmatically, as constituted through their encounters. We read the first *Critique* today in a way that Kant's contemporaries and immediate successors never could. That text now, as it could not have been then, determines the split between Hegel and Schopenhauer, the foundation of Bartlett's psychology, the end of the early modern period, and so on. But moreover, it is the text whose range of readings is determined by Hegel, by Schopenhauer, by Kemp Smith, by Wolff, and so on. *Mūlamadhya-makakārikā* is now, as it never could have been in the second century, the foundation of Madhyamaka, the text that determines the split between Svātantrika and Prāsaṅgika schools, and so on. Moreover, it is the text whose range of readings is determined by Āryadeva, Buddhapalitā, Bhāvaviveka, Candrakīrti, Chih-I, and so on. Eminent texts gain in significance with the passage of time.[11]

Time is special in another important respect. Traditions, even when conceived more loosely than they are by Heidegger, Gadamer, and their followers, share with human life a deeply temporal structure. Texts are composed in response to textual history, and with an eye to the future. This may seem like a truism. But inasmuch as we are comparing the temporal with the cultural dimension of distance, it is a truism of real significance. For we compose texts with the history of the tradition we regard as *ours* in mind differently from the way we hold what we regard as *other* traditions in mind. We usually—unless explicitly engaged in cross-cultural activity—write for those we regard as our fellows. When *others* enter our consciousness in this context, it is typically either in being written *about* or in being excluded.[12]

My encounters with Tibetan colleagues—cotemporal but transcultural encounters—who ask questions like "If Western philosophers do not think that philosophy can lead to liberation from cyclic existence, why do they do it?" and who respond with blank stares or laughs when I try to explain the intrinsic value of knowledge have led me to foreground and to examine the secular character (or secular pretensions) of contemporary Western philosophy and its vexed relation to science and to religion. (See chapter 14 of this volume for a continuation of this examination.) But this same encounter has also allowed my Tibetan colleagues to problematize the assumption that even all of *their* philosophical endeavor is of soteriological import. Distance seems to operate in this fashion symmetrically, independently of the dimension along which it is measured.

Moreover, distance in each dimension provides us with a greater sense of context for a work. The closer one is in time to a text within one's own tradition, the more difficult one has seeing its context, partly because many of the central intertextual relationships will connect the text to later texts, but partly also because those later texts and the intertextual relations they induce will also induce new relations of the text itself with its contemporaries and predecessors. Temporal distance illuminates these relationships and hence these dimensions of meaning. But cultural distance can accomplish this disclosure as well. So, for instance, I first noticed the successive addition of distinct ontological perspectives on objects within idealism represented by the evolution from Berkeley (who regards external objects as purely ideal) through Kant (who sees them as in one sense ideal, but also as having an empirical reality dependent upon the mind) to Schopenhauer (who grounds these two perspectives in a third providing an insight into the noumenal nature of phenomena) when I looked at these philosophers through the lens of Yogācāra doctrine, which thematizes these natures as understood from the standpoint of idealism. (See chapter 8 in this volume.) Since this is not thematized in the West, absent distance on the dimension of alterity, this particular evolutionary character of our tradition remains invisible if we restrict our purview to European texts. But once noted, it perhaps explains the progressive character of Western idealistic thought, and the curious fact that what begins as theistic immaterialism becomes a foundation for scientific realism.

THE PECULIARITIES OF ALTERITY

As we saw in the case of temporal distance, the advantages and disadvantages of alterity turn out to be two sides of a coin. We can note four distinct kinds of barriers to understanding posed by alterity, bearing in mind that these barriers are not thereby *defeaters*. First, and most obviously, alterity entails less access to the tradition in the context of which a text is most naturally situated, and this in two respects: first, the reader and the text will not share much by way of common heritage, and second, the reader will generally know much less of the background literature to which the text responds, and much less of the commentarial literature on the text than would someone steeped in its immediate cultural tradition.[13]

Second, language will often constitute an impediment to full understanding. A reader may be forced to read through translation, hence relying in part on the interpretations of others, and on the vagaries of indeterminate and competing translations. Third, the text and the reader are often at cross purposes where culture is not shared. When, for instance, at the close of a lengthy and very technical discussion of a debate concerning the nature of linguistic meaning and its connection with inner episodes—a discussion naturally read with relish by an analytic philosopher of mind as a piece of pure epistemology—rJe Tsong khapa wrote in fourteenth-century Tibet: "But of course the point of all of this is to attain enlightenment. Otherwise philosophy would be just for fun," one immediately feels the distance that separates a contemporary Western philosopher engaged in what is superficially the same debate from the author of *Drang nge legs bshad snying po*. Failure to appreciate the purport of a text can lead to a misreading, subordinating perhaps exactly those concerns that the tradition would foreground, or foregrounding those it would subordinate.[14]

Moreover, at the most abstract level, we encounter a puzzle that concerns the very structure of the reader-text relationship when recognized boundaries of tradition are transgressed. For as we saw above in our discussion of the hermeneutic circle marked out by reader and text, this relationship in its intratraditional context, where this is understood in something like Gadamer's terms, is essentially temporal and reciprocal. In the reading of alien texts, on this view, not only is an atemporal dimension added, but this circularity and reciprocity is, at least prima facie, disrupted: within a tradition we write in the anticipation that our work will be read by those who share our concerns, and whose views will be shaped in the delicate pas de deux of sameness and difference that a tradition mediates. We also write in the anticipation (or at least the vain hope!) that our text itself will evolve in response to subsequent readings, responses, and commentaries. The circular character of this relation between reader and text ensures that texts and readers are equally subject to transformation in the history of a tradition. But when we read an alien text, on this view, our alterity violates that authorial expectation regarding the nature of future readers and makes it impossible—or at least highly unlikely—that, however much we may be affected by the text in unanticipated ways, our own reading will similarly impinge upon the text itself. For to the extent that we remain outside of a tradition, our response to its texts will be irrelevant to their reception within the tradition. Understanding in such a case becomes not a phenomenon of a progressive spiral of mutual influence, but a peculiar psychological dead end. This complex problem is scouted by Panikkar:

> Diatopical hermeneutics is the required interpretation when the distance to overcome, needed for any understanding, is not just a distance within one single culture . . . or a temporal one . . . , but rather the distance

between two . . . cultures, which have independently developed in different spaces (*topoi*) in their own methods of philosophizing and ways of reaching intelligibility. . . .

The great problem in such a hermeneutical approach is the peculiar type of pre-understanding necessary to cross the boundaries of one's own philosophical world. This problem already exists within a single culture. But in our case we have something specifically different. Here we are under a different *mythos* or horizon of intelligibility. We understand because we are within the hermeneutic circle. But how can we understand something that does not belong to our circle? (Panikkar 1989, p. 130)

The fact that it is possible to have productive encounters across cultural boundaries, and that texts are successfully translated, read, and discussed by persons at some cultural remove should alert us to deficiencies of this approach to the hermeneutic task. The problem once again is simply that on this model any such success is miraculous, or at least mysterious. If, however, instead of focusing on the discovery of meaning in a text by a reader, we focus on the productive use of a text at a time by a reader or a possibly quite internally diverse community of colleagues and students and if we de-center the act of reading and interpretation of written texts, broadening our view to encompass discussion, commentary, and other forms of interchange, the mystery vanishes. The range of material available to such groups is far broader. Inevitable intersections facilitate conversation and learning. Texts can be productively used in a multiplicity of ways. Insurmountable barriers become merely challenging hurdles.

The Politics of Alterity

Given a powerful scholarly tradition practiced by the members of a politically and economically powerful group, it is indeed possible to come to know another culture by bringing it as object under the lens of one's own intellectual microscope. In doing so, however, one transforms that body of knowledge in fundamental ways. Indeed, the transformation is so complete that if it is successful, the alien culture becomes relegated to a merely historical phenomenon. The authority as readers and interpreters of its texts is shifted from those within the tradition to the alien experts. Alien commentaries gain ascendancy over traditional commentaries. The hermeneutic method of the conqueror becomes the standard means of reading the vanquished, and the vanquished tradition becomes, as the Ven Geshe Ngawang Samten put it in conversation, "the domain of curators." To the extent that we value a culturally distant set of texts and practices sufficiently to seriously consider active engagement with members of the community whose texts and practices they are, this is no option. Daya Krishna is particularly eloquent on this point:

Across the boundaries defined by the "we" and the "they," the world of comparative studies is inevitably an attempt to look at what, by definition, is "another reality" from the viewpoint of that which is not itself. . . . [It implies an] appeal to the universalism of the knowledge and the identification of the knowledge with the privileged "us" from whose viewpoint all "other" societies and cultures are judged and evaluated. The roots of the privileged position have generally lain in the political and economic powers of the society of which the viewer happened to be a member. . . . [C]omparative studies . . . were, by and large, an appendage of the extension of some Western European countries' political and economic powers over the globe. . . . As this expansion was accompanied not only by phenomenal growth in some of the traditional fields of knowledge but also by demarcation and consolidation of new areas designating new fields of knowledge, the feeling that the claim that all "knowledge" discovered by the West held universal validity was justified. It was seen, therefore, as a universal standard by which to judge all other societies and cultures anywhere in the world. . . .

Comparative studies, thus, meant in effect the comparison of all other societies and cultures in terms of the standard provided by the Western societies and cultures. . . . The scholars who belonged to these other societies or cultures, instead of looking at Western society and culture from their own perspective, accepted the norms provided by the Western scholars and tried to show that the achievements in various fields within their cultures paralleled those in the West, so they could not be regarded inferior in any way. This acceptance of bias hindered the emergence of what may be called "comparative 'comparative studies'" which might have led to more balanced perspectives in these fields.

Further, the so-called comparative studies were primarily a search for facts or the reporting of data in terms of conceptual structure already formulated in the West. The questions to which answer were being sought were already predetermined in the light of the relationships that were regarded as significant or the theories that were to be tested. (Krishna 1989, pp. 72–73)

There is another question to be raised, however: having abandoned a framework that treats traditions as discrete and mutually inaccessible for one in which we occupy positions distant from one another to varying degrees, we can then ask, Is it then appropriate for anyone to remain content with a particular location in that space? Or is there an epistemic and perhaps a moral imperative to move about a bit? Compare for a moment the temporal case. It would be the height of irrationality and epochal hubris for anyone to assert that whereas all previous historical moments were bound in error, ours alone has emerged into the light of truth. Just as the views of our predecessors have been superseded in all domains by more adequate or more revealing views, so too will ours by our successors. There is no privileged epistemic moment. The case should be even clearer with respect to cultural space. It is hard to seriously entertain the thought that Western music is *the* tradition that interprets aural beauty correctly, or that Japanese Buddhist philosophy is *the* standpoint from which to investigate the fundamental nature of reality, or that German hermeneutic theory is *the* uniquely adequate framework for interpretation and criticism. Given the availability of distinct positions in this cultural space, it then becomes something of an epistemic imperative to view matters from several rather than from one of them, just as a survey of physical terrain requires triangulation.

The imperative is moral and political as well. For the failure to take other standpoints seriously by those in powerful or prestigious positions stigmatizes those positions. The failure to admit those from other cultural positions into our dialogues makes a clear statement about the conditions of club membership. To the extent that these messages are not the ones we wish to send, we should think twice about cultural complacency. These concerns are even more compelling when raised in the contemporary postcolonial context. For from many of the traditions with which we are concerned legitimate complaints about exploitation on the one hand or marginalization on the other can be raised. Whether one approaches this from the standpoint of intellectual reparations or from that of remedial multiculturalism, a strong case can be made for a moral obligation on the part of Western intellectuals to engage seriously with the traditions of others. The bottom line, I think is that cross-cultural interaction is not only possible, but imperative. But how does one achieve this in a way that avoids the pitfalls of Orientalism?

The first thing to say is a kind of boring commonplace: collegiality is terribly important. This is of epistemological as well as political significance. The point is this: in encountering an alien tradition, we encounter not a fossilized sequence of texts but an active form of intellectual life. This requires genuine interaction with living scholars on terms of equality. They can be treated neither as "informants" nor as oracles. To interact as colleagues is to presume that in interchange we and our interlocutors come with questions, information, each with a legitimate purpose and interest. It is to be prepared to question, to answer, and to correct, and to be questioned, to be answered, and to be corrected. It sounds easy.

One of the reasons that it is not, in fact, easy is that in any such encounter, each party brings his or her own background of prejudices regarding the other. These require a certain degree of articulation and problematizing. (Many of my Western colleagues regard, antecedent to reading them, Buddhist philosophical texts as just so much religious mysticism without any philosophical merit, in contradistinction to the secular rigor of Augustine, Aquinas, and Descartes. But one of the most instructive experiences I had in this regard occurred when an eminent Tibetan scholar, responding to my offer to lecture on Western philosophy at the institute he directs, replied, "I can understand why you have come to India to study Buddhist philosophy. For our tradition is indeed deep and vast. But I frankly don't see what we have to learn from you. For Western philosophy is very superficial and addresses no important questions." Genuine dialogue requires that we begin by examining, questioning, and when necessary revising our own views of each other, and that we develop, rather than presuppose, the basis of our collegiality.[15]

THE PROBLEM OF TRANSLATION

Cross-cultural scholarship and interpretation inevitably implicate one in worries about translation. Indeterminacy is not a merely "theoretical" problem afflicting mythical jungle linguists charged with the creation of translation manuals for radically different languages. The moment one moves from tourist phrasebook to translation of eminent text, the polyvalence of the source text and its essential intertextuality conspire to make available an infinite number of equally bad translations and no good ones. Every reasonable proposal for an accurate translation will jostle with other equally reasonable proposals. For in translation one is always balancing a number of desiderata (things such as lexical associations, rhyme or prosody, anaphor, preservation of style or rhetorically important syntactic devices, ambiguities or puns) that inevitably turn out to be in conflict at every turn. Which desideratum receives precedence can often turn on one's reading of the text and its relation to context (see Bar-On 1993). And of course the way a text is translated in turn determines how it will later be read. Translation and interpretation are hence inextricably bound and are both radically indeterminate.

There is also an important political dimension to translation. Translation programs are typically asymmetric: We translate the texts of a tradition we are studying and typically, in studying that tradition we transfer expertise regarding it to the dominant tradition in which the study is being pursued. But rarely do we find the dominant, subject tradition translating its own texts into the language of the subordinate object tradition. This privileges the subject's language and hence reinforces the privileged status of the tradition of the subject, to the disparagement of the object tradition. The work of the subordinate tradition is hence assimilated as an object of study, while the superordinate tradition can congratulate itself on having "broadened its horizons," and having brought more within the scope of its own method. Daya Krishna depicts this situation graphically:

> [M]ost of the discussion about Indian philosophy is carried on in the European languages. Perforce, therefore, the Sanskritic terms have to be translated into their Western equivalents, giving the latter a magisterial status in deciding what the former mean or ought to mean. The converse situation normally does not take place; but recently when at Puna the

experiment was tried of translating some issues in Russell and Wittgenstein into Sanskrit so that responses might be elicited from persons trained in philosophy in the traditional manner, the difficulty became apparent. How were the pandits—philosophers trained on the Sanskrit classics in the traditional manner—to make sense of what Russell and Wittgenstein were saying? As most of them did not know English, the matter had to be translated into Sanskrit, but then those Sanskrit terms carried the usual connotations associated with them, and resisted the imposition of new meaning upon them. (Krishna 1989, p. 78)

Too often the task of translating the philosophical works of the dominant member of a cultural dyad into the language of the other is eschewed in favor of providing scholarships for students of the subordinate culture to study the language and texts of the dominant tradition. What would the consequence be of our recognition of authoritative translations of our works into the languages of "exotic" cultures, and of our recognition of the expertise of their scholars as interpreters of our own texts? Perhaps genuine interchange.

How to Hold a Productive Conversation

How are we to approach our alien colleague? There is always the possibility of the good old-fashioned way: we call him an "informant" and duly pump him for his views of the text and tradition, which then enter the field of knowledge when translated, indexed, analyzed, systematized, and reported as data within our own research. Not much needs to be said at this point regarding the odious character of this colonial approach to scholarship. On the other hand, we could do it in the (paradoxically denominated) New Age method: we can become disciples, accepting all that our new-found and suitably exotic guru says without criticism and with the greatest reverence. He is, after all, infallible. And even if he is not, who are we to question? (One does have to ask at some point just why alien cultures are so proficient at generating such oracular figures.)

One is tempted here to yet another truism, Be collegial! Neither more nor less. But if that requires either a common model of collegiality or a transcendent one, we would then be back to square one. Even collegial relations must be negotiated with due regard to the demands and presuppositions of each culture.[16] Matters are not simple here. For common purposes cannot be presupposed. Our goals in the discussion may not be the same, nor our presuppositions about what is possible or proper. Geshe Ngawang Samten, for instance, pointed out to me in conversation that in reading Western texts he proceeds with the understanding that they, unlike Buddhist texts, do not reflect a lineage grounded in an infallible canonical ground, and that they will contain a mixture of truth and error. Moreover, when reading them, he defers to Western interpretations and presumes neither his own "authority" to read these texts independently nor the "authenticity" of any reading he may develop. Authenticity and authority, from his standpoint and from that of the culture he represents, demand that one hold an appropriate lineage, and that one regard the text on which one is commenting as canonically expounded by one's lineage. The goal of commentary on his view is never to develop any original philosophical idea or interpretation, but rather to recover authorial intent. Debates in secondary literature are always debates about authorial intent, and the only criterion of interpretive success is the recovery of that intent. Hence, when he reads the work of Western commentators on Buddhist philosophy, the first question he asks is, "Who was this person's teacher?" Then, "Is this person commenting from the perspective of that lineage?" Only if the answers to these questions are satisfactory can the commentary be taken seriously. That is not to say that there might not be ideas to be drawn from a nonauthoritative text. But one's relation to that text will be very different from that which one would bear to an authoritative text. Tibetan scholars often find it odd and somewhat amusing that Western philosophers treat both their own texts and the work of Buddhist philosophers so differently, and that we give such autonomy to the text as opposed to the author, and so much latitude to interpreters. Geshe Ngawang Samten (in conversation) compares our view of the relation of author to text to the relation of a miner to gold: once he has dug it, it is up to others to make something out of it, and the miner is forgotten by the goldsmith. An apt metaphor.

Note then, that often, when a Western and a Tibetan scholar collaborate, different agendas are brought to the table: the Western scholar may feel comfortable importing a Buddhist text into her philosophical canon and repertoire: Plato, the Buddha, Aristotle, Nāgārjuna, Berkeley, Vasubandhu, Kant, Candrakīrti. . . . The traveler brings home souvenirs. The Tibetan scholar, on the other hand, may read the Western texts for insights into his own but leaves them where he found them. They remain alien. In this kind of intellectual tourism, the sights one sees remain abroad though the lessons they teach may be valuable once one reaches home. This difference is no bar to collaboration. But failure to attend to the differences may lead to misunderstanding. A productive conversation requires awareness of these differences, and a productive engagement with the literature of either culture by one who comes from a distance requires this same awareness. This, we might say, is a second-order hermeneutic distance, a distance of method superimposed on a distance of primary textual concern.

This indicates the necessity to read extensively in the tradition with which one hopes to interact, to learn its language(s), and to listen patiently and quietly to insiders as they expound their tradition. No matter what the attitude is in the United States to lineage, my understanding of the Buddhist texts I read is enhanced by appreciating that role in the Buddhist tradition, and my willingness to enter into a transmission lineage gives me an access to interactions otherwise unavailable, as well as new interpretive perspectives. Tibetans who interact extensively with us and our texts develop the ability to engage more productively in discussions of our texts, and in comparative interchange when they come to appreciate the difference in our interpretive practices. Just as Davidson has emphasized the illusory character of the scheme/content distinction, we must bear in mind that hermeneutic method and philosophical content are in the end parts of a seamless whole. To begin to negotiate a strategy for co-operation in hermeneutics, mutual methodological understanding is a prerequisite.

Do not be content to be a student of an alien tradition. Teach your own as well. For all of the demands of familiarity with the other that you face are faced by your interlocutors as well. Collegial interaction demands this kind of symmetry. Good manners demand that one contribute as well as learn. But moreover, in teaching, and hence in facing the difficulties involved in making one's own tradition clear to another, one attains a glimpse of its contours, and a deeper insight into the prejudices of the other. Nothing has changed my appreciation of Western political philosophy as much as teaching it at a Tibetan university. Reflective teaching not only gives one better colleagues but presents unique opportunities for understanding.

In this kind of genuine interchange between colleagues, the advantages of alterity emerge, as well as its differences from temporality as a dimension of hermeneutic distance. For in this arena the possibility of interactively placing one's own texts and concerns against another horizon, and of watching new texts and concerns emerge in outline as they interact with one's own is realized. The dynamic character of scholarly interchange is not incidental to this process, nor merely facilitative. It is essential. For again, understanding is actualized in the interaction between historically situated readers and texts and between interlocutors. This is no less true of inter-traditional understanding than it is of intratraditional understanding. Only by engaging in such actual interactions can we hope to benefit from the special kind of distance alterity provides. For there we see how we as recipients of our tradition and our interlocutor as a recipient of his each come to understand the work of the other. And in dialogue the dynamic interplay of our horizons can yield a perspective genuinely responsive to the presuppositions and insights of each.

Finally, and maybe most important, presume that anything of value must be transactionally obtained. To come to the task as a pirate, or as a distributor of intellectual charity, is to preclude understanding by precluding interaction. Only through a genuine openness can the flowering of two traditions, distant enough to permit perspective, yet close enough to talk, yield the fruits of cross-fertilization and render difference not a barrier to, but a facilitator of, understanding.

Philosophy, Religion, and the Hermeneutic Imperative

THIS IS AN ESSAY about the meaning of life. It is hence about our hermeneutical self-understanding. The word *meaning* notoriously has many meanings, and indeed in at least two senses of that term in its primary occurrence in the preceding sentence. And it might be thought that when we seek the meaning of a text and the meaning of our life we are seeking not simply different meanings, but different kinds of things entirely—that the first inquiry is properly hermeneutical and that the second is perhaps religious, or at least phenomenological. Among Gadamer's great achievements, he demonstrated that this is not so—that in coming to understand our lives as meaningful, we apply the same hermeneutical considerations to ourselves that we apply to understanding texts. That insight might seem to resolve the notoriously difficult problem of understanding the meaning of life into the prima facie easier problem of textual semantics. Unfortunately, however, it goes the other way around: the apparently unproblematic encounter with ink on the page or sound waves in the air turns out to be fraught with all of human being.

This essay is also about a curious hermeneutical and political phenomenon in the contemporary academy, one I will approach from personal experience, and experience I only came to understand through reflection on Gadamer's hermeneutic theory: I was brought up in the Western philosophical tradition, and more narrowly, primarily on what is called somewhat polemically and misleadingly "Anglo-American" philosophical literature. Throughout my education and early professional career, I never questioned nor was encouraged to question the presupposition that philosophy is a European phenomenon. (Nor, I might add, did I consciously *assert* that it is—the issue simply never arose.) Never did a Chinese, Japanese, Indian, Tibetan, or African philosopher or text enter my philosophical horizon until I began my teaching career and was led in that direction by the interests of my students. As it happens, my research interests have drifted Eastward, and now I spend a considerable portion of my professional time working on Indo-Tibetan Buddhist philosophy, and in collaboration with Tibetan philosophers.

The fact that I often work in this area has occasioned a number of interactions in which my Western colleagues say things like, "When you were still doing philosophy . . ." or "Now that you are working in religious studies. . . ." Now the questions I address when I work on texts and with scholars in this tradition are often pretty much those I address when I work on Western texts and with Western colleagues, give or take a bit—problems concerning the nature of causation, the nature of mind and intentionality, moral psychology, logic and the theory of justification, and so forth. Given this scenario, which is no secret, these encounters with Western colleagues suggest a peculiar attitude toward this work—more peculiar still given the fact that without exception those who preface their remarks in this way never read either my work in this area or the literature it addresses. But they know that it is not philosophy. And despite their epistemological sophistication, the juxtaposition of this knowledge claim with the manifest lack of evidence for it does not trouble them. Nor, I hasten to add, is this attitude somehow peculiar to my immediate acquaintances. One sees it reflected in philosophical curricula throughout the West, and in the fact that the vast majority of Western scholars of Asian philosophy are located not in departments of philosophy but in departments of religious studies, Asian studies, and so on.

I find that it does not trouble most Western philosophers that they have never so much as glanced at a text written in Asia, nor entered into dialogue with an Asian philosopher (mutatis mutandis for Africa, the Islamic world, and so on). Nor does it trouble many in our profession that academic departments in the West are often called "philosophy departments" when their academic coverage is limited to the Western philosophical tradition. Why not?

There are two comfortable answers that I hear most often when I raise this challenge. The first is this: "There is a world of difference between philosophy and religion, and what passes for 'Eastern philosophy' is in fact religion misnamed. Western philosophy is independent of religion, and is a rational, religiously disinterested inquiry into fundamental questions about the nature of reality, human life, and so on." But this distinction is supposed to deliver the result that St Thomas Aquinas's *Summa Theologica*, Descartes's *Meditations*, including the proofs of the existence of God, and Leibniz's discussion of theodicy are philosophical, while Dharmakīrti's investigations of the structure of induction and of the ontological status of universals, Tsong khapa's account of reference and meaning, and Nāgārjuna's critique of essence and analysis of the causal relation are religious. Anyone who has a passing familiarity with all of the relevant texts will agree that something has gone seriously wrong if this distinction is taken seriously.

The second reply is this: Western philosophers simply plead their lack of familiarity with the Asian texts, and inability to approach them, let alone to teach them or to use them in research. Those who offer this reply sometimes piously lament the presumably irremediable lacunae in their own philosophical training or their lack of competence in the relevant canonical languages. Better for the shoemaker to stick to his last, they say, then to lapse into charlatanism. This argument—however noble the scholarly sentiments to which it appeals—of course must rely on at least one of the following suppressed premises: (1) Asian philosophy is unreadable by anyone with European ancestry; (2) One should never read anything one has not already read or teach anything one has not been taught in graduate school; (3) One must never rely on a translation in teaching and research, and Asian languages are impossible to learn. I am not sure which of these options is more implausible, but many seem unembarrassed by reliance on at least one.

I find this second reply hard to take seriously as a theoretical position, though to be sure it demands political and rhetorical attention as a late moment in postcolonial racism. My real concern is with the first reply—that Asian philosophy, so-called, is really in some deep sense different in kind from Western philosophy—that it is religious in a sense that Western philosophy is not, and so with the relation between philosophy and religion and the connection of that relation with our understanding of the intellectual and geographical bounds of philosophy.

THE MEANING OF LIFE

Human self-understanding is always hermeneutical. It is by now a commonplace, thanks to the work of Professor Gadamer and of Heidegger before him, that for ink on a page to be more than an interruption in an expanse of white, for vocalizations to be more than "sound and fury, signifying nothing" and that for a work of art to be more than so much matter distributed in some physically describable way, crucial meaning-determining context is required, as well as interpretative commitment on the part of a reader or interlocutor. Just so for our human lives. From the standpoint of disinterested physical science, we are nothing but ephemeral, biologically driven organizations of matter: local, temporary, counter-entropic eddies in a vast indifferent universal flow to cold, homogenous darkness.

Our lives derive meaning, just as do our inscriptions, not from their intrinsic physical or biological properties, nor from any properties reducible to these, but from their context; not as solitary embodied texts but as moments in living traditions; and finally, not by virtue of anything available to the disinterested gaze, but only through the engagement made possible by interpretive commitment. The meaningfulness of any human life is hence always the collective achievement of the community in which that life is lived and of the tradition in terms of which that community understands itself and its members can understand themselves and each other. In this context we must remind ourselves that the relevant interpretive commitment—the willingness and determination to find meaning and to take that meaning as *important*—includes the commitment to take one's own life seriously as well as the reciprocal commitment to take others' seriously. *Dasein* is only possible in the context of *Mitsein*.[1]

For many cultures, including both the cultures descending from classical Greece and those descending from classical India and China, central to the traditions constituting the interpretive background against which their participants' lives gain meaning are textual traditions: extended sequences of written texts, written and oral replies to and commentaries on those texts; identifications of part of those traditions as canonical, and characterizations of what is excluded. More specifically, in all of these cultures, specific textual traditions take as their explicit problematic sorting out the canons of interpretation, accounts of the good, and so on in their respective cultures, and hence, we might say, working out the meaning of life. Among these textual traditions are those we identify as religious and philosophical traditions.

We must acknowledge that philosophy and religion as pretheoretically individuated share this hermeneutical role if we are to understand the curious ambivalence toward religion and religious traditions in contemporary Western philosophy. The antipathy that allows the use of *religious* as a dismissive epithet (again, bracketing for now its descriptive adequacy) for Asian philosophy is not in the first instance the antagonism toward that which is alien, but more an instance of the special vitriol that is reserved for members of the family or erupts in civil war but in this case is accidentally directed outward. The most significant difficulty with the dismissal of Asian philosophy as religion is not the fact that in the relevant sense (to which we shall shortly come) that charge is false, but that in that very sense, as well as in the deeper sense at which I am driving at here, Western philosophy is also profoundly religious.

PHILOSOPHY AND RELIGION AFTER THE ENLIGHTENMENT

Contemporary Western philosophy, despite its roots as old as classical Greece, derives much of its contemporary problematic and professional profile from the European Enlightenment. Even the most contemporary postmodern philosophical developments can only be understood as reactions and sequels to the upheavals of early modernity. European philosophy's professional self-understanding as, inter alia, an opposition to religion and its identification of its own canon and organon in contrast to those of religion also originates at that moment.[2] It is easy to make too much of individual figures or events salient in retrospect, and it is not good history to do so. But so long as we are careful not to take ourselves to be doing intellectual history but rather collective professional phenomenology, sketching the outlines of the self-understanding common to our tradition, it is not too much of a distortion to say that the Galileo affair forced philosophy to make a choice: science had at that moment thrown down the gauntlet at the church door, and there was never again to be a genuine coincidence or reconciliation between Western science and Semitic religion, as opposed to an uneasy and forced coexistence, abetted either by platitude or lame apology. Philosophy had to choose sides, and philosophy, of course, backed science.

The choice was indeed forced, and philosophy, to be sure, made the right decision. But the forced character of the choice and the correctness of the decision derives crucially from the specific character of the Semitic religions (principally, of course, Christianity) against which science was rebelling. First and foremost, these are *revealed* religions whose central tenets require that kind of faith Mark Twain characterized with his typical acidity as "believing what you know ain't so." Second, they are *theistic* religions, and hence religions which propose an account of reality according to which there is a terminus to explanation, and hence according to which there is a final horizon to all self-understanding. Given its own epistemic commitments, and given the success these commitments demonstrated and promised, science could never accommodate itself methodologically to revelation. And given the endless frontier of discovery it anticipated, a creator would be not only superfluous but also obstructive.

The progressive, empirical character of science, with its emphasis on the autonomy of reason and the consequent power to transform the natural world, gave rise to its image in a progressive humanism envisioning the possibility of endless reconceptualization of what it is to be human, progressively deeper self-understanding, and through this autonomous, empirical, and rational practice, the transformation and improvement of humanity itself. Modernity, so conceived, was a very good idea indeed, especially when contrasted with the available alternative. Academic philosophy could not but choose the side of science, and the great philosophical texts of that period, prominently including Descartes's *Meditations*, Kant's *Critique of Pure Reason*, as well as his essays "What Is Called Enlightenment" and "Conflict of the Faculties," document and confirm this choice.

In choosing to side with science, philosophy was hence emphatically choosing *against religion* and in doing so it was defining itself explicitly in contrast to religion. This emerges most clearly, of course, in Kant's critical philosophy in which the domains of reason and faith are so carefully circumscribed. In defining *itself* against religion, though, academic Western philosophy was also defining *religion* as its antithesis: philosophy is rational; religion dogmatic; philosophy progressive and humanistic; religion static and transcendental in its epistemic authority; philosophy atheistic, at least methodologically; religion theistic, particularly epistemologically.

Philosophy and religion so conceived are indeed as different as night and day. But the conception is misleading on two levels: first, we have to face squarely the fact that academic philosophy in the West never fully repudiates its Semitic religious background. The respects in which this is true are too numerous for complete enumeration, but here are some examples: Descartes finds it necessary to *prove* the existence of God, and Kant needs at least the *idea* of God; divine commands remain the model of morality in deontological ethics; liberal demo-cratic theory happily adopts a conception of human beings *self-evidently* "en-dowed by their Creator with certain inalienable rights"; the professional special-ization "philosophy of religion" invariably means "philosophical discussion of Christianity." I emphasize that these are only examples. For a more extended treatment, I advise reading Schopenhauer and Nietzsche, each eloquent on this point.[3]

So the divorce was never complete, and the religious roots of Western philos-ophy ensure that even its most recent fruits are Christian in character however determined the effort to occlude that fact. That this is so is partly to be explained by the deeper respect in which Western philosophy is religious: its purpose, after all, has been soteriological from its classical period (and though this was more explicitly articulated by Aristotle, the skeptics, and stoics than by modern and postmodern successors, it remains at the heart of the enterprise)—the articulation of the context in which we can give meaning to our lives. *Articulation* is here used in both senses of that term: through philosophy, as through religious thought, we both constitute and come to understand the ground of that meaning, and we do so through a hermeneutically self-conscious textual tradition. Para-phrasing Clausewicz, we can say that philosophy is the continuation of religion by other means, just as long as we also realize that those means are only ever so slightly "other."

PHILOSOPHY AND RELIGION ON THE PATH
TO ENLIGHTENMENT

The history of philosophy and its relation to religion is of course not uniform in the world's cultures. A comparison with Buddhist culture is instructive here (though it is important to bear in mind that we cannot simply generalize from the Buddhist context to any other Asian, let alone African or other non-Western context). The European enlightenment has no historical counterpart in India or China. There was never a cataclysmic rift between religion and science, and so philosophy never had to take sides. Buddhism is atheistic, rejects revelation as epistemically authoritative, and is committed to infinite human perfectibility through empirical inquiry and rational analysis, culminating in full awakening, or buddhahood. And most Buddhists follow Siddhartha Gautama in regarding this perfectibility as the individual responsibility of each person. Buddhism as a religion, of course, has the trappings and social functions we expect to find in a religion: prayer, spiritual practices, rituals, temples, festivals, and so on. Their efficacy or propriety can be questioned, and there could be good reason to reject any part or all of Buddhist religion as a rational or efficacious practice, just as there could be with respect to Christian religious practices.

Buddhist philosophy, like Western philosophy, aims to understand the fundamental nature of reality, the nature of human life, and so provides a hermeneutical context in which those in Buddhist cultures constitute and understand the meaning of their lives. Buddhist religious practice, like Christian religious practice, aims at similar goals. But in the Buddhist context, religious and philosophical practice have never been prised apart as distinct and independent cultural practices, as opposed to connected parts of a seamless cultural artefact. And this is true not simply because Western science was late to come to the Buddhist world or because when it did it had little impact. Its impact has indeed been marked. It is asked because the particular features of Semitic religions just adumbrated that generate the rift between philosophical and religious traditions in the West are simply not present in Buddhism.

This is, of course, neither a brief for Buddhism as a religion (many of its tenets and practices are every bit as scientifically problematic as any of those of Christianity, and its particular vision of human perfection may be no more plausible than Christian theism) nor a brief for Buddhist philosophy as in any sense superior to Western philosophy. Rather, it is an argument for the cultural specificity of the truth of the claim—even to the limited degree that it is true—that the categories of religious and philosophical discourse determine a dichotomy, which is in turn determined not by the respective characters of religious thought and philosophical thought per se, but rather by the particular methodological and substantive commitments of specific religious and philosophical traditions at particular historical junctures. Seen from the standpoint of their role in the project of human self-understanding, the continuity between religious and philosophical discourse—and indeed between them both and literary and historical discourse— is more dramatic than any differences.

We can now return to the facile dismissal of Buddhist or other Asian philosophy as "just religion." In doing so we can reconstruct a slightly more plausible, but still fallacious argument and can thereby diagnose the deeper errors committed by those who would be so dismissive: philosophy and religion represent distinct and incompatible hermeneutical and epistemic enterprises. Buddhism is manifestly a religion. Therefore any thought bound up with it is not properly philosophical. We can now see that it is the first premise that must go—falsified not only by the very case under consideration but also by the Western tradition itself, which is supposed to provide the best evidence. Our vision of philosophy as handmaiden to the sciences must be replaced with one of philosophy as a synoptic discipline providing the interpretive context for our full range of epistemic, artistic, and moral activities. Understanding philosophy in this way forces us to see that it also has a central role in constituting the narrative in the context of which we become persons and not mere physical objects. We then find that it joins a host of other allied hermeneutical activities in that position, and that it cannot help but be interpenetrated by them.

Philosophy must hence be seen as intimately bound to other humanistic, hermeneutic activities such as religion and history. It follows that the fact that in some Asian cultures philosophical and specifically religious practice remain more closely bound than they are in contemporary Western culture can in no way stand as a reason for disparaging the philosophical character or merit of those traditions.

Hermeneutic Practice, Humanism, and Human Life

I said at the outset that this chapter is about the meaning of life. That, of course, does not mean that it is an attempt to articulate that meaning. (Philosophers, after all, notoriously retreat from real, first-order questions to the safer ground of metatheory!) Instead I am concerned with the sense in which life can be found meaningful and the intellectual activity through which that meaning can be discovered. The crucial insight is provided by Gadamer's hermeneutical theories: the discovery of meaning is always a circular movement embracing the reciprocal relation between parts of texts and the whole that comprises them at the level of text and the larger image of this reciprocity in the relation between texts and the traditions that comprise them. Only the horizon of a text can determine the meaning of any part thereof; only the totality of the meanings of the parts can constitute the semantic horizon that text provides. Only the horizon of a tradition can determine the interpretation of any text; only the totality of texts a tradition comprises can constitute that larger semantic horizon. (See chapter 13 of this volume for a slightly more extended discussion of hermeneutic circles.)

We can conjoin this first insight with a second—that human beings, qua persons constitutively, though not of course exhaustively, are both bearers of meaning and creative participants in the set of meaning-bearing and meaning-determining practices that constitute the cultures and traditions in the context of which they live their lives. These cultures hence constitute the rich semantic horizon against which our lives come into relief as significant, and through that significance construct that very horizon. No sequence of words, however intelligently constructed and carefully printed and bound, absent a tradition in which it can be read and understood, can be interpreted as an eminent text and rise to real cultural significance. For exactly the same reasons, absent the hermeneutic context provided by a culture, no human life, whatever its internal structure, can be more than a "walking shadow . . . full of sound and fury and signifying nothing." Every bit as much as our literary and philosophical works depend for their meaning on their intertextuality, our lives each depend for their meaning on our interdependence with our fellows.

The hermeneutical counterpart of the collapse of the duality between conceptual scheme and empirical content is the collapse of anything pretending to be a duality of truth and method. Every tradition carries within it not only a set of texts demanding interpretation but a canon of interpretive practices that are themselves textually encoded and subject to interpretation. We encounter here yet another significant hermeneutic circle. This interweaving of object and method of interpretation is also, of course, present in the relation between human life and human culture. Our cultures do not only comprise sequences of interdependent lives calling for understanding, but also sets of practices encoded in those lives themselves through which lives are understood and in terms of which meaning is assigned and constituted. The variety of the interpretive practices involved in the assigning of meaning to lives in their cultural contexts is every bit as great as the variety of practices used in the assigning of meanings to texts in their traditional contexts. This variety is neither surprising, nor is it any insurmountable bar to cross-cultural understanding. In fact, such difference facilitates the kind of cross-cultural dialogue that ultimately leads to greater self-understanding. We recognize an initially alien form of interpretation not by finding it to be in all respects like our own (after all, it would then not be *alien*), but in virtue of recognizing a homology of function. It does for *its users* what ours does for *us*. This homology of function can then provide a fulcrum for understanding difference, for dialogue, and eventually, perhaps, for the fusion of horizons that can permit genuine collegiality and eventually the appreciation of those features of our own life invisible to us precisely because of their proximity.

In the modern and postmodern West, as in the textually articulated Hindu, Buddhist, T'aoist, and Confucian cultures of Asia, the practices centrally concerned with the interpretation of life are those of the humanities, including at least in the West philosophical, religious, historical, and text-critical practice. Again, any claim to universality of these precise disciplines, or especially the distinctions marked between them in twenty-first-century European, American, and Australasian universities and those patterned on them, would have to be tempered by the preceding reflections: we look for homologies of function, not mirror reflections of our own practices and commitments. But the homologies are real, reflecting a common purpose. Humanism, here understood as a commitment to that purpose *common* to these disciplines, is unavoidable, because human beings, qua persons, are committed to self-understanding; because all understanding presupposes meaning-constituting practices; because self-understanding requires practices constituting lives as meaningful; because only cultures comprising sets of interpretive practices that take as their object human life can do that. Rejection of the hermeneutic imperative is thus rejection of one's own humanity.

Now seen from this perspective, it is clear that this commitment—this humanism—binds philosophical and religious practice so tightly that they cannot be separated by any culturally contingent rift such as that caused by the particular interpretative practices espoused by the Christian church on the one hand, and the nascent natural sciences on the other, in the sixteenth and seventeenth centuries.[4] This is not to deny the real difference between the modes of interpretation encoded by Semitic religious traditions and the Western project of modernity and its aftermath in which Western academic philosophy is appropriately involved. It is instead to urge both that that distinction is in a larger context not so deep after all, and more important, that to expect that distinction to appear universally would be both ill motivated and a serious barrier to intercultural understanding, particularly in encounters with cultures in which no such distinction can be drawn. At its worst it permits us to ignore deep and important philosophical traditions, an ignorance that in the present postcolonial historical context has significant moral and political implications as well as more obvious intellectual problems.

Ignoring the philosophical traditions of other cultures in fact, whether we like it or not, continues the colonial project of subordinating those cultures to our own. That project was "justified" by the white man's burden of bringing civilization to the benighted heathen, a burden of which we can only make sense if we deny their manifestly existent intellectual traditions the epistemic status we grant ours. Giving the Western philosophical tradition pride of place as "philosophy" while marginalizing in our departments or in our individual life all other traditions, if the arguments I have offered are cogent, hence implicates us directly in institutional racism. Recognizing that we are so implicated and refraining from changing our individual practice and from working to change our institutional practice hence constitutes, however passive it may be, individual racism. It also constitutes a profound epistemic vice, that of willfully ignoring sources of knowledge we know to be relevant to our own activities. It is a measure of the importance of Professor Gadamer's hermeneutic theory that it allows us to come to see these failings in ourselves and to see our way to remedying them.

I further note that a fixation on this superficial distinction can also lead to a mis-taking of the role of philosophical activity itself, a mislocation of philosophy in the *Naturwissenschaften* and a failure to appreciate the essentially *soteriological* character of philosophical activity. For philosophy always begins in *aporia*, always aims at *noûs*, and always for the sake of *eudaimonia*. Or to put it another way, philosophy always begins in *avidya* and *saṃsāra*, always aims at *prajñā*, and always for the sake of *nirvāna*. This quest turns out to be built into *Dasein* itself.

Notes

1. Epochē and Śūnyatā

I thank Dick Garner, David Karnos, Dan Lloyd, and the members of the Propositional Attitudes Task Force, particularly Janet Gyatso, John Connolly, Kathryn Addelson, Bruce Aune, Lee Bowie, Istuyaque Haji, Murray Kiteley, Meredith Michaels, and Janice Moulton, for spirited discussion and for many useful comments and suggestions on an earlier draft of this essay. Thanks especially to Janet Gyatso for much enlightening conversation, for assistance and support in my efforts to understand and to interpret Buddhist philosophy, and for detailed criticism of my use of the Buddhist texts I discuss here. An earlier version of this chapter ("Waking Up to Regularity: Scepticism as a Meta Physick") was read to an NEH Summer Institute on Nagarjuna and Buddhist Thought, at the University of Hawaii in the summer of 1989. I thank David Kalupahana, Steve Odin, Kenneth Inada, and Arthur Herman for that opportunity and for their comments on the essay.

1. From here on, for the sake of brevity, I use the term *Buddhists* to refer specifically to the *Prāsaṅgika-Madhyamaka* school of Mahāyāna Buddhism. I will be primarily concerned with the work of Nāgārjuna, Candrakīrti, and Tsong khapa, all major figures of this school. Many of the arguments and the specific tenets I will discuss would be received and understood differently by philosophers in other schools of Buddhism.

2. Wittgenstein, of course, frequently denies that he is a skeptic: "Scepticism is *not* irrefutable, but obvious *nonsense*" (1979, p. 44). But I would argue that the position Wittgenstein denotes by "scepticism" is what I am calling here "nihilism." The type of response Wittgenstein repeatedly offers to the skeptical problems posed by nihilistic arguments is characteristically skeptical.

3. At least as the Yogācāra are interpreted by Candrakīrti and Tsong khapa. But the prāsaṅgika accounts of Yogācāra may well be uncharitable, and the idealism imputed to them and attacked by the prāsaṅgika may well be more extreme than any position the Yogācāra philosophers actually espouse. I take no position here on the correct resolution of the attendant hermeneutical disputes. In a similar vein, it may well be that a correct reading of Berkeley would recognize his idealism as more Kantian and transcendental than that "dogmatic idealism" Kant and most others impute to him. But these questions of interpretation, too, are beyond the scope of this discussion.

4. Note that I am lumping together ontological and epistemological claims. This is not to suggest that the rejection of the existence of the external world is the same as the

261

rejection of *knowledge* of the external world. It is merely to remind us that historically the route to nihilistic ontological claims has often been through the assessment of the objects of putative knowledge.

5. There are real philosophical and interpretive problems regarding my interpretation of Nāgārjuna as indicating by "material form" something akin to what Hume disparages as "material substance." This is not the place to defend this interpretation in detail, and in fact there are important differences between the ways substance and material form figure in their respective ontological positions. But these differences do not undermine the central claim that in the context of disputes concerning the reality and status of the material world, their respective conceptual roles are importantly analogous. It should be noted in this context that Nāgārjuna in the stanzas just quoted and elsewhere in his corpus discusses the emptiness of material form as a single central example of the emptiness of phenomena quite generally. But again, this rhetorical role of the discussion of form leaves the comparative point undisturbed.

6. My reading of Nāgārjuna's distinction between causes and conditions, and the account of causation and explanation I attribute to him is, I know, controversial; and Nāgārjuna's remarks on these topics are cryptic enough to sustain a number of plausible competing interpretations. The view I attribute to Nāgārjuna (developed in more detail later and in Garfield 1995), however, renders his account of causation, of the conditions of the nature of explanation in the world of saṃsāra, and of the ultimately empty nature of causation both compelling and remarkably similar in form to his more explicitly articulated views concerning the nature of self, of action, and of form. I acknowledge the somewhat tendentious nature of the reading, and the fact that it is hard to see these theses explicitly asserted in the texts, but I stand by the cogency of the interpretation.

7. The Prāsaṅgika conception of suspension is very much the same. Compare with the discussion of nonduality in Book 9 of the *Vimalakīrtinirdesa-sūtra* (Thurman 1976).

8. There is hence a similarity to Strawson's account of refusing to assert either that the present king of France is bald or that he is not bald, in virtue of rejecting the common presupposition that the two alternatives share—the existence of a present king of France.

9. This metaphor also appears in the Buddhist literature, both in the early sūtras and in the later Mahāyāna literature. Candrakirti quotes the *Ratnakūta sūtra*:

> Kasyapa, consider this example: If a doctor gives a patient medicine, and this medicine cures all of his illness, but stays in his stomach, do you think that suffering will not arise, Kasyapa? Do you think this man will be relieved of the illness in his belly? No way, blessed one! If the medicine, having cured all of his illnesses stays in his stomach, this man will certainly become seriously ill. The Blessed one said, "Kasyapa, you should see the insistence on any view in just this way. If emptiness is seen like that, Kasyapa, whoever sees emptiness like that, will be incurable. I have said that it is like that." (*Prasannapadā* 83b–84a)

10. In fact, this point is rather complicated, For while, as Tsong khapa argues, nihilism really is a philosopher's view—one to which the vulgar are not readily susceptible (Berkeley, to the contrary, notwithstanding)—reificationism comes in two versions. We might call these, with Tsong khapa, "ordinary" and "philosophical." For arguably, the person on the street thinks of the physical as substantial, thinks of causation as a real force, thinks of personal identity as grounded in a soul, and so forth. But these views are probably in the typical case rather inchoate. Philosophical reificationism can be seen as a careful conceptual refinement of this fallacy of everyday metaphysics. It is the job of the skeptic to cure both

the ordinary and the sophisticated forms of the disease. The relative prevalence of reificationism as opposed to nihilism in the streets probably also explains the common confusion of skepticism with nihilism, For given this reificationist epidemic, the arguments the skeptic must most frequently muster are quasi-nihilistic, to most effectively undermine that dogma.

11. I use the term *naturalistic* to denote relational, or nonindividualistic properties or predicates. The relations in question may be either intentional or nonintentional. The contrast is with *individualistic* properties or predicates—which apply to their subjects irrespective of any relations they may bear to other things.

12. These verses are explained in much more detail in Garfield 1995. This brief commentary is sufficient for present purposes.

13. Again, I emphasize that this interpretation of Nāgārjuna on causation and explanation is not defended in this chapter but at length in Garfield 1995. The extension of his expressed views on ordinary explanation to a theory of scientific explanation must be regarded as highly tendentious but strike me as a useful way to bring Madhyamaka philosophy into dialogue with contemporary philosophy of science and cognitive science.

14. Fodor never comes completely clean in expressing his commitment to this "cement of the universe" picture of causation. The view, however, emerges quite clearly both from the passages I have quoted and others such as this:

> Effects on causal powers require mediation by laws and/or mechanisms and in the Twin cases there are no such mechanisms and no such laws.
>
> If you are inclined to doubt this, notice that for any causal relation that holds between my mental states and the local water puddles, there must be a corresponding relation that holds between my neurological states and the local water pudles. (1987, 157, n.6 to p. 39)

And consider, "[Y]ou *can't* affect the causal powers of a person's mental states without affecting his physiology" (ibid., p. 39).

But even without an explicit endorsement of this view (a view that even Fodor might acknowledge sounds crazy when explicitly stated), we can note that Fodor is committed to it inasmuch as, without it, there is no way to *begin* to make the strong locality argument about causation or to draw the distinctions between *genuine* and *ersatz* causal relations Fodor is seeking.

15. This is, of course, a causal version of the "third man" argument.

16. Note, however, that the question regarding whether or not there are exceptionless natural laws (whatever an account of a natural law is) is independent of the question regarding individualism in the philosophy of science generally as well as that regarding individualism in psychology.

17. There is, as Lee Bowie has noted, another account of what physicists do: they posit particles as bearers of forces. But this is no comfort for the Fodorian causal realist. For the behavior of these particles, and the nature of their interactions with other fundamental particles, are again characterized by more-or-less exceptionless regularities, not by reference to the bonding powers of ghostly subatomic superglue.

18. Dick Garner and an anonymous reviewer each raise the following objections at this point: Sextus, they argue, is more circumspect regarding causal powers than I suggest, and in fact, they argue I am downright dogmatic about causal powers in insisting on their superfluity in scientific explanation. For, they point out, in his chapter in the *Outlines of Pyrrhonism* on causation, Sextus provides arguments both in support of the hypothesis

that there are causes, and in support of the hypothesis that nothing causes anything, concluding, "From this, then, we conclude finally that if plausibility attaches both to the arguments . . . [for and against the plausibility of the existence of causes] we must necessarily suspend judgement regarding the existence of cause" (Hallie, 1985 p. 116).

Admittedly, this is a strong exegetical case. But things are not so simple. Careful attention to the differences between the arguments in support of the causal hypothesis and those against it reveals an important methodological insight. The arguments *for* the existence of causation (ibid., p. 113) all hinge on one of two observations—the existence of natural regularities and our ability to exploit these regularities in explanation and prediction. *None of these arguments or observations is called into question in the succeeding discussion.* The arguments *against* the causal hypothesis all hinge either upon the conceptual connection between cause and effect or on the lack of evidence for the existence of any *tertium quid* between putative cause and putative effect. And each supposes the relativity and explanatory utility of putative causes and putative effects, denying only the efficacy or occult link between them. *And none of these arguments is called into question.* When the two sides are put together carefully, we have an argument for the lack of any necessity to assert the existence of occult powers in order to vouchsafe the explanatory utility of regularities.

Moreover, there is nothing dogmatic about this position. What is at issue is the existence of causal powers. Neither Sextus nor I assert or deny their *existence*. What we both deny is the need to posit them, and the view that they have any explanatory force. We suspend—as pointless—any judgment regarding them. But while doing so, we can accept the very scientific and explanatory practices the dogmatist thinks require the existence of causal powers.

2. Dependent Arising and the Emptiness of Emptiness

Thanks to the Ven. Lobzang Norbu Shastri and Janet Gyatso for a very thorough critical reading of and helpful critical comments on an earlier draft of this chapter and to G. Lee Bowie and Meredith Michaels for sound suggestions regarding that draft. This chapter has also benefited from the insightful questions posed by an audience at Mt. Holyoke College, and from the sound suggestions of Tom Wartenberg on that occasion. My deepest appreciation goes to the Ven. Geshe Yeshes Thab khas for his patient and lucid teaching of this text and discussion of Nāgārjuna's position and to the Central Institute of Higher Tibetan Studies, its director the Ven. Prof. Samdhong Rinpoche, and my many colleagues there, including those just mentioned and the Ven. Geshe Ngawang Samten and the Ven. Geshe Ngawang Sherab. Thanks also to my research assistant both at the Institute and at Hampshire College, Sri Yeshe Tashi Shastri and to the Indo-American fellowship program for grant support while working on these ideas.

1. A fine point, suggested by Janet Gyatso: though in the end, as we shall see, ultimate reality depends on our conventions in a way, it depends on our conventions in a very different way from that in which conventional reality does. Despite this difference in the structure of the relation between convention and reality in the two cases, however, it remains a distinctive feature of Nāgārjuna's system that it is impossible to speak coherently of reality independent of conventions.

2. The division into chapters is due to Candrakirti, introduced in his commentary *Prasannapadā*.

3. Some argue that there is no real difference between causes and conditions; others, that a cause is one kind of condition; still others, that efficient causes are causes, and all other causal factors contributing to an event are conditions. Some like my reading. I have found no unanimity on this interpretive question, either among Western Buddhologists or among Tibetan scholars. The canonical texts are equivocal as well. I do not argue that the distinction I here attribute to Nāgārjuna, which I defend on hermeneutical grounds, is necessarily drawn in the same way throughout the Buddhist philosophical world, or even throughout the *Prāsaṅgika-Madhyamaka* literature. But it is the one Nāgārjuna draws.

4. There are two kinds of case to be made for attributing this distinction to Nāgārjuna in this chapter: Most generally, there is the hermeneutical argument that this makes the best philosophical sense of the text. It portrays Nāgārjuna as drawing a distinction that is clearly suggested by his philosophical outlook and that lines up nicely with the technical terms he deploys. But we can get more textually fine grained as well: in the first verse, Nāgārjuna explicitly rejects the existence of efficacy and pointedly uses the word *cause*. He denies that there are such things. Nowhere in chapter 1 is there a parallel denial of the existence of conditions. On the contrary, in verse 2 he positively asserts that there are four kinds of condition. To be sure, this could be read as a mere partitioning of the class of effects that are described in Buddhist literature. But there are two reasons *not* to read it thus: first, Nāgārjuna does not couch the assertion in one of his "It might be said" locutions. Second, he never takes it back. The positive tone the text takes regarding conditions is continued in verses 4 and 5, where Nāgārjuna asserts that conditions are conceived without efficacy *in contrast with the causes rejected in 1*, and where he endorses a regularist view of conditions. So it seems that Nāgārjuna does use the "cause"/"condition" binary to distinguish between the kind of association he endorses as an analysis of dependent arising and one he rejects.

5. The Ven. Lobsang Norbu Shastri has pointed out to me that this verse may not in fact be original with Nāgārjuna but is a quotation from sūtra. It appears in the *Kamśika-prajñapāramitāsūtra* as well as in the *Madhyamaka-Śalistambasūtra*. Inasmuch as these are both late texts, their chronological relation to Nāgārjuna's text is not clear.

6. There is also a nice regress to be developed here that Nāgārjuna does not explicitly note in this chapter, though he does use it later in the *Mūlamadhyamakakārikā* (chapter 7): even if we did posit a causal power mediating between causes and their effects, we would have to explain how a cause event gives rise to or acquires that power, and how the power brings about the effect. And now we have two nexuses to explain, and now each one has an unobservable entity on one end. In chapter 1 of this volume, I explore this problem in more detail and note that it is explored both by Hume and by Wittgenstein in the *Tractatus*.

7. The Madhyamaka position implies that we should seek to explain regularities by reference to their embeddedness in other regularities, and so on. To ask why there are regularities at all, on such a view, would be an incoherent question: the fact of explanatorily useful regularities in nature is what makes explanation and investigation possible in the first place and is not something that can be explained itself. After all, there is only one universe, and truly singular phenomena, on such a view, are inexplicable in principle. This connects deeply to Buddha's insistence that questions concerning the beginning of the world are unanswerable.

8. A formula familiar in the sūtras of the Pali canon.

9. Though this is beyond the scope of this chapter, this last fact, the emptiness of the relation between the conventional world of dependently arisen phenomena and emptiness

itself is of extreme importance at another stage of the Madhyamaka dialectic and comes to salience in *Vigrahavyāvartanī* and in Candrakīrti's *Prasannapadā*. For this amounts to the emptiness of the central ontological tenet of Nāgārjuna's system and is what allows him to claim, despite all appearances, that he is positionlessness. That is, Nāgārjuna thereby has a ready reply to the following apparent *reductio* argument (reminiscent of classical Greek and subsequent Western challenges to Pyrrhonian skepticism): you say that all things are, from the ultimate standpoint, nonexistent. That must then apply to your own thesis. It, therefore is really nonexistent, and your words are hence only nominally true. Your own thesis, therefore, denies its own ground and is self-defeating. This objection would be a sound one against a view that in fact asserted its own inherent existence or grounded its truth on an inherently existing ontological basis. But, Nāgārjuna suggests here, that is not the case for his account. Rather, on his analysis, everything, including this very thesis, has only nominal truth, and nothing is either inherently existent, or true by virtue of designating an inherently existent fact. (See chapter 3 of this volume for a detailed discussion of this issue.)

10. This, of course, is the key to the soteriological character of the text: reification is the root of grasping and craving, and hence of all suffering. And it is perfectly natural, despite its incoherence. By understanding emptiness, Nāgārjuna intends one to break this habit and extirpate the root of suffering. But if in doing so one falls into the abyss of nihilism, nothing is achieved. For then action itself is impossible and senseless, and one's realization amounts to nothing. Or again, if one relinquishes the reification of phenomena but reifies emptiness, that issues in a new grasping and craving—the grasping of emptiness and the craving for nirvāna—and a new round of suffering. Only with the simultaneous realization of the emptiness but conventional reality of phenomena and of the emptiness of emptiness, argues Nāgārjuna, can suffering be wholly uprooted.

11. Paradox may appear to loom at this point. For, one might argue, if emptiness is empty, and to be empty is to be merely conventional, then the emptiness of any phenomenon is a merely conventional fact. Moreover, to say that entities are merely conventional is merely conventional. Hence it would appear optional, as all conventions are. Hence it would seem reasonable to say that things are in fact nonconventional, and hence nonempty. This would be a deep incoherence indeed at the heart of Nāgārjuna's system. But the paradox is merely apparent. The appearance of paradox derives from seeing *conventional* as functioning logically like a negation operator—a subtle version of the nihilistic reading Nāgārjuna is at pains to avoid, with a metalinguistic twist. For then, each iteration of *conventional* would cancel the previous occurrence, and the conventional character of the fact that things are conventional would amount to the claim that really they are not, or at least that they might not be. But in Nāgārjuna's philosophical approach, the sense of the term is more ontological than logical: to say of a phenomenon or of a fact that it is conventional is to characterize its mode of subsistence. It is to say that it lacks an independent nature. The fact that a phenomenon lacks independent nature is, to be sure, a further phenomenon, a higher order fact. But that fact, too, lacks an independent nature. It, too, is merely conventional. This is another way of expressing the strongly nominalistic character of Madhyamaka philosophy. So a Platonist, for instance, might urge (and the mādhyamika would agree) that a perceptible phenomenon is ultimately unreal. But the Platonist would assert that its properties are ultimately real. And if some Buddhist-influenced Platonist would note that among the properties of a perceptible phenomenon is its emptiness and its conventional reality, she or he would assert that these, as properties, are ultimately real. This is exactly where Nāgārjuna parts company with all forms of re-

alism. For he gives the properties a nominalistic construal, and asserts that they, including the properties of emptiness and conventionality, are, like all phenomena, merely nominal, merely empty, and merely conventional. And so on for their emptiness and conventionality. The nominalism undercuts the negative interpretation of *conventional* and so renders the regress harmless. (This is not to say that there are not other interesting, though also in the end harmless, paradoxes in the neighborhood. These more genuine paradoxes are explored in chapter 5 of this volume.)

3. Emptiness and Positionlessness

I am grateful to Kathy Addelson, Nalini Bhushan, and Janet Gyatso for comments on an earlier draft. I also give deep thanks to His Holiness the Dalai Lama, the Most Ven. Samdhong Rinpoche, the Most Ven. Khamtrul Rinpoche, the Ven. Geshe Lobzang Gyatso, and the Ven. Geshe Yeshe Thap-Khas for teachings on these questions and texts. Thanks also to Georges Dreyfus, the Ven. Gareth Sparham, the Ven. Graham Woodhouse, and the Ven. Sherab Gyatso for fruitful conversations and spirited arguments about these ideas. I also thank Jamie Hubbard and Philippe Goldin for detailed and helpful comments on this chapter, audiences at Marlboro College, the University of Helsinki, the University of Lund, Canterbury University, and Massey University for helpful comments. Thanks also to Sri Yeshi Tashi Shastri and to Jamyang Norbu for editorial assistance.

1. The text is full of passages such as this, where it is obvious that Nāgārjuna is suppressing such qualifications inasmuch as the context and the argument make their explicit inclusion superfluous and the metrical requirements of the poetic form would rule out their inclusion.

2. As Newland (1992) puts it:

> According to Ngok Lo-tsawa [Ngog blo ldan shes rab] and his followers mere appearance is the basis of division of the Two Truths. . . .
> . . . His position is that objects of knowledge, posited as the basis of division of the two truths by dGe lugs pa, is too narrow because ultimate truths—emptinesses—are not objects of knowledge . . . In his system, the unfindability of an object under analysis is *called* emptiness, but there is no existent or objects of knowledge to which "emptiness" refers; if emptiness were cognizable, it would (absurdly) have to be inherently existent. . . . (44)

3. The Most Ven. Khamtrul Rinpoche, personal communication. See also Newland 1992, Cabezon 1992.

4. Diogenes Laertius. Trans. R. D. Hicks. *Lives of Eminent Philosophers*, 474–76. 1991.

5. For more detailed discussions of these issues see Cabezón 1992; chapters 1, 2, 4 and 5 of this volume; Garfield 1995, Hopkins 1983, Huntingdon 1989; Napper 1992; or Newland 1992.

6. To see emptiness as nonexistence would be, absurdly, to treat ordinary reality, by virtue of the emptiness of its furniture, as nonexistent. It would also force an uncomfortable dilemma: either, by virtue of the emptiness of emptiness, emptiness itself would be nonexistent, in which case it would be hard to see how all phenomena could in fact be empty, or nonexistence would be the only thing that in fact exists—but in what sense it could exist would be hard to specify. On the other hand, to hypostasize emptiness as a reality behind illusion would be both to assert the nonexistence of the conventional and

to deny the emptiness of emptiness, which, by virtue of the necessary relation of emptiness to empty phenomena, would be unintelligible.

7. To say that things are empty is not to deny their actual, conventional existence. Conventionally existent phenomena are perfectly real. But it in no way follows that anything that lacks inherent existence therefore exists conventionally. Just as rabbits' horns exist in neither sense, so, as we shall see, propositions in the sense at issue exist in neither sense. So this denial of the mādhyamika that they hold a position should emphatically not be seen as a move toward the disparagement of the conventional. Rather it is a clearing of ontological and logical obstacles to the realization that the two truths are mutually supportive. See also Garfield 1995, pp. 250–53, 280–81, 352–59.

8. I will use feminine pronouns throughout to denote Nāgārjuna's opponent for the sake of referential clarity.

9. By "independently existent" in this context, I do not mean *inherently existent*, in the sense central to Madhyamaka philosophy. All I mean here is something that serves as the semantic value of a sentence but exists independently of the existence of any sentence whose meaning it is. Positing this kind of entity or a corresponding semantics leaves open the question of the mode of existence of the entities posited. Similarly, eschewing such a semantics leaves open the question of whether anything exists inherently.

10. We should not, however, *identify* the Nyῑya position with Frege's. In particular, the Nyāya would not hold that the semantic values of propositions are Fregan "third-world" entities, being resolutely first-world realists. It is also important to note in this context that *pratijñā* also denotes the conclusion of an argument—a thesis one is defending. It is therefore also tempting to read this discussion in the context of *svātantrika-prāsaṅgika* debates as one concerning the question whether the mādhyamika develops arguments in which she defends her own conclusions. It should be clear, however, that the remainder of the context undermines this reading. These issues are simply not raised.

11. Note that she does not anticipate and reply to a silly mistake with which she charges Nāgārjuna, that is, that the charge of question begging could be equally made on both sides of the self-refutation dispute.

12. See Ingalls 1949 and Chakrabarti 1995, esp. pp. 53ff.

13. Here we can also see that the common reading on which Nāgārjuna and his interlocutor are arguing about whether *anything exists* cannot be sustained. On that reading Nāgārjuna's thesis that all things are empty would be simply misunderstood by the Nyāya interlocutor as the self-refuting statement that everything is nonexistent (including that very statement). Then Nāgārjuna's reply to the interlocutor would have to be read as the charge that his statement would have be be similarly nonexistent, to which the interlocutor responds that he does not endorse the thesis of emptiness and so is not guilty of the same self-refutation. There is a lot wrong with this way of reading the text: first, it makes the debate just plain silly, on both sides. Nāgārjuna has already, in *Mūlamadhyamakakārikā* responded to the misunderstanding of emptiness as nonexistence (ch 24). Second, Nāgārjuna cannot want to be understood as thinking that the Nyāyika *shares* his semantic theory or ontology. *Third*, Nāgārjuna does not respond by urging that he *has* a proposition, as he would if he were charged with *denying* the *existence* of what he is saying, but rather by urging that he does *not*, a dialectical move that can only be understood if there is something *other* than his words at stake. Fourth, neither emptiness nor existence are even *mentioned* in this interchange, as they surely would be if the topic were a confusion of emptiness and nonexistence.

14. And moreover, *not* whether he has uttered *words*: that is an issue between him and

the opponent, as it would have to be were the issue about the existence, inherent existence or nonexistence, of a linguistic item.

15. It is, of course, this positive desideratum that drives dGe lugs pa philosophers to interpret Nāgārjuna as not repudiating all theses, and to regard emptiness as an object of knowledge, and hence as an entity. For on such a view, there is no problem in understanding how we can know that things are empty. But as we have seen, this does not square well with Nāgārjuna's own assertions or dialectical moves.

16. Moreover, a distinction must be drawn between knowing conventional truths and knowing ultimate truths. For it is central to any Buddhist understanding of the epistemological viewpoint that the nature of one's consciousness and cognition changes dramatically in enlightenment. Whereas in *saṃsāra* one knows objects conceptually, and they appear to one as inherently existent substantial entities, in nirvāna one knows things as they are, through direct, nonconceptual consciousness. Our account of what it is to relinquish all views, as well as our account of the status of emptiness, what one knows when one knows the ultimate, will have to respect this distinction.

Closely bound up with this, but perhaps creating more problems for us, is the apparent truism that when we know emptiness there must be something that we know. Tsong khapa and mKhas grub rje both make a good deal of this epistemological argument for an ontological conclusion. The point is this: the goal of Mahāyāna meditative practice and philosophical reasoning is to gain an understanding of emptiness—a knowledge grounded in careful analytical reasoning and ingrained into one's spontaneous cognitive set toward the world that all phenomena lack essence and are merely nominal and conventional in their identity, and hence in their existence-as-perceived. And the emptiness that a highly realized yogi perceives when he contemplates a table is the same emptiness that is known through reasoning to be the final nature of that table by a less meditatively accomplished but philosophically astute layperson. But for the latter, that emptiness is clearly known as an actual property. And so it must be for the yogi. Then, since it is a property that the table is known to possess, it must exist. For if it did not, it would be impossible to truly know that the table possesses it. (Hence the yogi's knowledge of emptiness, however different it might be from the layperson's in its epistemic structure and phenomenology, is nonetheless knowledge of an actual object.)

17. These points—familiar to anyone immersed in modern or postmodern epistemology or theory of perception—were also philosophical commonplaces in the Indian milieu in which Madhyamaka emerged. Worries about their implications for the construal of yogic states, direct awareness, and a Buddha's omniscience animate a lot of that philosophical enterprise. So, in unpacking these implications of the metaphor, we are doing nothing anachronistic.

18. I need not in virtue of so viewing it view it as having an essence. Though to be sure, a central point of the Madhyamaka critique both of prereflective awareness and of the analyses of substantialist philosophy is that we do often so view phenomena and then strive to understand the natures we naively attribute to them through our metaphysics. But I do view it as having characteristics from its side, and not merely through my (or our) attribution. That is to say, I view the paper as existing independently as an enduring substance that functions as the substratum of properties.

19. Here again, note the affinities to postmodern deconstruction not only of meaning and reference, but of epistemically privileged convention-independent standpoints, or privileged, transcendent ontologies.

20. Not, importantly, an ultimate existent. That would imply that when we analysed

emptiness, it would prove to be findable. But it does not. Hence its emptiness. Hence the impossibility of conceiving of ultimate existents, a conclusion agreed upon by all Madhyamaka schools, and all parties to this debate concerning the status of emptiness.

21. But though emptiness itself is what we find when we examine conventional entities, when emptiness itself is subjected to analysis, we find not it, but its emptiness, and so on all the way down. This is the emptiness of emptiness. So, in an important sense, when we ask whether all things have an ultimate nature, the answer, for Nāgārjuna, is "yes—emptiness." But when we ask whether that ultimate nature exists ultimately, the answer is a definite "no." Importantly, then, from the standpoint from which things are empty, there is no nature that they have. Nonetheless, since it is true, in an important sense, to say that all phenomena are empty, and indeed to say that emptiness is empty, it must be conventionally true, and so it would appear that emptiness must exist at least conventionally, as the possible subject of that predication, and indeed as the predicate as well.

22. Before going into any depth, I will note a terminological point that is always jarring to the ears of Western philosophers when they first encounter Buddhist philosophy. The term *truth* in this tradition does not always refer to one of the two truth-values that can be classically assigned to a sentence or a proposition. *Truth* can also refer to a way of characterizing reality (as in the Two Truths), or more to present purposes, to entities. So we can say that a table is a conventional truth—meaning an entity that can truly be said to exist within the framework of convention. We can then say that it is not an ultimate truth, meaning that from the point of view of one seeing reality as it is independent of conventions, the table does not exist. We can also say then that emptiness is an ultimate truth, because one who sees things as they are independently of convention sees their emptiness.

23. This point is made with the greatest of eloquence, and of obscurity in the *Heart Sūtra*: "Form is empty; emptiness is form. Emptiness is not other than form; form is not other than emptiness." But it is defended in more detail by Nāgārjuna in *Mūlamadhyamakakārikā*, where he argues for the identity of emptiness, dependently originated phenomena, and that the emptiness of emptiness just is its conventional existence. See Garfield 1995, esp. chapter 24.

24. Note that if emptiness were an existent in this sense, the contradiction in question would be vicious indeed, rendering the Madhyamaka position incoherent. For emptiness would be a positive characteristic, and the claim that things lack essence would be falsified. In chapter 5 Priest and I argue that there is in fact a contradiction here, but a *true* contradiction, and one that in fact underlies the *coherence* of Madhyamaka, despite its contradictory character.

25. Once again, this emphasis on the assertorial speech act in its very act of apparently asserting something whose sense transcends the conventional domain as, when correctly understood to undermine the very possibility of such assertion, has a curiously postmodern ring about it. This is explored more fully in chapter 5.

26. Note that there is inexpressibility and inexpressibility. This claim can easily be misunderstood to assert some kind of mysticism: that the ultimate nature of reality is fundamentally different from its conventional nature, and that this is the difference between reality and illusion: all of what we say in language, all that can be expressed, is literally false, and only silence can "express" the true nature of things. This moral, for instance, is sometimes drawn from the famous "Lion's Roar of Silence" in the *Vimalakīrtinirdeśa-sūtra*. The point should rather be understood as concerning the complete identity between the ultimate and the conventional truth: the ultimate truth about

things is that they are merely conventional in nature. But this issues in a limitation on expressibility: language and thought are always perspectival, and while reality outruns any perspective, and while that fact can be known, reality independent of perspective cannot be comprehended discursively.

27. Once we appreciate this point, it is a short jump to the conclusion that in an important sense, when propositions are understood in a particular way—as nonconventional entities that serve as the referents for linguistic expressions—no sentence expresses a proposition. And that is one important component of Nāgārjuna's thought. That is one more respect in which emptiness is on a cognitive par with other nominal entities. All linguistic and conceptual activity is implicated simultaneously in ontic constitution and assertion. On the other hand, while conventionally such entities, and hence such propositions exist, ultimately they do not. Once we see this, there is no harm in treating such sentences as asserting propositions *understood as nominal*. The problem with statements about emptiness is that it looks as though they are meant to assert propositions made true by the existence of an ultimate nature of phenomena. But that "nature," to the extent that things have it, cannot exist except as their very lacking of any nature, including that one. So there is *no* coherent interpretation of these sentences as assertorial in this sense.

28. Note that the points being made here about nonassertion are in one sense perfectly general, while in another content-relative. In the first sense, we can say that Nāgārjuna and his followers deny that any assertion should be understood as meaningful by virtue of expressing an extralinguistic proposition of the kind posited by the Nyāya or Fregean semanticist. That point is perfectly general. On the other hand, the understanding of the denial of the existence of a Mahāyāna *position*, or of a *proposition* asserted as not involving the implicit qualification "inherently existent" does not depend upon the subject matter. When a mādhyamika philosopher, for instance, denies the existence of a self or of a table, that qualifier is certainly in order inasmuch as such phenomena are argued by these philosophers to exist conventionally, but *not inherently*. Propositions, on the other hand, or emptiness as it is correctly understood, do not even exist conventionally. These can be denied existence without qualification.

4. Nāgārjuna's Theory of Causality

Thanks to Arindam Chakrabarti for provoking me, to the Ven. Geshe Ngawang Samten for debating this issue, and to Guy Newland and Mark Siderits for valuable contributions to the ensuing discussion from which this chapter emerges and to Mark for a valuable set of comments on an earlier draft. Thanks also to Georges Dreyfus for sending crucial texts and to the Ven. Sonam Thakchöe for checking and correcting translations and for further discussion of these issues. I also thank Cynthia Townley and Tricia Perry for editorial assistance.

1. I will not use the pejorative term *anti-realist*, for in the context of Madhyamaka that begs important questions both about the appropriate sense of *reality* and about what kinds of phenomena we might identify about which to be realists. Moreover, for a *prāsaṅgika-mādhyamika* like Nāgārjuna, there is an additional problem: how to identify the common object necessary to generate a realist/anti-realist debate.

2. Note that while this objection might appear to be a version of Smart's (1963) "cosmic coincidence" argument for scientific realism, it is not. For Nāgārjuna would agree with Smart that one must be (conventionally) realistic about anything one posits in an

explanation. His claim is simply that in fact we never really posit causal powers in explanations (compare Tsong khapa 1984, 1998 on the question of whether for a Prāsaṅgika—unlike a Svātantrika—we posit inherent existence even conventionally). The cosmic coincidence argument really does have its home in realism/anti-realism debates, and this is not one of those. The question here is whether or not the concept of causal powers actually has any content. The reificationist claims that it does; Nāgārjuna, that it does not.

3. The contemporary philosophers most explicit about this justification for ontological discrimination in science are Jerry Fodor (1984) and Paul Churchland (1978).

4. See also Kitcher 1993 for another contemporary argument for the claim that causal claims are grounded in explanations rather than vice versa. I thank Mark Siderits for calling this parallel to my attention.

5. Mark Siderits (personal communication) charges me with adopting my own dogmatic ideology of the disunity of science, in that I underestimate or ignore future theoretical unifications of the domains of these diverse sciences. This is not the place to fight this larger battle in the philosophy of science. I have said my piece elsewhere (Garfield 1988,). Briefly, though, while I endorse a broadly physicalistic view of the supervenience of the domains and theories of higher level sciences on those of more fundamental sciences (for example, psychology vs. physics), such supervenience does not entail for supervening sciences and domains either reduction to or absorption by the more fundamental sciences or domains, and the frequently relational, normative, or gerrymandered character of the ontologies and methodologies of higher level sciences often blocks such reduction or subsumption. Multiple styles and axes of explanations are often necessary to capture the irregular, multilevel character of reality. (See also Hardcastle 1996). Of course this point depends to a certain degree on what one counts as reduction. If reduction is to be distinguished from supervenience as I (1988) and others (Hardcastle 1996, Churchland 1978 to cite but two examples) have argued it must be, reduction cannot be simply defined as global supervenience. Whether it is understood as Nagel-style reduction by biconditional bridge laws or as inter-level definitions, systematic reduction as in Haugeland 1981 or Cummins 1983, or the preservation of roughly equipotent theoretical images (Churchland 1978, Hardcastle 1996), the point goes through: ontological dependence does not entail reducibility.

6. The Ven. Geshe Ngawang Samten, personal communication, and the Ven. Sonam Thackchöe, personal communication.

7. And the Jataka tales include stories of the Buddha doing prima facie bad things precisely because on those rare occasions they lead to the more rapid spiritual benefit of others.

8. I leave open the option of fighting the other issue out later.

9. The Ven. Geshe Ngawang Samten (personal communication) points out another reason for thinking that belief in rebirth is necessary in order to cultivate *bodhicitta*:

> One of the principal means of cultivation is the practice of visualizing all sentient beings as one's mother in past lives and developing a feeling of gratitude for their past kindness. If this method were necessary for cultivating *bodhicitta*, then belief in past lives would also be necessary for cultivating *bodhicitta*.

But he also points out that this is not the *only* method for cultivating *bodhicitta* recommended in the tradition, and that exchange of self for others does not require this belief, and is widely regarded as sufficient.

10. Mark Siderits (personal communication) notes that I, like Dharmakirti and rGyal

tshab, rely on causal processes to explain the possibility of Buddhahood, and so that I, like them, presuppose some confidence in causation as a ground of the possibility of *bodhicitta*, even as I reconceptualize that aspiration. So, he suggests, my view is really no different from theirs. Not so. There is a big difference: whereas the orthodox view I criticize requires (its own protestations to the contrary notwithstanding) a substantial basis for a causal relation, and hence more than mere *pratitya-samutpāda*, and something like *kriyā* (*bya ba*) proper of the kind Nāgārjuna so properly rejects, my account merely requires the kind of causal dependence with which Nāgārjuna properly suggests we should replace causal power and substance talk. What is at issue, I repeat, is neither faith in the existence of the past and the future, nor the view that buddhahood has causes and is difficult to achieve, but rather the claim that personal rebirth is a necessary condition of enlightenment and hence that faith therein is a necessary condition of *bodhicitta*. And here we differ.

5. *Nājārjuna and the Limits of Thought*

Thanks to Paul Harrison, Megan Howe, and Koji Tanaka for comments on earlier drafts of this chapter and to our audience at the 2000 meeting of the Australasian Association of Philosophy and the Australasian Society for Asian and Comparative Philosophy, especially Peter Forrest, Tim Oakley, and John Powers, for their comments and questions.

1. Gorampa, in fourteenth-century Tibet, may be an exception to this claim, for in *Nges don rab gsal* he argues that Nāgārjuna regards all thought and all conceptualization as necessarily totally false and deceptive. But even Gorampa agrees that Nāgārjuna argues (and indeed soundly) for that conclusion.

2. Tillemans (1999) takes Nāgārjuna's sincere endorsement of contradictions to be possible evidence that he endorses paraconsistent logic with regard to the ultimate while remaining classical with regard to the conventional. We think he is right about this.

3. For how this phenomenon plays out in the theories of Kripke, and Gupta and Herzberger, see Priest 1987, ch. 1; for the theory of Barwise and Etchemendy, see Priest 1993; and for McGee, see idem.

4. See Priest 1987 and 1995 for extended discussion.

5. The reason for the *qua* qualification will become clear in a minute. It will turn out that conventional and ultimate reality are, in a sense, the same.

6. See, for example, Chapters 2 and 3 of this book, 1995, 1997, Huntington and Wangchen 1989; Kasulis 1989.

7. These are taken up most notably in the Zen tradition (Kasulis 1989).

8. On the other hand, it is no doubt true that on Nāgārjuna's view many of our pretheoretical and philosophical conceptions regarding the world are indeed riddled with incoherence. Making them coherent is the task of *MMK*.

9. Though we take no position here on any debates in Sextus interpretation, or on whether Sextus is correct in characterizing his own method in this way.

10. The fact that Nāgārjuna's view is inconsistent does not, of course—on his own view or on ours—mean that it is *incoherent*.

11. See Hayes 1994 and Tillemans 1999 for excellent general discussions of the *catuskoti* and its role in Indian logic and epistemology.

12. On the paradoxical nature of being in Heidegger, see Priest (forthcoming).

13. Kasulis (1989) appropriately draws attention to the way in which Nāgārjuna's account of the way this traversal returns us to the conventional world, but with deeper insight

into its conventional character, is taken up by the great Zen philosopher Dōgen in his account of the great death and its consequent reaffirmation of all things.

6. Three Natures and Three Naturelessnesses

1. See chapters 1 and 2 in this volume and Garfield 1995 for more extensive discussion of this point.

2. I assume that Vasubandhu composed the root verses traditionally attibuted to Maitreyanātha. There is no mention of these verses prior to Vasubandhu's commentary. On the other hand, of course, there is no direct evidence regarding their authourship at at all, by Vasubandhu or anyone else (Asanga is another likely possibility). But the philosophical consonance of this root text with the remainder of Vasubandhu's distinctive corpus is strong prima facie evidence for this hypothesis.

3. This parallel is all the more striking, I would argue, civen that *MVB is* a text self-consciously about the middle path in the context of a philosophical break from the Madhyamaka tradition. The case for this self-conscious break can be made either from an internal philosophical standpoint as I do here, or from the standpoint of which sūtras are taken as definitive, as later Indian and Tibetan exegetes would prefer. Vasubandhu is clearly writing in reliance on the *SNS* and the *Lankāvatāra-sūtra*, whereas Nāgārjuna would, by this time, have been firmly identified with the *Prajñāpāramitā* literature.

4. There is a lot to be said about Tibetan Cittamātra doxography, and in particular a lot to be said about the ways that the location of Dharmakirti in that doxography affect Tibetan interpretations of Cittamātra, and about intersectarian debates regarding Cittamātra hermeneutics. But it is all beyond the scope of this chapter. It should also be noted that there is substantial non-dGe lugs Tibetan commentary on Cittamātra, both oral and written. There are interesting differences between schools regarding the interpretation of that school. Again, any comparison of those traditions is beyond the scope of this study.

5. Though some dGe lugs oral traditions hold the ninth (Maitreya) chapter to be a Second Turning chapter. This is by no means a universal view even within the dGe lugs tradition, however. Others hold it to be a Third Turning presentation of a Second Turning view

6. *SNS*, ch. 7, 104 (Powers 1995): Ascribing the imagined nature to the dependent nature and the consummate nature, sentient beings then apply the conventions of the imagined nature to the dependent nature and the consummate nature.

7. However, mKhas grub rje argues forcefully that the mādhyamika cannot accept the three naturelessnesses *as they are understood by the Cittamātra.* This is important. Once the doxography gets rolling, and the three naturelessnesses are understood in terms of the three natures, while the mādhyamika can still accept a verbal formulation of emptiness in terms of lack of distinguishing characteristics, dependence upon causes and conditions, and emptiness of the inherent existence naïvely imputed to things, their analysis of what these terms mean will differ from that of the Yogācāra.

8. I here sidestep the entire Tibetan controversy concerning whether *rang mtshan* is to be glossed as *rang gi mtshan nyid kyis grub pa*, as this takes us far afield into much later sectarian hermenutical debates. I prefer here to focus clearly on the origins of Vasubandhu's ideas.

9. For a more extensive and detailed discussion of this text, see chapter 7 of this volume.

10. This is indeed a core interpretive claim of the oral tradition regarding

Madhyamaka-Cittamātra debates: that while mādhyamikas reject the idealism of the Cittamātra (and in particular their distinction between the status of mind and that of external objects) they do not reject the three naturelessnesses. On the other hand, things become complicated regarding the three natures in this tradition, since, as we shall see, the dGe lugs, following Sthiramati, identify the natures and the naturelessnesses. They hence argue that mādhyamikas accept the three natures, but not as presented by Vasubandhu. I am indebted to the Ven Gen Lobsang Gyatso for this point (as well as for much else in this chapter, most of which he would regard as incorrect. mKhas grub's s *Tong thun chen mo* is an important source here.

11. The Ven Gen Lobsang Gyatso and the Most Ven Prof Samdhong Rinpoche, in conversation.

12. Note, however, that this is *not* an *identity* of view, merely a continuity in some respects. The yogācārin and mādhyamika disagree strongly about the precise analysis of emptiness, and about whether or not anything ultimately exists. A substantial polemical literature can be found on both sides. This is one reason for grave suspicion about Nagao's claim for a strong parallel.

13. The Ven Gen Lobsang Gyatso emphasizes that, in the dGe lugs oral tradition, this is the principal issue: the Third Turning sūtras, on this view, were taught for the sake of those who, hearing the *Prajñāpāramitā* doctrine of emptiness, reasoned that there is therefore no causality, and hence no possibility of spiritual progress (or degeneration) and hence fell into the abyss of nihilism. The central theme of the Third Turning then, according to this tradition, is precisely the establishment of the ultimate reality of causality. Similar considerations can be raised regarding the need to establish the ultimate reality of mind as the bearer of karma.

7. Vasubandhu's Treatise on the Three Natures

My reading of this text has developed as a result of many conversations with and instruction from teachers, students, and colleagues. I thank in particular Janet Gyatso for extended discussion of *Cittamātra* philosophy in general and this text in particular, the Ven. Geshe Yeshes Thab khas for several teaching sessions, the Ven. Gen Lobsang Gyatso for several useful conversations, and Karen Meyers for a number of spirited discussions of this text and of *Cittamātra* philosophy in general. Moira Nicholls read an earlier version and made a number of useful suggestions. Jens Schlieter has made many very helpful suggestions regarding both the translation and commentary. Both are much improved as a consequence. I also thank an anonymous reviewer for *Asian Philosophy* for pointing out lacunae in an earlier version. Thanks also to Sri Yeshi Tashi Shastri and Jamyang Norbu Gurung for research assistance.

1. See, for example Nāgārjuna's *Mūlamadhyamikakārikā* (Garfield 1995) or Candrakirti's *Madhyamakāvatāra* (translated in Huntington, and Wangchen 1989 p. 1989).

2. See also Vasubandhu's *Madhyāntavibhāgabhāsya* and *Triṃśikakārikā* in Kochumuttom 1982 and Anacker 1984 for further expositions of this view.

3. While such comparisons will prove useful, and while the affinities are real, one must be careful not to push the comparisons too far. There is a specifically Buddhist context to Vasubandhu's idealism, and the different philosophical milieus of medieval India and modern Europe generate distinct philosophical positions and moves. It is well beyond the scope of this commentary to address all of the relevant similarities and differences, or

even to spell out all of Vasubandhu's arguments or system. See chapter 8 of this volume for more on comparison between Vasubandhu's idealism and Western versions of that doctrine.

4. A possible reason may be that this text was written when Vasubandhu was quite advanced in years. It was probably composed at Ayodhya during the last year or two of his life.

5. Compare, for instance, the presentation of the three natures in the *Samdhinirmocana-sūtra* in which these ontological claims are completely absent.

6. See *Legs bshad snyings po*, translated in Thurman 1984.

7. See *sTong thun chen mo*, translated in Cabezón 1992.

8. See chapter 6 of this volume, for more on Cittamātra doxography and on the relation between the three natures and three naturelessnesses and chapter 9 for more on Sthiramati's commentary on *Triṃśikakākārikā*.

9. Translated in Huntingdon 1992, see esp. pp. 162–68).

10. This translation is from the Tibetan text. The principal version used is that in the sDe dge edition of the Tibetan canon (Si 12a–14a). The Peking edition was used for comparison, and is in complete concordance. Anacker (1984) and Wood 1991 each reprint the original Sanskrit text.

11. Again, it is interesting to contrast this presentation with that of the *Samdhinirmocana-sūtra*, where this dependence is explicitly characterized as dependence on other nonmental causes and conditions. Vasubandhu is clearly developing an idealistic position that contrasts with the strikingly nonidealistic ontology of the *Samdhinirmocana-sūtra*. It is in large part due to doxographic imperatives to unify the Yogācāra corpus theoretically that so many Tibetans read the *Samdhinirmocana-sūtra* as idealistic and that so many contemporary Western scholars have lately argued that Vasubandhu is *not* an idealist. (See chapters 8 and 9 for more on this topic.) Both imperatives should be resisted, as the tradition is internally diverse.

12. Kochumuttom 1982, Thurman 1984, Wood 1991, Powers 1995, Anacker 1984, Nagao 1991, and Cabezon, 1992, respectively.

13. Contrast this with the standard presentation of Cittamātra metaphysics in dGe lugs pa doxography, following Sthiramati, according to which the second and third are real, but the first—the imagined nature—is completely unreal. See rJe Tsong khapa in Thurman 1984, pp. 223–30 and mKhas grub rje in Cabezon 1992, pp. 47–61. See also Meyers 1995, ch. 2. On the other hand, as Tsong khapa and his followers correctly emphasize, there is something *special* about the second two natures. Each is established through its own characteristic, not from the side of the conceptual mind.

14. See Kant 1965 and Berkeley 1954.

15. Schopenhauer 1974, pp. 273ff., idem 1969 §4. See also "Criticism of the Kantian Philosophy" in Schopenhauer 1969.

16. Schopenhauer, 1969 §§19, 23–24.

17. This is not to say that Schopenhauer charges Kant with the failure to postulate a noumenon—only that he charges Kant with the failure to see that this noumenal character is a third nature of the object, one that is knowable immediately, without subject-object duality. Again, in this respect Vasubandhu's idealism is far closer to Schopenhauer's than it is to Kant's. I thank Dr Moira Nicholls for pointing out the need for clarity on this point.

18. See the analysis of time as the form of inner sense and hence of the empirical character of self-knowledge in the "Transcendental Aesthetic" (Kant 1965, b155–159).

19. It is not, however—to put it mildly—at all obvious that these etymological claims are at all accurate.

20. Again, the anticipation of Kant's account of empirical self-knowledge is striking.

21. This becomes complex and leads to an analysis of *saṁsāra* itself, and the sense in which everything in *saṁsāra* can be said to be afflicted—to be caused by and to be a cause of suffering, and in a deeper sense to have suffering and primal ignorance as part of its very ontological structure; and then to an analysis of a specifically Yogācāra understanding of *saṁsāra*. But that is beyond the scope of this commentary.

22. In the scholastic or Cartesian sense—the character of the mental object itself.

23. Note how this account of the ultimate nature of a phenomenon contrasts with that given by mādhyamika philosophers such as Nāgārjuna or Candrakirti, according to whom not even the emptiness of the cup can be said to exist in this sense. It is at this crucial point in ontology that Cittamātra and Madhyamaka are utterly discontinuous. See Siderits, 1996 and chapter 9 of this volume. But see Nagao 1991, n.13, for a contrary view.

24. This contrasts once again with the standard dGe lugs pa view according to which the important ontological divide is between the imagined nature and the other two. On this view, the imagined nature is wholly false, while the other-dependent and consummate natures are both truly existent.

25. See, for instance, mKhas grub rJe in Cabezón 1992, p. 50 n.13.

26. The one significant ontological doctrine associated with Cittamātra philosophy that does not appear here is the theory of the Three *Naturelessnesses (trinisvabhāva/ngo bo nyid med gsum)* that takes center stage in the *Samdhinirmocana-sūtra*. In *Trimśikakākārikā* Vasubandhu connects this doctrine to *trisvabhāva* theory, arguing that each nature is natureless in one of these senses. Sthiramati, in his commentary on this text, argues that in fact the Three Natures and the Three Naturelessnesses are the same—a view adopted by such Tibetan exegetes as Tsong khapa and mKhas grub. This is not a view that Vasubandhu ever articulates, however, and while he uses the *trinisvabhāva* in explicating emptiness in *Madhyāntavibhagabhāsya*, it is not, on his view, a doctrine specifically connected to idealism and so has no role in the present text. See chapter 6 for more on the relation between the Three Natures and the Three Naturelessnesses.

8. Western Idealism through Indian Eyes

I thank Moira Nicholls, Frank White, and Angela Round for helpful comments on an earlier draft, and the late Ven Gen Lobzang Gyatso, Janet Gyatso and Karin Meyers for many helpful discussions of Cittamātra and its relation to Western Idealism. I am also deeply grateful to the Ven Prof Gareth Sparham for comments on an earlier draft of this chapter, for valuable suggestions regarding translations, and for extensive interchange regarding Cittamātra philosophy and texts. Thanks also to two anonymous referees for *Sophia* for extremely helpful suggestions.

1. See Klein 1995 for more on cross-cultural hermeneutics and dialogue.

2. See also Powers 1996a. Lusthaus 1996a,b even lumps Sthiramati in as a nonidealist exponent of Yogācāra and emphasizes that in his view *no* early Yogācāra writer (anybody preceding Dharmakirti) is an idealist in any sense. Though it would take us well beyond the scope of this paper, it is hard to imagine how anyone reading Sthiramati's commentary on the *Trimsikakārikā* could come to this conclusion.

3. See chapters 6 and 7 of this volume for more on this point.

4. The purpose of this essay is neither to engage in a philological examination of

Vasubandhu's corpus or the commentarial literature it inspires nor to survey Vasubandhu's entire corpus for evidence of his idealism. I here restrict my gaze to those passages most directly relevant to the comparative enterprise at hand.

5. A full exposition of Vasubandhu's treatment of the dual character of mind is beyond the scope of this essay. See chapter 7 for a compete translation and detailed exposition of *Trisvabhāvanirdeśa*. For now suffice it to say that Vasubandhu, like Kant, argues that the mind figures both as subject and as object. Inasmuch as the mind appears to itself in introspection, it appears with subject-object duality, and the object that appears in such an awareness is for Vasubandhu of exactly the same status as any external object so appearing. On the other hand, he argues, in order to make sense of appearance at all, whether of an external object or the mind, we must posit an independently existing mental continuum in which the appearance is located. Vasubandhu argues that we come to realize the illusory character of the mind as object through first understanding the easier-to-grasp illusory character of external phenomena. But his analysis of the mind as it appears to itself does not undermine in any way his insistence on the reality of the more fundamental, purely subjective mind.

6. While there is general agreement that Vasubandhu is the author of the commentary that constitutes the bulk of this text, the authorship of the root verses of *Madhyāntavibhāga* is uncertain. They are traditionally attributed to Maitreya, dictated to Vasubandhu's brother Asaṅga. They may have been composed by a fifth- or sixth-century philosopher named Maitreyanātha. They may have been composed by Asaṅga. Or they may have been composed by Vasubandhu. I take no position in this debate, but Vasubandhu clearly endorses their content and takes his commentary to provide both an exposition and defense of the position they articulate.

7. Here I agree with Anacker's reading of this verse, reading the Tibetan / jig rten 'das pa'i ye shes med / as / jig rten 'das pa'i ye shes. This appears to be the only coherent reading.

8. This position differs from the Madhyamaka position of Nāgārjuna or Candrakīrti, according to which both subject and object are empty of essence yet conventionally existent. It would take us far afield to enter into a detailed comparison of these two philosophical schools or to explore their interchanges or the exquisite doxography they inspire. For now suffice it to say that whereas the Madhyamaka assign identical ontological status to the mind and its objects and argue that both are empirically real, the Cittamātra sharply distinguish their status, assigning a more fundamental reality to the subject than to its objects. See chapter 1 for an exposition of Nāgārjuna's position and Huntington and Wangchen 1989 for an exposition of Candrakirti's powerful refutation of Vasubandhu. See also Cabezón 1992 and Hopkins 2000 for a sense of the Tibetan doxography.

9. Another interesting difference between Cittamātra and Madhyamaka metaphysics: *paratantra* involves the notion of causal dependence and is significantly different from the *parikalpitā* in this respect. As Sthiramati emphasizes in his *Triṃśikābhāṣya*, in the *parikalpitā*, inasmuch as the imagined objects do not even exist, they are not connected by causal links to one another. *Paratantra-svabhāva*, though, is causal in two senses: first, the apparent objects depend upon psychological episodes; second, the successive mental episodes that represent the objects of experience are causally related to each other. This causal continuum of mental episodes is the evolving and endlessly transforming mind. For the decidedly nonidealistic Madhyamaka, on the other hand, all empirical phenomena, whether mental or physical, are linked in the endless webs of interdependence constituting the world of *pratītya-sammutpāda*, or dependent origination.

10. See Nagao 1991 for more on the Janus-like character of the *paratantra-svabhāva*.

11. See also Sellars 1992 for a fine discussion of the interpenetration of metaphysics and epistemology in the context of analyzing mental representation.

12. I should also acknowledge a point at which Kant departs from Vasubandhu, and a way in which he is perhaps closer to Candrakīrti: while Berkeley and Vasubandhu emphasize the *difference* in ontological status between external phenomena and mind, Kant (following Hume), like Candrakīrti, emphasizes the *homogeneity* in ontological status between the outer and inner. Just as Candrakīrti emphasizes that phenomena and the self are equally conventionally real and ultimately empty, in contradistinction to Vasubandhu's reification of self and consequent nihilism with respect to phenomena, Kant emphasizes the empirical reality of both external objects and the self, as well as the transcendental ideality of both, arguing that Berkeley reifies the latter and is nihilistic about the former. Both Kant and Candrakīrti emphasize that these two extreme views are themselves opposite sides of the coin of a too-radical idealism. See chapter 1 of this volume for a more detailed discussion of this point.

13. But see Priest 1995 for a more subtle discussion of Kant's predicament regarding the noumenon. Priest argues that Kant is committed both to the knowability and to the unknowability of the noumemon and is in fact committed to a contradiction on this point by virtue of the introduction of the noumenon.

14. I say this despite the fact that it is clear that for a variety of reasons—some of them good, and some a bit confused—Kant himself no doubt was committed to an ontological role for noumena.

15. The fact that Schopenhauer himself completely confused advaita Vedanta with Buddhism and had no sense of the internal diversity of the Buddhist tradition means that it is inevitably tendentious to ascribe to him commitment to any particular Indian school. His frequent adoption of Vedanta terminology would in fact suggest that to the extent that such an attribution would be fair at all, one would have to locate him as an advaita Vedanta philosopher. But my task here is not that of Schoepenhauer exegesis, per se, or at least not from a disinterested perspective, but rather that of seeing how Schopenhauer and his predecessors would be read from the vantage point of Cittamātra philosophy. And the Cittamātra elements I identify in Schopenhauer, I would maintain, despite Schopenhauer's own blindness to them, or at least to their distinctness from other Indian perspectives, are very much there.

16. See, for example, Schopenhauer 1969, vol. I, pp 98–99, 119.

17. To use the term *force* here is dangerous inasmuch as Schopenhauer himself (1969, vol. 1, p. 111, trans. Payne) explicitly eschews it. In that eschewal, however, he is concerned to avoid the implication that the Will is somehow on an ontological par with *forces of nature* of the kind posited in physics, by virtue of either one of them or being the single force of some future grand unifying theory. He would argue instead that *those* forces are all phenomenal manifestations of Will. He prefers terms such as *drive* or *impulse*. These, too, have their disadvantages, suggesting intentional content or consciousness, suggestions he also would wish to avoid. So it is important to understand the term *force* here in a sense not indicating forces of nature, but rather a kind of metaphysical force prior to nature.

18. One should not be misled here into identifying Schopenhauer's Will with the *ālaya-vijñāna* of the Cittamātra. That would be a mistake. The Will is not conscious. Nor is it personal. But then the *ālaya-vijñāna* is not an aspect of representation. Rather, I am identifying Schopenhauer's assertion that the fundamental nature of all phenomena is Will, and hence nondual, non-spatio-temporal, and so on with Vasubandhu's that the consum-

mate nature of all phenomena is to be empty of externality, duality, and so on and their respective assertions that to be a representation is to have, in addition to an empirical, or imagined, nature and a nature as dependent upon mind, a third nature more fundamental than these two in which the dualities implicated in those first two vanish. In fact, if space permitted, it would be fascinating to explore the relation between Schopenhauer's account of the transcendental subject—as opposed to the Will—and Vasubandhu's account of the foundation consciousness.

9. *Sounds of Silence*

1. Some will object to my use of the pejorative term *hinayāna* here. There are two reasons for using it: first, from the standpoint of this sūtra, Śariputra very much represents a *lesser* vehicle. But more than that, there is no alternative term (perhaps save "non-Mahāyāna," which itself, when unpacked semantically is every bit as pejorative) to encompass all of the non-Mahāyāna schools. *Theravada*, while fine for talking about contemporary non-Mahāyāna schools, denotes but one of the schools extant in classical India that would have been denoted by Mahāyana philosophers as *hinayāna*.

2. Here I have in mind principally the "Maitreya" texts, the short verse treatises of Vasubandhu as well as his commentary on *Madhyāntavibhāga* and the commentaries of Sthiramati. It is important to bear in mind both that the Yogācāra school is internally quite diverse and is interpreted in a range of ways. There is at present substantial disagreement among Western scholars concerning whether Yogācāra is idealist. If we restrict our purview to these texts, I have argued in chapters 6 through 8 that the answer is unequivocally "yes."

10. *Human Rights and Compassion*

1. See esp. H.H. the Dalai Lama 1984, 1992.

2. See especially Baier 1994a, ed, e, f, 1992; Tronto 1993, Noddings 1984, and Garner (1994).

3. See, for example, Care 1987 or Kohlberg 1981, 1984 as well as Flanagan and Jackson 1987.

4. See Hohfeld 1923, Thomson 1986.

5. The right to vote might be urged as a counterexample here. This appears to be a positive right, fundamental in the requisite sense. Matters become complicated here, but here is a quick sketch of a reply: one might argue that the right to vote is not universal; it is a right that one has by virtue of living in a democracy It is not obvious that democracy is the only morally acceptable way for persons to organize their lives, though it may indeed be the best. On the other hand, one might argue that to the degree the right to vote is fundamental, it is also negative: it is the right *not to have one's vote interfered with.*

6. Of course, the framework of rights is not the *only* framework within which moral criticism is possible. I return to this point below. But it is a framework that has proved remarkably effective as a platform for moral criticism and has often been mistakenly believed by those who think the alternative is mindless relativism to be the only framework from which such criticism is possible.

7. See for example, Janiak 1994 for a good discussion of the liberal response to relativism on this score, and Rawls 1971 or Care 1987 for a powerful defense of the universal claims of liberalism.

8. See Rawls 1971, Gibbard 1990, Thomson 1986, and Feinberg 1990.

9. This is not to say that, whether within a classic liberal theory or in some other moral framework—there are no rights children may assert against their parents, or vice versa. Assuredly there are. Rather, the point is that to try to accommodate everything that is morally significant about family life, or friendship, within the framework of rights will inevitably result in a sterile picture of this domain. For too much of what amounts to, for example, good parenting involves acts and attitudes that are neither supererogatory nor the objects of plausibly enforceable claims.

10. See Tronto 1993, Noddings 1987, and Janiak 1994 for more detailed exposition of this point. It is, however, important not to overemphasize it: liberal moral theorists do not deny that moral considerations other than rights have a place in moral discourse. Rather they accord primacy to rights and to rights claims and only a subsidiary role to other considerations. I thank Prof. Ernest Alleva for emphasizing this point in conversation.

11. This is especially clear in "What is Enlightenment?" where Kant writes: "Enlightenment is man's release from his self-incurred tutelage. Tutelage is man's inability to make use of his understanding without direction from another. . . . *Sapere aude!* 'Have courage to use your own reason!' That is the motto of enlightenment" from Kant 1959, p. 41. Thanks to Andrew Janiak for drawing my attention to this passage.

12. Privacy theory is very complex and very much contested terrain. This is not the place to survey the literature of the debates it comprises. See Inness 1992, Allen 1988, Schoeman 1984, and Feinberg 1980 for excellent perspectives on privacy in liberal moral and legal theory.

13. Griswold vs. Connecticut (381 U.S. 479, 1965), *Roe vs. Wade* (410 U.S 113, 1973).

14. *Union Pacific Railway vs. Botsford* 141 U.S. 250 (1981).

15. See MacKinnon 1984.

16. See O'Neill 1989 for an excellent discussion of the connection between liberalism and privacy, as well as MacKinnon 1984. Care 1987 attempts to construct a moral theory blending rights and compassion by retaining the basic liberal framework but abrogating the right to privacy under circumstances of great distress in the world. Janiak 1994 argues persuasively that this attempt is incoherent. Liberalism without privacy is oxymoronic.

Another important category of privacy theory deserves note. Inness 1992 has articulated this with the greatest clarity. She notes that privacy can be understood as protecting a sphere of particularly intimate aspects of individual expression and life: "[P]rivacy . . . amounts to the state of the agent having control over decisions concerning matters that draw their meaning and value from the agent's love, liking, or care . . . Therefore, privacy claims are claims to possess autonomy with respect to our expression of love, liking, and care" [91] While I agree with Inness that these are central components in of privacy whether it is a zone demarcated by liberal moral theory or accorded, as I will suggest below, through a compassion-based ethic, I think that her characterization is a bit too narrow. Much of what is "intimate" in the morally relevant sense goes beyond matters of "love, liking and care," and, for instance, includes religious, artistic, or political thought.

17. Prof. Ernest Alleva has persuaded me to be fairer to liberalism on this score. I am aware that these few remarks do not do justice to the full range of liberal replies to the implicit critique of liberalism this chapter represents. But to discuss those matters fully would take us far afield.

18. O'Neill 1989 states the point this way:

Since the discourse of rights requires that obligations are owed to all others or to specified others, unallocated right action, which is owed to unspecified others, drops out of sight. It may be right to help those in need, or to treat others with courtesy—but if these traditional obligations lack counterpart rights they will not be recognized by theories that treat rights as basic. (286) . . . Suppose we think there are both rights not to be tortured and rights to food. In the absence of enforcement, A tortures B, we are quite clear who has violated B's right; but if A does not provide B with food, nor even with an aliquot morsel of food, we are not sure whether A has violated B's rights. There nothing shows that it is *against* A that B's claim to food should be lodged or enforced. (296)

Thomson, in "A Defense of Abortion," argues strenuously for such an understanding of rights and defends such a framework throughout (1986). See also Benhabib 1987.

19. As I note previously, this does overstate the case slightly. But the important point remains intact once necessary qualifications are noted: concerns about character are, for the liberal, derivative of concerns about rights; any intrusion into the private is to be justified by public concerns.

20. See Baier 1994a, c, g, Noddings 1984 and Tronto 1993. Kohlberg (1984), responding to this criticism, writes, "The spheres of kinship, love, friendship, and sex, all eliciting considerations of care, are usually understood to be the spheres of personal decision-making, as are, for instance, the problems of marriage and divorce" (230). But this just restates the problem. For the liberal, to say that these are "personal" matters is to exclude them from the domain of moral discourse and criticism. For the moral theorist who takes compassion as foundational, it is to put them at the very center of that domain. The challenge for the liberal is to explain the seriousness of these issues; for the theorist of compassion it is to show how the rights the liberal correctly articulates can be recovered without reconstructing this zone of privacy. Baier writes in "The Need for More than Justice" (Baier 1994i):

For the moral tradition which developed the concept of rights, autonomy, and justice is the same tradition that provided "justifications" of the oppression of those whom the primary rights-holders depended on to do the sort of work they themselves preferred not to do . . . As long as women could be got to assume responsibility for the care of home and children and to train their children to continue the sexist system, the liberal morality could continue to be the official morality, by turning its eyes away from the contribution made by those it excluded. (25)

21. Principal figures in this tradition are Rousseau 1947, Locke 1988, and Hobbes 1909. For excellent discussions of the structure of social contract theory, see Care 1969 and Rawls 1971.

22. See Baier 1994, Tronto 1993, and Noddings 1987. But see also HH the Dalai Lama 1992.

23. Baier emphasizes this with great force in (1994 e, g, and h). In "Trust and Anti-Trust," she writes:

A complete moral philosophy would tell us how and why we should act and feel toward others in relationships of shifting and varying power asymmetry and shifting and varying intimacy . . . [T]hese relationships . . . such as parent and child . . . make up much of our lives, and they, as much as our relations to equals, determine the state of moral health or corruption in which we are content to live. (300–301)

24. Janiak 1994 makes this point with particular force and clarity.

25. In "The Need for More than Justice" (Baier 1994i) Baier emphasizes this:

One cannot regard any version of morality that does not ensure that caring for children gets well done as an adequate "minimal morality," anymore than we could so regard one that left any concern for more distant future generations as an optional extra. A moral theory . . . cannot regard concern for new and future persons as an optional charity left for those with a taste for it. (29)

26. Another way to put this point is that from the standpoint of compassion-based moral theories, to be human is to participate in compassion. Tsong khapa expresses the idea this way:

Indeed, the joy and glory of humans, as well as the skill of humans, are the principle of carrying the burden of others' aim, because staying only in one's own aim is shared with the animals. For that reason, the character of the great ones is limited to the benefit and happiness of others." (Tsong khapa Lam rim chen mo Wayman 1991, p. 26)

27. Prof. Ernest Alleva points out (personal communication) that there are two other important differences between liberal moral theory and moral theory grounded in compassion worthy of note: first of all (and this consideration is very important for Schopenhauer in his criticism of rights-based moral theory), rights theories typically do not extend moral consideration to nonhuman animals, or, to the extent that they do, justify such consideration in highly artificial or problematic ways. Given the necessary conditions rights theories typically require for moral standing, it is very difficult to grant animals any genuine moral standing. Morality grounded in compassion allows us to account much more directly not only for our actual moral sentiments with regard to infrahuman animals, but also to explain why these sentiments are correct, and why all creatures have some moral standing and claim to our moral recognition.

Second, rights-based moral theories, with their strong emphasis on individual autonomy, typically render highly problematic any "paternalistic" (I prefer *parentalistic*) interference in the affairs of others—that is, the restriction of the autonomy of others for their own good. Debates regarding parentalism are extremely complex, and certainly beyond the scope of this essay. But I would argue that the straightforward prohibition against such action that emerges from rights-based theories does less justice to the complexity of such situations than the more textured considerations that compassion brings into play: it is often wrong to intervene in such circumstances, but more often because of a lack of sufficient skill on the part of the person intervening to bring about genuinely favorable outcomes. Where such skill is in place, however, and where appropriate knowledge is brought to bear, with appropriate motivations, parentalistic intervention is often laudable.

28. A number of recent Kantian apologists (most notably O'Neil 1989, 1996, Baron 1995, and Korsgaard 1996) have argued that Kantian moral theory places greater emphasis on compassion and other virtues than I accord it. It is true that Kant offers a theory of virtue and reckons the virtues to be of great moral significance. But they remain nonetheless in the domain of the supererogatory. See Garfield 2001 for a more extensive discussion of this point.

29. Schopenhauer puts this point eloquently: "As soon as this compassion is aroused, the weal and woe of another are nearest to my heart in exactly the same way . . . as my own. Hence the difference between him and me is now no longer absolute" (1965, p. 144)

30. See Schopenhauer (ibid., p. 205) on the illusory character of the difference between individuals:

> This conception that underlies egoism is, *empirically* considered, strictly justified. According to experience, the *difference* between my own person and another's appears to be absolute. The difference in space and time that separates me from him, separates me also from his weal and woe. (205 trans. Payne)

> Accordingly, if plurality and separateness belong only to the *phenomenon*, and if it is one and the same essence that manifests itself in all living things, than that conception that abolishes the difference between ego and non-ego is not erroneous, but, on the contrary, the opposite conception must be. . . . Accordingly, it would be the metaphysical basis of ethics and consists in *one* individual's again recognizing in *another* his own self, his own true inner nature. Thus practical wisdom, doing right and doing good, would in the end harmonize with the profoundest teaching . . . (ibid., p. 209)

> "[I]ndividuation is real." . . . Each individual is a being radically different from all others . . . This . . . lies at the root of all egoism . . ."

> "Individualism is a mere phenomenon or appearance . . . My true inner being exists in every living thing as directly as it makes itself known in my self-consciousness only to me." . . . It is this that bursts through as *compassion* on which all genuine . . . virtue therefore depends." (ibid., p. 210 trans. Payne *passim*)

and Śantideva in *Bodhicaryāvatāra:*

> But if I do find happiness in his happiness
> Then surely I should feel the same way towards all. 6: 96 ab

> There is no doubt that those with the nature of compassion
> Regard those beings as the same as themselves. 6: 126 ab

31. This insight is in the West original to Hume. But in recent moral theory, Baier (1994a), Noddings (1984) and Tronto (1993) have developed and defended it with great force. In Tibetan Buddhist philosophy it is old, represented in the literature on visualizing each sentient being as one's mother, and on the exchange of self for others. Here the use of moral imagination is urged as a primary vehicle for extending natural sympathy into universal compassion. Tsong khapa writes:

> [T]he cultivation of sentient beings as kinsfolk is for generating gratitude. Now, the ultimate kin is the mother. Therefore, the three, mother-contemplative repetition, mindfulness of kindness, and show of return gratitude . . . generate compassion. (LRCM in Wayman 1991, p. 43)

> See also Kensur Lekden in Hopkins 1980, pp. 37–38 for detailed instructions on visualizing others as one's mother, and for cultivating and transferring appreciation of the mother's boundless kindness. He sums this discussion up thus:

Why should one make all neutral persons and enemies equal to one's mother? If she had fallen into a ravine or a river, or into a chasm made by an earthquake, and if her own child whom she had helped from the time of his entry into her womb would not help her, who would? (45)

32. Baier (1994i) notes:

> It is however also true that the moral theories that made the concept of a person's rights central were not just the instruments for excluding some persons but also the instruments used by those who demanded that more and more persons be included in the favored group. Abolitionists, reformers, women, used the language of rights to assert their claims to inclusion in the group of full members of a community. (26)

33. This does *not* create *duties* to, for example, give to particular beggars, or correlative *rights* on the part of, for example, some or all beggars to alms from some or all persons. Rather, it establishes a moral *ideal* that includes *generosity* and a compassionate regard for others as components, which ideal is relevant to *anyone* whether or not she or he acknowledges its relevance, just as intelligence is part of an intellectual ideal even for those who do not care how smart they are. This is important, because the liberal might fear the following consequence from the elimination of the fundamental status of privacy: it could turn out that we are so overwhelmed, in view of the universal demands of compassion, by a sea of new duties—such as those to give to each beggar who could thereby benefit—that it becomes impossible to lead a rational, coherent life. This is akin to the difficulty that Williams (1973) shows to afflict utilitarianism. Integrity becomes impossible under such circumstances, as does the attainment of any goal requiring singleness of purpose. But this problem does not beset the current account, because the foundational status of compassion requires only the development and expression of a set of virtues, and because compassion itself requires that we respect an, albeit more circumscribed, zone of privacy. I thank Laurie Smith for calling my attention to this problem.

34. This view contrasts somewhat with Inness's account (1992). I agree that privacy is important because it protects autonomy in a sphere particularly central to self-expression and self-development. But beyond the disagreement noted previously, regarding the *content* of that sphere, I disagree regarding the *basis* of that protection. Here Inness is closer to classical liberalism than am I. She writes:

> Privacy protects our autonomy with respect to our expressions of love, care and liking. There are two possible explanations of the positive value we accord to this sphere of individual autonomy. The first of these is a consequentialist "relationship-creation" explanation. According to this explanation, privacy promotes the creation and growth of positively valued human relationships dependent on the agent's love, liking and care. (ibid., 95)

But she rejects this explanation (which I clearly endorse, suitably modified):

> Relationship-promotion explanations of privacy's value also fail to accord with out intuitions about privacy's consequence-independent value. If its value flows from the relationships it produces, it is clear privacy will be positively valued only in the world where it does promote close relationships. . . . However, this inverts our intuitions about privacy's value . . . [P]rivacy is valued *just*

because it can halt the intrusions of the external world. (ibid., 101) (emphasis in original)

These "intuitions," I would argue (though space prohibits developing this point here), are classical liberal intuitions, not shared by adherents to other moral frameworks, and invoking them here begs the question against compassion-based moral theory. Compassion theorists, I would argue, secure the goods the liberal cares about, but secure them for the right reason—that they promote individual and collective happiness.

So when Inness continues,

Privacy's positive value stems from a principle of respect for persons as autonomous beings with the capacity for love, care, and liking, beings with an invaluable capacity for freely chosen close relationships; this principle dictates the positive value we accord to the agent's control over intimate decisions about her own actions and her decisions about intimate access to herself. (ibid., 112),

I would argue that the emphasis on autonomy as foundational inverts the correct order of moral explanation.

11. Buddhism and Democracy

I thank Anna Alomes, the Ven Geshe Ngawang Samten, Jeffrey Wallen, and Mark Siderits for comments on earlier drafts and for helpful conversations on this topic.

1. Violence, from a Buddhist perspective, can be directed either outward, toward others, or toward oneself. Though here I am emphasizing the former, given my concern for social policy in this chapter, in most canonical literature, concerned as such literature is for individual spirtual development, the emphasis is on the latter. In that context, these five proscriptions are most explicitly linked by their tendency to inflame passion and hence to impede spiritual progress. This, too, is a form of violence, albeit more subtle, and is seen in the tradition as the seed of more explicit violence in speech and action.

12. The "Satya" in Satyagraha

Thanks to the Ven. Geshe Ngawang Samten and to Anna Alomes for comments on an earlier draft and for many helpful conversations. I am deeply indebted for the ideas expressed in this essay to the most Ven Prof Samdhong Rinpoche and to Anna Alomes.

13. Temporality and Alterity

I thank Kathryn Addelson, Janet Gyatso, Meredith Michaels, and Jeffrey Wallen for extensive and valuable comments on earlier drafts of this chapter. I am especially grateful to the Ven. Geshe Ngawang Samten for several vigorous and illuminating conversations on these topics. He has taught me much over the years about cross-cultural interpretation and exchange. It is hard to imagine the last five years without his collaboration.

1. One might, of course, invoke the claim that what is called "Asian philosophy" is not truly philosophical but is somehow essentially *religious* in character. There is not time to thoroughly explore this unfortunate and dated move here. It will have to suffice to note

three insuperable difficulties with this strategy: first, so much of Indian, Chinese, Tibetan, and Japanese philosophical writing is so directly concerned with what anyone can recognize as quintessentially philosophical questions, such as the relation between substance and attributes; the nature of causality, personal identity, freedom, and determinism; the nature of time, and so forth; and pursues those questions through such recognizable philosophical analysis that nobody who has seriously examined these texts could say with a straight face that they are any less philosophical then Western treatises on these topics. Second, this move ignores the fact that much of Western philosophy is religious, and derives its point specifically from religious concerns. Consider not only the works of Augustine, Aquinas, Scotus, Ockham, and other Catholic medieval philosophers, but also the work of such modern figures as Berkeley, Descartes, and Kant. Third, this move presumes a clear demarcation between the philsophical and the religious treatment of philosophical and religious problems, and a clear conception of what it is for a work to be religious. This is dangerous, particularly if the model of religion one has in mind is essentially Semitic. For the opposition between academic philosophy and religion that characterizes modern and postmodern intellectual life in the West has no analogue in Asia. But that can hardly impugn the philosophical status of Asian traditions, unless we want to urge that Western philosophy begins not in Greece but in Königsberg. See chapter 14 of this volume for a more extensive exploration of this question.

2. This requires immediate qualification: these presuppositions are not true. Hermetic isolation was never possible for any Asian, or for any European tradition. But even if one thought that it was at one time, it surely is not so now.

3. See Deutsch 1989 and Smart 1989 for useful discussions of the difficulties in applying Western hermeneutic methods to Asian philosophical traditions or Lopez 1988 and Cabezón 1994 for good discussions of the very different hermeneutic approaches characteristic of Buddhist traditions.

4. We would probably do well to ask ourselves just *why* we wish to do so, as well. For motivations in this field are often themselves problematic.

5. This presupposition is not, of course, the assumption that the meaning of a text is stable historically—but rather that the text itself is not only identifiable across changes in meanings but is also the appropriate unit of hermeneutic analysis: it is texts that we seek to understand.

6. And to the extent that our mode of being is historical, of our being the beings we are.

7. Given my enterprise, the concept of an alien is problematic here. Here is one way to put the point: if we take the integrity and insularity of traditions for granted, the concept of an alien is straightforward. She or he is anyone who is not a member of our own historical tradition. But once boundaries between traditions are blurred, alterity becomes a matter of degree.

8. This is simply a consequence of the twin semantic theses of the compositionality and the contextuality of meaning. Just as the meaning of any semantic whole depends upon the meanings of its parts—on pain of a magical theory of understanding—any semantic marker can only be ascribed a meaning by virtue of its systematic relations to the meaningful terms in whose neighborhood it functions, on pain of a magical theory of significance. In defending an interpretation of a term, we appeal only to the fact that when the term is so interpreted, it, and the text in which it is situated make more sense than either would on any competing interpretation. When we defend an interpretation of an

entire text, we do so only by showing that that interpretation is determined by those we offer of its constituent terms. No other interpretive strategies are sane.

9. Now, that is not to say that our blindnesses and prejudices can never themselves come to awareness through hermeneutic practice. That bringing-to-the-foreground is in fact one of the most important purposes of such practice, and of our entering into dialogue. But the structure of our investigation of these blindnesses and prejudices is no different from the structure that makes them inevitable. That is, these come to consciousness only against still more background. To put the point in terms of the Heideggerian-Gadamerian metaphor, phenomena only come to explicit consciousness against a horizon constituted by our tradition and prejudices. One can always approach an object on the horizon and bring it to the foreground, but always against yet another horizon.

10. And I have in mind here as much the epistemic issues raised in *On Certainty* as the semantic issues raised in *Philosophical Investigations*.

11. The point is not simply that we have historical knowledge that the authors of or early commentators on these texts necessarily lacked—knowledge about the events occurring between the composition of those texts and the present—nor that our philosophical method or insight is somehow better than theirs. The texts themselves, if regarded in the way I urge here, are themselves determined by their intertextual relations, by their readings, and by the conversations among their readers. Such texts are always incomplete and are hence always better understood by posterity.

12. This relation of the other to the home tradition in writing is terribly complex and demands independent study. There is the matter of self-definition by contrast; the matter of selective appropriation of material, authority, objectification, and so forth. I leave all of these aside for the moment.

13. Though this last is by no means a universal predicament.

14. The fact that the same point can be made with regard to our reading of Western texts whose horizons are markedly different only reinforces the point that "traditions" are hardly monolithic.

15. This is not to say that collegiality is ever unproblematic in an intracultural context. Why should one suspect that it would be, given the range of space any culture makes available, and the concrete facts of interpersonal relationships? One should not expect that collegial relationships in the cross-cultural context would be any less problematic. But simply to engender *collegial,* as opposed to interrogator-informant, or guru-disciple relationships, is a huge step forward.

16. Panikkar fleshes out this suggestion:

> [W]e forge the common language, we reach a mutual comprehension, we cross the boundaries. This is what I call dialogical philosophy. It is not the imposition of one philosophy or one mode of understanding, but the forging of a common universe of discourse in the very encounter, in the dialogical dialogue taking place not once for all, but in the actual encounter.
>
> We do not assume here any hermeneutical circle. We create that circle through the existential encounter. We do not start a dialectical dialogue, which accepts *a priori* some rules before dialogue takes place. This theory cannot be severed from the praxis.
>
> Diatopical hermeneutics is not just theory. The rules here do not precede the understanding nor the theory the praxis. At the same time, the praxis implies the theories of the meeting partners. . . .

In sum, how can we reduce to zero, or at least shorten the distance between the two *topoi* of diatopical hermeneutics? The answer here is one in which theory and praxis meet. Only those persons who, for one reason or another, have existentially crossed the borders of at least two cultures and are at home in either, shall be able first to understand, and then to translate. Diatopical hermeneutics are not universal. They function, generally speaking, between two different *topoi*, not between many. They bring one culture, language, philosophy, into another culture, language or religion, making it understandable. Diatopical hermeneutics is an art as much as a science, a praxis as much as a theory. It is a creative encounter and there is no blueprint for creativity.

Diatopical hermeneutics cannot prescribe specific rules of interpretation. If we want to interpret another basically different philosophy we will have to attend the school of that philosophy and immerse ourselves in its universe of discourse as far as is possible for us. We will have to overcome our parameters and plunge into a participatory process of which we may not be able to foresee the outcome. The process may be likened to that of learning a new language. At the beginning we translate by comparing with the mother tongue, but when we become proficient we think and speak directly in that other linguistic universe. The *topoi* are connected by simply going over there and actualizing the encounter. The process could be likened to an authentic process of conversation (with the other philosophy). Mutual fecundations may take place. (Panikkar 1989, pp. 132–33)

14. *Philosophy, Religion, and the Hermeneutic Imperative*

I thank Tricia Perry, Susan Levin, and the Ven Geshe Ngawang Samten for comments on earlier drafts.

1. Lynne Rudder Baker (personal communication) points out that hermits can lead very meaningful lives without any regular interactions with their cultures or with others. But this is not a true counterexample, for the meaningulness of the hermetic life is itself culturally constructed, and the institutions of hermitages are social institutions, even if the relations in question are highly unusual and even attenuated. Even life outside of society, paradoxically, is a form of social life. Only a truly feral life would be a life without *Mitsein*, but such a life, I would argue, would not be human, and would, in the relevant sense, utterly lack meaning.

2. This is not precisely true. There is a complex relationship between philosophy and religion in ancient Greece, with philosophical thought sometimes deriving content and problematic from explicitly religious ideas (Xenophanes) and philosophy sometimes taking religion to task (Plato). But that history is not directly relevant to the issues with which we are concerned here, as they are historically quite discontinuous with the present relationship between philosophy and religion in the West, and certainly not relevant to the relationship between Asian and Western philosophy.

3. There are actually two distinct levels at which we here note the affinity between specifically philosophical and specifically religious thought: on the one hand we often detect *residues* of religious ideas preserved unwittingly, or prereflectively in philosophical discourse (the categorical imperative). This is, to be sure, significant in demonstrating the pervasive impact of Semitic religious thought on "secular" philosophy. But more important

for our purposes is the fact that philosophy and religion, as we will argue later in this chapter, share important hermeneutic roles, even in the post-Enlightenment West (and this is explicitly acknowledged, for instance, in Kant's understanding of the mission of the first *Critique* as circumscribing reason in order to make room for faith).

4. And here we see that second and deeper level of affinity at work.

References

Allen, A. 1988. *Uneasy Access*. New York: Rowan and Littlefield.

Alomes, A. 1998. *Stepping Out of the River: A Proposal for Nonviolence Today*. Ph.D. dissertation, University of Tasmania; forthcoming, Ithaca: Snow Lion.

Anacker, S. 1984. *Seven Works of Vasubandhu: The Buddhist Psychological Doctor*. New Delhi: Motilal Banarsidass.

Āryadeva. *Four Hundred Stanzas*. Trans. K. Lang in *Aryadeva's Catuhsataka* 1986. Copenhagen: Akademisk Forlag.

Baier, A. 1992. *A Progress of Sentiments: Reflections on Hume's* Treatise. Cambridge, Mass.: Harvard University Press.

———. 1994a. *Moral Prejudices*. Cambridge, Mass.: Harvard University Press.

——— 1994b. "Hume: A Women's Moral Theorist?" in Baier 1994a: pp. 31–75.

———. 1994c. "Morals and Cruelty: Reflections on Hume and Kant." In Baier 1994a: pp. 268–2.

———. 1994d. "Sustaining Trust." In Baier 1994a: pp. 152–182.

———. 1994e. "Trust and Anti-Trust." In Baier 1994a: pp. 95–129.

———. 1994f. "Trust and Its Vulnerabilities." In Baier 1994a: pp. 130–5.

———. 1994g. "Unsafe Loves." In Baier 1994a: pp. 33–50.

———. 1994h. "What Do Women Want in a Moral Theory?" In Baier 1994a: pp. 1–17.

———. 1994i. "The Need for More than Justice." In Baier 1994a: 18–32.

Baker, L. R. 1988. *Saving Belief: A Critique of Physicalism*. Princeton: Princeton University Press.

Bar-On, D. 1993. "Indeterminacy of Translation: Theory and Practice."*Philosophy and Phenomenological Research* 53, 4, pp. 718–810.

Baron, M. 1995. *Kantian Ethics Almost without Apology*. Ithaca: Cornell University Press.

Barwise, J., and J. Etchemendy. 1987. *The Liar*. Oxford: Oxford University Press.

Benhabib, S. 1987. "The Generalized and the Concrete Other: Implications of the Kohlberg-Gilligan Debate." In E. Kittay and D. Meyers, eds., *Women and Moral Theory*. New York: Rowman an Littlefield.

Berkeley, G. 1954. *Three Dialogues between Hylas and Philonous*. Ed. C. Turbayne. Indianapolis: Bobbs-Merrill.

Bhattacharya, K., E. H. Johnston, and A. Kunst 1985. *The Dialectical Method of Nāgārjuna: Vigrahavyāvartanī*. New Delhi: Motilal Banarsidass.

Burge, T. 1979 "Individualism and the Mental." *Midwest Studies in Philosophy 4*, 73–121.

Cabezón, J. 1992. *A Dose of Emptiness: An Annotated Translation of the sTong thun chen mo of mKhas grub dGelegs dpal bzang.* Albany: State University of New York Press.

———. 1994. *Buddhism and Language: A Study of Indo-Tibetan Scholasticism.* Albany: State University of New York Press.

Candrakīrti. 1989. *Madhyamakāvatāra.* Trans. in C. Huntington and Geshe Namgyal Wangchen, *The Emptiness of Emptiness.* Honolulu: University of Hawaii Press.

———. 1994. *dBu ma la 'jugs pa'I ran 'grel.* Sarnath: Gleugpa Student Welfare Committee.

———. *Prasannapadā.* sDe dge edition of the Tibetan Canon. Vol 'a, 2–399. Dharamsala: Paljor Press, Tibetan Government Printing Office.

Card, C. 1992. "Caring and Evil." *Hypatia 5*(1), 1–8.

Care, N. 1969. "Contractualism and Moral Criticism." *The Review of Metaphysics 23*, 83–101.

———. 1987. *On Sharing Fate.* Philadelphia: Temple University Press.

Cartwright, N. 1978. *How the Laws of Physics Lie.* Oxford: Oxford University Press.

Chakrabarti, K. K. 1995. *Definition and Induction: A Historical and Comparative Study.* Society for Asian and Comparative Philosophy, monograph no. 13. Honolulu: University of Hawaii Press.

Churchland, P. 1978. *Scientific Realism and the Plasticity of Mind.* Cambridge: Cambridge University Press.

Cummins, R. 1983. *The Nature of Psychological Explanation.* Cambridge, Mass.: MIT Press/ Bradford Books.

Davidson, D. 1974. "On the Very Idea of a Conceptual Scheme." *Proceedings and Addresses of the APA 47*, 5–20.

Deutsch, E. 1989. "Knowledge and the Tradition Text in Indian Philosophy." In Larson and Deutsch 1989, 165–73.

———. ed. 1991. *Culture and Modernity: East-West Philosophic Perspectives.* Honolulu: University of Hawaii Press.

Diogenes Laertius, 1991. *Lives of Eminent Philosophers.* Trans. R. D. Hicks. Cambridge, Mass.: Harvard University Press.

Dunne, J. 1996. "Yogācāra Idealism." Contribution to *Buddha-L, Buddhist Academic Discussion Forum*, June 30 (BUDDHA–L @ULKYVM.LOUISVILLE.EDU).

Feinberg, J. 1990. *Rights, Justice and the Bounds of Liberty.* Princeton: Princeton University Press.

Flanagan, O., and K. Jackson. 1987. "Justice, Care and Gender: The Kohlberg-Gilligan Debate Revisited." *Ethics 97*, 622–45.

Fodor, J. 1987. *Psychosemantics: The Problem of Meaning in the Philosophy of Mind.* Cambridge, Mass.: MIT Press/Bradford Books.

Gadamer, H-G. 1975. *Truth and Method.* New York: Seabury Press.

———. 1976. *Philosophical Hermeneutics.* Berkeley: University of California Press.

Garfield, J. 1988. *Belief in Psychology.* Cambridge, Mass.: MIT Press.

———. 1993. "Eliminativism and Substantialism." Levett-Spenser Lecture, Union College.

———. 1995. *Fundamental Wisdom of the Middle Way: Nāgārjuna's Mūlamadhyamakakārikā.* New York: Oxford University Press.

———. 1997. *Western Idealism and Its Critics.* Hobart: Pyrrho Press; forthcoming in Tibetan, Central Institute of Higher Tibetan Studies Press.

————. 2000. "Thought as Language: A Metaphor Too Far." In *Protosoziology* 14 (http://www.rz.uni-frankfurt.de/protosociology).

————. 2001. "Particularity and Principle: The Structure of Moral Knowledge." In M. Little and B. Hooker, eds., *Moral Particularism*. Oxford: Oxford University Press, pp. 178–204.

Garner, R. 1994. *Beyond Morality*. Philadelphia: Temple University Press.

Gibbard, A. 1990. *Wise Feelings: Apt Choices*. Cambridge, Mass.: Harvard University Press.

Gilligan, C. 1982. *In a Different Voice: Psychological Theory and Women's Moral Development*. Cambridge: Harvard University Press.

Gorampa. 1990. *Nges don ran gsal*. Sarnath: Sakya Students' Union.

Gupta, A., and N. Belnap. 1993. *The Revision Theory of Truth*. Cambridge, Mass.: MIT Press.

Hallie, G., ed. 1985. *Sextus Empiricus: Selected Writings on Scepticism, Man and God*. Engelwood Cliffs: Prentice-Hall.

Hardcastle, V. 1996. *How to Build a Theory in Cognitive Science*. Albany: State University of New York Press.

Haugeland, J. 1981. "The Nature and Plausibility of Cognitivism." *Behavioral and Brain Sciences* 1, 218–26.

Hayes, R. 1994. "Nàgàrjuna's Appeal." *Journal of Indian Philosophy* 22, 299–378.

Heidegger, M. 1958. "What Is Philosophy?" New York: Twayne.

————. 1962. *Being and Time*. London: SCM Press.

Henkin, L. 1974. "Privacy and Autonomy." *Columbia Law Review 74*, 1410–33.

HH the Dalai Lama (1984). *Kindness, Clarity and Insight*. Ithaca: Snow Lion Press.

————. 1992. *The Global Community and the Need for Universal Responsibility*. Boston: Wisdom Publications.

Hobbes, T. 1909. *Leviathan*. Oxford: Clarendon Press.

Hohfeld, W. 1923. *Fundamental Legal Conceptions*. New Haven: Yale University Press.

Hopkins, J. 1980. *Compassion in Tibetan Buddhism*. Ithaca: Snow Lion.

————. 1983. *Meditation on Emptiness*. Boston: Wisdom Publications.

————. 2000. *Emptiness in the Mind-Only School of Tibetan Buddhism*. Berkeley: University of California Press.

Hume, D. 1978. *A Treatise of Human Nature*. Ed. L. A. Selby Bigge and P. H. Nidditch. Oxford: Oxford University Press.

Huntington, C., and Geshe N. Wangchen. 1989. *The Emptiness of Emptiness: Candrakīrti's Madhyamakāvatāra*. Honolulu: University of Hawaii Press.

Ingalls, D.H.H. 1949. *Materials for the study of Navya-Nyāya Logic*. Delhi: Motilal Banarsidass.

Inness, J. 1992. *Privacy, Intimacy and Isolation*. New York: Oxford University Press.

Janiak, A. 1994 *Assessing a Contemporary Challenge to Ethical Liberalism*. Amherst, Mass.: Hampshire College division III thesis.

Kalupahana, D. 1986. *Nāgārjuna: The Philosophy of the Middle Way*. Albany: State University of New York Press.

————. 1987. *Principles of Buddhist Psychology*. Albany: State University of New York Press.

Kant, I. 1959. "What Is Enlightenment?" In *Perpetual Peace and Other Essays*. Trans. T. Humphrey. Cambridge: Hackett: 41–48.

————. 1965. *Critique of Pure Reason*. Ed. and trans. N. Kemp-Smith. New York: St. Martins Press.

————. 1979. "The Conflict of the Faculties." Trans. M. J. Gregor. New York: Abacus.

————. 1983. *Perpetual Peace and Other Essays*. Trans. Ted Humphrey. Cambridge: Hackett.

Kasulis, T. 1989. *Zen Action/Zen Person*. Honolulu: University of Hawaii Press.

Kitcher, P. 1993. *The Advancement of Science*. New York: Oxford University Press.

Klein, A. 1995. *Path to the Middle: The Oral Scholarship of Kensur Yeshe Thupden*. Albany: State University of New York Press.

Kochumuttom, T. 1982. *The Buddhist Doctrine of Experience: A New Translation and Interpretation of the Works of Vasubandhu the Yogacārin*. New Delhi: Motilal Banarsidass.

Kohlberg, L. 1981. *Essays in Moral Development I: Moral Stages and the Idea of Justice*. San Francisco: Harper and Row.

————. 1984. *Essays in Moral Development II: The Nature and Validity of Moral Stages*. San Francisco: Harper and Row.

Komito, D. 1987. *Nāgārjuna's "Seventy Stanzas": A Buddhist Psychology of Emptiness*. Ithaca: Snow Lion.

Korsgaard, H. 1996. *Bringing about the Kingdom of Ends*. Cambridge: Cambridge University Press.

Kripke, S. 1975. "Outline of a Theory of Truth." *The Journal of Philosophy* 72, 690–716.

————. 1982. *Wittgenstein on Rules and Private Language*. Cambridge, Mass.: Harvard University Press.

Krishna, D. 1989. "Comparative Philosophy: What It Is and What It Ought To Be." In Larson and Deutsch 1989, 71–83.

Larson, G. J. and E. Deutsch, eds. 1989. *Interpreting across Boundaries: New Essays in Comparative Philosophy*. Delhi: Motilal Banarsidass.

Locke, J. 1988. *Two Treatises on Government*. Cambridge: Cambridge University Press.

Lopez, D. 1988. *Buddhist Hermeneutics*. Honolulu: University of Hawaii Press.

Lusthaus, D. 1996a. "Yogācāra Idealism." Contribution to *Buddha-L, Buddhist Academic Discussion Forum*, June 26 (BUDDHA-L @ULKYVM.LOUISVILLE.EDU).

————. 1996b. "Yogācāra Idealism." Contribution to *Buddha-L, Buddhist Academic Discussion Forum*, June 27 (BUDDHA-L @ULKYVM.LOUISVILLE.EDU).

MacKinnon, C. 1984. "*Roe v. Wade*: A Study in Male Ideology." in J. Garfield and P. Hennessey, eds. *Abortion: Moral and Legal Perspectives*. Amherst: University of Massachusetts Press, 45–54.

Mehta, J. L. 1985a. *India and the West: The Problem of Understanding*. Cambridge, Mass.: Harvard University Press.

————. (1985b). "Understanding and Tradition." In Mehta 1985, 134–59.

Meyers, K. 1995. *Empty Talk: Tsong khapa's Elucidation of the Buddha's Intention as a Matter of Semantics*. Amherst, Mass.: Hampshire College division III thesis.

Michaels, M. 1985. "The Woman in the Supermarket and the Man on the Street." Amherst, Mass., Hampshire College Philosophy Colloquium.

Milikan, R. 1987. "What Is Behavior?" Paper deliver at the annual meeting, the Society for the Philosophy of Psychology, Toronto.

Murti, T.R.V. 1955. *The Central Philosophy of Buddhism*. London: Allen and Unwyn.

Nagao, G. 1991. *Mādhyāmika and Yogācāra*. Albany: State University of New York Press.

Nāgārjuna. *Śunyatāsaptatikārikā*. SDe dge edition of the Tibetan canon. Vol. tsa, 241d–73g. Dharamsala: Paljor Press, Tibetan Government Printing Office.

Nāgārjuna. *Vigrahavyāvartanīkārikā* (70 Verses on Emptiness with Commentary). SDe dge edition of the Tibetan canon. Vol. dBu ma Tsa, 219d–41c. Dharamsala: Paljor Press, Tibetan Government Printing Office.

Nāgārjuna. *Vigrahavyāvartanīvṛtti*. SDe dge edition of the Tibetan canon. Vol. tsa, 241d–73g. Dharamsala: Paljor Press, Tibetan Government Printing Office.

Napper, E. 1993. *Dependent Arising and Emptiness*. Boston: Wisdom Publications.

Newland, G. 1992. *The Two Truths*. Boston: Wisdom Publications.

Noddings, Nel. 1984. *Caring: A Feminine Approach to Ethics and Moral Education*. Berkeley: University of California Press.

O'Neill O. 1989. *Constructions of Reason*. Cambridge: Cambridge University Press.

———. 1996. *Towards Justice and Virtue: A Reconstructive Account of Practical Reasoning*. Cambridge: Cambridge University Press.

Owens, J. 1988. "The Causal Thesis." Annual meeting, the Society for the Philosophy of Psychology, Chapel Hill, N.C., 1988.

Pannikar, R. 1989. "What Is Comparative Philosophy Comparing?" In Larson and Deutsch 1989. 116–136.

Powers, J. 1995. *Wisdom of the Buddha: The Saṁdhinirmocana-sūtra*. Berkeley: Dharma Press.

———. (1996a). "Yogācāra Idealism." Contribution to *Buddha-L, Buddhist Academic Discussion Forum*, July 1 (BUDDHA-L@ULKYVM.LOUISVILLE.EDU).

———. (1996b). "Yogācāra Idealism." Contribution to *Buddha-L, Buddhist Academic Discussion Forum*, September 30 BUDDHA-L @ULKYVM.LOUISVILLE.EDU).

Priest, G. 1987. *In Contradiction*. Dordrecht: Kluwer.

———. 1995. *Beyond the Limits of Thought*. Cambridge: Cambridge University Press.

———. (forthcoming). "The Grammar of Being." In R. Gaskin, ed., *Grammar and the World*. New York: Routledge.

Rabten, G., and S. Batchelor. 1983. *Echoes of Voidness*. Boston: Wisdom Publications.

Rawls, J. 1971. *A Theory of Justice*. Cambridge, Mass.: Harvard University Press.

rGyal tshab rje 1990. *rNam 'grel thar lam gsal byed*. Sarnath: Central Institute of Higher Tibetan Studies Gelugpa Student Welfare Committee.

Robinson, R. 1957. "Some Logical Aspects of Nāgārjuna's System." *Philosophy East and West* 6, 291–308.

———. 1972. "Did Nāgārjuna Really Refute all Philosophical Views?" *Philosophy East and West* 22, 325–31.

Rousseau. J. 1947. *The Social Contract*. Trans. C. Frankel. New York: Abner.

Ruegg, D. S. 1977. "The Uses of Four Positions in the Catuṣkoṭi and the Problem of the Description of Reality of Mahāyāna Buddhism." *Journal of Indian Philosophy* 5(1), 1–71.

Śantideva. *Bodhicaryāvatāra*. SDe dge edition of the Tibetan Canon. Vol. La, pp. 1–94. Dharamsala: Paljor Press, Tibetan Government Printing Office.

Schoeman, F., ed. 1984. *Philosophical Dimensions of Privacy: An Anthology*. New York: Cambridge University Press.

Schopenhauer, A. 1892. In T. B. Saunders, trans., *Essays of Schopenhauer*. "On Our Relations to Others." New York: A. Burt, 141–168.

———. 1965. *On the Basis of Morality*. Trans. E.F.J. Payne. Indianapolis: Bobbs-Merrill.

———. 1969. *The World as Will and Representation*. 2 vols. Trans. E.F.J. Payne. New York: Dover.

————. 1974. *The Fourfold Root of the Principle of Sufficient Reason*. Ed. and trans. E.F.J. Payne. Chicago: Open Court.

Sellars, W. 1992. *The Metaphysics of Epistemology*. Santa Cruz: Ridgeview Press.

————. 1997. *Empiricism and the Philosophy of Mind*. Cambridge: Harvard University Press.

Siderits, M. 1988. "Nāgārjuna as an Anti-Realist." *Journal of Indian Philosophy* 16, 311–25.

————. 1989. "Thinking on Empty: Madhyamaka Anti-Realism and the Canons of Rationality." In S. Biderman and B-A Scharfstein, eds., *Rationality in Question: On Eastern and Western Views of Rationality*. Dordrecht: Brill.

————. 1996. "On the Continuity Thesis." Australia-New Zealand Joint Religious Studies Conference, Christchurch.

Smart, J. 1963. *Philosophy and Scientific Realism*. London: Routledge and Kegan Paul.

Smart, N. 1989. "The Analogy of Meaning and the Tasks of Comparative Philosophy." In Larson and Deutsch 1989. pp. 174–183.

Sparham, G. 1994. *Ocean of Eloquence: Tsong khapa's Commentary on the Yogācāra Doctrine of Mind*. Albany: State University of New York Press.

Sprung, M. 1979. *Lucid Exposition of the Middle Way: The Essential Chapters from the Prasannapadā of Candrakīrti*.

Sthiramati. *Trimsikābhasya (Sum chu pa 'bral shad)*. sDe dge edition of the Tibetan Canon. Vol. Shi, pp. 292–342. Dharamsala: Paljor Press, Tibetan Government Printing Office.

Thomson, J. 1986. *Rights, Restitution and Risk*. Cambridge, Mass.: Harvard University Press.

Thurman, R. 1984. *Tsong khapa's Speech of Gold in the Essence of True Eloquence*. Princeton: Princeton University Press.

————. 1976. *The Holy Teaching of Vimalakīrti*. University Park: Pennsylvania State University Press.

Tillemans, T. 1999. "Is Buddhist Logic Non-classical or Deviant?" In Tillemans, *Scripture, Logic, Language*. pp. 187–205. Boston: Wisdom Publications, 187–205.

Tronto, J. 1993. *Moral Boundaries: A Political Argument for an Ethic of Care*. New York: Routledge.

Tsong khapa. 1997. *Drang ba dang nges pa'i don mam par 'byed pa'i bstan beas legs bashal snying po*. Sarnath: Central Institute of Higher Tibetan Studies Press.

————. 1998. *Drang nge Legs bshad snying po*. In Geshe Yeshes Thap-khas, *Drang nges legs bshad snying po*. Sarnath: Central Institute of Higher Tibetan Studies Press.

Tuck, A. 1990. *Comparative Philosophy and the Philosophy of Scholarship*. New York: Oxford University Press.

Van Fraassen, B. 1980. *The Scientific Image*. Oxford: Clarendon Press.

Van Gulick, R. 1989. "Metaphysical Arguments for Internalism and Why They Don't Work." In S. Silvers, ed., *Representation*, Dordrecht: Kluwer, pp. 151–160.

Vasubandhu. *Madhyāntavibhāgabhāsya (Dbus dang mtha' rnam par 'byed pa'i 'grel pa)*. SDe dge edition of the Tibetan Buddhist Canon. Vol. Bi 2a–535. Dharamsala: Paljor Press, Tibetan Government Printing Office.

Vasubandhu. *Trimsikākārikā (gSum cu pa)*. Tibetan Buddhist Canon. Vol. Shi, pp 2–5. Dharamsala: Paljor Press, Tibetan Government Printing Office.

Vasubandhu. *Trisvabhāvanirdesa (Rang bzhin gsum gnes par bstan pa)*. Tibetan Buddhist Canon. Vol. Shi, 19c–22d. Dharamsala: Paljor Press, Tibetan Government Printing Office.

Vasubandhu. *Viṃsātikā* (*Nyi shu pa*). Tibetan Buddhist Canon. Vol. Shi. Dharamsala: Paljor Press, Tibetan Government Printing Office.

Vinitadeva. *Trimsikatika*. sDe dge edition of the Tibetan Canon. Vol. Hi, pp. 2–125.2a–125g. Dharamsala: Paljor Press, Tibetan Government Printing Office.

Von Eckardt, B. 1988. "Constraints on a Theory of Content Determination." Annual meeting, the Society for the Philosophy of Psychology, Chapel Hill, N.C.

———. (1995). *What Is Cognitive Science?* Cambridge: MIT Press.

Wayman, A. 1991. *The Ethics of Tibet*. Albany: State University of New York Press.

Williams, B. 1973. "A Critique of Utilitarianism." In J.J.C. Smart and B. Williams, *Utilitariansim For and Against*. Cambridge: Cambridge University Press, pp 77–150.

Wittgenstein, L. 1922. *Tractatus Logico-Philosophicus*. Trans. B. F. McGuiness. London: Routledge and Kegan Paul.

———. 1958. *Philosophical Investigations* Trans. G.E.M. Anscombe, Englewood Cliffs: Prentice Hall.

———. 1969. *On Certainty*. Translated and ed. G. H. Von Wright and G. E. Anscombe. New York: Harper Torchbooks.

———. 1979. *Notebooks 1914–1916*. Oxford: Oxford University Press.

Wood, T. M. 1991. *Mind Only: A Philosophical and Doctrinal Analysis of the Vijñānavāda*. Honolulu: University of Hawaii Press.

———. 1994. *Nagarjunian Disputations: A Philosophical Journey through an Indian Looking-Glass*. Society for Asian and Comparative Philosophy, monograph no. 11. Honolulu: University of Hawaii Press.

Index